Macmillan/McGraw-Hill Edition

# McGRAW-HILL READING

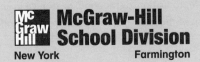

**McGraw-Hill School Division**

New York      Farmington

**Contributors**

The Princeton Review, Time Magazine, Accelerated Reader

The Princeton Review is not
affiliated with Princeton
University or ETS.

# McGraw-Hill School Division

### A Division of The McGraw·Hill Companies

McGraw-Hill School Division
Two Penn Plaza
New York, New York 10121

Printed in the United States of America

ISBN 0-02-184750-9/1, Bk.4, U.1

2 3 4 5 6 7 8 9  043/071  04 03 02 01 00 99

# McGRAW-HILL READING

**McGraw-Hill
School Division**

New York          Farmington

Selected Quizzes Prepared by 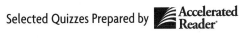 Accelerated Reader®

# McGraw-Hill Reading
# Authors
## Make the Difference...

**Dr. James Flood**

**Ms. Angela Shelf Medearis**

**Dr. Jan E. Hasbrouck**

**Dr. Scott Paris**

**Dr. James V. Hoffman**

**Dr. Steven Stahl**

**Dr. Diane Lapp**

**Dr. Josefina Villamil Tinajero**

**Dr. Karen D. Wood**

# Contributing
# Authors

**Dr. Barbara Coulter**

**Ms. Frankie Dungan**

**Dr. Joseph B. Rubin**

**Dr. Carl B. Smith**

**Dr. Shirley Wright**

iv

**Part 1**
## START TOGETHER

### Focus on Reading and Skills

**All students start with the SAME:**

- Read Aloud
- Pretaught Skills
  Phonics
  Comprehension
- Build Background
- Selection Vocabulary

# ...Never hold a child back. Never leave a child behind.

**Part 2**
## MEET INDIVIDUAL NEEDS

### Read the Literature

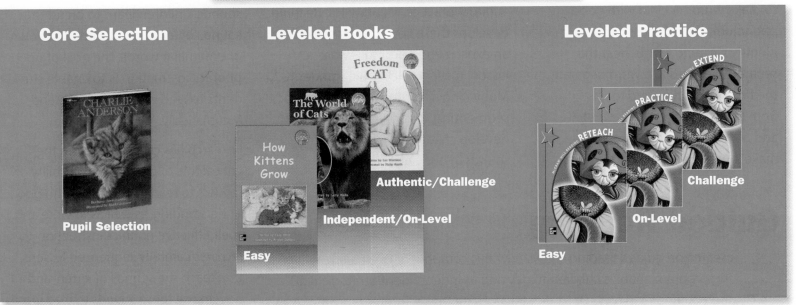

**Core Selection**

Pupil Selection

**Leveled Books**

Authentic/Challenge

Independent/On-Level

Easy

**Leveled Practice**

EXTEND

PRACTICE

RETEACH

Challenge

On-Level

Easy

Examples Taken From Grade 2

**Part 3**
## FINISH TOGETHER

### Build Skills

**All students finish with the SAME:**

- Phonics
- Comprehension
- Vocabulary
- Study Skills
- Assessment

# McGraw-Hill Reading Applying the Research

## Phonological Awareness

**P**honological awareness is the ability to hear the sounds in spoken language. It includes the ability to separate spoken words into discrete sounds as well as the ability to blend sounds together to make words. A child with good phonological awareness can identify rhyming words, hear the separate syllables in a word, separate the first sound in a word (onset) from the rest of the word (rime), and blend sounds together to make words.

Recent research findings have strongly concluded that children with good phonological awareness skills are more likely to learn to read well. These skills can be improved through systematic, explicit instruction involving auditory practice. McGraw-Hill Reading develops these key skills by providing an explicit Phonological Awareness lesson in every selection at grades K-2. Motivating activities such as blending, segmenting, and rhyming help to develop children's awareness of the sounds in our language.

## Guided Reading

**R**esearch on guided reading shows how this component of a balanced reading program enables children to develop as independent, strategic readers. Through guided reading lessons that incorporate the reciprocal teaching model of Palincsar and the Gay Su Pinnell model, teachers model strategic thinking, questioning, clarifying, and problem-solving strategies. Ultimately, the goal is to encourage children to learn to question, clarify, make predictions, and summarize text themselves with less and less teacher support.

The McGraw-Hill Reading program offers a Guided Reading lesson for each core piece of literature as well as each leveled reader selection. These lessons incorporate interactive questioning prompts that are modeled by the teacher. The McGraw-Hill Reading program assures that this interaction between text reading and good teaching builds a strong literacy foundation for all children.

## Phonics

**O**ur language system uses an alphabetic code to communicate meaning from writing. Phonics involves learning the phonemes or sounds that letters make and the symbols or letters that represent those sounds. Children learn to blend the sounds of letters to decode unknown or unfamiliar words. The goal of good phonics instruction is to enable students to read words accurately and automatically.

Research has clearly identified the critical role of phonics in the ability of readers to read fluently and with good understanding, as well as to write and spell. Effective phonics instruction requires carefully sequenced lessons that teach the sounds of letters and how to use these sounds to read words. The McGraw-Hill program provides daily explicit and systematic phonics instruction to teach the letter sounds and blending. There are three explicit Phonics and Decoding lessons for every selection. Daily Phonics Routines are provided for quick reinforcement, in addition to activities in the Phonics Workbook and technology components. This combination of direct skills instruction and applied practice leads to reading success.

# Curriculum Connections

**A**s in the child's real-world environment, boundaries between disciplines must be dissolved. Recent research emphasizes the need to make connections between and across subject areas. McGraw-Hill Reading is committed to this approach. Each reading selection offers activities that tie in with social studies, language arts, geography, science, mathematics, art, music, health, and physical education. The program threads numerous research and inquiry activities that encourage the child to use the library and the Internet to seek out information. Reading and language skills are applied to a variety of genres, balancing fiction and nonfiction.

# Integrated Language Arts

**S**uccess in developing communication skills is greatly enhanced by integrating the language arts in connected and purposeful ways. This allows students to understand the need for proper writing, grammar, and spelling. McGraw-Hill Reading sets the stage for meaningful learning. Each week a full writing-process lesson is provided. This lesson is supported by a 5-day spelling plan, emphasizing spelling patterns and spelling rules, and a 5-day grammar plan, focusing on proper grammar, mechanics, and usage.

# Meeting Individual Needs

**E**very classroom is a microcosm of a world composed of diverse individuals with unique needs and abilities. Research points out that such needs must be addressed with frequent intensive opportunities to learn with engaging materials. McGraw-Hill Reading makes reading a successful experience for every child by providing a rich collection of leveled books for easy, independent, and challenging reading. Leveled practice is provided in Reteach, Practice, and Extend skills books. To address various learning styles and language needs, the program offers alternative teaching strategies, prevention/intervention techniques, language support activities, and ESL teaching suggestions.

# Assessment

**F**requent assessment in the classroom makes it easier for teachers to identify problems and to find remedies for them. McGraw-Hill Reading makes assessment an important component of instruction. Formal and informal opportunities are a part of each lesson. Minilessons, prevention/intervention strategies, and informal checklists, as well as student self-assessments, provide many informal assessment opportunities. Formal assessments, such as weekly selection tests and criterion-referenced unit tests, help to monitor students' knowledge of important skills and concepts. McGraw-Hill Reading also addresses how to adapt instruction based on student performance with resources such as the Alternate Teaching Strategies. Weekly lessons on test preparation, including test preparation practice books, help students to transfer skills to new contexts and to become better test takers.

McGraw-Hill School
**TECHNOLOGY**

*inter*NET CONNECTION For information on research that supports this program, visit **www.mhschool.com/reading/eric**

# McGraw-Hill Reading

## Theme Chart

### MULTI-AGE Classroom

Using the same global themes at each grade level facilitates the use of materials in multi-age classrooms.

| GRADE LEVEL | Experience<br>Experiences can tell us about ourselves and our world. | Connections<br>Making connections develops new understandings. |
|---|---|---|
| Kindergarten | **My World**<br>We learn a lot from all the things we see and do at home and in school. | **All Kinds of Friends**<br>When we work and play together, we learn more about ourselves. |
| Subtheme 1 | At Home | Working Together |
| Subtheme 2 | School Days | Playing Together |
| 1 | **Day by Day**<br>Each day brings new experiences. | **Together Is Better**<br>We like to share ideas and experiences with others. |
| 2 | **What's New?**<br>With each day, we learn something new. | **Just Between Us**<br>Family and friends help us see the world in new ways. |
| 3 | **Great Adventures**<br>Life is made up of big and small experiences. | **Nature Links**<br>Nature can give us new ideas. |
| 4 | **Reflections**<br>Stories let us share the experiences of others. | **Something in Common**<br>Sharing ideas can lead to meaningful cooperation. |
| 5 | **Time of My Life**<br>We sometimes find memorable experiences in unexpected places. | **Building Bridges**<br>Knowing what we have in common helps us appreciate our differences. |
| 6 | **Pathways**<br>Reflecting on life's experiences can lead to new understandings. | **A Common Thread**<br>A look beneath the surface may uncover hidden connections. |

# Themes: Kindergarten – Grade 6

**Six Units IN EVERY GRADE**

| Expression | Inquiry | Problem Solving | Making Decisions |
|---|---|---|---|
| There are many styles and forms for expressing ourselves. | By exploring and asking questions, we make discoveries. | Analyzing information can help us solve problems. | Using what we know helps us evaluate situations. |
| **Time to Shine**<br>We can use our ideas and our imagination to do many wonderful things. | **I Wonder**<br>We can make discoveries about the wonders of nature in our own backyard. | **Let's Work It Out**<br>Working as part of a team can help me find a way to solve problems. | **Choices**<br>We can make many good choices and decisions every day. |
| Great Ideas | In My Backyard | Try and Try Again | Good Choices |
| Let's Pretend | Wonders of Nature | Teamwork | Let's Decide |
| **Stories to Tell**<br>Each one of us has a different story to tell. | **Let's Find Out!**<br>Looking for answers is an adventure. | **Think About It!**<br>It takes time to solve problems. | **Many Paths**<br>Each decision opens the door to a new path. |
| **Express Yourself**<br>We share our ideas in many ways. | **Look Around**<br>There are surprises all around us. | **Figure It Out**<br>We can solve problems by working together. | **Starting Now**<br>Unexpected events can lead to new decisions. |
| **Be Creative!**<br>We can all express ourselves in creative, wonderful ways. | **Tell Me More**<br>Looking and listening closely will help us find out the facts. | **Think It Through**<br>Solutions come in many shapes and sizes. | **Turning Points**<br>We make new judgments based on our experiences. |
| **Our Voices**<br>We can each use our talents to communicate ideas. | **Just Curious**<br>We can find answers in surprising places. | **Make a Plan**<br>Often we have to think carefully about a problem in order to solve it. | **Sorting It Out**<br>We make decisions that can lead to new ideas and discoveries. |
| **Imagine That**<br>The way we express our thoughts and feelings can take different forms. | **Investigate!**<br>We never know where the search for answers might lead us. | **Bright Ideas**<br>Some problems require unusual approaches. | **Crossroads**<br>Decisions cause changes that can enrich our lives. |
| **With Flying Colors**<br>Creative people help us see the world from different perspectives. | **Seek and Discover**<br>To make new discoveries, we must observe and explore. | **Brainstorms**<br>We can meet any challenge with determination and ingenuity. | **All Things Considered**<br>Encountering new places and people can help us make decisions. |

# Let's Find Out!

*Looking for answers is an adventure.*

## Contents

   *"To the Top"* a poem by *Sandra Liatsos*

*written by* **Gary Apple**
*illustrated by* **Shirley Beckes**

| SKILLS | | | |
|---|---|---|---|
| **Phonics** | **Comprehension** | **Vocabulary** | **Study Skill** |
| • **Introduce** Long *i: i-e* <br> • **Review** Long *i-e, a-e* | • **Introduce** Cause and Effect | • **Review** Inflectional Ending -s and -es | • Charts |

**A HUMOROUS STORY**

*written by* **Barbara Bottner**
*illustrated by* **Dominic Catalano**

| SKILLS | | | |
|---|---|---|---|
| **Phonics** | **Comprehension** | **Vocabulary** | **Study Skill** |
| • **Introduce** Long *o: o-e* <br> • **Review** Long *o-e, i-e, a-e* | • **Review** Cause and Effect | • **Review** Inflectional Ending -ed | • Charts |

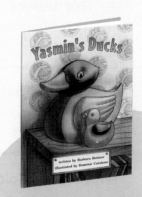

**A SCIENCE STORY**

| SKILLS | | | |
|---|---|---|---|
| Phonics | Comprehension | Vocabulary | Study Skill |
| • **Introduce** Long *u: u-e*<br>• **Review** *u-e, o-e, i-e, a-e* | • **Introduce** Make Inferences | • **Introduce** Inflectional Endings *-er* and *-est* | • Charts |

**A PLAY**

| SKILLS | | | |
|---|---|---|---|
| Phonics | Comprehension | Vocabulary | Study Skill |
| • **Introduce** Long *a: ai, ay*<br>• **Review** *ai, ay; u-e, o-e* | • **Review** Make Inferences | • **Review** Inflectional Endings *-er, -est* | • Charts |

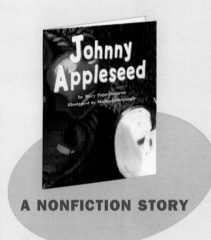

**A NONFICTION STORY**

| SKILLS | | | |
|---|---|---|---|
| Phonics | Comprehension | Vocabulary | Study Skill |
| • **Review** *ai, ay; u-e, o-e, i-e, a-e* | • **Review** Cause and Effect<br>• **Review** Make Inferences | • **Review** Inflectional Endings *-s, -es*<br>• **Review** Inflectional Endings *-er, -est* | • Charts |

**A STORY**

# Unit Planner

| | **WEEK 1** The Shopping List | **WEEK 2** Yasmin's Ducks |
|---|---|---|
| **Leveled Books** | Easy: *A Pet for Max*<br>Independent: *The Big Secret*<br>Authentic: *Who Took the Farmer's Hat?* | Easy: *Spot's Tricks*<br>Independent: *Show-and-Tell Rose*<br>Authentic: *My Best Friend* |
| ✓ **Tested Skills** | ☑ **Phonics**<br>Introduce Long *i: i-e,* 10A–10B<br>Review Long *i: i-e,* 37E–37F<br>Review *i-e, a-e,* 37G–37H<br><br>☑ **Comprehension**<br>Introduce Cause and Effect, 37I–37J<br><br>☑ **Vocabulary**<br>Review Inflectional Endings *-s, es,* 37K–37L<br><br>☑ **Study Skills**<br>Charts, 36 | ☑ **Phonics**<br>Introduce Long *o: o-e,* 40A–40B<br>Review Long *o: o-e,* 65E–65F<br>Review *o-e, i-e, a-e,* 65G–65H<br><br>☑ **Comprehension**<br>Review Cause and Effect, 65I–65J<br><br>☑ **Vocabulary**<br>Review Inflectional Ending *-ed,* 65K–65L<br><br>☑ **Study Skills**<br>Charts, 64 |
| **Minilessons** | **Phonics and Decoding:** Blends, 13; Short *a, e, i, o, u,* 19<br>**Make Inferences,** 17<br>**Context Clues,** 23<br>**Plot and Character,** 25<br>**Sequence of Events,** 27<br>**Summarize,** 31 | **Final Sound /k/, *ck,*** 43<br>**Context Clues,** 47<br>**Make Inferences,** 51<br>**High-Frequency Words,** 55<br>**Main Idea,** 59 |
| **Language Arts** | **Writing:** Persuasive Writing, 37M<br>**Grammar:** *Was* and *Were,* 37O<br>**Spelling:** Words with Long *i: i-e,* 37Q | **Writing:** Persuasive Writing, 65M<br>**Grammar:** *Has* and *Have,* 65O<br>**Spelling:** Words with Long *o: o-e,* 65Q |

## Activities

| Curriculum Connections | | The Shopping List | Yasmin's Ducks |
|---|---|---|---|
| | Social Studies | Read Aloud: "General Store," 8E | Read Aloud: "Drawing Ducks," 38E |
| | Mathematics | Phonics Rhyme: "Wish List," 8/9 | Phonics Rhyme: "My Phone," 38/39 |
| | Science | Math: Shape Graphs, 12 | Science: Fish, 44 |
| | Music | Social Studies: Food Geography, 20 | Math: Weight, 48 |
| | Art | Science: Recycling, 22 | Social Studies: Map Skills, 58 |
| | Drama | Math: Rhyme Song, 26 | |
| | Language Arts | | |
| **CULTURAL PERSPECTIVES** | | Colors/Los Colores, 24 | Down Feathers, 42 |

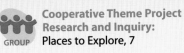

# WEEK 3 — The Knee-High Man

**Easy:** *Fun Run*
**Independent:** *A Bigger House For June*
**Authentic:** *Pete's Chicken*

☑ **Phonics**
Introduce Long *u: u-e*, 68A–68B
Review Long *u: u-e*, 95E–95F
Review *u-e, o-e, i-e, a-e*, 95G–95H

☑ **Comprehension**
Introduce Make Inferences, 95I–95J

☑ **Vocabulary**
Inflectional Endings *-er, -est*, 95K–95L

☑ **Study Skills**
Charts, 94

**Phonics and Decoding:** Long *o: o-e*, 73
**Context Clues**, 75
**High-Frequency Words**, 77
**Make Inferences**, 79
**Main Idea**, 89

**Writing:** Persuasive Writing, 95M
**Grammar:** *Go* and *Do*, 95O
**Spelling:** Words with Long *u: u-e*, 95Q

**Read Aloud:** "Timimoto," 66E

**Phonics Rhyme:** "Duck the Ant," 66/67

**Math:** Inch by Inch, 76

**Science:** Frogs, 80

**Social Studies:** Peaceful Solutions, 86

Corn Varieties, 72

# WEEK 4 — Johnny Appleseed

**Easy:** *Fall is Fun!*
**Independent:** *The Land*
**Authentic:** *Down by the Bay*

☑ **Phonics**
Introduce Long *a: ay, ai*, 98A–98B
Review Long *a: ay, ai*, 123E–123F
Review *ai, ay; u-e, o-e*, 123G–123H

☑ **Comprehension**
Review Make Inferences, 123I–123J

☑ **Vocabulary**
Review Inflectional Endings *-er, -est*, 123K–123L

☑ **Study Skills**
Charts, 122

**Context Clues**, 101
**Vowels**, 105
**Setting**, 107
**Character**, 109
**Cause and Effect**, 115
**Summarize**, 117

**Writing:** Persuasive Writing, 123M
**Grammar:** *See* and *Say*, 123O
**Spelling:** Words with Long *a: ai, ay*, 123Q

**Read Aloud:** "The Great Big Enormous Turnip," 96E

**Phonics Rhyme:** "The Gift," 96/97

**Science:** Plant a Seed, 102

**Art:** Color Theory, 104

**Social Studies:** Family Farming, 106

**Math:** Estimation, 110

Apples, 100

# WEEK 5 — Ring, Ring, Ring!

Self-Selected Reading of Leveled Books

☑ **Phonics**
Review *ai, ay; u-e, o-e, i-e, a-e*, 126A–126B

☑ **Comprehension**
Review Cause and Effect, 133E–133F
Review Make Inferences, 133G–133H

☑ **Vocabulary**
Review Inflectional Endings *-s, -es*, 133I–133J
Review Inflectional Endings *-er, -est*, 133K–133L

☑ **Study Skills**
Charts, 132

**Writing:** Persuasive Writing, 133M
**Grammar:** More Contractions with *Not*, 133O
**Spelling:** Words from Social Studies, 133Q

**Read Aloud:** "The Brave Ones," 124E

**Phonics Rhyme:** "Fire Pups," 124/125

# WEEK 6 — Review, Writing Process, Assessment

Self-Selected Reading

☑ **Assess Skills**
Long *i: i-e*
Long *o: o-e*
Long *u: u-e*
Long *a: ay, ai*
Cause and Effect
Make Inferences
Inflectional Endings *-s, -es*
Inflectional Ending *-ed*
Charts

☑ **Assess Grammar and Spelling**
Review Verbs, 135G
Review Spelling Patterns, 135H

☑ **Unit Progress Assessment**

☑ **Standardized Test Preparation**

**Unit Writing Process:** Persuasive Writing, 135A–135F

**GROUP** — *Cooperative Theme Project Research and Inquiry:* Places to Explore, 7

## Unit Resources

### LITERATURE

**LEVELED BOOKS**

**Easy:**
- *A Pet For Max*
- *Spot's Trick*
- *Fun Run*
- *Fall is Fun!*

**Independent:**
- *The Big Secret*
- *Show and Tell Rose*
- *A Bigger House For June*
- *The Land*

**Authentic:**
- *Who Took the Farmer's Hat?*
- *My Best Friend*
- *Pete's Chicken*
- *Down by the Bay*

**THEME BIG BOOK**
Share *Fish Faces* to set the unit theme and make content-area connections.

**STUDENT LISTENING LIBRARY AUDIOCASSETTE**
Recordings of the student book selections and poetry.

### SKILLS

**LEVELED PRACTICE**

**Practice Book:** Student practice for phonics, comprehension, vocabulary and study skills; plus practice for instructional vocabulary and story comprehension. Take-Home Story included for each lesson.

**Reteach:** Reteaching opportunities for students who need more help with each assessed skill.

**Extend:** Extension activities for vocabulary, comprehension, story and study skills.

**TEACHING CHARTS**
Instructional charts for modeling vocabulary and tested skills. Also available as transparencies.

**WORD BUILDING BOOK**
Letter and word cards to utilize phonics and build instructional vocabulary.

**LANGUAGE SUPPORT BOOK**
**ESL** Parallel teaching lessons and appropriate practice activities for students needing language support.

**PHONICS PRACTICE BOOK**
Additional practice focusing on vowel sounds, phonograms, blends, digraphs, and key phonetic elements.

### LANGUAGE ARTS

**GRAMMAR PRACTICE BOOK**
Provides practice for grammar and mechanics lessons.

**SPELLING PRACTICE BOOK**
Provides practice with the word list and spelling patterns. Includes home involvement activities.

**DAILY LANGUAGE ACTIVITIES**
Sentence activities that provide brief, regular practice and reinforcement of grammar, mechanics, and usage skills. Available as blackline masters and transparencies.

**McGraw-Hill School TECHNOLOGY**

*Phonics* **CD-ROM**
Provides extra phonics support.

*inter***NET** **CONNECTION** Extends lesson activities through Research and Inquiry ideas.

Visit **www.mhschool.com/reading.**

# Resources for
# Meeting Individual Needs

| EASY | INDEPENDENT | CHALLENGE | LANGUAGE SUPPORT |
|------|-------------|-----------|------------------|

## BOOK 4

**The Shopping List**

**Leveled Book:**
*A Pet for Max*
Reteach, 127–134
**Alternate Teaching Strategies,** T64–T72
 **Writing:** Draw a Map, 37M–37N
 **CD-ROM**

**Leveled Book:**
*The Big Secret*
Practice, 127–134
**Alternate Teaching Strategies,** T64–T72
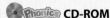 **Writing:** Write an Ad, 37M–37N
 **CD-ROM**

**Leveled Book:**
*Who Took the Farmer's Hat?*
Extend, 127–134
 **Writing:** Make a Journal Entry, 37M–37N
 **CD-ROM**

**Teaching Strategies,** 10C, 11, 13, 15, 16, 19, 23, 28, 30, 37A, 37B, 37C, 37N
Language Support, 136–144
**Alternate Teaching Strategies,** T64–T72
**Writing:** Write a Letter, 37M–37N
**CD-ROM**

---

**Yasmin's Ducks**

**Leveled Book:**
*Spot's Trick*
Reteach, 135–142
**Alternate Teaching Strategies,** T64–T72
 **Writing:** Draw a Scene, 65M–65N
 **CD-ROM**

**Leveled Book:**
*Show and Tell Rose*
Practice, 135–142
**Alternate Teaching Strategies,** T64–T72
 **Writing:** Write a Plan, 65M–65N
**CD-ROM**

**Leveled Book:**
*My Best Friend*
Extend, 135–142
 **Writing:** Make a Journal Entry, 65M–65N
**CD-ROM**

**Teaching Strategies,** 40C, 41, 47, 53, 57, 65A, 65B, 65C, 65N
Language Support, 145–153
**Alternate Teaching Strategies,** T64–T72
**Writing:** Write a Letter, 65M–65N
**CD-ROM**

---

**The Knee-High Man**

**Leveled Book:**
*Fun Run*
Reteach, 143–150
**Alternate Teaching Strategies,** T64–T72
**Writing:** Draw a Scene, 95M–95N
**CD-ROM**

**Leveled Book:**
*A Bigger House for June*
Practice, 143–150
**Alternate Teaching Strategies,** T64–T72
 **Writing:** Record a Dream, 95M–95N
 **CD-ROM**

**Leveled Book:**
*Pete's Chicken*
Extend, 143–150
 **Writing:** Make a Journal Entry, 95M–95N
**CD-ROM**

**Teaching Strategies,** 68C, 69, 71, 79, 85, 95A, 95B, 95C, 95N
Language Support, 154–162
**AlternateTeaching Strategies,** T64–T72
**Writing:** Write a Letter, 95M–95N
 **CD-ROM**

---

**Johnny Appleseed**

**Leveled Book:**
*Fall Is Fun!*
Reteach, 151–158
**Alternate Teaching Strategies,** T64–T72
**Writing:** Draw a Scene, 123M–123N
**CD-ROM**

**Leveled Book:**
*The Land*
Practice, 151–158
**Alternate Teaching Strategies,** T64–T72
**Writing:** Write a Handbook, 123M–123N
**CD-ROM**

**Leveled Book:**
*Down by the Bay*
Extend, 151–158
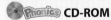 **Writing:** Make a Journal Entry, 123M–123N
 **CD-ROM**

**Teaching Strategies,** 98C, 99, 107, 109, 115, 116, 123A, 123B, 123C, 123N
Language Support, 163–171
**Alternate Teaching Strategies,** T64–T72
**Writing:** Write a Letter, 123M–123N
 **CD-ROM**

---

**Put Out the Fire!**

**Review**
Reteach, 159–166
**Alternate Teaching Strategies,** T64–T72
**Writing:** Draw a Fire Scene, 133M–133N
**CD-ROM**

**Review**
Practice, 159–166
**Alternate Teaching Strategies,** T64–T72
**Writing:** Write a Description of a Fire Scene, 133M–133N
**CD-ROM**

**Review**
Extend, 159–166
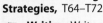 **Writing:** Make a Journal Entry, 133M–133N
**CD-ROM**

**Teaching Strategies,** 126C, 127, 133N
Language Support, 172–180
**Alternate Teaching Strategies,** T64–T72
**Writing:** Write a Speech, 133M–133N
  **CD-ROM**

## INFORMAL

### Informal Assessment

- Phonics, 10B, 33, 37F, 37H; 40B, 61, 65F, 65H; 68B, 91, 95F, 95H; 98B, 119, 123F, 123H; 126B, 129
- Comprehension, 32, 33, 37J; 60, 61, 65J; 90, 91, 95J; 118, 119, 123J; 128, 129, 133F, 133H
- Vocabulary, 37L, 65L, 95L, 123L, 133J, 133L

### Performance Assessment

- Scoring Rubrics, 37N, 65N, 95N, 123N, 133N, 135F
- Research and Inquiry, 7, 135
- Listening, Speaking, Viewing Activities, 8E, 8/9, 10C, 10–37, 37D, 37M–N; 38E, 38/39, 40C, 40–65, 65D, 65M–N; 66E, 66/67, 68C, 68–95, 95D, 95M–N; 96E, 96/97, 98C, 98–123, 123D, 123M–N; 124E, 124/125, 126C, 126–133, 133D, 133M–N
- Portfolio
- Writing, 37M–N, 65M–N, 95M–N, 123M–N, 133M–N, 135A–F

### Leveled Practice

**Practice, Reteach, Extend**

- **Phonics and Decoding**
  Long *i: i-e,* 127, 131, 132, 140, 148, 159
  Long *o: o-e,* 135, 139, 140, 148, 156, 159
  Long *u: u-e,* 143, 147, 148, 156, 159
  Long *a: ay, ai,* 151, 155, 156, 159
- **Comprehension**
  Cause and Effect, 133, 141, 163
  Make Inferences, 149, 157, 164
- **Vocabulary Strategies**
  Inflectional Endings *-s, -es,* 134, 165
  Inflectional Ending *-ed,* 142, 165
  Inflectional Endings *-er, -est,* 150, 158, 166
- **Study Skills**
  Charts, 130, 138, 146, 154, 162

## FORMAL

### Selection Tests

- **Skills and Vocabulary Words**
  *The Shopping List, 31–32*
  *Yasmin's Ducks, 33–34*
  *The Knee-High Man, 35–36*
  *Johnny Appleseed, 37–38*
  *Put Out the Fire! 39–40*

### Unit 3 Assessment

- **Phonics and Decoding**
  Long *i: i-e*
  Long *o: o-e*
  Long *u: u-e*
  Long *a: ay, ai*
- **Comprehension**
  Cause and Effect
  Make Inferences
- **Vocabulary Strategies**
  Inflectional Endings *-s, -es*
  Inflectional Ending *-ed*
  Inflectional Endings *-er, -est*

### Grammar and Spelling Assessment

- **Grammar**
  Verbs, 101, 107, 113, 119, 125, 127–128
- **Spelling**
  Words with Long *i: i-e,* 102
  Words with Long *o: o-e,* 108
  Words with Long *u: u-e,* 114
  Words with Long *a: ay, ai,* 120
  Words from Social Studies, 126
  Unit Assessment, 127–128

### Diagnostic/Placement Evaluation

- Individual Reading Inventory, 15–16
- Running Record, 17–18
- Phonics and Decoding Inventory, 101–102
- Grade K Diagnostic/Placement
- Grade 1 Diagnostic/Placement
- Grade 2 Diagnostic/Placement
- Grade 3 Diagnostic/Placement

### Test Preparation

- TAAS Preparation and Practice Booklet, 35–44
- See also Test Power in Teacher's Edition, 37, 65, 95, 123, 133

# Assessment Checklist

**Student** ................................. **Grade** ..........

**Teacher** .................................

| | The Shopping List | Yasmin's Ducks | The Knee-High Man | Johnny Appleseed | Put Out the Fire! | Assessment Summary |
|---|---|---|---|---|---|---|
| **LISTENING/SPEAKING** | | | | | | |
| Participates in oral language experiences | | | | | | |
| Listens and speaks to gain knowledge of culture | | | | | | |
| Speaks appropriately to audiences for different purposes | | | | | | |
| Communicates clearly | | | | | | |
| **READING** | | | | | | |
| Uses a variety of word identification strategies: | | | | | | |
| • Phonics and decoding: long *i: i-e* | | | | | | |
| • Phonics and decoding: long *o: o-e* | | | | | | |
| • Phonics and decoding: long *u: u-e* | | | | | | |
| • Phonics and decoding: long *a: ay, ai* | | | | | | |
| • Inflectional Endings *-s, -es* | | | | | | |
| • Inflectional Ending *-ed* | | | | | | |
| • Inflectional Endings *-er, -est* | | | | | | |
| Reads with fluency and understanding | | | | | | |
| Reads widely for different purposes in varied sources | | | | | | |
| Develops an extensive vocabulary | | | | | | |
| Uses a variety of strategies to comprehend selections: | | | | | | |
| • Cause and Effect | | | | | | |
| • Make Inferences | | | | | | |
| Responds to various texts | | | | | | |
| Analyzes the characteristics of various types of texts: | | | | | | |
| Conducts research using various sources: | | | | | | |
| • Charts | | | | | | |
| Reads to increase knowledge | | | | | | |
| **WRITING** | | | | | | |
| Writes for a variety of audiences and purposes | | | | | | |
| Composes original texts using the conventions of written language such as capitalization and penmanship | | | | | | |
| Spells proficiently | | | | | | |
| Composes texts applying knowledge of grammar and usage | | | | | | |
| Uses writing processes | | | | | | |
| Evaluates own writing and writing of others | | | | | | |

+ Observed      − Not Observed

# Introducing the Theme

### Let's Find Out!

*Looking for answers is an adventure.*

**PRESENT THE THEME** Read the theme statement to the children. Have children discuss how they find answers to questions. Whom do they ask? What books do they look at? What are some other ways they find answers to questions? Give, or have children provide, specific questions, such as "How old is this town?" or "How many children are in this school?" and have children tell how they would search for answers.

**READ THE POEM** Tell children that poems are often about people exploring, asking for questions, or searching for answers. Read aloud "To the Top." Ask children what kind of adventure the poet is describing. What question does the poet ask about the adventure?

 **STUDENT LISTENING LIBRARY AUDIOCASSETTES**

**MAKE CONNECTIONS** Have children preview the unit by reading the selection titles and looking at the illustrations. Then have them work in small groups to brainstorm a list of ways that the stories, poems, and the *Time for Kids* magazine article relate to the theme Let's Find Out!

Groups can then compare their lists as they share them with the class.

6

## THEME SUMMARY

Each of the five selections relates to the unit theme Let's Find Out! as well as the global theme Inquiry. These thematic links will help children to make connections across texts.

*The Shopping List* People at a store help a boy recall what he was supposed to get.

*Yasmin's Ducks* A girl explains her interest in ducks to her friends.

*The Knee-High Man* A small man asks big animals how he can become big, too.

*Johnny Appleseed* A man helps settlers to plant apple trees.

*Ring! Ring! Ring! Put Out the Fire!* Firefighting is an important job.

# Let's Find Out

## To the Top

We're climbing and climbing
The trail is so high
that I think we'll be climbing
right up to the sky.
I want it to end
and my poor feet to stop.
Oh, when will we reach
the mountaintop?

*by Sandra Liatsos*

7

## LEARNING ABOUT POETRY

**Literary Devices: Imagery** Read "To the Top" to children. As you read the poem, have children visualize the trail. Is it steep? Long? What words in the poem make you think so?

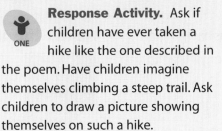

**Response Activity.** Ask if children have ever taken a hike like the one described in the poem. Have children imagine themselves climbing a steep trail. Ask children to draw a picture showing themselves on such a hike.

# Research and *Inquiry*

**Theme Project: Places to Explore** Have teams brainstorm lists of places they would like to explore, such as a city or another planet. They will then choose a place as the basis for a project that will tell about the place, why they want to explore it, and what they hope to find out.

**List What They Know** Once children have picked a place to explore, have them list what they already know about it.

**Ask Questions and Identify Resources** Ask children to brainstorm some questions that tell what they want to know about the place they want to explore. Have them list possible resources.

| QUESTIONS | POSSIBLE RESOURCES |
|---|---|
| • What would it be like to walk on Mars?<br>• How cold or hot is it there?<br>• What does it look like there? | • Encyclopedia<br>• Book<br>• Search on Internet |

**inter NET CONNECTION** Go to *www.mhschool.com /reading* for links to sites about cities and planets.

**Create a Presentation** When their research is complete, children will present their project to the class. Have children make a poster about their place, give a talk, or put on a play. Encourage children to use visuals.

**See Wrap-Up the Theme, page 135**

# The Shopping List

**Selection Summary** Children will read about what happens when a boy forgets one item on his shopping list. With the help of other customers, the boy eventually remembers what he was supposed to get, but not before his father's grocery store is turned upside down.

**Student Listening Library Audiocassette**

**INSTRUCTIONAL**
Pages 10–37

**About the Author** Gary Apple has always liked to write stories that are funny. "I like to write about things that make me laugh," he says. "I think that if something makes me laugh, then it will make other people laugh too."

**About the Illustrator** Shirley Beckes is an illustrator of children's books, puzzles, and games. She and her husband live in Wisconsin, where they have their own design and illustration studio.

# Resources for Meeting Individual Needs

**EASY**
Pages 37A–37D

DECODABLE

**INDEPENDENT**
Pages 37B–37D

Take-Home version available

**CHALLENGE**
Pages 37C–37D

## LEVELED PRACTICE

**Reteach, 127–134**

blackline masters with reteaching opportunities for each assessed skill

**Practice, 127–134**

workbook with Take-Home Stories and practice opportunities for each assessed skill and story comprehension

**Extend, 127–134**

blackline masters that offer challenge activities for each assessed skill

## ADDITIONAL RESOURCES

- **Language Support Book** 136–144
- **Take-Home Story, Practice** pp. 128a–128b
- **Alternate Teaching Strategies** T64–T72

McGraw-Hill School
**TECHNOLOGY**

Phonics **CD-ROM** provides extra phonics support.

**interNET**
CONNECTION Research & Inquiry ideas. Visit **www.mhschool.com/reading.**

*The Shopping List*
by Gary Apple
Illustrated by Shirley Beckes

## Suggested
# Lesson Planner

 **Available on CD-ROM**

| READING AND LANGUAGE ARTS |  DAY **1** *Focus on Reading and Skills* |  DAY **2** *Read the Literature* |
|---|---|---|
| ● **Phonics Daily Routines** | Daily  Routine: **Blending,** 10B <br><br>  CD-ROM | Daily **Phonics** Routines: **Segmenting,** 10C <br><br> **Phonics** CD-ROM |
| ● **Phonological Awareness** <br><br> ● **Phonics** *Long i* <br><br> ● **Comprehension** <br><br> ● **Vocabulary** <br><br> ● **Study Skills** <br><br> ● **Listening, Speaking, Viewing, Representing** | **Read** **Read Aloud and Motivate,** 8E <br> *General Store* <br><br> **Develop Phonological Awareness,** 8/9 <br> Long *i: i-e* <br> *Wish List* <br><br> ☑ **Introduce Long *i: i-e,*** 10A–10B <br> **Reteach, Practice, Extend,** 127 <br> Phonics Workbook, 139–142 | **Build Background,** 10C <br> Develop Oral Language <br><br> **Vocabulary,** 10D <br><br> *after*    *always*    *blue* <br> *were*    *who* <br><br> Vocabulary Cards <br> Teaching Chart 94 <br> **Reteach, Practice, Extend,** 128 <br><br> **Read** **Read the Selection,** 10-33 <br> Guided Reading <br> ☑ Long *i: i-e* <br><br> **Minilessons,** 13, 17, 19, 23, 25, 27, 29 <br><br> **Cultural Perspectives,** 24 |
| ● **Curriculum Connections** |  **Link** Language Arts, 8E |  **Activity** Math, 12 |
| ● **Writing** |  **Writing Prompt:** Write about a time you went shopping. Tell how you found where everything was. |  **Writing Prompt:** Imagine that you were once a clerk in a store. Write about a child you watched shopping. <br><br>  **Journal Writing** <br> Quick-Write, 33 |
| ● **Grammar** | **Introduce the Concept:** *Was* and *Were,* 37O <br> Daily Language Activity: Use *was* and *were* correctly. <br> **Grammar Practice Book,** 97 | **Teach the Concept:** *Was* and *Were,* 37O <br> Daily Language Activity: Use *was* and *were* correctly. <br> **Grammar Practice Book,** 98 |
| ● **Spelling** *Long i* | **Pretest: Words with Long *i: i-e,*** 37Q <br><br> **Spelling Practice Book,** 97–98 | **Explore the Pattern: Words with Long *i: i-e,*** 37Q <br><br> **Spelling Practice Book,** 99 |

**Meeting Individual Needs**

☑ = **Skill Assessed in Unit Test**

---

 **DAY 3** — *Read the Literature*

 Daily **Phonics** Routine:
**Writing,** 35

**Phonics** CD-ROM

**Reread for Fluency,** 32

**Story Questions,** 34
Reteach, Practice, Extend, 129
**Story Activities,** 35

**Study Skill,** 36
☑ Charts
**Teaching Chart 95**
Reteach, Practice, Extend, 130

 **Read**

**Read the Leveled Books,**
Guided Reading
☑ Long *i: i-e*
☑ High-Frequency Words

**Activity** Social Studies, 20

 **Writing Prompt:** Write a story about a cat who went to a store with a shopping list. What was the cat like? What did it buy?

**Journal Writing,** 37D

**Review and Practice:** *Was* and *Were,* 37P
Daily Language Activity: Use *was* and *were* correctly.

**Grammar Practice Book,** 99

**Practice and Extend: Words with Long *i: i-e*,** 37R

**Spelling Practice Book,** 100

---

 **DAY 4** — *Build Skills*

Daily **Phonics** Routine:
**Fluency,** 37F

**Phonics** CD-ROM

**Read** **Read the Leveled Books and Self-Selected Books**

☑ **Review Long *i: i-e*,** 37E–37F
**Teaching Chart 96**
Reteach, Practice, Extend, 131
**Language Support,** 141
Phonics Workbook, 139–142

☑ **Review *i-e, a-e*,** 37G–37H
Teaching Chart 97
Reteach, Practice, Extend, 132
**Language Support,** 142
Phonics Workbook, 139–142

**Activity** Science, 22

**Writing Prompt:** Describe a holiday gift you bought for someone.

**Persuasive Writing,** 37M
Prewrite, Draft

**Meeting Individual Needs for Writing,** 37N

**Review and Practice:** *Was* and *Were,* 37P
Daily Language Activity: Use *was* and *were* correctly.

**Grammar Practice Book,** 100

**Proofread and Write: Words with Long *i: i-e*,** 37R

**Spelling Practice Book,** 101

---

**DAY 5** — *Build Skills*

Daily **Phonics** Routine:
**Letter Substitution,** 37H

**Phonics** CD-ROM

**Read** **Read Self-Selected Books**

☑ **Introduce Cause and Effect,** 37I–37J
**Teaching Chart 98**
Reteach, Practice, Extend, 133
**Language Support,** 143

☑ **Review Inflectional Endings -s, -es,** 37K–37L
**Teaching Chart 99**
Reteach, Practice, Extend, 134
**Language Support,** 144

**Listening, Speaking, Viewing, Representing,** 37N
Illustrate the List
Convince the Class

**Minilessons,** 13, 17, 19, 23, 25, 27, 29

**Activity** Music, 26

**Writing Prompt:** Pretend you once stayed overnight in a store when nobody else was there. Write a story about how you felt and what you did.

**Persuasive Writing,** 37M
Revise, Edit, Proofread, Publish

**Assess and Reteach:** *Was* and *Were,* 37P
Daily Language Activity: Use *was* and *were* correctly.

**Grammar Practice Book,** 101–102

**Assess and Reteach: Words with Long *i: i-e*,** 37R

**Spelling Practice Book,** 102

**8D**

**Link**

**Language Arts**

# Read Aloud and Motivate

## General Store

a poem by
Rachel Field

**S**omeday I'm going to have a store

With a tinkly bell hung over the door,

With real glass cases and counters wide

And drawers all spilly with things inside.

There'll be a little of everything:

Bolts of calico; balls of string;

Jars of peppermint; tins of tea;

Pots and kettles and crockery;

Seeds in packets; scissors bright;

Kegs of sugar, brown and white;

Sarsaparilla for picnic lunches,

Bananas and rubber boots in bunches.

I'll fix the window and dust each shelf,

And take the money all in myself,

It will be my store and I will say:

"What can I do for you to-day?"

## Oral Comprehension

**LISTENING AND SPEAKING** Motivate children to think about setting by reading this poem in which the poet imagines having a general store. Ask children to picture the store and everything in it, as you read the poem aloud. When you are done, ask: "Where does the poem take place? What are some things that are in the store? Would you like to have a store like that? Why or why not?"

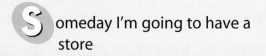 Ask children to draw the scene described in "General Store." Help children by bringing in pictures of items with which they may not be familiar, such as calico. Encourage them to include as many details as they can from the poem. When children have finished, have them compare their pictures.

▶ **Visual**

# Develop Phonological Awareness

Anthology pages 8–9

## Wish List

I made a silly shopping list
Of things I want to get:
Five limes, a kite, a bike,
Four plums (they have to be ripe),
A snake that slides, and skates that shine.

Do you think I could get all this
With a dime?

## Objective: Listen for Long *i*

**RHYMING** Read "Wish List." As you reread the poem, have children clap each time they hear words with the /i/ sound, such as *time*.

**Phonemic Awareness** Blending Using the poem context, ask children to blend together sounds to identify words. Example: *I want a* /k/ /ī/ /t/. *What do I want?* (a kite) Have children look at the word in their texts. Point out that the final *-e* is silent.

Repeat with **five, bike, ripe, slides, shine,** and **dime.**

**Phonemic Awareness** **SEGMENTING** Have children segment initial and final sounds.

Use letter cards to build the word *five.*

• Say the word *five.*

Take away the *v* and *e* cards.

• Say *five* without the letters /v/ and /e/.

Replace the *v* and *e* cards. Take away the *f* card.

• Say *five* without the letter /f/.

Repeat with **kite, bike, ripe, shine,** and **dime.**

## Introduce Long i: *i-e*

**OBJECTIVES**

Children will:

* identify long *i-e* words.
* blend and read long *i-e* words.
* review consonants, blends, and digraphs.

**MATERIALS**

* letter cards long *i* cards, and word building boxes from the **Word Building Manipulative Cards**

**SPELLING/PHONICS CONNECTIONS**

Words with long *i-e*: See the 5-Day Spelling Plan, pages 37Q–37R.

**TEACHING TIP**

**INSTRUCTIONAL** In blending, cover up the silent "e" and have children read the word; then have them read it again with the "e" uncovered.

**Identify *i-e* as a Symbol for /ī/**   Let children know they will learn to read words with the letters *i-e* where the letter *i* sounds like /ī/ and the *e* on the end is silent.

* Display the *i-e* letter card. Point to the *i* and say /ī/.
* Explain to children that a consonant needs to go in the space between the two letters.

i ___ e

**BLENDING Model and Guide Practice with Long *i-e* Words**

* Point to the *i* on the letter card, say /ī/, and have children repeat after you.
* Place the *p* letter card on the space between the *i* and the *e*.
* Point to the letters as you blend the sounds to read *ipe*. Have children repeat after you.

 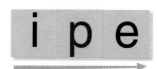

* Place the *r* letter card in front of the letter *i*.
* Have children blend the sounds and read the word *ripe* with you as you move your hand below the word. Remind children that the final *e* is silent.

 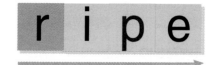

**Use the Word in Context**   • Use the word in context to reinforce its meaning. Example: *The ripe apples fell from the tree.*

**Repeat the Procedure**   Use the following words to continue modeling and guided practice with long *i: i-e*.

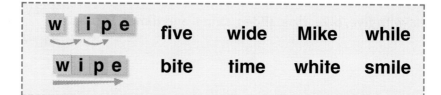

| w i p e | five | wide | Mike | while |
| w i p e | bite | time | white | smile |

## PRACTICE

**LETTER SUBSTITUTION**
Build Long *i-e* Words with Letter Cards

**GROUP**

Display the *i-e* letter card. Point to the *i* and say /ī/. Remind children that the *e* is silent. Add a *t* between the *i* and *e*, and a *k* at the beginning. Build and read the word *kite*, then ask children to read it. Continue by having children substitute letters and build, read, and write the following words: *bite, bike, like, life, wife, wipe, dive.*

▶ **Linguistic/Kinesthetic**

## ASSESS/CLOSE

**Read and Write Long *i-e* Words**

To assess children's ability to blend and read long *i-e* words, observe them as they build and read the words in the Practice activity. Then have them turn to page 8 in their books and read "Wish List" aloud with them. Ask them to write two long *i-e* words from the rhyme.

## ADDITIONAL PHONICS RESOURCES

**Phonics/Phonemic Awareness Practice Book, pages 139–142**
**PHONICS KIT**
Hands-on Activities and Practice

McGraw-Hill School
**TECHNOLOGY**
**Phonics CD-ROM**
activities for practice with Blending and Segmenting

# Meeting Individual Needs for Phonics

| EASY | ON-LEVEL | CHALLENGE |
|---|---|---|
| Name_____ Date_____ Reteach 127 | Name_____ Date_____ Practice 127 | Name_____ Date_____ Extend 127 |
| **Long i: i-e** | **Long i: i-e** | **Long i: i-e** |

**EASY**

Read the sentence.
Would you **like** to **bite** a **lime**?

Circle the word that completes the sentence. Then write the word.

1. I ___smile___ when I am glad.
   (smile)   bite   gripe

2. He wants to ___write___ a letter.
   (write)   wide   live

3. I like her ___white___ dress.
   mile   drive   (white)

4. My cat had ___five___ kittens.
   rice   bride   (five)

Book 1.4
The Shopping List    4
At Home: Say a long *i* word, such as *wipe*. Have children name words that rhyme with it such as *pipe* or *stripe*.    127

**ON-LEVEL**

Use the words in the box to answer the riddles.

| five | smile | time | rice | ripe |

1. Six is after me. What am I? ___five___

2. You do this with your lips. What am I? ___smile___

3. A good plum is this way. What am I? ___ripe___

4. A clock tells you about me. What am I? ___time___

5. You can eat me. What am I? ___rice___

Book 1.4
The Shopping List    5
At Home: Have children make up sentences using each of the words in the box.    127

**CHALLENGE**

Read the words in the box. Find them in the puzzle. Circle them.

| like | white | ride | ripe | Mike | nice | smile |

```
A N I C E N O
M I K E E I M
I R I D E K L
V F R I P E X
E C W H I T E
L I K E O C P
S M I L E Z A
```

Choose a word from the box. Write a sentence with that word.

Answers will vary but should include a word from the box.

Think of your own **i-e** word. Use it in a sentence.

Possible answers include price, pile, and lime.

Book 1.4
The Shopping List
At Home: Write *-ite, -ice, -ipe, -ive, -ike,* and *-ile* on separate cards. Take turns picking cards and filling in letters to create new words. Example: *-ice, nice; -ipe, ripe;* and *-ile, bile.*    127

Reteach, 127        Practice, 127        Extend, 127

## Daily Routines

**DAY 1 Blending** Write the spelling of each sound in *smile* as you say the word. Have children blend the sounds and repeat the word. Do the same with *drive* and *prize.*

**DAY 2 Letter Substitution** Give children the *i-e* and consonant letter cards. Say *dime* aloud, and show how to build the word. Have children listen to the sounds and replace consonant cards to build the words *time* and *hive.*

**DAY 3 Writing** Have children write labels on simple pictures using the appropriate word from this list: *kite, tire, bike, five.*

**DAY 4 Fluency** Write the following list of long *i-e* words on the chalkboard: *mine, hike, drive, smile, ride.* Ask children to first read the list silently and then read it aloud.

**DAY 5 Rhyming** Using the *i-e* and consonant cards, have pairs of children build sets of ryhming words.

**PHONICS KIT**
HANDS-ON ACTIVITIES AND PRACTICE

**10B**

# Build Background

 **Link**

Social Studies

## Anthology and Leveled Books

### Evaluate Prior Knowledge

**CONCEPT: SHOPPING** Ask children to share their experiences going to the grocery store. Use the following activity to give them more information about grocery shopping.

**MAKE A SHOPPING LIST** Help children record items they would like to buy at the grocery store. ▶ **Visual/Linguistic**

**DRAW A PICTURE** Invite children to draw pictures of something they would like to get at the grocery store. Encourage them to use the list for ideas. Have children label drawings with the sentence: *I like to get ___ at the store.*

### Develop Oral Language

**CONNECT WORDS AND ACTIONS** Have **ESL** children follow simple instructions to act out a trip to the grocery store. For example:

- *Write a list.*
- *Drive to the store.*
- *Push the cart.*
- *Pay the money.*

Encourage children to talk about their trip as they act it out. Ask:

- *What are you doing?*
- *Where are you right now?*
- *Who are you paying?*
  ▶ **Kinesthetic/Linguistic**

## DAILY **Phonics** ROUTINES

**DAY 2** **Letter Substitution**
Give children the *i-e* an consonant letter cards. Say *dime* aloud and show how to build the word. Have children listen to the sounds and replace consonant cards to build the words *time* and *hive.*

**Phonics CD-ROM**

---

### LANGUAGE SUPPORT

To build more background and help develop understanding and recognition of High-Frequency Words, see pages 136–139 in the **Language Support Book.**

# Vocabulary

## High-Frequency Words

**Shopping**

I always take a shopping list.
It helps me not forget.
I got red grapes. I got blue plums.
But I'm not finished yet.
Milk and chips were jotted down.
And after them, a bun.
Who gets to eat this soup I got?
I bet it will be good and hot.
I like my shopping list a lot.
Shopping is such fun!

Teaching Chart 94

### High-Frequency Words

| after | blue |
| always | were |
| who | |

### SPELLING/VOCABULARY CONNECTIONS

The words *after, always, blue, were,* and *who* are Challenge Words. See page 37Q for Day 1 of the 5-Day Spelling Plan.

## Auditory

**LISTEN TO WORDS** Without displaying it, read aloud "Shopping" on **Teaching Chart 94**. Ask children to imagine what other things were on the poet's shopping list. Then have them talk about their own experiences shopping with a list.

**FIND ANTONYMS FOR HIGH-FREQUENCY WORDS** Have children aurally identify each high-frequency word using the following activity:

- Say aloud one of the high-frequency words. Read a line of the poem where the word appears.

- Ask children if they can think of a word that means the opposite of the high-frequency word. (always/never, were/weren't, after/before) Then have them use the words in a sentence.

- Repeat this activity with other high-frequency words.

## Visual

**READ WORDS** Display "Shopping" on **Teaching Chart 94**. Read the poem, tracking the print with your finger as you read. Then hold up Vocabulary Cards one at a time and have children circle the high-frequency words on the chart.

after
blue  who
were  always

Vocabulary Cards

### MAKE A SHOPPING LIST OF WORDS

 **GROUP** Have each group make a shopping list of the vocabulary words. Then put the Vocabulary Cards in different places in the room. Have the groups go "shopping" to find the cards. They can check off the word on their list by using it in a sentence.

**ON-LEVEL**

Name_____ Date_____ Practice 128
High-Frequency Words

Write the word from the box that completes each sentence.

| after | always | blue | were | who |

1. The cat runs _____after_____ the dog.

2. _____Who_____ has my hat?

3. My toys _____were_____ in the box.

4. The chicks _____always_____ eat.

5. The water is _____blue_____.

128

Take-Home Story 128a
Reteach 128
Practice 128 • Extend 128

**10D**

# Guided Instruction

## Preview and Predict

Point to and read aloud the names of the author and illustrator. Take a **picture walk** to discuss what children see, stopping after eight or ten pages. Using words from the story, talk about the illustrations. Point out a few long *i: i-e* words as you go (*Mike, ripe*). Have children make predictions about the story. Discuss questions such as these:

- Who do you think the story is about?
- What do you think is going to happen?

Chart children's predictions about plot and character and read them aloud.

| PREDICTIONS | WHAT HAPPENED |
|---|---|
| The story is about a boy. | |
| People try to help the boy remember what he forgot. | |

## Set Purposes

Ask children what they want to find out by reading the story. For example:

- Why does the store get so untidy?
- What did the boy forget?

READ TOGETHER

**Meet Gary Apple**

When Gary Apple was a little boy, he liked to write funny stories. Now that he is grown up, he still likes to write funny stories. Today, he writes funny books, plays, and TV shows.

**Meet Shirley Becke**

Shirley Beckes is an illustrator of children's books, puzzles, and game She owns her own design studio in Wisconsin.

10

---

# Meeting Individual Needs • Grouping Suggestions for Strategic Reading

| EASY | ON-LEVEL | CHALLENGE |
|---|---|---|
| **Shared Reading** Read the story aloud as you model directionality and track print with your finger. Invite children to join in on repetitive words and phrases. As you read each page, discuss the illustrations. | **Guided Reading** Read the story with children, using the Guided Reading. Monitor any reading difficulties the children have in order to determine which parts of the Guided Reading to emphasize. After reading the story with children, have them reread it, using the rereading suggestions on page 32. | **Read Independently** Have children set purposes before they read. After reading, have children retell the story. Children can use the questions on page 34 for a group discussion. |

# The Shopping List

by Gary Apple

illustrated by Shirley Beckes

11

# Guided Instruction

 **Phonics** **Long *i: i-e***

**Strategic Reading** Tell children that paying attention to what characters say in a story will help them understand what happens. Explain that they will use a map of a grocery store to keep track of the information in the story.

**1** We are going to read *The Shopping List,* by Gary Apple. Do you think Mr. Apple used his experiences in grocery stores to write this book? *Concept of a Book: Author*

**2** Do people in your family write lists? Why do you think it is a good idea? (You won't forget things.)

---

### TEACHING TIP

**INSTRUCTIONAL** The following chart indicates words from the story that children have learned to decode and high-frequency words that have been taught in a previous lesson.

| Decodable | | High-Frequency |
|-----------|-----|----------------|
| fire | time | after |
| Mike | wide | always |
| ripe | | blue |
| smile | | were |
| while | | who |

---

## LANGUAGE SUPPORT

A blackline master for making a map of Dad's store can be found in the **Language Support Book**. Children can draw in the missing produce as they read the story. At the end they can draw what Mike was really forgetting—his Dad.

**LANGUAGE SUPPORT, 140**

**11**

# Guided Instruction

**③** Phonics **LONG *i*: *i-e* WORDS**
This word looks like it might be some-one's name. Let's see what it is. I'm going to read it as a long *i*, silent *e* word. I can say the letter sounds and blend them together: M i k(e) Mike. The name is *Mike*. *Blending*

**④** Which person in the picture is Mike? (the boy) How do you know? (The other person is his dad.) *Make Inferences*

**⑤** Why did Mike go to the store? (to shop for his mom) Why did he find Dad there? (It's his dad's store.) *Plot and Character*

---

### TEACHING TIP

**MANAGEMENT** If containers are limited, children can work in pairs or small groups. You may also invite volunteers to draw and label their own containers (box or can).

---

**③**
**④**
**⑤** 12

One day Mike went to his dad's store with a list.

---

## Activity

## Cross Curricular: Math

**SHAPE GRAPHS** Show children some empty food boxes and cans.

- Have children identify each shape by name as you sort it: *This is a ___.* (box/can)

- Make a graph on the chalkboard to show how many of each shape.

- Use the graph to talk about *more, fewer.*

Make a grid on the floor with a large piece of paper and a marker. Have each child select one of the empty containers. Invite children to create a floor graph to show whether more boxes or more cans were chosen. ▶ **Visual/Spatial**

Dad was always glad to see Mike.

"Hi, there, Mike!" said Dad with a grin.

"Hi!" said Mike. "Mom sent me to get some things."

13

# Guided Instruction

**6** What can you tell about Dad from the way his store looks? (He's neat; he works hard; he likes things to look nice and tidy.) *Analyze Character/Use Illustrations*

**7** Why is Dad grinning? (He's glad to see Mike.) *Cause and Effect*

## Minilesson
### REVIEW
### Phonics: Blends

Tell children you want to play a game called "What is the beginning? What is the ending?" Tell them you will say a word and ask one of the two questions. Use the following words:

- *list (st)*
- *glad (gl)*
- *grin (gr)*
- *sent (nt)*

Once children identify the blend, write the word on the board and underline the blend.

**Activity** Write a sentence on the board using the blend words and ask children to find the blend.

## LANGUAGE SUPPORT

**ESL** Help children with the concept of *always* by contrasting it with *sometimes* and *never*. Use the three words orally in context. Invite children to make up sentences or stories using the words. Examples: *I always brush my teeth at night. Sometimes I also take a shower. My dog never takes a shower. She always shakes off the water when she's wet.*

Have children draw pictures to illustrate their sentences or stories.

**13**

# Guided Instruction

**(8)** **Phonics** **LONG** *i: i-e* **WORDS**
Long vowels are easy to remember because they say their own name. What letter am I pointing to? *(i)* Yes, /i/. The name of the letter and the sound are the same. There are some long *i: i-e* words on this page. The first one is *Mike*. I'm going to blend the sounds to read the next one: r i p(e) *ripe*. Who can spot the last long *i: i-e* word? Let's blend the sounds to read it: f i v(e) *five*. *Blending*

**(P/i)** **VOCABULARY STRATEGIES** Point to the word in the first sentence that tells what Mike is doing. What is the root word of *checked*? *(check)*

Mike checked his list. "Let's see," he said. "Mom wants me to get jam and rice.
**(8)** She needs five ripe plums, too."

14

---

**(P/i)** **PREVENTION/INTERVENTION**

**VOCABULARY STRATEGIES** Help children decode *-ed* words by reminding them that the *-ed* ending signals time: it says that an action happened in the past. The rest of the word tells the action. Write *-ed* words and ask children to find and read the action (root) word. Then have them read the whole word. Examples: *asked (ask), mixed (mix), locked (lock), bumped (bump), thanked (thank).*

Dad got the rice, the jam, and the five ripe plums.

"Thanks a lot!" said Mike.

Mike packed them in a big bag.

15

# Guided Instruction

**9** Why did Dad get the rice, jam, and plums? (Mike asked for them; Mom wanted them.)

**10** What kinds of containers do rice, jam, and plums usually come in? (rice: box, bag; jam: jar; plums: bag, nothing)

**11** Now it's time to draw the rice, jam, and five plums on our map of Dad's grocery store. Look at the illustration. Who can tell me where the rice, jam, and plums should go?

## LANGUAGE SUPPORT

**ESL** The long *i: i-e* sound may be difficult for some children to identify. Reinforce the sound of long *i: i-e* by giving children rhyming words. Write these words on the chalkboard: *bike, hike, like, Mike, spike, strike*. Let children say or chant pairs of words together.

# Guided Instruction

 **12** Which sentence helps us know why Mike cannot remember what Mom wants? ("*I didn't write it down.*") ***Cause and Effect***

**13** How do you think Mike is feeling? (He is puzzled/upset/confused because he forgot what Mom wants.) ***Make Inferences***

"There was something else I had to get," said Mike

"What is it?" asked Dad.

 **12** "I didn't write it down," said Mike. "I can't remember now."

**13**

16

# Guided Instruction

"I can help you," said Dad. "Did Mom ask for fresh fish?"

"No, it was not fish," said Mike.

17

**14** What does Dad think that Mike forgot? (fish) Why are the fish lying on ice? (so they will stay fresh) Find the fish section on your map of Dad's store. Draw some fish in the empty space.

**BLENDING SHORT *i* WORDS** What short *i* words can you read on this page? (did, fish, it)

## PREVENTION/INTERVENTION

**BLENDING SHORT *i* WORDS**
Review with children the sound of short *i*. Then write the word *fish* on the chalkboard. Review the blending process as you run your finger under the sounds in the word f i sh fish. Then give children word cards and ask them to work in pairs. One child shows a word card and the other blends the sounds to read the word aloud. Have children take turns. Examples: *wish, this, hid, lick.*

## Minilesson

### REVIEW

### Make Inferences

Remind children that they can look at people's expressions and actions to learn more about what is happening in a story.

- How do you think Dad is feeling? (glad/happy) How does the picture help you know? (Dad has his arm around Mike.)
- Mike seems proud of his dad in the picture. Why do you think so? (Dad can help; Dad owns a clean and tidy store.)

**Activity** Have children draw a picture of someone feeling happy, sad, angry, or scared. Have children label the pictures and display them under the appropriate heading on the bulletin board.

# Guided Instruction

**15** What foods do you see here? (grapes and other fruits) Where would you see these in a grocery store? (in the fruit section)

**15** "Well, did Mom want you to get some grapes?" asked Dad.

"No, she didn't ask for grapes," said Mike.

18

**16**

"Is it punch? Is it milk? Is it something to drink?" **17**
asked Dad.
"No. It was not something to drink," said Mike.

19

# Guided Instruction

**16** Is Dad taking the containers out of the case or putting them back in? (taking them out) Why do you think so? (He is showing them to Mike.)

**17** Which new foods does Dad think Mike is forgetting? (grapes, milk, punch) Where do these go in the grocery store? (in the fruit section; in the cooler) Find the fruit section on your map and draw in some grapes. Then find and draw in some milk and punch.

## Minilesson
### REVIEW

### Short *a, i, o, u*

Have children identify and sort short *a, i, o, u* words. Ask them to find:

- 2 short-*a* words (*asked, Dad*)
- 4 short-*i* words (*milk, drink, it, is*)
- 1 short-*o* word (*not*)
- 1 short-*u* word (*punch*)

**Activity** Ask children to draw a picture of four things they like to eat or drink that have the short *a, i, o,* and *u* sound. Have them label their pictures.

**Phonics CD-ROM** Have children use the interactive activities on the Phonics CD-ROM for reinforcement.

## LANGUAGE SUPPORT

**ESL** Children may have difficulty with *didn't* and other contractions. Ask a volunteer to tell what two words *didn't* stands for. (*did not*) Write *did not* and *didn't* on the chalkboard. Then write *was not* on the chalkboard. Invite children to say the contraction these two words make. (*wasn't*) Read the words aloud. Continue with other contractions: *are not* (*aren't*), *isn't* (*is not*).

**19**

# Guided Instruction

**18** How does Miss Lin know that something is "going on"? (Mike's expression; the store is untidy) *Make Inferences*

**19** What does the word *can't* tell us in the third sentence? (Mike is unable to remember.)

## SELF-MONITORING

### STRATEGY

**REREAD** Remind children that rereading part of the story can help them understand the main idea.

***MODEL*** I read that Miss Lin came in and asked what was going on. She can see that Mike and Dad are upset. Then she says "Maybe I can help." I don't remember how she knows what is going on. Oh, I see. Dad says, "Mike can't remember what he came to get." So Dad explains the problem to Miss Lin.

**18**

Just then, Miss Lin came in.
"What's going on?" she asked.
**19** "Mike can't remember what he came to get," said Dad.

20

## Activity

### Cross Curricular: Social Studies

**FOOD GEOGRAPHY** Explain that many foods we think of as ordinary are not native to North America. Potatoes come from South America. Rice was first grown in Asia. Broccoli is native to Europe. Peanuts are from Africa. Help children find these continents on a map or globe.

▶ **Visual/Linguistic**

**RESEARCH AND INQUIRY** Let children look through cookbooks and other books and magazines about food.

*inter*NET **CONNECTION** To access sites about foods grown around the world, have children log on to **www.mhschool.com/reading**.

"Maybe I can help," said Miss Lin. "Does it **(20)** come in a big box?"

"Does it come in a small sack?" asked Dad. **(21)**

21

# Guided Instruction

**(20)** Do Miss Lin and Dad name a food? (no) What do they suggest? (possible containers: box and sack)

**(21)** How are a box and a sack alike? (Both hold things.) How are they different? (A box is harder and has square corners.) *Compare and Contrast*

**BLENDING SHORT *a, o* WORDS** Find and read the short *a* words on this page. *(can, sack, Dad)* Now find and read the short *o* word on this page. *(box)*

---

### TEACHING TIP

**MANAGEMENT** Observe which children are having difficulty with the Prevention/Intervention prompt. After Guided Readings of the story, reinforce blending of short a and o words with these children. Have the rest of the class reread the story for fluency development.

---

 **PREVENTION/INTERVENTION**

**BLENDING SHORT *a, o* WORDS**
Have children blend the sounds in *box* and *sack* as you move your hand beneath the letters in each word. Give children word-building boxes and write these incomplete words on the chalkboard: *gl-d, th-t, p-th, c-p, st-p, ch-p, tr-t, l-g*. Ask children to blend and fill in a missing short *o* or short *a*. Read the words together.

# Guided Instruction

**22** Let's look back through the pictures up to page 22. What has happened to the store? (It is getting untidy.) Why does it look so different from the way it did at the beginning? (People are searching for what Mike forgot.) *Use Illustrations*

**23** Do you think Mike will remember what Mom wanted him to get? (yes/no) Why or why not? Let's add a new prediction to our chart. *Make Predictions*

**24** Look at the picture. How would you describe the expression on Mike's face? (confused) On Dad's face? (frustrated) *Use Illustrations*

"Does it come in tin cans or glass jars?" asked Miss Lin.
But Mike still could not remember.

22

## Activity

### Cross Curricular: Science

**RECYCLING** Recycling turns garbage into something useful. Children can see recycled glass sparkling in roads and sidewalks. Paper waste finds new life in roofing and building materials. Cans break down to form other metal products. Recycling conserves our planet's natural resources and reduces pollution.

**RESEARCH AND INQUIRY** Have children find out where waste goes and how to recycle at school. ▶ **Visual**

**interNET CONNECTION** To access links to various sites about recycling, log on to **www.mhschool.com/reading**.

Then Fran and Ann Gomez came in. (26)
Soon, they were trying to help, too.

23

# Guided Instruction

**25** Why did Fran and Ann Gomez come into the store? (to get groceries) What happened to change their plan? (They found out about Mike's problem and decided to stay and help.) *Sequence of Events*

**26** What do you notice about Fran and Ann's last name? (It is the same.) Does this mean they are in the same family? (probably) How do you think they are related? (They are sisters/sisters-in-law/mother and daughter/cousins.) *Make Inferences*

## Minilesson
### REVIEW
### Context Clues

Remind children that they can use clues in the story and the last sounds of a word to help identify and read it. Ask:

- Which word on page 23 is Gomez?
- What is the sound of the first letter? (/g/)
- How do you know it is a character's last name? (It comes after the name Ann; it is capitalized.)

**Activity** Ask children to write their first names on slips of paper. Put all the names in a hat. Have a volunteer pull a name from the hat and read it by using the first and/or last sounds in the word and the names they know of children in the classroom.

## LANGUAGE SUPPORT

**ESL** Draw the map of Dad's store and produce on the board. Label the five ripe plums, but leave a space for the *i* in *five* and *ripe*. Tell children that the name of the picture contains a long-vowel sound.

Ask them to read the name and say the words to themselves. Tell them to listen to the long vowel say its own name. Ask them to tell you what the long vowel is in each word.

# Guided Instruction

**27** Help me blend the sounds to read the second word here: c o l o r .
*Blending*

**28** When Fran asks *What color is it?* what is the *it* she is talking about? (the thing Mike can't remember)

**29** **Phonics** LONG *i: i-e* Hmm . . . I know red and blue are colors, maybe this word names a color too. The word begins with /wh/. Then I see *i-t-e.* I'm going to blend this word as a long *i,* silent *e* word. w h i te white. *Blending*

---

**TEACHING TIP**

**MANAGEMENT** You may wish to pair children who speak different languages so they can guide each other in the cultural activity. Have other children form a chorus to chant the English word after each new language word.

---

**27** "What color is it?" asked Fran.
"Is it red, blue, white, or black?" asked Ann.

**28**

**29** 24

---

 **CULTURAL PERSPECTIVES**

**COLORS/LOS COLORES** Ask children who know a second language to share the words for *red, blue, white,* or *black.*

**Activity** On the chalkboard write:

red  blue  white  black
rojo  azúl  blanco  negro

Teach children these words in Spanish. (Say: *ro*-ho, ah-*ssul, blahnk*-o, *nay*-gro.) Then pick one word and play "I Spy Something ___ " (*rojo*).

▶ **Auditory/Linguistic**

rojo

Then Miss Lin jumped in. "Is it **30**
carrots, muffins, or bread?"
"No, no, and no!" said Mike. **31**

25

# Guided Instruction

**30** Why does Mike say *no* three times? (Miss Lin asks about three foods, but they are not what Mike forgot.) How do you think Mike feels at this point in the story? (sad; angry; more confused by other people's help) *Character and Plot*

 **PHONOLOGICAL AWARENESS**
Listen to the second sentence. Which word starts with the same sound that *Miss* and *Mike* start with? (*muffins*)

**31** What are the foods Miss Lin suggests? (Miss Lin said carrots, muffins, and bread.) Let's find the bakery section on our maps of Dad's store and add muffins and bread to the picture. Where would the carrots go? (in the vegetable section) Let's add carrots to our map as well. *Story Props*

## Minilesson

### REVIEW

### Plot and Character

Help children see how the story plot develops because of what people do *not* do (as well as what people do). Ask:

- Tell something that Mike did *not* do that made him forget. (He did *not* write everything down.)
- What problem has Mike created by *not* remembering? (Everyone is messing up the store and getting excited.)
- What could Mike do now to change the situation? (Remember what he forgot!)

**Activity** Briefly describe an unusual event. For example: A gigantic tub of ice cream is found floating in the pool. Invite children to suggest what happened just before the event and what might (not) happen after it. Let children draw their "plot."

 **PREVENTION/INTERVENTION**

**PHONOLOGICAL AWARENESS**
Ask children to identify words that begin with the same sounds. Examples: What word in the sentences " Is it carrots, muffins, or bread?" start with the same sound as *color*? (*carrots*) What word begins with the same sound as *bright* and *break*? (*bread*) Encourage children to contribute other words that start with the /k/c or /br/ sounds: *cut, came, corn, cake; brook, bring, brown, brave.*

# Guided Instruction

**32** As we read the last line, show me how you are going to "cut" and "chop". This is how I do it. Watch me cut and chop as I read the last line. Now we'll read it again and cut and chop together. *Pantomime*

**33** How are the ideas of "cut" and "chop" alike? (Both are ways of preparing food.) How do cut and chopped foods look the same? (Both are in pieces.) How are they different? (They have different shapes and sizes.) *Compare and Contrast*

### TEACHING TIP

**INSTRUCTIONAL** Help children see that names also begin with a capital letter, but they do not always start a sentence. Invite volunteers to point out names within the sentence.

Then together, Fran, Ann, Dad, and Miss Lin spoke. "Is it this or that?
**32** Is it that or this? Do you cut it?
**33** Do you chop it?"

26

## Activity

### Cross Curricular: Music

**RHYME SONG** Write the words *pipe* and *ripe* on the board. Read them aloud. Sing the following poem it to the tune of "Twinkle Twinkle, Little Star."

We know a word that rhymes with ___. (pipe)
But it's not another ___. (pipe)

You are right if you guess ___. (ripe)
That's a word that rhymes with ___. (pipe)

Repeat with other rhyming long *i: i-e* words on the chalkboard. Examples: *five, hive, drive; file, mile, pile; ripe, pipe, stripe; spike, bike, hike.*

"I know!" said Miss Lin. "You were sent to get dog food!"

"Who needs that?" asked Mike.

"We do not have a dog!"

27

# Guided Instruction

**34** Why doesn't Mike need dog food? (He has no dog.)

**CONCEPTS OF PRINT** How many sentences are there on page 216? (five) How many are on page 217? (four) How do you know when a new sentence begins? (It starts with a capital letter.)

## Minilesson
### REVIEW

## Sequence of Events

Remind children that they can understand a story by thinking about what happened first, next, and so on.

* Ask children to tell the first thing that happened to Mike.
* Ask them to continue telling the main events in sequence.
* Help children differentiate between main events and details.
* Lead a discussion about how the separate events are building up to create a feeling of frustration.

**Activity** Invite children to draw a picture of something that could happen next.

# Guided Instruction

**35** Why is everyone running around and showing things to Mike? (They're trying to jog his memory.) *Make Inferences*

**36** How is the store different from the way it was at the beginning of the story? (It is now topsy-turvy.) What do you think Dad will be doing in his store tomorrow? (cleaning up) *Make Predictions*

Dad looked in every row.

Miss Lin looked on every shelf.

Fran looked up and down.

Ann looked down and up!

28

---

## Visual Literacy

### VIEWING AND REPRESENTING

Discuss the illustration on page 28. What view do you get of the store? Explain. (The artist drew it like a tunnel to show the entire store.) Why is Miss Lin's face so much larger than the other faces? (For perspective: People look bigger when they are standing in front of other people or objects.)

Ask: Why do you think the illustrator drew the picture from this point of view? (to show that all the people are looking; to show the amount of chaos up and down the store)

---

## LANGUAGE SUPPORT

**ESL** Play a game to help children who are having trouble with directions. Ask children to stand beside their chairs. Say "Reach up!" as you stretch your arms overhead. Say "Reach down!" as you bend and reach toward the floor. Straighten back up and hold your arms out in front of you. Say "Reach in front!" Hold your arms in back and say "Reach behind!" Continue modeling direction.

After they had looked everywhere,
Miss Lin said, "I give up!"
"And we give up, too!" said Ann and Fran.

29

# Guided Instruction

**37** When did Miss Lin give up? (after they had looked everywhere) Did Ann and Fran give up before or after Miss Lin? (after Miss Lin) *Sequence of Events*

**CONCEPTS OF PRINT** What do Ann and Fran say? ("And we give up, too!") How do you know they are saying this? (There are quotation marks before and after what they say.)

## Minilesson
### REVIEW
## Make Predictions

Tell children that they can sometimes guess how a person is going to act by how that person has acted or felt in the past. Ask: At this point, which person in the story is most likely to help Mike? Why?

- Is it Miss Lin, Ann, or Fran? (No. They've given up; they've become too frustrated by looking everywhere.)

- What about Dad? (Maybe. He's been calmer than everyone; he knows what his family usually buys.)

- How about Mom? (Sure, but she's not there.)

- Who does that leave? (Mike himself!)

**Activity** Invite the class to brainstorm ideas about what people can do to remember or help others remember.

## PREVENTION/INTERVENTION

**CONCEPTS OF PRINT** Remind children that quotation marks are used before and after what someone says to show that someone is speaking. Ask children how they like the story. Then write *"We think this story is funny!" said the children.* Have volunteers come to the board. Have one child point to the beginning quotes and the other child point to the ending quotes to frame the sentence. Invite the class to read the sentence aloud.

✦ *TEKS ELA 1.5:G*

# Guided Instruction

**38** Look closely at the illustration. How does it help you know that Mike is thinking? (His hand is on his chin.) What shows you that Dad wants to help? (He is touching Mike's shoulder.) *Use Illustrations*

**39** Why do you think the artist drew this picture as a close-up of Mike and Dad? (Mike might remember what he forgot.) *Concept of a Book/Illustrator*

**38** "Think, Mike, think!" said Dad. "What were you sent to get?"

**39** Mike said, "Let me think."

30

Mike looked at the messy store.
Then Mike looked at Dad.
A wide smile filled Mike's face.

31

# Guided Instruction

**40** Why is Mike smiling? (He just remembered what he forgot.) When was the last time he looked this happy? (when he first came into the store) *Make Inferences*

**CONCEPTS OF PRINT** The name *Mike* appears three times on this page. The third *Mike* has a mark and the letter *s* after it. What does this ending tell us? (Mike has or owns the thing that follows.)

## Minilesson

### REVIEW

### Summarizing

Remind children that summarizing means telling a story's main parts and leaving out the details. They should include the main idea, the most important events, and how the story ends. Ask:

- In a summary, do you mention every suggestion that people made to Mike? (no)
- Do you mention Dad in the story? (yes)
- Do you mention that Mike didn't own a dog? (no)
- Do you mention that Mike remembered what Mom wanted? (yes)

**Activity** Have children form news teams to make up a headline that tells the entire story. Example: "Mike Remembers Food; Forgets Dad!" Let children write their headlines on banner paper.

WRITING

---

**p/i PREVENTION/INTERVENTION**

**CONCEPTS OF PRINT** Remind children that apostrophe -*s* shows possession. In this case, it tells us that the face belongs to Mike. Help children find the possessive on page 12. (*Dad's store*) Encourage children to then think of something they own and say their name and the item. Example: *Mary's dog.*

# Guided Instruction

**41** So what was it that Mike finally remembered? (his Dad)

**42** Let's look at our maps of Dad's store. Where would be a good place to draw Dad? (next to Mike) Let's add Dad to the picture. *Story Props*

**RETELL THE STORY**  Ask children to work in groups of five to act out the story. After they decide on what to say in their retelling, have them choose roles. One child can retell the story as the others act out the events. Remind children to refer to the map of Dad's Store to help them remember grocery items and what happened in the store. *Summarize/Story Props*

## STUDENT SELF-ASSESSMENT

Have children ask themselves the following questions to assess how they are reading:

- How did I use what I already know about grocery shopping to understand the story?
- How did I use letters and sounds I already know to help me read the words?
- How did I use the pictures and words to understand what is happening?

**TRANSFERRING THE STRATEGIES**

- How can I use these strategies to help me read other stories?

"Mom wanted me to get…!" he said.
"What is it?" yelled Miss Lin.
"Tell us!" yelled Fran and Ann.

32

## REREADING FOR *Fluency*

**GROUP**  Children who need fluency practice can read along silently or aloud as they listen to the story being read.

**READING RATE** You may want to evaluate individual children's reading rates. Have the child read aloud from *The Shopping List* for one minute. Then have the child place a self-stick note after the last word read aloud. Count

how many words the child has read.

Alternatively, you could assess small groups or the whole class together by having children count words and record their own scores.

A Running Record form provides in **Diagnostic/Placement Evaluation** will help you evaluate reading rate(s).

Mike smiled and said, "Mom asked me  to get YOU, Dad. It's time for supper!"

33

# Guided Instruction

## Return to Predictions and Purposes

Reread children's predictions about the story and discuss them. Ask if they need to revise any predictions about the story, and if their questions were answered.

Have children talk about the strategy of using the map of Dad's store. Did it help them follow what the characters said, where the story took place, and what happened in the story?

| PREDICTIONS | WHAT HAPPENED |
|---|---|
| The story is about a boy. | The story is about Mike, who visits his dad's grocery store. |
| People try to help the boy find something. | People give Mike many ideas, but they are unsuccessful. |
| In the end, Mike does not remember what he forgot. | Mike finally remembers on his own: Get Dad! |

### INFORMAL ASSESSMENT

 **LONG *i: i-e*** Have children find and read three long *i: i-e* words in the story. *(five, Mike, ripe, time white, smile)*

**FOLLOW UP**

**Phonics** **LONG *i: i-e*** Continue to model blending the sounds in long *i: i-e* words in the story for children who are having difficulty.

## LITERARY RESPONSE

**QUICK-WRITE** Have children write in their journals about a character or a part of the story they found interesting. They can use the map of Dad's store or ask for help with difficult words.

**ORAL RESPONSE** Have children use their journal entries to discuss these questions:

• Choose a role for yourself in the story. Which character do you want to be, and why?

• Imagine you are Dad or Mike at the supper table. You are telling Mom what happened. What do you say?

• Think about another ending for the story. What happens if Mike never remembers?

# Story Questions

Tell children that now they will read some questions about the story. Help children read the questions. Discuss possible answers.

**Answers:**

1. jam, rice, 5 ripe plums *Literal*

2. Dad's store became a big mess. *Inferential/Make Inferences*

3. Answers may vary. (One response: because the item Mike forgot was not food.) *Inferential/Make Inferences*

4. Accept appropriate responses. *Critical/Summarize*

5. Meg forgot to bring her rain gear when she went outside in the rain to catch the bus. *Critical/Reading Across Texts*

**Write a Food Label** For a full writing-process lesson related to this writing suggestion, see the lesson on expository writing on pages 37M–37N.

## Story Questions & Activities

*READ TOGETHER*

1 What foods were on Mike's list?

2 What happened to Dad's store?

3 Why do you think Mike forgot?

4 Pretend you are Mike and tell about your day.

5 Tell how Meg from "Splash!" also forgot something.

## Write a Food Label

Think about your favorite food.
Draw a box for it.
Write its name on the box.
Tell why it is good to buy.
Put a price on your box.

$1.00
Bran Puffs
It tastes good.

# Meeting Individual Needs

## EASY

Name_____ Date_____ Reteach 129

**Story Comprehension**

Think about "The Shopping List." Fill in the chart below.

First: Mike goes to the store with a
shopping list.

Then: Mike can't remember one thing he had to get.

Next: Miss Lin, Fran, and Ann try to help Mike.

Finally: Mike remembers what is not on the list.
Mom wants Dad to come home with Mike.

Book 1.4
The Shopping List
At Home: Help children make a list of things they might want to have at a party.
129

## ON-LEVEL

Name_____ Date_____ Practice 129

**Story Comprehension**

Think about what happened in "The Shopping List." Write **T** if the sentence is **true**. Write **F** if the sentence is **false**.

1. _T_ Mike has a list.

2. _F_ His dad drives a bus.

3. _T_ Dad wants to know what Mike forgot.

4. _T_ Dad hunts and hunts.

5. _T_ Fran and Ann try to help Mike.

6. _T_ At last, Miss Lin gives up.

7. _F_ Mike gets sad and goes away.

8. _T_ Mom wants Mike to tell Dad it is time to eat.

Book 1.4
The Shopping List
At Home: Help children to write a shopping list for a meal you are planning together.
129

## CHALLENGE

Name_____ Date_____ Extend 129

**Story Comprehension**

What do you put on a shopping list? Look at the pictures. Make a list of things to buy. Then add more things. Draw a picture, too.

**SHOPPING LIST**

cake

milk

grapes

Book 1.4
The Shopping List
At Home: Invite children to identify the fruits and vegetables and their colors. Make a shopping list together.
129

Reteach, 129          Practice, 129          Extend, 129

# Play a Memory Game

Play in a group.
One person begins:

"I went to the store to buy soap."

The next person says:

"I went to the store to buy soap and bananas."

Keep playing.
See how many items you remember.

# Find Out More

Find out about one food that is good for you.
Tell about the food and how it helps you.

35

# Story Activities

### Memory Game

Read the directions aloud. Help children who have questions. Are there any things they want to buy at the store? Are these items for the kitchen or another room in the house?

**GROUP** After the children have played the memory game in groups, have them make a list of the items they "bought" at the store. Then have them illustrate their shopping lists.

### Find Out More

**RESEARCH AND INQUIRY** Again, read the directions aloud, and help children who have questions. Then have them **GROUP** work in pairs.

Partners should choose one food together that is good for them. Have them write a list about why this food helps them grow and stay healthy. Invite children to illustrate their findings and present them to the class.

inter**NET** **CONNECTION** Have children log on to **www.mhschool.com/reading**, where they can access sites about food.

**FORMAL** **A**SSESSMENT

See the Selection Assessment Test for Book 4.1.

DAILY **Phonics** ROUTINES

**DAY 3** **Writing** Have children write labels on simple pictures using the appropriate word from this list: *kite, tire, bike, five.*

 **Phonics** CD-ROM

**35**

# Study Skills

## READ A CHART

### OBJECTIVES

**Children will:**

• learn to read a chart to gather information.

**PREPARE** Preview the chart with children, pointing out that a chart presents information in columns or lists. Display **Teaching Chart 95.**

**TEACH** Review how to get information from a chart. Have children read the labels and look at the illustrations.

**PRACTICE** Have children answer questions 1–2. Review the answers with them.
**1.** a peach, a plum, and a cherry **2.** a carrot

**ASSESS/CLOSE** Have children draw conclusions from the chart and write their conclusions in a sentence or two.

## Study Skills

READ TOGETHER

### Fruit or Vegetable?

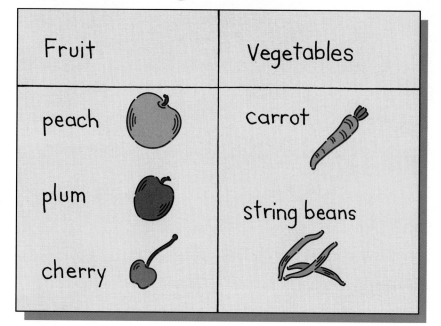

## Look at the Chart

**1** What are listed as fruits?

**2** Name an orange vegetable.

## Meeting Individual Needs

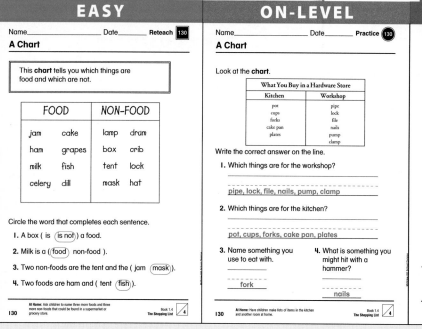

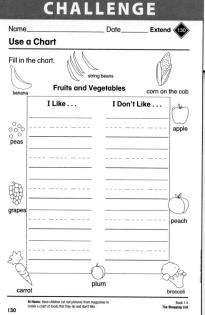

| Reteach, 130 | Practice, 130 | Extend, 130 |
|---|---|---|

# TEST POWER

## Test Power

THE PRINCETON REVIEW

### Mike's Pet

Mike has a fish.
It lives in a fish tank.
Mike feeds his fish everyday.
The food sits on top of the water.
The fish swims to the top to eat the food.
Then it swims back down to the bottom.

Why does the fish swim to the top?

○ To say hello to Mike

● To eat the food

Ask yourself: "What does the story tell me?"

### Read the Page

Explain to children that you will be reading this story as a group. You will read the story, and they will follow in their books.

Request that children put pens, pencils, and markers away, since they will not be writing in their books.

### Discuss the Question

Discuss with children what constitutes an answer to a "why" question. Have them reread the story, find the place where the fish swims to the top, and put their fingers on the reason why the fish swims to the top.

### Test-Tip

Always look back to the story to find the answer. The answer is always somewhere in the passage.

37

For The Princeton Review test preparation practice for **TerraNova, ITBS,** and **SAT-9,** visit the McGraw-Hill School Division Web site. See also McGraw-Hill's *Standardized Test Preparation Book.*

# Leveled Books

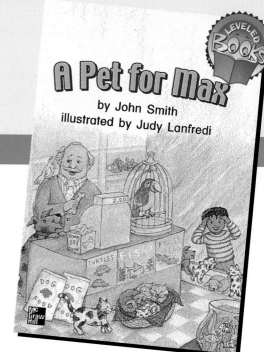

**A Pet for Max**
by John Smith
illustrated by Judy Lanfredi

## EASY

### A Pet for Max

☑  **Long *i*: *i-e***
☑ **High-Frequency Words:** *after, always, blue, were, who*

## Guided Reading

**PREVIEW AND PREDICT** Discuss each illustration up to page 9, using the high-frequency words. As you take the **picture walk**, have children predict what the story will be about and chart their ideas.

**SET PURPOSES** Have children write or draw why they want to read *A Pet for Max*. For example: I want to find out what pet Max got.

**READ THE BOOK** Use questions like the following as children read or once they have read the story independently.

**Pages 2–7:** Model: The second sentence on page 2 says, *A pet is …* I'm not sure what this word is, but I can blend the letters together to read it. The first letter is *f*. It stands for the sound /f/. The middle letter is *i*. It has the long *i* sound, /ī/. The next letter is *n*, for the /n/ sound. The final letter is silent *e*. I can blend the sounds together f i ne fine. The word is *fine*. Who sees another word with long *i* and silent *e* on page 3? *(like)* What does Max want after visiting Kim? (a cat) Why? (because she has one) *Cause and Effect*

**Pages 8–13:** What pet does Max want after visiting Nick? (a duck) Why? (because Nick says it's a fun pet) Who sees a word with long *i* and silent *e* on page 8? *(bike)* On page 10? *(dive) Cause and Effect, Phonics and Decoding*

**Pages 14–16:** Who sees two vocabulary words we just learned on pages 14 and 15? *(who)* On page 15? *(blue)* Where does Max finally see the pet he wants? (in a pet store) *High-Frequency Words/Use Illustrations*

**RETURN TO PREDICTIONS AND PURPOSES** Discuss children's predictions and review their purposes for reading. Ask which were close to the story and why. Did they find out what pet Max got?

**LITERARY RESPONSE** Focus children's responses by asking:

- Why do people have all kinds of pets?
- Do you have a pet? Tell about it.

Also see the story questions and writing activity in *A Pet for Max*.

See the **Phonics CD-ROM** for practice with blends.

---

**Answers to Story Questions**
1. A pet
2. A bird (parrot)
3. Answers will vary.
4. Kim had a cat. Dave had a dog. Nick had a duck.
5. *Max, the Cat, Quack, One Good Pup, Splash*

**Story Questions and Writing Activity**
**A Pet for Max**
1. What did Max want?
2. Who said, "Look at me!"?
3. Why do a lot of people like pets?
4. Tell about the pets Max's friends had.
5. What other stories have you read about pets?

**A Pet Page**
Find pictures of pets in magazines, or use pictures of a pet you know. Cut and paste them onto a page. Write a sentence for your Pet Page.

*from A Pet for Max*

# Leveled Books

**The Big Secret**

by Tim Kane
Illustrated by Kristine Goeters

## INDEPENDENT

### The Big Secret

☑  **Phonics** Long *i*: *i-e*

☑ **High-Frequency Words:**
*after, always, blue, were, who*

## Guided Reading

**PREVIEW AND PREDICT** Discuss each illustration up to page 9, using the high-frequency words. As you take the **picture walk**, have children predict what the story will be about and chart their ideas in their journals.

**SET PURPOSES** Have children write or draw why they want to read *The Big Secret*. For example: I want to find out what the big secret is.

**READ THE BOOK** Ask questions like the following as children read or once they have read the story independently.

**Pages 2–7:** Let's look at the pictures and read the third sentence on page 3. Model: *I don't have …* I'm not sure what this word is, but I can blend the letters together to read it. The first letter is *t*. It stands for the sound /t/. The middle letter is *i*. It has the long *i* sound. The next letter is *m*, for the /m/ sound. The final letter is silent *e*. I can blend the sounds together t i me time. The word is *time*. Why do you think everyone is busy? (getting ready for Dan's party) Why? (It's his birthday.) *Phonics and Decoding, Draw Conclusions*

**Pages 8–13:** Who sees a vocabulary word we just learned on page 9? *(blue)* Who has a big white box? (Meg) Who has two red boxes? (Miss Kent) *High-Frequency Words/ Use Illustrations*

**Pages 14–16:** What was the big secret? (There is a birthday party for Dan.) What does Dan get that he wanted? (a blue bike) *Confirm Predictions/Use Illustrations*

**RETURN TO PREDICTIONS AND PURPOSES** Discuss children's predictions and review their purposes. Ask which were close to the story and why. Did they find out what the big secret was?

**LITERARY RESPONSE** Focus children's responses by asking:

• How did Dan help with his own party?

• Have you ever kept a secret?

Also see the story questions and writing activity in *The Big Secret*.

See the  **Phonics** CD-ROM for practice with blends.

### Answers to Story Questions

1. Shopping
2. There was a party for Dan.
3. Answers will vary.
4. Dan wakes up, goes outside, goes shopping, sees a bike in a shop, sees Meg, and sees Miss Kent.
5. Answers may vary: *The Shopping List*.

### Story Questions
**The Big Secret**

1. Where did Dan go with Gran?
2. What was the big secret?
3. Why do people sometimes keep party secrets?
4. Tell four things about Dan's day?
5. In what other story that you have read did someone go to a store?

### Make a Birthday Card

Make a birthday card.
Use construction paper and markers.
Make a birthday card for someone whose birthday is this month.

*from The Big Secret*

# Leveled Books

**ESL** Have children read up to page 11 independently. Then discuss any words or concepts with which they may have had difficulty and the strategies they can use to help them understand the story. Then encourage the children to continue reading independently.

**AUTHENTIC**

## Who Took the Farmer's Hat?

☑ **Phonics** Long *i*: *i-e*

WHO TOOK THE FARMER'S HAT?
LEVELED BOOKS
by Joan L. Nôdset pictures by Fritz Siebel

**Answers to Story Questions**

1. The wind.
2. A bird used it for a nest.
3. Answers will vary.
4. The wind took the farmer's hat. He looked for the hat. None of the animals he asked saw the hat. Bird had the hat and used it as a nest. The farmer got a new hat.
5. Both stories are about friendship.

**Story Questions**

**Who Took the Farmer's Hat?**

1. Who took the farmer's hat?
2. Why does the farmer get a new hat?
3. What does this story tell you about sharing?
4. Tell the story in your own words.
5. How is this story like *The Cow That Went OINK*?

**Make a Card**

Pretend you are a bird. Write a thank-you card for the farmer.

from *Who Took the Farmer's Hat?*

# Guided Reading

**PREVIEW AND PREDICT** Discuss each illustration up to page 15. As you take the **picture walk**, have children predict what the story is about and chart their ideas in their journals.

**SET PURPOSES** Have children write or draw why they want to read *Who Took the Farmer's Hat?* For example: I want to find out who took that hat.

**READ THE BOOK** Ask questions like the following as children read or once they have read the story independently.

**Pages 1–13:** Model: *Oh, how he … I'm not sure what this next word is, but I can blend the letters together. The first letter is l. It stands for the /l/ sound. The next letter is i. It has the long i sound. The next letter is k. It has the /k/ sound. The ending is ed. Let's blend the sounds of these letters to read the word l i k ed liked. The word is liked.* **Phonics and Decoding, Main Idea and Details, Analyze Character and Plot**

**Pages 14–23:** Who did the farmer ask after the duck? (the bird) Did the bird see the hat? (No, but she saw a nice brown nest that was really the hat.) **Details**

**Pages 24–27:** Did the farmer ever find his hat? (No, he got a new one.) **Use Illustrations, Details**

**RETURN TO PREDICTIONS AND PURPOSES** Discuss children's predictions. Ask which were close to the story and why. Have children review their purposes for reading. Did they find out who took the farmer's hat?

**LITERARY RESPONSE** Focus children's responses by asking:

• Why didn't the farmer take his hat away from the bird?

• Have you ever lost something you liked a lot? Tell about it.

Also see the story questions and writing activity in *Who Took the Farmer's Hat?*

# Activities
## Anthology and Leveled Books

## Connecting Texts

**STORY CHARTS**
Write the story titles on the chalkboard. Discuss with children what the character in each story is shopping for. Have children construct a word web that describes the shopping items in each story.

Use the chart to talk about shopping.

**A Pet for Max**
a pet bird

**The Big Secret**
birthday gifts
a blue bike

**Shopping**

**Who Took the Farmer's Hat?**
A hat

**The Shopping List**
jam, rice, five ripe plums

## Viewing/Representing

**GROUP PRESENTATIONS** Divide the class into groups, one for each of the four books. (For *The Shopping List,* combine children of different reading levels.) Have each group draw pictures of the shopping items and orally summarize the book. Have each group present its pictures and summary.

**AUDIENCE RESPONSE**
Ask children to pay attention to each group's presentation. Allow time for questions after each group presents.

## Research and Inquiry

**MORE ABOUT SHOPPING** Have children ask themselves: What else would I like to know about shopping? Then invite them to do the following:

• Bring in shopping catalogues from home.

• Ask a grown-up in the retail industry to come and speak about it.

inter**NET** **CONNECTION** Have children log on to **www.mhschool.com/reading** for links to Web pages about shopping.

JOURNAL Children can draw pictures representing what they learned in their journals.

Children will:

- identify long *i: i-e* words.
- blend and read long *i: i-e* words.
- review consonants

. . . . . . . . . . . . . . . . . . . . . . . . .

**MATERIALS**

- **Teaching Chart 96**
- long *i* cards from the **Word Building Manipulative Cards**

**SPELLING/PHONICS**
**CONNECTIONS**

Words with long *i: i-e;* See the 5-Day Spelling Plan, pages 37Q-37R.

**ALTERNATE TEACHING**
**STRATEGY**

. . . . . . . . . . . . . . . . . . . . . . . . .

**PHONICS: LONG *i: i-e***

For a different approach to teaching this skill, see page T64.

**TEACHING TIP**

**INSTRUCTIONAL** Remind children that the *e* at the end of words spelled *i-e* is silent and helps the vowel *i* say its name.

# Review Long *i: i_e*

**PREPARE**

**Listen for the Long *i* Sound**

Read the following sentence aloud and ask children to tap their feet when they hear a word with the long *i: i-e* sound:

- If you <u>like</u>, we will <u>dine</u> on grape jam and <u>lime</u> <u>ice</u>.

**TEACH**

**Review the Letters *i-e* as Symbols for /ī/**

- Tell children that they will review the vowel pattern *i-e* and the long *i* sound it makes.

- Display the letter card *i-e*. Remind children that the space between the letters *i-e* is for a consonant letter. Together the letters make a long *i* sound.

**BLENDING Model and Guide Practice with Long *i* Words**

- Say /ī/. Have children repeat after you. Display **Teaching Chart 96.**

- Run your hand under the letters *ive* and blend them together. Have children repeat after you. i v e ive

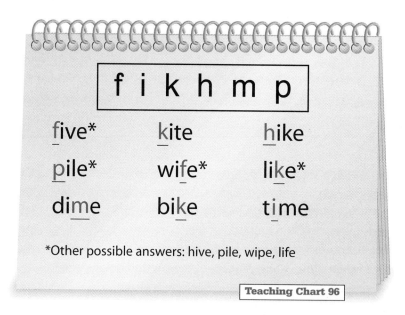

*Teaching Chart 96*

- Write the letter *f* in the blank space. Run your hand under the letters again, blending them to read the word *five*. f ive five

- Erase the *f* and have the children choose another letter from the box to complete the word.

**Use the Word in Context**

Have volunteers say the word in a sentence to reinforce its meaning. Example : *I saw five children in the park.*

**Repeat the Procedure**

Continue by having children substitute other letters to complete words on the chart.

## PRACTICE

**BLENDING**
**Build Long *i*: *i-e*
Words with
Letter Banks**

**PARTNERS**

Write the following letter banks on the chalkboard:

| b f l |
| p s h |

| i __ e |

| d f k |
| l n t |

Ask children to work in pairs. One child writes *i-e* on the paper and then chooses a letter from the first letter bank to begin a long *i*: *i-e* word. The partner chooses another letter from the third letter bank to complete the long *i*: *i-e* word. Partners can then reverse roles. Have children keep a list of the words they make. ▶ **Auditory/Linguistic**

## ASSESS/CLOSE

**Read Long *i*: *i-e*
Words**

To assess children's mastery of blending and reading long *i*: *i-e* words, check the words they built in the Practice activity. Ask them to read some of the words from their lists.

### ADDITIONAL PHONICS RESOURCES

**Phonics/Phonemic Awareness
Practice Book,
pages 135–142**

*McGraw-Hill School*
**TECHNOLOGY**

**Phonics CD-ROM**

**Activities for practice with
Blending and Segmenting**

### DAILY Phonics ROUTINES

**DAY 4**

**Fluency** Write the following list of long *i-e* words on the chalkboard: *mine, hike, drive, smile, ride*. Ask children to first read the list silently and then read it aloud.

**Phonics CD-ROM**

### SELF-SELECTED
## Reading

Children may choose from
the following titles.

**ANTHOLOGY**

- *The Shopping List*

**LEVELED BOOKS**

- *A Pet for Max*
- *The Big Secret*
- *Who Took the Farmer's Hat?*

Bibliography, page T92

---

# Meeting Individual Needs for Phonics

## EASY

Name_____ Date_____ **Reteach 131**

**Long *i*: *i-e***

Say the number. Listen to the long **i** sound made by the letters **i** and **e**.    9    nine

Write the letters **i** and **e** to make a word.
Write each word under the picture it names.

r _i_ c _e_        t _i_ m _e_

r _i_ d _e_        f _i_ r _e_

k _i_ t _e_        pr _i_ z _e_

kite        prize

time        rice

fire        ride

Book 1.4
**The Shopping List**    **12**
**At Home:** Help children think of other words that contain the long i sound.    131

## ON-LEVEL

Name_____ Date_____ **Practice 131**

**Long *i*: *i-e***

Write the words in each group that have the same middle sound as in **hide**.

1. bike    nine    take
   _bike_    _nine_    _____

2. lime    pine    cane
   _lime_    _pine_    _____

3. late    slide    kite
   _____    _slide_    _kite_

4. write    wide    wade
   _write_    _wide_    _____

5. tire    ride    tale
   _tire_    _ride_    _____

Book 1.4
**The Shopping List**    **5**
**At Home:** Ask children to choose a word with the long i sound and use it in a sentence.    131

## CHALLENGE

Name_____ Date_____ **Extend 131**

**Long *i*: *i-e***

Make a word. Put the letter **i** or **e** in each blank. Then write a word that rhymes with the word you made.
Sample answers are given.

| Word | Rhyming Words |

r _i_ p _e_        pipe

n _i_ c _e_        ice

wr _i_ t _e_       kite

9  n _i_ n _e_     fine

sl _i_ d _e_       ride

Book 1.4
**The Shopping List**    **At Home:** Invite children to create tongue twisters using the words in the exercise. For example: Ice is very nice. She rides a slippery slide.    131

## LANGUAGE SUPPORT

Name_____ Date_____

**Word Frame in a Can**

r    c    wh    t

wr    t    f    v

r    p    m    k

_____ i _____ e

Grade 1    Language Support/Blackline Master 77 • The Shopping List **141**

---

## <sup>TESTED</sup> ✓BJECTIVES

**Children will:**

- review long *a: a-e* and long *i: i-e.*
- blend and read long *a: a-e* and long *i: i-e* words.
- review blends and digraphs.

.................................................

### MATERIALS

- **Teaching Chart 97**
- letter cards long *a* and long *i* cards from the **Word Building Manipulative Cards**

---

**TEACHING TIP**

**INSTRUCTIONAL**

Challenge children to come up with long *a* and *i* CVCe words which share the same consonants, such as *bike* and *bake*.

---

# Review Long *i-e, a-e*

**PREPARE**

**Identify *i-e* and *a-e* as Symbols for /ī/, /ā/**    Write the letters *a-e* and *i-e* on the chalkboard and say their sounds aloud. Have children repeat the sounds after you.

**Discriminate Between /ā/ *a-e* and /ī/ *i-e* Words**    Display the word cards or list words on the chalkboard for *a-e* and *i-e*. Ask volunteers to read the words with the /ā/ sound. Do the same for words with the /ī/ sound.

**TEACH**

**BLENDING Model and Guide Practice with Long *a* and Long *i* Words**    **Display Teaching Chart 97.** Point to the letters *a* and *i* at the top.

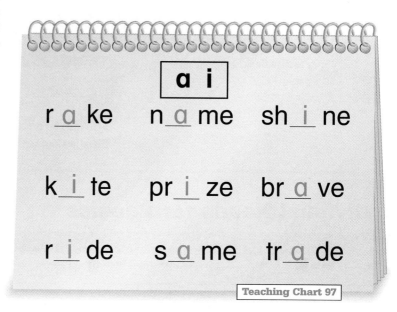

r_a_ke    n_a_me    sh_i_ne

k_i_te    pr_i_ze    br_a_ve

r_i_de    s_a_me    tr_a_de

Teaching Chart 97

- Write the letter *a* in the blank space: r_ke. Cover the first letter *r* and blend the remaining sounds, a k(e) ake. Have children repeat after you. Uncover the letter *r* and blend the whole word together. Have children repeat.

  **r ake        rake**

- Replace the letter *a* with *i* and repeat the blending process.
- Ask which letter forms a real word. (*a*)

**Use the Word in Context**    • Invite volunteers to use the word in a sentence to reinforce its meaning. Example: *I like to rake leaves in the fall.*

**Repeat the Procedure**    • Continue by asking volunteers to complete words and blend sounds together to read the words aloud.

## PRACTICE

**BLENDING**
**Build and Sort**
**Long *a-e*, *i-e***
**Words**

**PARTNERS**

Have children work in pairs using the letter cards and long vowel cards to build words. One child builds long *a*: *a-e* words and the partner builds long *i*: *i-e* words. Have children write two lists for the words they build. Pairs can switch lists to see if they can think of any new words their partner may have missed. ▶ **Linguistic/Kinesthetic**

## ASSESS/CLOSE

**Draw and Label**
**a Picture**

Use your observations from the Practice activity to determine if children need more reinforcement with long *ai, a-e* and long *i: i-e* words. Have children choose a word, draw a picture of it, and label it with the word.

**DAY 5** Rhyming Using the *i-e* and consonant cards, have pairs of children build sets of rhyming words.

**Phonics** CD-ROM

### ADDITIONAL PHONICS RESOURCES

**Phonics/Phonemic Awareness**
**Practice Book,**
**pages 135–142**

*McGraw-Hill School*
**TECHNOLOGY**
**Phonics** CD-ROM

**activities for practice with**
**Blending and Segmenting**

**ALTERNATE TEACHING**
# STRATEGY

**PHONICS: LONG i:** *i-e*
For a different approach to teaching this skill, see page T64.

# Meeting Individual Needs for Phonics

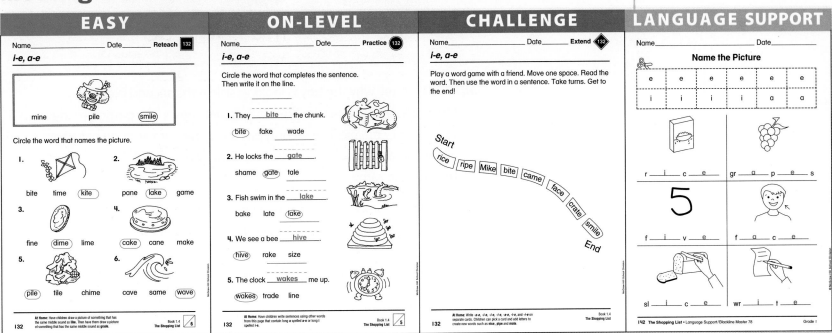

| | | | |
|---|---|---|---|
| Reteach, 132 | Practice, 132 | Extend, 132 | Language Support, 142 |

## OBJECTIVES

Children will use words and pictures to identify cause and effect.

MATERIALS
• Teaching Chart 98

### TEACHING TIP

**INSTRUCTIONAL**

Encourage children to share examples of cause-and-effect events in their own lives. They can share these examples with a partner or make a drawing depicting a cause-and-effect event.

# Introduce Cause and Effect

### PREPARE

**Introduce the Concept of Cause and Effect**

Tell children that they can understand a story better by seeing that some things happen as a result of other things that happened before them.

### TEACH

**Identify Cause and Effect**

Display **Teaching Chart 98.** Encourage children to look carefully at the first set of pictures and think about the cause-and-effect relationship.

Ann plants seeds.  Her seeds grow pretty flowers.

Jeb eats lots of pie!  Jeb feels sick.

Teaching Chart 98

*MODEL* I can tell why the boy is looking sick in the second picture by looking at the first picture. The first picture shows him getting ready to eat a very big pie. The second picture shows him after he has eaten all the pie, and now he has a tummy ache. When I read the sentences, they tell the same story.

Have children look at the second set of pictures on the chart. Point out to children how the first picture shows *why* something happened—the cause—and the second picture shows *what* happened—the effect. Invite children to tell in their own words the events shown in that set of pictures. Encourage them to identify the cause and the effect. Ask volunteers to circle the "cause" sentences and underline the "effect" sentences.

## PRACTICE

**Act Out Cause and Effect**

GROUP

Have children think about another cause-and-effect event, such as some things that could happen as a result of a snowfall. (building a snowman, shoveling the sidewalk, and so on.) Have volunteers act out possible effects based on the cause. Invite the class to guess what the volunteers are pantomiming. ▶ **Visual/Kinesthetic**

## ASSESS/CLOSE

**Think of a Different Cause or Effect**

Review children's skits to determine how well they have understood the concept of cause and effect. To reinforce understanding, ask them to look again at the pictures on **Teaching Chart 98.** Invite volunteers to make up a different cause or effect than the obvious one. Example: *Jeb is upset because someone else ate his lime pie.*

### ALTERNATE TEACHING STRATEGY

••••••••••••••••••••••••••••

**CAUSE AND EFFECT**

For a different approach to teaching this skill, see page T66.

### LOOKING AHEAD

Children will apply this skill as they read the next selection, *Yasmin's Ducks*.

# Meeting Individual Needs for Comprehension

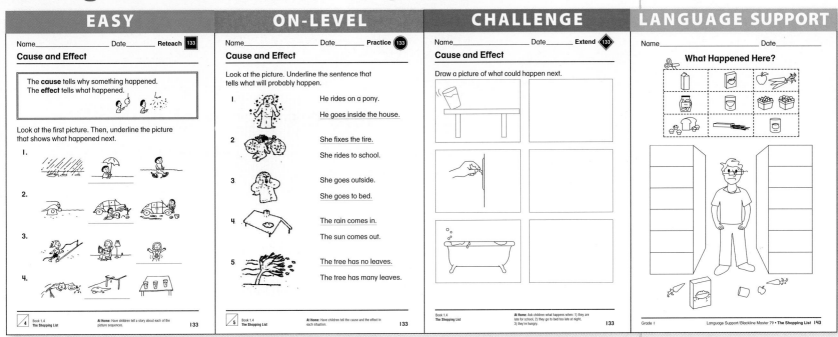

**Reteach, 133**  **Practice, 133**  **Extend, 133**  **Language Support, 143**

### OBJECTIVES

Children will read words that end in *-s* and *-es*.

MATERIALS

- **Teaching Chart 99**
- index cards

---

**TEACHING TIP**

**INSTRUCTIONAL** Point out to children that when a word ends in *sh*, *ch*, *x*, or *ss*, the plural is always formed by adding *-es*.

---

# Review Inflectional Endings -s, -es

**PREPARE**

**Introduce the Concept of Endings -s, -es**

Write the word *can* on the chalkboard. Ask a volunteer to pantomime handing you one can, then another. Say: *I had one can, now I have two cans.* Write *-s* after *can* and explaining that we add *-s* or *-es* to many words to show more than one. Pretend to pull a nut from one can and eat it. Say: *I ate one nut.* Then repeat your action and say: *I ate two nuts.* Write the word *nut* on the board, then add the letter *-s*.

**TEACH**

**Identify Base Words**

Track each sentence on **Teaching Chart 99** as you read it with children. Invite volunteers to identify the words ending in *-s* or *-es* and then underline the base word in each. Model for children how understanding inflectional endings can help them read.

Here are cans of nuts.

Here are bunches of grapes.

Here are dishes of plums.

Teaching Chart 99

**MODEL** I can use what I know to help me recognize *-s* and *-es* words. I know the word *can*. I can see the word *can* with an *-s* at the end. I know that sometimes when this letter appears at the end of a word, it means more than one. The word is *cans*.

benches

## PRACTICE

**Add -s, -es**

**PARTNERS**

Distribute index cards to children. Then write *benches, dresses, frogs, boxes, dolls,* and *wishes* on the chalkboard. Have children read each word, indentifying the part of the word they know first. Then ask children to write each word on an index card. Direct them to turn the card over and write the word without the *-s* or *-es* ending. Have pairs practice reading all the words and using them in sentences.

▶ **Visual/Representing**

dolls

## ASSESS/CLOSE

**Use the Words in Context**

Invite pairs of children to make up stories using their words. Children can tell their stories. They may wish to act them out as well. Call on other children to identify the base words.

**ALTERNATE TEACHING STRATEGY**
································

**INFLECTIONAL ENDINGS**
*-s, -es*

For a different approach to learning this skill, see page T67.

---

# Meeting Individual Needs for Vocabulary

| EASY | ON-LEVEL | CHALLENGE | LANGUAGE SUPPORT |
|---|---|---|---|

**EASY**

Name_____ Date_____ Reteach **134**

**Inflectional Ending -s, -es**

Add **-s** or **-es** to what one person or thing does.

Dan and Pam hike up the hill.
hike + **s** = hikes
Dad hike**s** up the hill.

If the word ends in **e** or most consonants, add **-s**.
If the word ends in **sh**, **ch**, **x**, or **ss**, add **-es**.

Underline the word that finishes each sentence.

1. Dan ____ to see Pam.
   want     **wants**

2. He ____ to Pam's house.
   run     **runs**

3. Pam ___ in.
   dash     dashesit     sits

5. Dan ___ Pam an apple.
   pass     **passes**

_At Home:_ Choose two more verbs with **-s** or **-es** endings,
and help children to use them in sentences.

134

Book 1.4
**The Shopping List** 5

**ON-LEVEL**

Name_____ Date_____ Practice **134**

**Inflectional Endings -s, -es**

Add **-s** or **-es** to tell what only one person or thing does.

When a word ends in **e** or most consonants, add **-s**.
When a word ends in **sh, ch, x,** or **ss**, add **-es**.

Circle the word that completes each sentence.
Then write the word on the line.

1. Nick ___brushes___   2. She ___gives___ me a
   his pup.                ring.
   brush (brushes)        give (gives)

3. They ___            4. The mouse ___
   ___shop___ for food.    ___munches___
   (shop) hops            munch (munches)

5. Bob and Jen ___    6. The boy ___
   ___wish___ for fish.    ___yanks___ the gate.
   (wish) wishes         yank (yanks)

_At Home:_ Challenge children to use three of the uncircled
word choices in sentences.

134

Book 1.4
**The Shopping List** 6

**CHALLENGE**

Name_____ Date_____ Extend **134**

**Inflectional Endings -s, -es**

Choose one of the two words. Use it in a sentence.
Circle the word you used.   Sample answers are given.

can   cans
_____
I will buy a can of soup.

grape   grapes
_____
Here are the red grapes.

muffin   muffins
_____
I like corn muffins.

plum   plums
_____
Plums taste good.

Look at the picture. Write a sentence about it. Use
one of the words in the box.

| duck   ducks |

_____
The mother duck swims in the front.

_At Home:_ Have children use words such as bench/benches,
doll/dolls, wing/wings, and frog/frogs in sentences.

134

Book 1.4
**The Shopping List**

**LANGUAGE SUPPORT**

Name_____ Date_____

**Pick an Ending**

| s | s | s | es | es |

1. ___ ate the grape___s___.

2. ___ has five can___s___.

3. ___ has two box___es___.

4. ___ takes the ripe plum___es___.

5. ___ puts away a can of peach___s___.

144  The Shopping List • Language Support/Blackline Master 80

Grade 1

---

**Reteach, 134**          **Practice, 134**          **Extend, 134**          Language Support, 144

**GRAMMAR/SPELLING**
**CONNECTIONS**

See the 5-Day Grammar and Usage Plan on *was* and *were*, pages 37O–37P.

See the 5-Day Spelling Plan on Words with Long *i: i–e* (silent *e* rule), pages 37Q–37R.

# Persuasive Writing

## Prewrite

**WRITE A LETTER** Present this writing assignment: Write a letter to a family member telling him or her what you would like to put on a grocery shopping list. Name the things you want, and tell why each item would be a good thing to have.

**BRAINSTORM IDEAS** Have children brainstorm ideas for things they might like to put on the list in their letter. What kinds of things does their family buy at the market? Why do they buy each thing?

**Strategy: Make a List** Have children list the things they want to put on their shopping list, and explain why. Suggest the following:

- In one column, list the items you want to buy.

- In another column, list the reasons you want to buy each item.

- Decide on the order of importance for the items on the shopping list. Use numbers to show the order.

## Draft

**USE THE LIST** Guide children to write full sentences telling about each item on their list and elaborating on why they want to buy it. They should put the items in order of importance. Encourage children to use convincing, vivid words to make each item seem attractive. Letters should include a heading with the writer's address, the date, a greeting, and a closing signature.

## Revise

**SELF-QUESTIONING** Ask children to assess their drafts.

- Did I put items in order of importance?

- Did I give a reason to buy each item?

**PARTNERS** Have children trade letters with a partner. Have each partner make sure that the shopping list includes clear reasons for buying each item. Are the reasons clear?

## Edit/Proofread

**CHECK FOR ERRORS** Children should reread their letters for spelling, grammar, punctuation, and letter format.

## Publish

**SHARE LETTERS** Children can "mail" their letters to one another. Recipients can tell writers what they will "buy" and why.

---

Joe Kidd
18 Main Street
Anytown, TX 00000
January 11, 20___

Dear Mom,

I want to put milk on my shopping list. Milk is good to drink all day.

I want to put grapes on my list, too. They are fun to eat. They are good for you, too. I like the red ones.

We all like rolls I think we should get the ones that are big. They are good to have with dinner.

Do not forget food for our dog. He likes to eat all the time. We want him to be happy and well.

Sincerely,

Joe

---

**TEACHING TIP**

A spell-checker won't catch a word that has been used incorrectly, such as a homophone. Use the spell-checker, but proofread the letter, too.

# Presentation Ideas

**ILLUSTRATE THE LIST** Have children draw pictures of the items they put on their shopping lists. ▶ **Viewing/Representing**

**CONVINCE THE CLASS** Have children try to convince the class to buy something on their list. Encourage the rest of the children to ask questions. ▶ **Speaking/Listening**

Consider children's creative efforts, possibly adding a plus (+) for originality, wit, and imagination.

## Scoring Rubric

| Excellent | Good | Fair | Unsatisfactory |
|---|---|---|---|
| **4:** The writer<br>• crafts full sentences for each item, with vivid descriptions.<br>• provides very convincing reasons why each item should be bought.<br>• uses correct letter format. | **3:** The writer<br>• presents clear, full sentences for each item.<br>• provides good reasons why each item should be bought.<br>• uses letter format. | **2:** The writer<br>• lists each item, but may not use full sentences.<br>• may give vague or unconvincing reasons for buying the items.<br>• may use only partial letter format. | **1:** The writer<br>• may not propose a shopping list.<br>• may offer few, or no reasons to buy items.<br>• does not use letter format. |

# Meeting Individual Needs for Writing

| EASY | ON-LEVEL | CHALLENGE |
|---|---|---|
| **Draw a Map** Have children invent an aisle in a grocery store and draw the shelves, labeling some of the items. | **Write an Ad** Have children write an ad for a grocery store, naming two or three items and telling why the shoppers might want to buy them. | **Make a Journal Entry** Have children write a journal entry about a grocery shopping trip. Who were they with? What did they buy? How did they decide what to buy? How much did some of the things cost? What did the other people in the store do? |

# 5 Day Grammar and Usage Plan

**ESL** Some English learners may have trouble recognizing plural and singular subjects. Review the rules for plural nouns, as well as irregular plural nouns such as *children, feet, men, teeth,* and *mice.*

## DAILY LANGUAGE ACTIVITIES

Write the Daily Language Activities on the chalkboard each day or use **Transparency 1**. Have children correct the sentences orally.

### Day 1

1. The store were small. was
2. Mike were glad. was
3. Dad were happy, too. was

### Day 2

1. The boxes was neat. were
2. The sisters was twins. were
3. The bag were big. was

### Day 3

1. Miss Lin were old. was
2. The twins was girls. were
3. They was not old. were

### Day 4

1. The plums was ripe. were
2. The jam were red. was
3. The cans was full. were

### Day 5

1. The sack were tan. was
2. The store were a mess. was
3. They was late. were

**Daily Language Transparency 1**

---

## DAY 1 Introduce the Concept

**Oral Warm-Up** Say the following sentences aloud: *The boy is fine. Yesterday, the boy was fine.* Ask children what changed in the second sentence. (*is* changed to *was*) Repeat with these sentences: *The boys are fine. Yesterday, the boys were fine.* (*are* changed to *were*)

**Introduce *Was* and *Were*** Discuss with children:

> ### Was and Were
>
> * The words *was* and *were* are verbs that tell about the past.
> * The word *was* tells about one person, one place, or one thing.

Present the Daily Language Activity and have students correct the sentences orally. Then have children write a sentence using *was.*

 **WRITING** Assign the daily Writing Prompt on page 8C.

Name_____ Date_____ **LEARN GRAMMAR 97**

**Was and Were**

* The words *was* and *were* are verbs that tell about the past.
* The word *was* tells about one person, place, or thing.

Mike **was** in his Dad's store

Read the sentences. Write *was* in each sentence.

1. Dad _____ was _____ happy.

2. Mike _____ was _____ in the store.

3. No one _____ was _____ home.

4. Miss Lin _____ was _____ with Mike.

5. The store _____ was _____ full of people.

Book 1.4
The Shopping List
EXTENSION: Ask students to use the words *was* and *were* to write sentences about what they did yesterday. 97

**GRAMMAR PRACTICE BOOK, PAGE 97**

---

## DAY 2 Teach the Concept

**Introduce *Were*** Remind children that yesterday they learned about using *was.*

**Review *Was*** Write the following sentence on the chalkboard: *Meg was fast.* Ask children which word is a verb and tells something about Meg. (was)

**Introduce *Were*** Write the following sentences on the chalkboard: *The ham was thick. The hams were thick.* Read the sentences aloud. Ask children which sentence tells about one thing (the first) and which tells about more than one thing (the second). Discuss with children:

> ### Was and Were
>
> * The word *were* tells about more than one person, place, or thing.

Present the Daily Language Activity. Have students correct the sentences orally. Then have children write a sentence using *were.*

 **WRITING** Assign the daily Writing Prompt on page 8C.

Name_____ Date_____ **LEARN AND PRACTICE GRAMMAR 98**

**Was and Were**

* The words *was* and *were* are verbs that tell about the past.
* The word *was* tells about one person, place, or thing.
* The word *were* tells about more than one person, place, or thing.

Gran and Ann **were** in the store.

Read the sentence about each picture.
Circle the verb for more than one person, place, or thing.

1. Mom and Dad (were) happy.

2. The jam and rice (were) for supper.

3. Mike and Dad (were) smiling.

4. The five plums (were) in a bag.

5. Grapes (were) on the list.

EXTENSION: Have children think of sentences about shopping for groceries. The sentences should be about more than one person, place, or thing.

98
Book 1.4
The Shopping List

**GRAMMAR PRACTICE BOOK, PAGE 98**

---

# Was and Were

## DAY 3 — Review and Practice

**Learn from the Literature** Review *was* and *were* with children. Then read the first sentence on page 12 of *The Shopping List:*

**Dad was always glad to see Mike.**

Ask children why *was* is used instead of *were*. (Dad is only one person, so the correct verb is *was*.) Then write this: The twins _____ always glad to see Mike. Ask children to fill in the blank orally using *was* or *were*. Then ask them why *were* is the correct choice. (The twins are more than one person, so the correct verb is *were*.)

**Use *Was* and *Were*** Present the Daily Language Activity and have children correct orally. Then have children write two sentences using *was* and *were* about people or things in *The Shopping List*.

 **WRITING** Assign the daily Writing Prompt on page 8D.

## DAY 4 — Review and Practice

**Review *Was* and *Were*** Write the following sentence on the chalkboard: *The jets was fast.* Ask children if the sentence is correct. (no) Why not? (The verb should be *were*.) Why? (because there is more than one jet) Correct the sentence on the chalkboard, then present the Daily Language Activity for Day 4.

**Mechanics and Usage** Before children begin the daily Writing Prompt on page 8D, review proper nouns. Display and discuss:

> **Proper Nouns**
> - The name of each day begins with a capital letter.
> - The name of each month begins with a capital letter.
> - The name of a holiday begins with a capital letter.

 **WRITING** Assign the daily Writing Prompt on page 8D.

## DAY 5 — Assess and Reteach

**Assess** Use the Daily Language Activity and page 101 of the **Grammar Practice Book** for assessment.

**Reteach** Have children look through magazines and find two pictures: one of one person, place, or thing and one of more than one person, place, or thing. Then have children write a sentence describing each picture, using *was* or *were*.

Children can create a classroom word wall with the sentences they have written.

Use page 102 of the **Grammar Practice Book** for additional reteaching.

 **WRITING** Assign the daily Writing Prompt on page 8D.

---

**Name_____ Date_____ PRACTICE AND WRITE GRAMMAR 99**

### Was and Were

- The words *was* and *were* are verbs that tell about the past.
- The word *was* tells about one person, place, or thing.

  Mike **was** smiling.
- The word *were* tells about more than one person, place, or thing.

  Fran and Ann **were** smiling.

Read the sentences. Write *was* for one person, place, or thing. Write *were* for more than one person, place, or thing.

1. Mike _____ was _____ in the store.

2. Fran _____ was _____ in the store.

3. Fran and Ann _____ were _____ there.

4. Tin cans and glass jars _____ were _____ on the shelves.

5. Fran and Ann _____ were _____ trying to help.

Book 1.4
The Shopping List

EXTENSION: Have the children change the sentences with one person, place, or thing to sentences with more than one. **99**

**GRAMMAR PRACTICE BOOK, PAGE 99**

---

**Name_____ Date_____ MECHANICS GRAMMAR 100**

### Capital Letters

- The name of each day begins with a capital letter.
- The name of each month begins with a capital letter.
- The name of a holiday begins with a capital letter.

Read the sentences. Circle each word that should begin with a capital letter.

1. Ann Gomez was home on (thursday).

2. Last (april) was Mike's birthday.

3. Ann and Fran were at the (thanksgiving) dinner.

4. Miss Lin was celebrating (new year's day).

5. Mike was looking for birthday presents on (sunday).

6. It was cold last (november).

Book 1.4
The Shopping List

EXTENSION: Have the students write sentences that use names of days, months, and holidays. **100**

**GRAMMAR PRACTICE BOOK, PAGE 100**

---

**Name_____ Date_____ TEST GRAMMAR 101**

### Test

Circle *was* or *were* to complete each sentence.

1. Mike _____ was _____ glad to see Mom.

   (was)  were

2. Miss Lin and Dad _____ were _____ helping.

   was  (were)

3. Ann and Fran _____ were _____ helping.

   was  (were)

4. There _____ was _____ something else to get.

   (was)  were

5. It _____ was _____ not milk.

   (was)  were

Book 1.4
The Shopping List

**101**

**GRAMMAR PRACTICE BOOK, PAGE 101**

# 5 Day Spelling Plan

**ESL** Children may be unfamiliar with the concept of "long" versus "short" vowels. The "silent *e*" rule may confuse them further. For those children who have difficulty, have them chant the following: *I have a wide smile.* Explain that *I, wide,* and *smile* all have the long *i* sound.

## DICTATION SENTENCES

### Spelling Words

1. She likes your smile.
2. I have a white cat.
3. The path is wide.
4. We can look while we ride.
5. The cat could bite.
6. We can hide in the shed.

### Challenge Words

7. You can ride after me.
8. Look at the blue hat!
9. What were you looking for?
10. Who said we could go?

---

## DAY 1 Pretest

**Assess Prior Knowledge** Use the Dictation Sentences at left and **Spelling Practice Book** page 97 for the pretest. Allow children to correct their own papers. If children have trouble, have partners give each other a midweek test on Day 3. Children who require a modified list may be tested on the first eight words.

| Spelling Words | | Challenge Words | |
|---|---|---|---|
| 1. **smile** | 4. while | 7. **after** | 9. **were** |
| 2. **white** | 5. bite | 8. **blue** | 10. **who** |
| 3. **wide** | 6. hide | | |

*Note: Words in **dark type** are from the story.*

**Word Study** On page 98 of the **Spelling Practice Book** are word study steps and an at-home activity.

### Spelling Practice Book page 97

Name_____ Date_____ **PRETEST SPELLING** 97

**Words with Long i : i-e**

**Pretest Directions**
Fold back the paper along the dotted line. Use the blanks to write each word as it is read aloud. When you finish the test, unfold the paper. Use the list at the right to correct any spelling mistakes. Practice the words you missed for the Posttest.

1. _____ | 1. smile
2. _____ | 2. white
3. _____ | 3. wide
4. _____ | 4. while
5. _____ | 5. bite
6. _____ | 6. hide

Challenge Words

_____ | after
_____ | blue
_____ | were
_____ | who

**To Parents**
Here are the results of your child's weekly spelling Pretest. You can help your child study for the Posttest by following these simple steps for each word on the list:
1. Read the word to your child.
2. Have your child write the word, saying each letter as it is written.
3. Say each letter of the word as your child checks the spelling.
4. If a mistake has been made, have your child read each letter of the correctly spelled word aloud, and then repeat steps 1-3.

5 Book 1.4 The Shopping List | 97

**SPELLING PRACTICE BOOK, PAGE 97**

**WORD STUDY STEPS AND ACTIVITY, PAGE 98**

---

## DAY 2 Explore the Pattern

**Sort and Spell Words** Say *hid* and *hide.* Ask children what vowel sound they hear in each word. Write the words on the chalkboard and circle the *i-e* pattern as you repeat the word *hide.* Repeat with the following pairs: *bit/bite; kit/kite; fin/fine; pin, pine.*

Ask children to read aloud the six spelling words before sorting them according to the spelling pattern.

| Words ending with | | |
|---|---|---|
| *-ite* | *-ile* | *-ide* |
| bite | smile | wide |
| white | while | hide |

**Word Wall** As children read other stories and texts, have them look for new words with long-vowel sounds that follow the silent *e* rule. Add them to a classroom word wall, underlining the vowel and the silent *e.*

### Spelling Practice Book page 99

Name_____ Date_____ **EXPLORE THE PATTERN SPELLING** 99

**Words with Long i : i-e**

Look at the spelling words in the box.

| smile | white | wide | while | bite | hide |

Write the two letters that are found in every spelling word.

1. ___i___ | 2. ___e___

Write the words that end with ite.

3. ___white___ | 4. ___bite___

Write the words that end with ile.

5. ___smile___ | 6. ___while___

Write the words that end with ide.

7. ___wide___ | 8. ___hide___

6 Book 1.4 The Shopping List | 99

**SPELLING PRACTICE BOOK, PAGE 99**

---

# Words with Long i̅: -ile

## DAY 3 Practice and Extend

**Word Meaning: Add -s** Remind children that we can add -s to a verb to show an action that one person or thing does now. Ask children to add -s to the following spelling words and write sentences using the words: *smile, bite, hide*.

**Identify Spelling Patterns** Write this sentence on the chalkboard: *Who can smile for a while?* Have a volunteer read it and tell which words follow the -ile spelling pattern and which word is a Challenge Word. Repeat with the spelling patterns -ite, ide, using these sentences:

*The cat does not bite after she eats.*

*The sky is blue and wide.*

Then have children write other sentences using the Challenge Words.

## DAY 4 Proofread and Write

**Proofread Sentences** Write these sentences on the chalkboard, including the misspelled words. Ask children to proofread, circling incorrect spellings and writing the correct spellings. There are two errors in each sentence.

> **We can hid for a whil.** (hide, while)
>
> **I made a wid smil.** (wide, smile)
>
> **I took a bit of whit bread.** (bite, white)

Have children create additional sentences with errors for partners to correct.

**WRITING** Have children use as many Spelling Words as possible in the daily Writing Prompt on page 8D. Remind children to proofread their writing for errors in spelling, grammar, and punctuation.

## DAY 5 Assess

**Assess Children's Knowledge** Use page 102 of the **Spelling Practice Book** or the Dictation Sentences on page 37Q for the posttest.

**Personal Word List** If children have trouble with any words in the lesson, have them create a personal list of troublesome words in their journals. Have children write a short poem with the words.

Children should refer to their word lists during later writing activities.

---

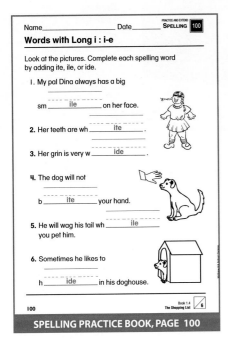

Name_____ Date_____ PRACTICE AND EXTEND SPELLING 100

**Words with Long i : i-e**

Look at the pictures. Complete each spelling word by adding ite, ile, or ide.

1. My pal Dina always has a big
   sm___ile___ on her face.

2. Her teeth are wh___ite___.

3. Her grin is very w___ide___.

4. The dog will not
   b___ite___ your hand.

5. He will wag his tail wh___ile___ you pet him.

6. Sometimes he likes to
   h___ide___ in his doghouse.

100
Book 1.4
The Shopping List 6

**SPELLING PRACTICE BOOK, PAGE 100**

---

Name_____ Date_____ PROOFREAD AND WRITE SPELLING 101

**Words with Long i : i-e**

Finding Mistakes
Read the poem. There are six spelling mistakes. Circle the mistakes. Write the words correctly on the lines.

A tent that is (whide)
Is a good place to (hyd)
All the (whyle),
I sit and (smil)
I take a (bitte)
Of cake so (wite)

1. ___wide___    2. ___hide___
3. ___while___    4. ___smile___
5. ___bite___    6. ___white___

Write a sentence using two words you wrote.
_____
_____

Book 1.4
The Shopping List 6    101

**SPELLING PRACTICE BOOK, PAGE 101**

---

Name_____ Date_____ POSTTEST SPELLING 102

**Words with Long i : i-e**

Look at the words in each set. One word in each set is spelled correctly. Use a pencil to color in the circle in front of that word. Before you begin, look at the sample sets of words. Sample A has been done for you. Do Sample B by yourself. When you are sure you know what to do, you may go on with the rest of the page.

Sample A
Ⓐ side
Ⓑ sid
Ⓒ sidde

Sample B
Ⓓ lak
Ⓔ lacke
Ⓕ lake

1. Ⓐ byt
   Ⓑ biet
   Ⓒ bite

2. Ⓓ while
   Ⓔ wile
   Ⓕ whyl

3. Ⓐ wid
   Ⓑ wide
   Ⓒ wyde

4. Ⓓ hyde
   Ⓔ heid
   Ⓕ hide

5. Ⓐ smyl
   Ⓑ smile
   Ⓒ smil

6. Ⓓ wite
   Ⓔ white
   Ⓕ whyte

102
Book 1.4
The Shopping List 6

**SPELLING PRACTICE BOOK, PAGE 102**

# Yasmin's Ducks

**Selection Summary** Yasmin discovers the value and joy of teaching as she tells her friends what she has learned about ducks.

**Student Listening Library Audiocassette**

**INSTRUCTIONAL**
Pages 40–65

**About the Author** As a young woman, Barbara Bottner dreamed of becoming an actress. While recovering from a broken leg, Ms. Bottner realized how much she loved to draw. She began to illustrate children's books. Soon she was writing stories, too.

**About the Illustrator** Dominic Catalano has illustrated several children's books. He is also a musician. Mr. Catalano owns his own design studio.

# Resources for Meeting Individual Needs

**EASY**
Pages 65A, 65D

DECODABLE

**INDEPENDENT**
Pages 65B, 65D

🏠 *Take-Home version available*

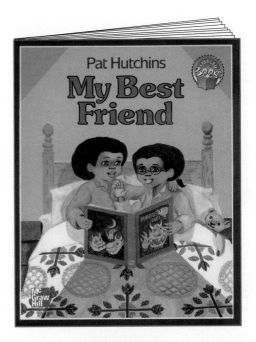

**AUTHENTIC**
Pages 65C, 65D

## LEVELED PRACTICE

**Reteach,** 135–142

blackline masters with reteaching opportunities for each assessed skill

**Practice,** 135–142

workbook with Take-Home Stories and practice opportunities for each assessed skill and story comprehension

**Extend,** 135–142

blackline masters that offer challenge activities for each assessed skill

## ADDITIONAL RESOURCES

- **Language Support Book** 145–153
- **Take-Home Story, Practice** pp. 136a–136b
- **Alternate Teaching Strategies** T64–T72

McGraw-Hill School
**TECHNOLOGY**

💿 Phonics **CD-ROM** provides extra phonics support.

**interNET** Research & Inquiry ideas. Visit
**CONNECTION** **www.mhschool.com/reading.**

 **Suggested**
# Lesson Planner

| READING AND LANGUAGE ARTS | DAY 1 — *Focus on Reading and Skills* | DAY 2 — *Read the Literature* |
|---|---|---|
| ● **Phonics Daily Routines** | Daily  **Routine:** **Segmenting,** 40B <br><br>  **CD-ROM** | Daily **Phonics Routines:** **Blending,** 40C <br><br> **CD-ROM** |
| ● **Phonological Awareness** <br><br> ● **Phonics** *Long o* <br><br> ● **Comprehension** <br><br> ● **Vocabulary** <br><br> ● **Study Skills** <br><br> ● **Listening, Speaking, Viewing, Representing** |  **Read Aloud and Motivate,** 38E <br> *Drawing Ducks* <br><br> **Develop Phonological Awareness,** 38/39 <br> Long *o: o-e* <br> *My Phone* <br><br> ☑ **Introduce Long o: o-e,** 40A–40B <br> Reteach, Practice, Extend, 135 <br> Phonics Workbook, 143–146 | **Build Background,** 40C <br> Develop Oral Language <br><br> **Vocabulary,** 40D <br> <table><tr><td>*work*</td><td>*because*</td><td>*buy*</td></tr><tr><td>*found*</td><td>*some*</td><td></td></tr></table> **Vocabulary Cards** <br> **Teaching Chart 100** <br> Reteach, Practice, Extend, 136 <br><br>  **Read the Selection,** 40–61 <br> Guided Reading <br> ☑ Long *o: o-e* <br> ☑ Cause and Effect <br><br> **Minilessons,** 43, 47, 51, 55, 59 <br><br> **Cultural Perspectives,** 42 |
| ● **Curriculum Connections** |  Science, 38E |  Science, 40C |
| ● **Writing** |  **Writing Prompt:** Write about the pets you have, or the pets you would like to have. |  **Writing Prompt:** Write a short article comparing a dog and a duck. <br><br>  **Journal Writing** <br> Quick-Write, 61 |
| ● **Grammar** | **Introduce the Concept:** *Has* and *Have,* 65O <br> Daily Language Activity: Use *has* and *have* correctly. <br> **Grammar Practice Book,** 103 | **Teach the Concept:** *Has* and *Have,* 65O <br> Daily Language Activity: Use *has* and *have* correctly. <br> **Grammar Practice Book,** 104 |
| ● **Spelling** *Long o* | **Pretest: Words with Long o: o-e,** 65Q <br><br> **Spelling Practice Book,** 103, 104 | **Explore the Pattern: Words with Long o: o-e,** 65Q <br><br> **Spelling Practice Book,** 105 |

## DAY 3 — Read the Literature

Daily  **Routine:**
**Fluency,** 63

 **CD-ROM**

**Reread for Fluency,** 60

**Story Questions,** 62
Reteach, Practice, Extend, 137
**Story Activities,** 63

**Study Skill,** 64
☑ Charts
**Teaching Chart 101**
Reteach, Practice, Extend, 138

**Test Power,** 65

 **Read the Leveled Books,**
Guided Reading
☑ Read Words with Long *o: o-e*
☑ Cause and Effect
☑ High-Frequency Words

 **Science,** 44

**Writing Prompt:** Think of an art project you could do with your friends. Which friends own art supplies? Write about your project, and tell what your friends have that they can use.

**Journal Writing,** 65D

**Review and Practice:** *Has* and *Have,* 65P
Daily Language Activity: Identify the correct use of *has* and *have.*

**Grammar Practice Book,** 105

**Practice and Extend: Words with Long *o: o-e*,** 65R

**Spelling Practice Book,** 106

## DAY 4 — Build Skills

Daily  **Routine:**
**Writing,** 65F

 **CD-ROM**

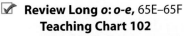 **Read Self-Selected Books**

☑ **Review Long *o: o-e*,** 65E–65F
**Teaching Chart 102**
Reteach, Practice, Extend, 139
Language Support, 150
Phonics Workbook, 143–146

☑ **Review *o-e, i-e, a-e*,** 65G–65H
**Teaching Chart 103**
Reteach, Practice, Extend, 140
Language Support, 151
Phonics Workbook, 143–146

 **Math,** 48

**Writing Prompt:** Interview a friend. Ask about your friend's pets. Write your questions and his or her answers.

**Persuasive Writing,** 65M
Prewrite Draft

**Meeting Individual Needs for Writing,** 65N

**Review and Practice:** *Has* and *Have,* 65P
Daily Language Activity: Identify the correct use of *has* and *have.*

**Grammar Practice Book,** 106

**Proofread and Write: Words with Long *o: o-e*,** 65R

**Spelling Practice Book,** 107

## DAY 5 — Build Skills

Daily  **Routine:**
**Letter Substitution,** 65H

**Phonics CD-ROM**

 **Read Self-Selected Books**

☑ **Review Cause and Effect,** 65I–65J
**Teaching Chart 104**
Reteach, Practice, Extend, 141
Language Support, 152

☑ **Review Inflectional Ending *-ed*,** 65K–65L
**Teaching Chart 105**
Reteach, Practice, Extend, 142
Language Support, 153

**Listening, Speaking, Viewing, Representing,** 65N

**Minilessons,** 43, 47, 51, 55, 59

 **Social Studies,** 58

**Writing Prompt:** Pretend you're a duck planning a poster about people. Describe how people are different from you.

**Persuasive Writing,** 65M
Revise, Edit, Proofread, Publish

**Assess and Reteach:** *Has* and *Have,* 65P
Daily Language Activity: Identify the correct use of *has* and *have.*

**Grammar Practice Book,** 107, 108

**Assess and Reteach: Words with Long *o: o-e*,** 65R

**Spelling Practice Book,** 108

**Link**

Science

# Read Aloud and Motivate

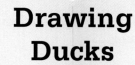

## Drawing Ducks

A poem by
Constance Levy

I'm really good at drawing ducks

I make them very yellow

I always make them following

the leader in a row

I always make them walking left—

and then I wonder *where they go!*

I give each one an orange bill

Each eye I dot just so . . .

and then they look at me so hard

it makes me wonder

*what they know!*

## Oral Comprehension

**LISTENING AND SPEAKING** Motivate children to think about the images in a poem by reading this poem about drawing ducks. Ask children to picture the ducks as you read the poem. When you are done, ask: "How are the ducks in the picture lined up? What does that make the poet wonder?" Then ask: "What else are the ducks in the picture doing? In what direction are the ducks in the picture walking?"

**Activity** Have children draw or paint the scene described in "Drawing Ducks." Encourage them to make their pictures or paintings as much like the poem as they can. ▶ **Visual**

# Develop Phonological Awareness

**Anthology pages 38–39**

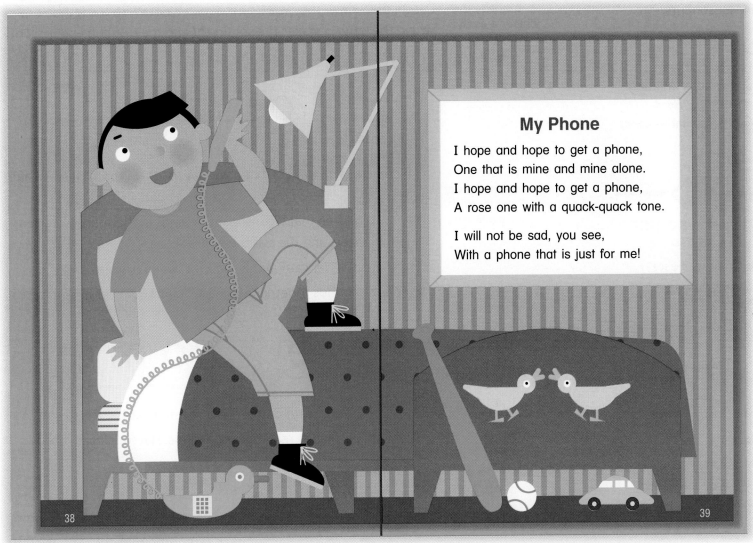

## My Phone

I hope and hope to get a phone,
One that is mine and mine alone.
I hope and hope to get a phone,
A rose one with a quack-quack tone.

I will not be sad, you see,
With a phone that is just for me!

## Objective: Listen for Long *o*

**RHYMING** Read "My Phone." As you reread the poem, have children clap each time they hear words that rhyme with *cone*.

**Phonemic Awareness** **BLENDING** Write the spelling of each sound in *hope* as you say it. Have children repeat after you. Explain that the final -*e* is silent, but tells you that the vowel sound is long, as in *hope* instead of *hop*. Ask children to blend the sounds to read the word.

Repeat with **alone** and **tone**.

**Phonemic Awareness** **SEGMENTING** Have children segment initial and final sounds.

Use letter cards to build the word *hope*.

• Say the word *hope*.

Take away the *p* and *e* cards.

• Say *hope* without the letters *p* and *e*.

Replace the *p* and *e* cards. Take away the *h* card.

• Say *hope* without the letter *h*.

Repeat with **rose**.

## OBJECTIVES

**Children will:**

- identify words with long *o: o-e.*
- blend and read words with long *o: o-e.*
- review consonants.

--------

### MATERIALS

- letter cards and long *o* cards, and word building boxes from the **Word Building Manipulative Cards**

### SPELLING/PHONICS CONNECTIONS

Words with long *o: o-e* see 5-Day Spelling Plan, pages 65Q–65R.

---

### TEACHING TIP

**INSTRUCTIONAL** To help children become more aware of the long *o* sound, ask them to concentrate on the position of their mouths as they pronounce it. Have them notice that their mouth makes an *o* shape when they say /ō/.

---

## Introduce Long o: o-e

> **TEACH**

**Identify the Letter o as the Symbol for the Sound /ō/**

Let children know they will learn to read words with the letters o-e, where the letter *o* makes the sound /ō/ and the *e* on the end is silent.

- Display the *o-e* letter card and say /ō/.

$$\boxed{\text{o } \_ \text{ e}}$$

**BLENDING Model and Guide Practice with Long o Words**

- Point to the *o* on the letter card and say /ō/. Have children repeat after you.
- Remind children that a consonant belongs in the space between the two letters and the *e* at the end is silent.
- Place the *m* letter card in the space between *o* and *e*.
- Blend the sounds together and have children repeat after you.

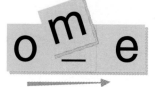

- Place the *h* letter card before the *o_e* letter card.
- Blend the sounds to read the word *home*. Have children repeat after you.

 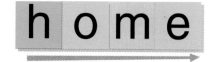

**Use the Word in Context**

- Use the word in context to reinforce its meaning. Example: *I walk home from school.*

**Repeat the Procedure**

- Use the following words to continue modeling and guided practice with long *o*.

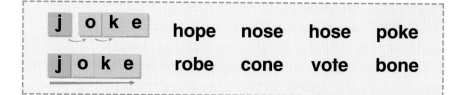

| j o k e | hope | nose | hose | poke |
| j o k e | robe | cone | vote | bone |

## PRACTICE

**LETTER SUBSITUTION**
**Build Long o Words with Letter Cards**

ONE

Build the word *mope*, asking children to repeat after you. Change the word to *hope* by replacing the *m* with *h*. Have children repeat after you. Next, ask children to build and read the following words, substituting the appropriate letter: *hose, nose, rose, rope, robe.*

▶ **Spatial/Kinesthetic**

## ASSESS/CLOSE

**Read and Write Long o Words**

To assess children's ability to blend and read long *o* words, observe children as they build words in the practice activity. Have children turn to page 38 and read "*My Phone.*" Then have them write two long *o* words from "*My Phone.*"

### ADDITIONAL PHONICS RESOURCES

**Phonics/Phonemic Awareness Practice Book, pages 143–146**

**PHONICS KIT**
Hands-on Activities and Practice

McGraw-Hill School
**TECHNOLOGY**
**Phonics CD-ROM**

activities for practice with
**Blending and Segmenting**

## Meeting Individual Needs for Phonics and Decoding

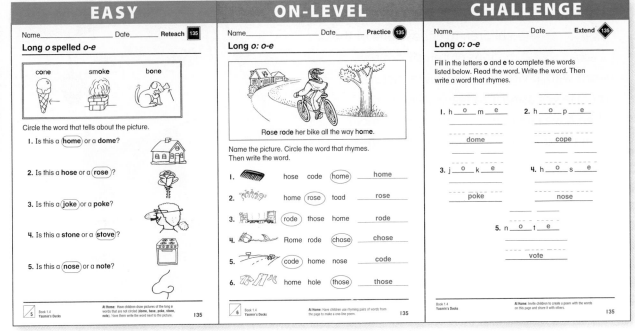

Reteach, 135     Practice, 135     Extend, 135

### Daily Routines

**DAY 1** **Segmenting** Distribute word building boxes. Say a word with long *o* and silent *e*. Have children write the spelling of each sound in the appropriate box. (Use *hope, nope, joke, home, vote.*)

**DAY 2** **Blending** Write the spelling of each sound in *cone* as you say it. Ask children to blend the sounds to read the word. Repeat with *poke* and *woke.*

**DAY 3** **Fluency** Write a list of words with long *o* and silent *e*. Point to each word, asking children to blend the sounds silently. Ask a volunteer to read each word aloud.

**DAY 4** **Writing** Have children choose three words with long *o* and silent *e* and write a sentence using each word.

**DAY 5** **Letter Substitution** Using the letter and long *o* cards, have pairs of children build *bone*. Taking turns, one child is to change a letter to build a new word, asking the partner to read it.

**PHONICS KIT**
HANDS-ON ACTIVITIES AND PRACTICE

**40B**

❖ TEKS ELA 1.20:A; 1.5:D,H

**DAILY**  **ROUTINES**

**DAY 2** **Blending** Write the spelling of each sound in *cone* as you say it. Ask children to blend the sounds to read the word. Repeat with *poke* and *woke*.

 **CD-ROM**

**LANGUAGE SUPPORT**

To build more background and help develop understanding and recognition of high-frequency words, see pages 145–148 in the **Language Support Book**.

# Build Background

 **Anthology and Leveled Books**

Social Studies

## Evaluate Prior Knowledge

**CONCEPT: TEACHING** Ask children to think of something they can do. How would they teach this to someone else? Have children perform the following activities to help them become more aware of the teaching and learning process.

**MAKE A WORD WEB FOR TEACHING** Ask the class to brainstorm a list of actions and items they can use to help teach a fact or skill. Make a word web of their ideas.

▶ **Linguistic/Visual**

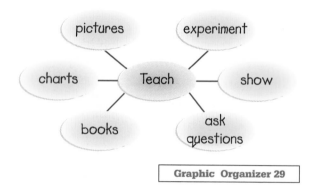

Graphic Organizer 29

**MAKE A TEACHING-AID PICTURE** Ask   children to choose one of the actions of items from the word web. Invite them to draw a pictured of themselves using it to teach a fact or skill. Then have children write a sentence under their illustration to explain how they are using that item to teach.

## Develop Oral Language

**CONNECT WORDS AND ACTIONS**

**ESL** Have children pretend to be schoolteachers and follow simple instructions such as:

• Greet the class.

• Tell the class what you will teach today.

• Write some facts on the board.

Prompt children to say what they are doing by asking:

• What are you doing?

• What will you teach today?

• What items will you use to help you teach the class?

▶ **Kinesthetic/Linguistic**

# Vocabulary

## High-Frequency Words

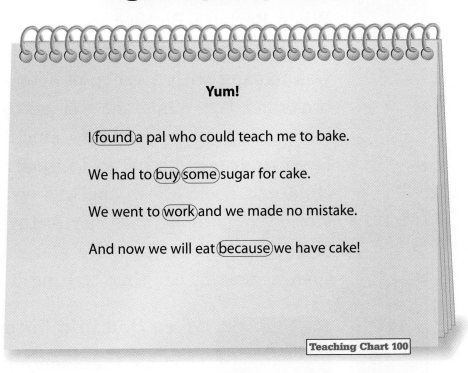

**Yum!**

I found a pal who could teach me to bake.

We had to buy some sugar for cake.

We went to work and we made no mistake.

And now we will eat because we have cake!

Teaching Chart 100

**SPELLING/VOCABULARY CONNECTIONS**

The words *work, because, buy, found,* and *some* are Challenge Words. See page 65Q for Day 1 of the 5-Day Spelling Plan.

---

## Auditory

**LISTEN TO WORDS** Without displaying it, read aloud "Yum!" on **Teaching Chart 100.** Ask children if they ever had a friend who taught them something, or if they ever taught a friend something. What was it? How did they teach it?

**SAY "YUM!" FOR HIGH-FREQUENCY WORDS** Have children aurally identify each high-frequency word using the following activity.

- Say aloud one of the high-frequency words. Read a line of the poem where the word appears.

- Before you read the line again, ask children to say the high-frequency word with you, then say "Yum!" Then read the line again, pausing at the word.

- Repeat this activity with each of the high-frequency words.

## Visual

**READ WORDS** Display "Yum!" on **Teaching Chart 100.** Read the poem, tracking the print with your finger as you read. Then hold up Vocabulary Cards one at a time and have children circle the high-frequency words on the chart.

work    because    found    buy    some

Vocabulary Cards

**CREATE SENTENCES** Have partners write the vocabulary words on separate index cards. They turn their cards upside-down in a pile, and mix them up. Ask the partners to take turns picking two cards, reading the words, and using them in a spoken sentence. (NOTE: If both words are the same, they can pick again.)

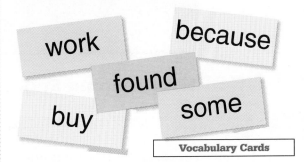

**ON-LEVEL**

Name_____ Date_____ Practice **136**

**High-Frequency Words**

Write the words from the box to finish the sentences.

| some | found | work | because | buy |

1. Dad went to ____work____

2. We ____found____ our cat.

3. I will ____buy____ it at the store.

4. Jane is sad ____because____ she lost her ball.

5. Pam wants ____some____ chips.

Take-Home Story 136a–136b
Reteach 136
Practice 136 • Extend 136

**40D**

# Guided Instruction

## Preview and Predict

Point to and read aloud the names of the author and illustrator. Discuss the roles of each person. Then take a **picture walk** through the illustrations, stopping at page 48. Using words from the story, talk about the details of each illustration.

- What will this story be about?
- What animal might we learn facts about?
- Will this story be a realistic one or a fantasy? (The drawings suggest a realistic story.) *Genre*
- Where does this story take place?

Have children make predictions about the story using the class chart.

| PREDICTIONS | WHAT HAPPENED |
|---|---|
| The story will be about why a girl likes ducks. | |
| We will learn facts about ducks. | |

## Set Purposes

Ask children what they want to find out.

- What do Yasmin and her friends talk about?
- Why is Yasmin drawing pictures of ducks?

---

**READ TOGETHER**

### Meet Barbara Bottner

When Barbara Bottner was a young woman, she was an actress. When she was touring with a group of actors, she broke her leg. While she was getting better, Bottner realized how much she loved to draw. She began to illustrate children's books. Soon she was writing stories to go along with her pictures. Now Bottner loves to write and she spends most of her time writing.

**1**

### Meet Dominic Catalano

Dominic Catalano has illustrated several children's books. He is also a musician. Catalano owns a design studio.

40

---

# Meeting Individual Needs • Grouping Suggestions for Strategic Reading

### EASY

**Shared Reading** Read the story aloud as you track print and model directionality. As you read with children, model using the strategy of understanding cause and effect. Use Guided Reading and other intervention prompts for additional help with decoding, vocabulary, and comprehension.

### ON-LEVEL

**Guided Reading** Ask children to read the story with you. Monitor children to identify difficulties with reading they may have and to determine which prompts from the Guided Reading to emphasize. After reading the story, have children reread it alone, using the rereading suggestions on page 60.

### CHALLENGE

**Independent Reading** Have children set purposes before they read. Remind them that thinking about why things happen can help them understand the story. After reading, have children tell why Yasmin likes ducks and why ducks don't get wet. Children can use the questions on page 60 for group discussion.

# Yasmin's Ducks

written by Barbara Bottner

illustrated by Dominic Catalano

41

# Guided Instruction

☑  **Long** *o*

☑ **Cause and Effect**

**Strategic Reading** Explain to children that to help them understand the story, they can think about how one event causes another event to happen.

**1** Let's look at page 40 again. What did the author do before she became a writer? (She was an actress.) What does the illustrator do besides draw pictures? (He is a musician.) *Concept of a Book: Author/Illustrator*

**2** **CAUSE AND EFFECT** Let's make Cause-and-Effect charts. We will fill them in as we read the story.

| What Happens | ▶ | Why It Happens |
|---|---|---|
| | ▶ | |

## Story Words

The words below may be unfamiliar. Have children check their meanings and pronunciations on page 12.

- ducks, p. 42
- rocket, p. 47
- feathers, p. 52

## LANGUAGE SUPPORT

This chart is available as a blackline master in the **Language Support Book.**

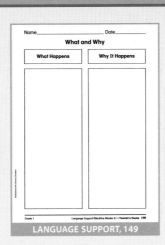

# Guided Instruction

**3** What is the first thing Yasmin says? ("These are the best ducks I ever made!") How do you know that she is speaking? (There are quotation marks.) *Concepts of Print*

**4** How do you think Yasmin feels about ducks? (She is interested in ducks; she likes ducks.) How do you know? (Yasmin has drawn ducks more than once; these are the best ducks she has ever drawn.) *Make Inferences*

**3** "These are the best ducks I have ever made!" said Yasmin.
"I can just see them in the lake. They swim around and quack. Quack, quack, quack," said Yasmin.

42

## CULTURAL PERSPECTIVES

**DOWN FEATHERS** Tell children that small feathers from ducks and geese, called down, are often used for warmth in blankets and clothing. In Scandinavian countries, where it can get very cold, eiderdown is collected from ducks. Display a world map or globe and point out Norway, Sweden, and Denmark.

**Activity** Invite children to find out more about Scandinavian customs and clothing. Ask each child to illustrate and label an item that has down feathers.

▶ **Visual/Logical**

My blanket is puffy.

My coat keeps me warm.

"Ducks, ducks, ducks!" said Ben. **6**
"I like your ducks."

43

# Guided Instruction

**5** **CAUSE AND EFFECT** Look back at Yasmin on page 42. What did she make? (a picture of ducks) Why do you think she draws ducks? (because she likes them) Let's write this on our Cause-and-Effect charts.

| What Happens | | Why It Happens |
|---|---|---|
| Yasmin draws a picture of ducks. | | She likes ducks. |
| | | |
| | | |

**6** Look at the first thing Ben says. How many commas are there? (2) *Concepts of Print*

## Minilesson
### REVIEW

### Final Sound /k/*ck*

As you read the word *duck* on page 42, emphasize the final /k/. Write the letters *ck* on the chalkboard. Then ask children to do the following:

Find each word on page 42 and 43 that ends with /k/ and the letters *ck*.

Brainstorm a list of other words that end with the same sound and letters at the end of *duck* and *quack*.

**Activity** Invite volunteers to frame the letters *ck* in each word on your brainstormed list while pronouncing /k/.

 **Phonics** **CD-ROM** Have children use the interactive phonics activities on the **CD-ROM** for more reinforcement with *ck*.

**43**

# Guided Instruction

**7** Let's read the first sentence on page 44 again. What punctuation mark comes after the word *ducks*? (question mark) What does a question mark mean? (Someone is asking a question.) *Concepts of Print*

**8** What is the first thing Yasmin did in the story? (drew a picture of ducks) What has she done now? (showed the picture to her mother) What will she do next? (take the picture to school to show to her class) *Sequence of Events*

**7** "Look, Mom, do you like my ducks?" asked Yasmin.

"Yes, they are fine ducks," she said.

"I will take them to class. It's show-and-tell day," said Yasmin.

44

## Activity

### Cross Curricular: Science

**FISH** After children read page 45, have them name different fish they have heard of or seen. Prompt them by asking:

• What are some very big fish?

• What are some very small fish?

▶ **Linguistic/Logical**

**RESEARCH AND INQUIRY** Invite children to look through books and magazines to find some examples of different fish.

**inter**NET **CONNECTION** For more information about fish, help children log on to **www.mhschool.com/reading**.

Miss Rome's class held up their work.　⑨

Tim made pictures of fish with fins.
"I like to make my fish with lots of colors,"
said Tim. "I have five blue and white fish
at home. I hope to buy a red fish."

45

# Guided Instruction

⑨ **Phonics** LONG *o* *"Miss…"* I'm not sure what this word is. Let's blend the sounds of the letters together to read it. R o m e Rome Let's read the word *hope* the same way. *Blending*

⑩ Let's look at the pictures that Yasmin and Tim drew. How are the pictures alike? (They both show animals.) **How are the pictures different?** (Yasmin's picture shows ducks. Tim's picture shows fish.) *Compare and Contrast*

**NOUNS** Let's look at the second sentence on page 45. How many nouns, or naming words, are there? (4) What are they? (*Tim, pictures, fish, fins*)

---

### *p/i* PREVENTION/INTERVENTION

**NOUNS** Remind children that a noun is a word that names a person, place, or thing. Write the sentence *The boy made pictures of fish with fins.* on the chalkboard. Invite a volunteer to the board to circle one noun in the sentence and explain why it is a noun. (*boy* is a person; *pictures, fish,* and *fins* are things.) Repeat this activity until all four nouns in the sentence have been circled. Continue to identify nouns by pointing to objects in the classroom, and ask children to call out the name of each object and explain why it is a noun. Explain to children that in the second sentence, *Tim* is a special kind of noun. It is a proper noun because it names the boy.

# Guided Instruction

**11** **Phonics** **LONG** *o* Look at the last word in the first sentence and point to it with your finger. Let's blend the sounds of the letters together to read it. h o s e s, hoses. *Blending*

**12** **CAUSE AND EFFECT** Why does Kate like to make big red fire trucks? (Her dad is a fireman.)

## Fluency

**READ WITH EXPRESSION**

**GROUP** Point out the punctuation marks at the ends of Mack's sentences on page 47. Discuss the differences between a statement and an exclamation.

Have children read Mack's statement aloud.

Then ask them to read Mack's exclamation aloud, reminding them to show excitement.

Invite children to read the two sentences again, displaying the proper changes in expression.

**11** Kate made fire trucks with big hoses. "I like to make big red fire trucks. My dad **12** is a fireman. He is very brave," said Kate.

46

 13

Mack said, "I like to make rocket ships. They can go around the globe and back!" 14

47

# Guided Instruction

**13** Look at Mack on this page. How do you think he feels? (excited) What are some reasons he might feel that way? (He could be looking forward to talking about his picture.) *Make Inferences*

**14** **Phonics** LONG *o* "*They can go around the* . . ." I'm not sure what this word is. Let's blend the sounds of the letters together to read it. g l o be, globe *Blending*

## Minilesson
### REVIEW
### Context Clues

Tell children that sometimes they will see words they don't know. Remind them that they can use pictures and other words in the sentence to help them figure out new words.

Have children look at page 46. Point out the word *hoses.*

Ask children to point to the hoses in the picture. Invite volunteers to explain what a hose is.

**Activity** Point out the word *globe.* Ask children to write a definition of the word *globe.* Then invite children to draw a picture above their definition.

## LANGUAGE SUPPORT

**ESL** Some children may have difficulty pronouncing /sh/ in words. Ask children to sound out /sh/ and draw it out, as if they were hushing someone. Then invite them to slowly add a vowel sound after /sh/, concentrating on how only their tongues change position. Practice saying *rocket ship* with children until they are comfortable blending the letters *sh* with the short *i.*

Invite children to write their own tongue twisters with /sh/. Remind children that correct pronunciation of the sound is more important than speed in reciting their tongue twisters.

# Guided Instruction

**15** What is Yasmin doing on this page? (She is showing her picture of ducks to the class.) *Use Illustrations*

**16** How does Yasmin feel as she talks about ducks? (excited) How do you know? (Her sentences end with exclamation marks.) *Character and Plot/Concepts of Print*

**15**

**16**

Yasmin held up her ducks. "I like ducks the best," she said. "I want to make ducks with wings that shine! I want to make ducks that swim and quack!"

48

---

## Cross Curricular: Math

**WEIGHT** Explain that most ducks weigh between two and four pounds.

Create a chart with the following heads: Weighs More than a Duck, Weighs Less than a Duck. Have children cut out pictures of animals to place in their charts.

▶ **Mathematical/Visual**

**RESEARCH AND INQUIRY** Have children research the actual weights of the animals in their charts.

*inter***NET** **CONNECTION** To find out about animals, have children log on to **www.mhschool.com/reading**.

"Why do you like to make ducks?"
Tim, Kate, and Mack asked.

49

# Guided Instruction

**17** Look at the picture on this page. What do you see? (children, a slide, the sun, and the grass) Where are the children? (at a playground) *Setting*

**18** Who are Tim, Kate, and Mack talking to on this page? (Yasmin) *Make Inferences*

**CONCEPTS OF PRINT** Look at the first sentence. There are punctuation marks at the beginning and end of it. What do these marks mean? (They show that someone is talking.)

## PREVENTION/INTERVENTION

**CONCEPTS OF PRINT** Write the sentence *"Why do you like to make ducks?" Tim asked.* on the chalkboard and read it with children. Ask children who is speaking. (Tim) Ask children to read what he is saying. To reinforce the separation between what is being said and the speaker, invite a volunteer to come to the board and frame the words between the quotation marks. Repeat this activity with other examples from the story.

**49**

# Guided Instruction

**(19)** **CAUSE AND EFFECT** What did Yasmin just do? (She read a good book on ducks.) Why did she read a book about ducks? (because she wanted to learn more about them) Let's write this in our Cause-and-Effect charts.

**(20)** Look at the picture on this page. What are Yasmin and her friends doing? (playing on the swings) *Use Illustrations*

| What Happens | | Why It Happens |
|---|---|---|
| Yasmin draws a picture of ducks. | | She likes ducks. |
| Yasmin read about ducks. | | She wanted to learn about them. |

## TEACHING TIP

**INSTRUCTIONAL** To help children focus more closely, help them understand that this process names the effect and then looks for its cause. Stress that they are "working backwards" by stating what happened and then asking why it happened. Make sure that children realize that the cause always occurs first and the effect always follows.

**(19)** "Well, I just read a good book on ducks. I found out a lot about them," said Yasmin.

"What did you learn?" Kate asked.

50

"Did you know that ducks don't get wet?" Yasmin asked.

"Wow," Yasmin's pals said.

"It's no joke," Yasmin added.

"How come they don't get wet?" Kate asked.

51

# Guided Instruction

**21** Yasmin tells her friends that ducks don't get wet. Are Yasmin's friends surprised? (yes) How do you know? (They say "Wow.") *Make Inferences*

**p/i** **CONTRACTIONS** Look at the last sentence on page 51. Point to the word *don't*. What does the apostrophe mean? (One or more letters have been taken out of the word.) Read it with me.

## Minilesson
### REVIEW
## Make Inferences

Remind children that they can use clues from illustrations to understand how characters are feeling.

Have children look carefully at the expressions on the characters' faces on pages 50 and 51.

Then ask them to brainstorm a list of words describing how each character might be feeling.

**Activity** Invite a volunteer to pantomime a character's expression. Suggest that the volunteer refer to the illustration as well as the list of words the class just brainstormed. The rest of the class can infer what the volunteer is feeling and call out descriptions of the volunteer's expression.

**p/i** **PREVENTION/INTERVENTION**

**CONTRACTIONS** Write the word *don't* on the chalkboard. Invite children to read it with you. Then write the words *do not* below it. Ask children what letter was removed from *do not* and replaced by the apostrophe in *don't*. (the second *o*) Ask children to use *don't* and then replace it with *do not* in the same sentence. Repeat this procedure with the words *can't, it's,* and *I'm*.

# Guided Instruction

**22** **CAUSE AND EFFECT** What do ducks do to their feathers? (Ducks wipe oil on their feathers.) What effect does this have? (It keeps the ducks dry because oil and water don't mix.) Let's write this in our Cause-and-Effect charts.

| What Happens | Why It Happens |
|---|---|
| Yasmin draws a picture of ducks. | She likes ducks. |
| Yasmin read about ducks. | She wanted to learn about them. |
| Ducks wipe oil on their feathers. | The oil keeps them dry. |

**23** How does Yasmin know so many facts about ducks? (She has just read a book about ducks.) *Character/Plot*

**RHYMING WORDS** Ask children to find a word on the page that rhymes with *sack*. (*back*)

## SELF-MONITORING

**ASK FOR HELP** Sometimes you might not understand what you read. You can ask questions about what you don't understand. First think of the things you do understand, then ask a friend or ask your teacher to explain what you don't understand.

*MODEL* I understand that a duck has oil next to its tail. I have heard that oil and water don't mix. But I don't know how the duck wipes the oil on its feathers in order to keep dry. I wipe with my hands, but ducks don't have hands. How does a duck wipe oil on its feathers without hands? I will ask the teacher to explain it to me.

**23**

"A duck has oil next to its tail," said Yasmin. "It wipes the oil all around its **22** feathers. The duck's feathers don't get wet ┃because┃ water and oil don't mix. The water rolls off its back," Yasmin said.

52

## P/I PREVENTION/INTERVENTION

**RHYMING WORDS** Write the words *sack* and *back* on the chalkboard. Ask a volunteer to underline the part of each word that is the same. (*-ack*) Then ask children to name other words that rhyme with *sack* and *back*. (*Jack, pack, quack, rack, tack*)

**24** Where was Yasmin at the beginning of the story? (at home) Where did she go next? (to school) Where will Yasmin and her friends go after school? (to Yasmin's house) *Sequence of Events*

**25** What do you think Yasmin and her friends will do at Yasmin's house? (Maybe they will try to mix water and oil.) *Make Predictions*

"That's cool," Mack said.

"Let's all go to my house after school," Yasmin said. "I'll show you how ducks don't get wet."

53

---

## LANGUAGE SUPPORT

**ESL** Help children read what Mack says on page 53. (*"That's cool."*) Discuss with children what he means. Explain that some phrases are common expressions that people use when they speak. Point out that sometimes phrases we use are not always meant literally.

For instance, the duck is not literally cool or cold when it puts oil on its feathers. Invite children to share other common expressions they use that are not always meant literally and list them on the board.

# Guided Instruction

**26** **Phonics** **LONG** *o* Read the first sentence aloud. Ask children to raise their hands when they hear a long *o* word as you reread the sentence slowly. *(home)* Still using the first sentence, have children read silently as you track print and ask them to raise their hands when you reach the long *o* word. *Nonverbal Response*

**BLENDING WITH SHORT** *o* Look at the first sentence. Find the word *got* and point to it with your finger. Now read the word with me, using your finger to help you remember to blend the sounds of the letters together.

When they got home, Yasmin got out her book on ducks. "We need two bags and salad oil," said Yasmin.

54

## *P/i* PREVENTION/INTERVENTION

**BLENDING WITH SHORT** *o* Write the following words on a piece of chart paper: *got, not, dot, mop,* and *hop.* Cover the first and last letters of each word with a self-stick note so that only the short *o* shows. Have children practice saying the short *o* sound. Then, starting with the first word, have a volunteer pull off one of the self-stick notes and blend the letters together. Invite another child to pull off the second note and blend all the letters together to read the word. Then have children smoothly read the word with you as you run your hand underneath it. Repeat this activity with the rest of the words.

"First, you put the oil on one lunch bag. Then you put some water on both bags," said Yasmin.  **27**

"Look at that!" Tim said.

"That bag isn't wet," Kate said. **28**

"The water drips off!" Tim said.

55

# Guided Instruction

**27** Let's go through Yasmin's demonstration again. **What materials did she get first?** (her book on ducks, two paper lunch bags, and some oil) **What did Yasmin do next?** (put oil on one bag) **After she put oil on one bag, what did she do?** (put some water on both of the bags) *Sequence of Events*

**28** **What happened to the paper bags?** (One got wet and one stayed dry.) **How do you know?** (Kate says, *"That bag isn't wet."*) *Draw Conclusions*

# Guided Instruction

**(29)** **CAUSE AND EFFECT** Let's write about Yasmin's demonstration in our Cause-and-Effect charts. What did she put on one paper bag? (oil) What happened when she put water on that bag? (The water rolled off the bag, the bag stayed dry.)

| What Happens | | Why It Happens |
|---|---|---|
| Yasmin draws a picture of ducks. | | She likes ducks. |
| Yasmin read about ducks. | | She wanted to learn about them. |
| Ducks wipe oil on their feathers. | | The oil keeps them dry. |
| Yasmin puts oil on a paper bag. | | She shows how oil keeps it dry. |

## TEACHING TIP

**MANAGEMENT** If you have a Science Corner in your classroom, make sure it is stocked with blank writing paper. When children have a question that can be answered with an experiment or demonstration, invite them to write the question on the scrap paper and provide an illustration if they choose. This will help inspire hands-on activities and inquiring minds.

"Water and oil really don't mix," Mack said.

56

"What about this? Did you know that ducks can dive to the bottom of very deep lakes?" Yasmin asked.

"And they don't get wet!" Yasmin's pals said.

"Nope! They don't," Yasmin said.

57

# Guided Instruction

**30** Look at the picture in Yasmin's book on this page. What does the picture show? (a duck diving to the bottom of a deep lake) *Use Illustrations*

**31** When the duck dives underwater, why doesn't it get wet? (because of the oil on its feathers) *Draw Conclusions*

## LANGUAGE SUPPORT

**ESL** As children read, have them place self-stick notes on any words they do not know. Remind children that to help understand these words, they can use pictures on the page, think about the sentence that the word is in, or ask a partner or the teacher. You may wish to model using context clues to help children figure out the meaning of the word *dive* on page 57. Have children figure out what dive means by looking at the illustration. Ask children:

- What is the duck doing? (swimming downward in the water)
- What do you think the word *dive* means, based on what you see in the picture? (swim down or swim underwater)

# Guided Instruction

**32** **CAUSE AND EFFECT** What happens to the lake in the fall? (It gets cold.) How does this affect the ducks? (They have no plants to eat so they fly south.) Let's write this in our Cause-and-Effect charts. *Story Props*

| What Happens | | Why It Happens |
|---|---|---|
| Yasmin draws a picture of ducks. | | She likes ducks. |
| Yasmin read about ducks. | | She wanted to learn about them. |
| Ducks wipe oil on their feathers. | | The oil keeps them dry. |
| Yasmin puts oil on a paper bag. | | She shows how oil keeps it dry. |
| Ducks fly south in the fall. | | It is cold and there's no food. |

**33** Why do you think ducks would fly south rather than north to find plants to eat? (because the south is usually warmer and plants grow where it is warm) *Make Inferences*

"Did you know that ducks fly south in the fall?" asked Yasmin.

**32** "When it's fall, the ducks can't get plants to eat because the lake is cold. They go

**33** south where they can eat."

58

## Activity

### Cross Curricular: Social Studies

**MAP SKILLS** Display a map of your state. Label North, East, South, and West around the edges of the map. Point out the major cities, such as Austin, Dallas, Houston, Galveston, Midland, and El Paso. Invite a volunteer to the map to find a city in the western part of the state. Repeat this activity for all directions.
▶ **Visual/Spatial**

**Activity** Locate your town on the map. Then invite children to locate towns or points that are north, south, west, and east of your town.

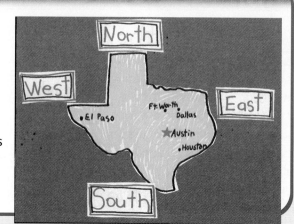

"They fly in a big flock," said Mack.
"I saw them last fall."

59

# Guided Instruction

**34** Look at the picture on this page. Do you think Yasmin's friends are now interested in ducks? (yes) How do you know? (They are drawing pictures of ducks.) *Make Inferences*

**35** What else do you see in this picture? (children, art supplies, books, tea, and rice) Where do you think Yasmin and her friends are? (in the kitchen) *Use Illustrations*

## Minilesson

### REVIEW

### Main Idea

Remind children that the main idea describes what a story is about and can be told in two or three sentences. Work with children to write a few sentences that tell the main idea of the story. Guide results by asking the following questions:

- What is the title of the story?
- What does Yasmin do with her friends?
- How do her friends feel about ducks at the end of the story?

**Activity** Ask children to write the title of the story and the main idea sentences on a piece of paper. Then invite them to illustrate their sentences by drawing three separate pictures underneath. You may wish to hang these "mini book reports" in a bulletin-board display.

# Guided Instruction

**CAUSE AND EFFECT** Why do you think Tim and Kate have started to like ducks?
(because Yasmin has taught them about ducks)

| What Happens | | Why It Happens |
|---|---|---|
| Yasmin draws a picture of ducks. | | She likes ducks. |
| Yasmin read about ducks. | | She wanted to learn about them. |
| Ducks wipe oil on their feathers. | | The oil keeps them dry. |
| Yasmin puts oil on a bag. | | She shows how oil keeps it dry. |
| Ducks fly south. | | It is cold and there's no food. |
| Tim and Kate like ducks. | | Yasmin taught them about ducks. |

**RETELL THE STORY** Using their Cause-and-Effect charts, have small groups of children talk about what happens in the story and why. *Summarize*

## STUDENT SELF-ASSESSMENT

Have children ask themselves the following questions to assess how they are reading:

- How did I use what Yasmin taught her friends to help me understand the story?

- How did I make sure I understood why things happened in the story?

- How did I use the pictures and the letters and the sounds I know to help me read the words in the story?

### TRANSFERRING THE STRATEGIES

- How can I use these strategies to help me read other stories?

"I think I like ducks, too," Tim said.

"Me, too. I wish I didn't have to go home now," said Kate.

"It's raining out," Yasmin said.

60

---

### REREADING FOR *Fluency*

**PARTNERS** Have partners take turns reading every page aloud while practicing appropriate rate and pausing.

**READING RATE** You may want to evaluate individual children's reading rates. Have the child read aloud from Yasmin's Ducks for one minute. When the minute is up, have the child place a self-stick note after the last word read. Then count the number of words the child has read.

Alternatively, you could assess small groups or the whole class together by having children count words and record their own scores.

A Running Record form provided in **Diagnostic/Placement Evaluation** will help you evaluate reading rate(s).

"Too bad we're not ducks!" Tim said.
"Then we would not get wet!"

Yasmin and her pals smiled.
"Quack, quack, quack, quack!"

61

# Guided Instruction

## Return to Predictions and Purposes

Reread children's predictions about the story. Ask children whether the story answered all the questions they had before they read it. Discuss their predictions, noting which needed to be revised.

Have children talk about the strategy of listing causes and effects in a chart. How did using their charts help them understand what and why things happened in the story?

### INFORMAL ASSESSMENT

#### HOW TO ASSESS

**Phonics** LONG *o* Have children turn to page 51. Have them point to and read the word *joke*. Then have them turn to page 57 and repeat the activity with the word *Nope*.

**CAUSE AND EFFECT** Have children describe an event in the story. Ask them to state one cause and its effect that they learned by referring to their Cause-and-Effect charts.

#### FOLLOW UP

**Phonics** LONG *o* Continue to model blending long *o* words that end in silent *e* for children who are having difficulty.

**CAUSE AND EFFECT** Children who are having difficulty can review the story and ask themselves "What happened?" to pinpoint one effect. To find the cause, children should then ask themselves "Why did it happen?"

## LITERARY RESPONSE

**QUICK-WRITE** Have children draw a picture of a duck in their journals. Ask them to describe what they find interesting about ducks and why. Then invite children to write about how Yasmin has inspired them.

**ORAL RESPONSE** Have children use their journal entries to discuss these questions:

- What is most interesting to you about ducks? Why?
- What words would you use to describe Yasmin?
- Have you read other stories about ducks?

# Story Questions

Tell children that now they will read some questions about the story. Help children read the questions and discuss possible answers.

**Answers:**

1. fly south *Critical/Sequence of Events*

2. to demonstrate that oil and water don't mix *Critical*

3. Answers will vary. Possible answer: It is raining and they will get wet. *Inferential/Make Inferences*

4. Reading helped Yasmin learn interesting facts about ducks. *Critical/Summarize*

5. In both stories, children learn about nature. *Critical/Reading Across Texts*

**Write a Letter** For a full writing process lesson related to writing a letter, see the lesson that compares on page 65K–65L.

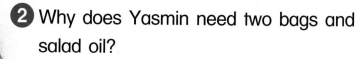
### Story Questions & Activities
READ TOGETHER

1. What do ducks do in the fall?

2. Why does Yasmin need two bags and salad oil?

3. Why don't the children want to go home?

4. What did you learn from this story?

5. Is "What Bug Is It?" like this story?

## Write a Letter

Pretend you are Yasmin's friend.
Write her a letter.
Tell her what you learned from her.
Draw a picture of one thing
you learned.

Dear Yasmin,
How are you? I learned that ducks don't get wet. It is fun to learn.
Do you like my drawing?
...friend, Bert

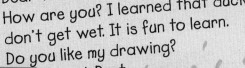

## Meeting Individual Needs

| EASY | ON-LEVEL | CHALLENGE |
|---|---|---|

**EASY**

Name_____ Date_____ Reteach 137
Story Comprehension

Draw a line from the children to their pictures.

1. Tim
2. Kate
3. Mack
4. Yasmin

Book 1.4
Yasmin's Ducks    At Home: Ask children to draw and label a picture of something they like.    137

**ON-LEVEL**

Name_____ Date_____ Practice 137
Story Comprehension

Think about "Yasmin's Ducks." Finish each sentence by circling the picture that tells the answer.

1. Yasmin likes to draw ___.
   a.   b.
2. Yasmin saw ducks in a ___.
   a.   b.
3. Ducks stay dry by ___.
   a.   b.
4. Ducks can dive in a ___.
   a.   b.
5. The ducks can't eat when the lake is ___.
   a.   b.

Book 1.4
Yasmin's Ducks    At Home: Have children tell what was their favorite part of the story.    137

**CHALLENGE**

Name_____ Date_____ Extend 137
Story Comprehension

Yasmin learned a lot from her book on ducks. What did you learn?

Read each sentence. Write **Yes** or **No**.

| Oil and water mix. | No |
| Ducks have wings. | Yes |
| Ducks can't swim. | No |
| Ducks don't get wet. | Yes |
| A duck wipes oil on its body. | Yes |
| Kids do not get wet in rain. | No |
| Ducks go south in the fall for food. | Yes |

Book 1.4
Yasmin's Ducks    At Home: Invite children to correct the incorrect facts. Have them rewrite the statements so that they are true.    137

Reteach, 137          Practice, 137          Extend, 137

# Play Duck, Duck, Goose

Sit in a circle.

Think of names of birds.

Play Duck, Duck, Goose.

Play again and use other bird names.

Have fun!

## Find Out More

Find out about another water bird.

How is it like a duck?

How is it different from a duck?

63

# Story Activities

### Play "Duck, Duck, Goose"

**GROUP** Read the directions aloud. Have volunteers explain how to play "Duck, Duck, Goose." Invite children to name different birds and to list them on the chalkboard.

### Find Out More

Brainstorm a list of other birds that live on or near the water. Select one of the birds listed and create a Venn diagram with its name above one circle and "Duck" above the other circle. Then ask children to compare and contrast the two birds by calling out features that each one has. (For instance, a "Duck" has a bill and short legs; "Both" have feathers; a "Crane" has a beak and long legs.)

**GROUP** **RESEARCH AND INQUIRY** Ask children how they could find out more about ducks and other water birds. Is there a place nearby where children could observe them? Have any children gone on nature hikes and watched water birds? Invite volunteers to describe water birds they have seen.

**inter NET CONNECTION** For more information on water birds, go to
***www.mhschool.com/reading***.

## FORMAL ASSESSMENT

After page 63, see the Selection Assessment.

**DAILY Phonics ROUTINES**

**DAY 3** **Fluency** Write a list of words with long *o* and silent *e*. Point to each word, asking children to blend the sounds silently. Ask a volunteer to read each word.

**Phonics CD-ROM**

# Study Skills

## GRAPHIC AIDS

### OBJECTIVES

Children will practice reading a tally chart of a class vote.

Remind children that they have just read a story about some friends who like to draw different things. Tell them that they will now read a tally chart that shows what some children like to draw. Explain that the tally chart shows the actual number of votes made for the animal the children liked to draw. Demonstrate by taking a quick vote on how many students enjoy drawing ducks.

Have children read the sentences and the title of the tally chart with you. Review how to read tallies and how to use tallies to show "5" (draw 4 vertical lines with a diagonal slash through them). Point to the column for "Fish" and ask how many children on the tally chart like to draw fish (2). Then help them read the questions below the diagram.

✦ TEKS ELA 1.10:B TAAS 3R2,5 (1.10:B)

## STUDY SKILLS

READ TOGETHER

## A Class Vote

This chart shows what some children draw.
Count the lines.
See how many children draw each thing.

| What Do You Like to Draw? | |
|---|---|
| ducks | \|\|\|\| |
| fish | \|\| |
| fire trucks | 卌 卌 |
| jets | 卌 |
| hats | \|\|\|\| |

## Look at the Chart

❶ How many children like to draw jets?

❷ Which thing do the most children like to draw?

## Meeting Individual Needs

### EASY

Name_____ Date_____ Reteach **138**

**A Chart**

This **chart** shows some children's toys. Under the name of each toy are **tally marks**. Each mark stands for a child who chose that toy as his or her favorite.

| What Toy Do I Like Best? | | | | | |
|---|---|---|---|---|---|
| Kites | Bikes | Trucks | Planes | Dolls | Drums |
| \|\|\|\|\|\| | \|\|\|\|\|\| | \|\|\|\|\| | \|\|\|\| | \|\|\|\|\|\| | \|\|\|\|\| |

Underline the word or words that answer the question.

1. Which two toys had five tally marks each?
   bikes and planes   <u>drums and trucks</u>

2. Which two toys had six marks?
   dolls and planes   <u>dolls and kites</u>

3. Which toy was the favorite of eight children?
   <u>bikes</u>   trucks

4. Which toy was the favorite of the most children?
   <u>bikes</u>   kites

**At Home:** Ask children to name each toy and count the number of tally marks under it.

138   Book 1.4 Yasmin's Ducks **4**

**Reteach, 138**

### ON-LEVEL

Name_____ Date_____ Practice **138**

**A Chart**

Look at the tally chart below.

| What Pets Do You Like Best? | | | |
|---|---|---|---|
| Mice | \|\|\|\|\|\| | Rats | \|\|\|\|\| |
| Cats | \|\|\|\|\|\|\|\|\| | Birds | \|\|\|\| |
| Dogs | \|\|\|\|\|\| | Fish | \|\|\|\|\| |

This chart shows some children's favorite pets. Count the marks next to each item. Then you will know which pets the children like best.

Write the correct word to complete each sentence.

1. The favorite pet of most of the children is a ___<u>cat</u>___

2. ___<u>Five</u>___ children like rats best.

3. Mice and dogs each have ___<u>six</u>___ tally marks.

4. Birds have ___<u>four</u>___ tally marks.

**At Home:** Help children to make a tally sheet to record people's preferences about something that interests them.

138   Book 1.4 Yasmin's Ducks **4**

**Practice, 138**

### CHALLENGE

Name_____ Date_____ Extend **138**

**Use a Chart**

Take a class vote. Find what children like to draw.

| What Do You Like to Draw? | |
|---|---|
| _____ | _____ |
| _____ | _____ |
| _____ | _____ |
| _____ | _____ |
| _____ | _____ |
| _____ | _____ |
| _____ | _____ |

Look at the chart. What do children like to draw best?

_____ Answer should be based on the chart. _____

**At Home:** Ask children other questions about the chart they made, such as: How many children chose [object] to draw?

138   Book 1.4 Yasmin's Ducks

**Extend, 138**

# TEST POWER

## Jasmin and Her Kite

Jasmin takes her kite outside.
She finds a place with no trees.
She unrolls her kite string.
She holds her kite up high.
The wind picks up the kite.
The kite begins to fly.
Soon it is high in the sky.

Why does Jasmin's kite fly?
- ● The wind picks it up.
- ○ There are no trees.

Ask yourself the question in your own words.

65

## Test Power

THE PRINCETON REVIEW

### Read the Page

Explain to children that you will be reading this story as a group. You will read the story, and they will follow in their books.

Request that children put pens, pencils, and markers away, since they will not be writing in their books.

### Discuss the Question

Discuss with children what constitutes an answer to a "why" question. Have them reread the story, find the place where the kite starts to fly, and put their fingers on the reason why the kite flies.

### Test-Tip

It's a good idea to restate the question in your own words to make sure that you understand it completely.

For The Princeton Review test preparation practice for **TerraNova, ITBS,** and **SAT-9,** visit the McGraw-Hill School Division Web site. See also McGraw-Hill's *Standardized Test Preparation Book.*

PUPIL SELECTION

**EASY**
DECODABLE

# Leveled Books

## EASY

### Spot's Trick

☑ **Phonics** Long *o*: *o-e*

☑ Cause and Effect

☑ High-Frequency Words:
*work, because, buy, found, some*

by Judy Nayer
illustrated by Key Wilde

## Guided Reading

**PREVIEW AND PREDICT** Discuss each illustration up to page 9, using the high-frequency words. As you take the **picture walk**, have children predict what the story will be about and record their ideas in their journals.

**SET PURPOSES** Have children write or draw why they want to read *Spot's Trick*. For example: I want to find out what trick Spot can do.

**READ THE BOOK** Use questions like the following to guide children's reading or after they have read the story independently.

**Pages 2–4:** Who sees some vocabulary words we just learned on page 2? *(buy, found, because)* On page 4? *(work)* *High-Frequency Words*

**Page 7:** Point to the word on this page that tells what Kate wants Spot to dig up. Model: If I don't recognize this word, I can read it by blending the sounds of the letters together as I run my finger under the word. b o n(e)  bone The word is *bone*.

Now read the word with me. Now let's use this strategy to find out what Spot dug up. r o ses  roses. *Phonics and Decoding*

**Pages 8–13:** What is happening so far in the story? (Kate wants Spot to do tricks, but he won't.) Is Kate proud of Spot? Why or why not? (No, she wants her dog to do tricks.) *High-Frequency Words/Main Idea and Details*

**Pages 14–16:** What happens when Spot jumps up on the bench with paint on his paws? (He makes paw prints on the bench; he paints the bench.) *Cause and Effect*

**RETURN TO PREDICTIONS AND PURPOSES** Discuss children's predictions. Ask which were close to the story. Have children review their purposes for reading. Did they find out what Spot's trick was?

**LITERARY RESPONSE** The following questions will help focus children's responses:

- Was Spot a good dog? What do you think would help Kate teach Spot a trick?

- Has someone ever wanted you to do something you couldn't do? Tell about it.

Also see the story questions and writing activity in *Spot's Trick*.

**Phonics** CD-ROM

---

**Answers to Story Questions**

1. A trick
2. Frustrated, upset
3. No.
4. Kate got a dog and tried to teach him a trick. He didn't learn any. The next day, when Greg came over, Kate asked Spot to do a trick. Spot jumped up on the bench Kate was painting and that was his trick.
5. Answers will vary.

**Story Questions and Writing Activity**

1. What does Kate want Spot to do?
2. How does Kate feel when Spot does not do those things?
3. Did Kate tell Spot to paint?
4. Tell what happened in the story.
5. What other pets have you read about?

**Pick a Pet**

Your Mom and Dad say you can have a pet!

What pet do you want? Draw a picture of it.

Give it a name.

Tell what it is and why you picked it.

*from Spot's Trick*

# Leveled Books

## INDEPENDENT

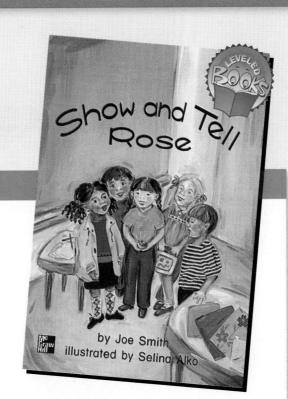

### Show and Tell Rose

☑  Long *o: o-e*

☑ Cause and Effect

☑ High-Frequency Words: *work, because, buy, found, some*

**PUPIL SELECTION**

INDEPENDENT
DECODABLE

# Guided Reading

**PREVIEW AND PREDICT** Discuss each illustration up to page 9, using the high-frequency words. As you take the **picture walk**, have children predict what the story will be about and chart their ideas in their journals.

**SET PURPOSES** Have children write or draw why they want to read *Show and Tell Rose*. For example: I want to find out what Rose shows and tells.

**READ THE BOOK** Use questions like the following to guide children's reading or after they have read the story independently.

**Pages 2–3:** How many words can you find on page 3 with long *o* and silent *e*? (four) Read them for me. Remember to blend the sounds of the letters together if you need to. (*Rose, hope, drove, home*) *Phonics and Decoding*

**Pages 4–7:** Who sees some vocabulary words we just learned on page 4? (*found*) On page 5? (*because, some*) Page 6? (*work*) *High-Frequency Words*

**Pages 8–13:** Why was Rose happy to meet Mr. Lin Chan? (She liked his cooking; he taught her to make paper things.) What will Rose bring for show and tell? (a paper flower) *Cause and Effect/Make Predictions*

**Pages 14–16:** How did learning how to make paper things help Rose? (It gave her a new skill she liked; it gave her a new friend at home and friends at school.) *Cause and Effect*

**RETURN TO PREDICTIONS AND PURPOSES** Discuss children's predictions. Ask which were close to the story and why. Have children review their purposes for reading. Did they find out what Rose brought for show and tell?

**LITERARY RESPONSE** The following questions will help focus children's responses:

• How did Mr. Lin Chan help Rose?

• Have you ever taught anyone to do something new? Tell about it.

Also see the story questions and writing activity in *Show and Tell Rose*.

 **CD-ROM**

**Answers to Story Questions**

1. Make something for show and tell.
2. She was new and she didn't make any friends yet.
3. Make paper roses.
4. She feels good.
5. Answers will vary.

---

**Story Questions and Writing Activity**

1. What does Rose have to do for class?
2. Why is Rose a bit sad in class?
3. What does Rose learn how to do?
4. How does Rose feel about her new school now?
5. What are some things you can bring for show and tell?

**Make Something with Paper**

Get some paper.

Work with a partner.

Show your partner how to make something with paper.

You can write, color, or cut the paper.

Then your partner can take a turn.

*from Show and Tell Rose*

**65B**

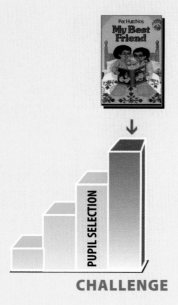

PUPIL SELECTION

**CHALLENGE**

# Leveled Books

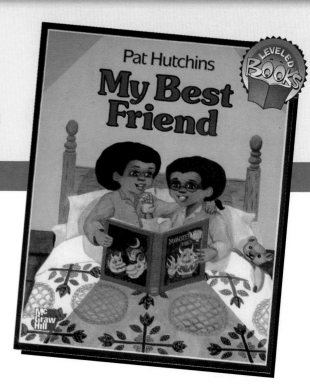

## AUTHENTIC

### My Best Friend

☑ **Phonics** Long *o*: *o-e*
☑ **Cause and Effect**

## Guided Reading

**PREVIEW AND PREDICT** Discuss each illustration up to page 15. As you take the **picture walk**, have children predict what the story will be about and list their ideas.

**SET PURPOSES** Have children write or draw why they want to read *My Best Friend*. For example: I want to find out more about the best friend.

**READ THE BOOK** Use questions like the following to guide children's reading or after they have read the story independently.

**Pages 2–13:** Let's read these pages together and look at the pictures. What is this book about? (two best friends) Why is the girl glad to have a best friend? (Her friend knows how to do things she can't do.) What can her friend do? (run fast, climb high) *Cause and Effect*

**Pages 17–24:** What else can the best friend do well? (untie her shoelaces, do up her buttons) What about the girl? (She can't do those things very well.) What is the friend afraid of? (monsters) Is the girl afraid? (no) *Details*

**Page 27:** Find the long *o* word on this page and point to it. Let's read it together. Remember that *s* can sometimes make the sound /z/.

**Pages 28–30:** What made the monster? (the wind blowing the curtains) How does the girl make the monster go away? (She closes the window.) *Cause and Effect*

**RETURN TO PREDICTIONS AND PURPOSES** Discuss children's predictions. Ask which were close to the story and why. Have children review their purposes for reading. Did they find out more about the best friends?

**LITERARY RESPONSE** The following questions will help focus children's responses:

- Are you good at something no one else can do? Tell about it.

- Can your friend do something you can't? Do you like that? Why or why not?

Also see the story questions and writing activity in *My Best Friend*.

**Phonics CD-ROM**

---

**Answers to Story Questions**

1. Jump, eat spaghetti, paint, read
2. She thinks the wind is a monster.
3. Answers will vary.
4. Two best friends
5. Both stories are about children who are friends.

**Story Questions and Writing Activity**

1. Name three things the friends do.
2. Why is the girl in the story afraid?
3. What makes a friend special?
4. What is this story about?
5. How is this story like *Big Brother Little Brother*?

**Your Special Friend**

Draw a picture of a special friend. Write a sentence that tells why your friend is special.

**from My Best Friend**

# Activities

## Anthology and Leveled Books

## Connecting Texts

| CLASS DISCUSSION | CHARACTER WEB |
|---|---|
| Lead a discussion of how the unit theme of Teaching applies to each of the stories. Have children construct a word web that describes what characters teach or what they learn from their own experiences or from others. | Have children create a web to compare the characters from their stories, their traits and what they do. |

**Yasmin's Ducks**
Yasmin teaches her friends about ducks.

**Spot's Tricks**
Kate teaches spot a trick by accident

**Teaching**

**Show and tell Rose**
Mr. Lin Chan teaches Rose to make origami.

**My Best Friend**
A girl teaches her best friend not to be afraid.

## Viewing/Representing

**GROUP PRESENTATIONS** Divide the class into groups, one for each of the four books. (For *Yasmin's Ducks,* combine children of different reading levels.) Have each group draw pictures of the main events and orally summarize the book. Have each group present its pictures and summary.

**AUDIENCE RESPONSE**
Ask children to pay attention to each group's presentation. Allow time for questions after each group presents.

## Research and Inquiry

**MORE ABOUT TEACHING** Have children ask themselves: What is something I would like a friend or relative to teach me? Then invite them to:

- have a show and tell in class, describing something that can be taught and who could teach it.

- ask a teacher of music, dance, or art to come and speak about it.

*inter*NET CONNECTION  Have children log on to **www.mhschool.com/reading** for more information about teachers.

 JOURNAL  Children can draw pictures representing what they learned in their journals.

**65D**

## Review **Long o: o-e**

### OBJECTIVES

**Children will:**

- identify /ō/o words with final *e*.
- blend and read long *o* words.
- review consonants.

**MATERIALS**

- **Teaching Chart 102**
- long *o* vowel card from the **Word Building Manipulative Cards**

### SPELLING/PHONICS CONNECTIONS

Words with long *o*: See 5-Day Spelling Plan, pages 65Q–65R.

---

### TEACHING TIP

**INSTRUCTIONAL** After children use the **Teaching Chart** words in sentences, ask them to act out the sentences.

---

### ALTERNATE TEACHING STRATEGY

**LONG o: o-e**

For a different approach to teaching this skill, see page T68.

---

**PREPARE**

**Listen for Long o** Read the following sentences and have children raise their hands whenever they hear a word with the long *o* sound.

- *I wrote a note. It has lots of jokes. I hope my note is funny.*

**TEACH**

**Review the letter o_e as symbols for the sound /o/**

- Tell children they will review vowel pattern *o_e* and the long *o* sound it makes.

- Display the long vowel card *o_e*. Remind children that the space between the letters is for a consonant letter. Together the letters make a long *o* sound.

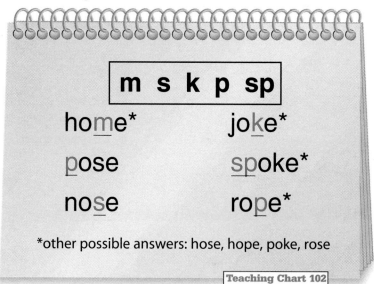

| m s k p sp |
| --- |

home*          joke*

pose          spoke*

nose          rope*

*other possible answers: hose, hope, poke, rose

Teaching Chart 102

**BLENDING Model and Guide Practice with Long o Words**

- Display **Teaching Chart 102**. Cover the letter *h* in the first example. Run your finger under the letters *o-e* and say /ō/.

- Choose the letter *m* from the box at the top of the chart and write it in the blank space. Blend the sounds together to say *o me*.

- Uncover the letter *h*. Run your finger under the letters again and have children blend the sounds and read the word *home*. home

**Use the Word in Context** Have volunteers use the word in a sentence to reinforce its meaning. Example: *Let's go home.*

**Repeat the Procedure** Erase *m* and model blending with *s* and the word *hose*. Continue by having children substitute other letters to complete words on the chart.

 **PRACTICE**

 **BLENDING**
**Build long _o_**
**Words with Letter**
**Banks**

**PARTNERS**

Write the following letter banks on the chalkboard as shown:

| h | j | r |
|---|---|---|
| p | w | n |

| o |
|---|

| ke | me | de |
|---|---|---|
| pe | l | se |

Have a child choose a letter from the first bank, write it down, and then write the letter _o_. Have another child choose a pair of letters from the third bank to form a word. Ask children to read the word.

▶ **Spatial/Linguistic**

**ASSESS/CLOSE**

**Read Long _o_**
**Words**

To assess children's mastery of blending and reading long _o_ words, observe them as they build words in the Practice activity. Ask each child to read three or four words aloud from their list.

### ADDITIONAL PHONICS RESOURCES

**Phonics/Phonemic Awareness Practice Book, pages 143–146**

McGraw-Hill School **TECHNOLOGY**

**Phonics CD-ROM**

**activities for practice with Blending and Segmenting**

 **DAILY Phonics ROUTINES**

**DAY 4** **Writing** Have children choose three words with long _o_ and silent _e_ and write a sentence using each word.

**Phonics CD-ROM**

**SELECTION**
**Connection**

Children may choose from the following titles for independent reading.

- _Yasmin's Ducks_
- _Spot's Trick_
- _Show and Tell Rose_
- _My Best Friend_

Bibliography, pages T92–T93

Bookshelf Library

## Meeting Individual Needs for Phonics

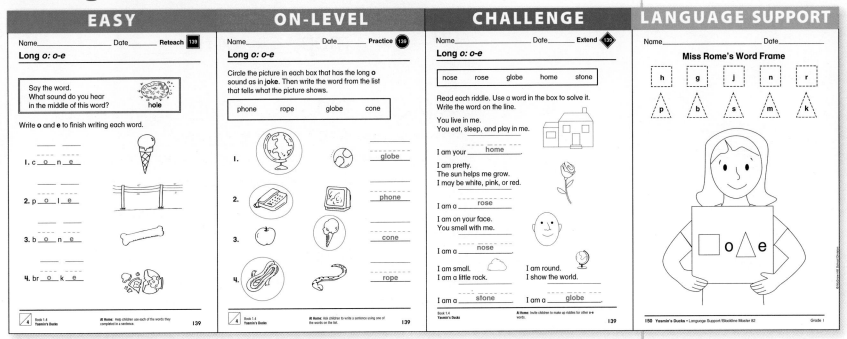

| EASY | ON-LEVEL | CHALLENGE | LANGUAGE SUPPORT |
|---|---|---|---|
| Reteach, 139 | Practice, 139 | Extend, 139 | Language Support, 150 |

**65F**

**OBJECTIVES**

**Children will:**

- review /ō/o, /ī/i, /ā/a in words with final *e*.

- blend and read long *o, i,* and *a* in words with final *e*.

- discriminate between long and short *o, i,* and *a* sounds.

. . . . . . . . . . . . . . . . . . . . . .

**MATERIALS**

- **Teaching Chart 103**

---

**TEACHING TIP**

**INSTRUCTIONAL** Children can make their own version of **Teaching Chart 103**. Help them write these and other CVCe words that are valid without the final *e*. Tell children to use self-stick notes to cover and uncover the final *e* for practicing on their own.

---

# Review *o-e, i-e, a-e*

**PREPARE**

**Discriminate Between Long and Short *o, i, a***  Write the following long *o, i,* and *a* words with final *e* on the chalkboard: *rope, bike,* and *cake.* Ask a volunteer for a word that has the same /ō/ sound as in *rope.* Then ask another volunteer for a word in which *o* makes the short sound. Repeat the activity for long and short *i* and *a.*

**TEACH**

**BLENDING Model and Guide Practice in Discriminating Long and Short *o, i,* and *a***

- Display **Teaching Chart 103**. Explain that the chart shows nine words. Children can make nine more words by adding *e* to the end of each word.

- Blend the first word on the chart with children.

  h  o  p   hop

- Write an *e* at the end of the first word and blend the word with children.

  h  o  pe   hope

Teaching Chart 103

**Use the Word in Context**  Ask a volunteer to use both words in a sentence to reinforce their meanings. Example: *I hope I can hop on one foot.*

**Repeat the Procedure**  Continue with **Teaching Chart 103**. Have children blend the sounds aloud and say the word. Then add an *e* to the end of the word and have them blend the sounds to say the new word.

## PRACTICE

**BLENDING**
**Build Words with Long and Short o, i, and a**

**PARTNERS**

Have children work in pairs. Ask one partner to write as many words with long o as possible, while the other partner writes as many words with short o as possible. Have partners check each other's work. Repeat with long and short i and a. Have partners compare their word lists to lists that other pairs have created.

▶ **Linguistic/Visual**

## ASSESS/CLOSE

**Read Words with Long and Short o, i, a**

Use your observations from the Practice activity to determine if children need more reinforcement discriminating between long and short o, i, and a. Have children choose a long o word and a short o word, and then read the words aloud. Repeat with long and short i and a.

### ADDITIONAL PHONICS RESOURCES

**Phonics/Phonemic Awareness Practice Book, pages 143–146**

*McGraw-Hill School* **TECHNOLOGY**

Phonics **CD-ROM**

**activities for practice with Blending and Segmenting**

**DAY 5 — Letter Substitution**
Using the letter and long o cards, have pairs of children build *bone*. Taking turns, one child is to change a letter to build a new word, asking the partner to read it.

Phonics **CD-ROM**

**ALTERNATE TEACHING STRATEGY**

**DISCRIMINATION BETWEEN LONG AND SHORT o, i, AND a**

For a different approach to teaching this skill, see pages T64, T68, and T72.

## Meeting Individual Needs for Phonics

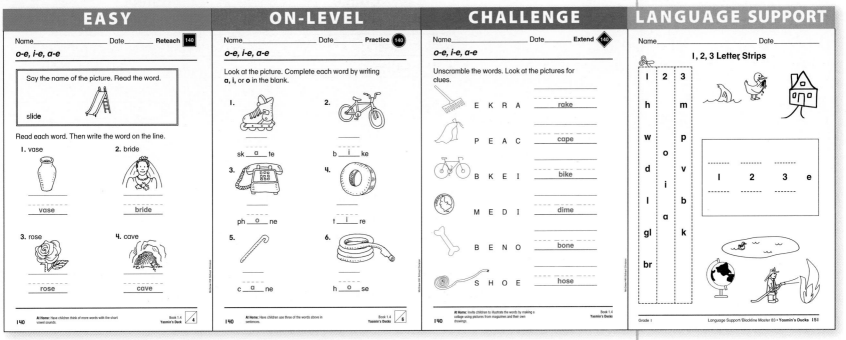

| EASY | ON-LEVEL | CHALLENGE | LANGUAGE SUPPORT |
|---|---|---|---|
| Reteach, 140 | Practice, 140 | Extend, 140 | Language Support, 151 |

**OBJECTIVES**

Children will identify cause and effect.

....................................................

**MATERIALS**

• Teaching Chart 104

---

**TEACHING TIP**

**INSTRUCTIONAL** Say a simple cause-and-effect statement aloud. As you repeat the sentence, ask children to raise their hands when they hear the cause and clap their hands when they hear the effect. For example, *It was snowing* (cause) *so I stayed at home.* (effect)

---

# Review Cause and Effect

> **PREPARE**

**Review Cause and Effect**    Remind children that as they read or listen, they should think about how one thing can cause another thing to happen.

> **TEACH**

**Identify Cause and Effect**    Display **Teaching Chart 104**. Read the first set of sentences aloud, tracking the print as you read. Ask children to think about why Yasmin put on her coat.

---

1. It is cold.
   Yasmin puts on her coat.

2. It is raining.
   Yasmin brings her umbrella.

3. It is sunny.
   Yasmin puts on her hat.

| Cause | Effect |
|-------|--------|
| 1. It is cold. | 1. Yasmin puts on her coat. |
| 2. It is raining. | 2. Yasmin brings her umbrella. |
| 3. It is sunny. | 3. Yasmin puts on her hat. |

Teaching Chart 104

---

*MODEL*    As I read the first two sentences, I need to figure out why Yasmin put on her coat. She put on her coat because it is cold. So the cause is the cold, and the effect is that Yasmin put on her coat.

Follow the same procedure for the other sets of sentences on the chart. Have volunteers write the causes and effects on **Teaching Chart 104.**

## PRACTICE

**Create a Cause and Effect Chart**

**GROUP**

Have children reread *Yasmin's Ducks,* or other stories they have read, and look for causes and effects. Make another cause and effect chart. Ask children to write sentences on the chart showing causes and effects. ▶ **Logical/Logistic**

## ASSESS/CLOSE

**Identify Cause and Effect**

Brainstorm with children events that happen each day. Then write sentences on the chalkboard that tell each event and its effect. For example: *The alarm clock went off and I woke up. I was hot so I opened the window.* Have volunteers circle the cause and underline the effect in each sentence. Ask if there were any clue words that helped them to determine which was the cause and which was the effect.

## ALTERNATE TEACHING STRATEGY

**CAUSE AND EFFECT**

For a different approach to teaching this skill, see page T66.

**LOOKING AHEAD**

Children will apply this skill as they read the next selection, *The Knee-High Man.*

# Meeting Individual Needs for Comprehension

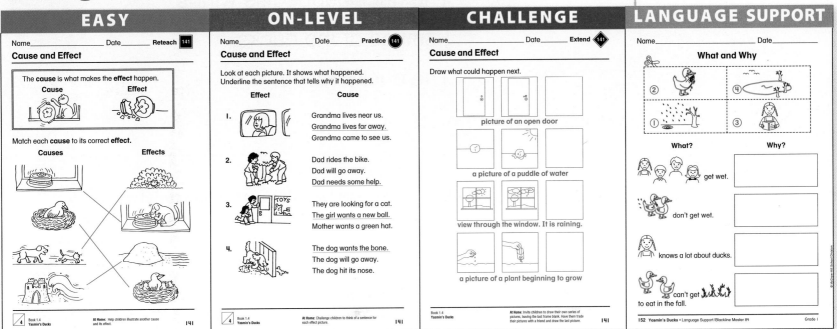

Reteach, 141      Practice, 141      Extend, 141      Language Support, 152

**OBJECTIVES**

Children will review reading words with the inflectional ending *-ed*, including words with a double consonant or a dropped *-e*.

**MATERIALS**

• **Teaching Chart 105**
• index cards

---

**LANGUAGE SUPPORT**

**ESL** If children are having difficulty remember rules for the *-ed* ending, have them list only words that need a double consonant on one page. Then have them list only words that drop the final *-e* on a separate page.

---

# Review Inflectional Ending -ed

**PREPARE**

**Introduce the Concept**   Write the word *flap* on the chalkboard. Have children pretend they are ducks and are flapping their wings. As they tell what they just did, add *-ped*. Explain that often *-ed* is added to words that show that something already happened. Point out that with some words, like *flap*, the last letter must be doubled before the *-ed* is added.

Repeat the procedure with the word *smile*. Explain that with some words, like *smile*, the final *e* must be dropped before the *-ed* is added.

**TEACH**

**Identify Base Words**   Track the first sentence on **Teaching Chart 105** as you read it with children. Then point to the word *flapped* on the chart. Ask children if they recognize part of the word. *(flap)* Model for children how understanding inflectional endings can help them read.

## I Like Ducks

The duck <u>flap</u>ped its wings.

I <u>smiled</u> at the ducks.

The ducks <u>raced</u>.

Teaching Chart 105

*MODEL*   I can use what I already know to help me read words I don't recognize. I know the word *flap*. I know that sometimes when you add *-ed* to the end of a word, you have to double the last letter of the word. That's where the extra *p* comes from. The *-ed* shows that the action happened in the past. The word is *flapped*.

Repeat this activity with the other two sentences. Then call on children to come up and draw a line under the base word in each sentence.

## PRACTICE

**Add -ed**

PARTNERS

Write *added, hiked,* and *smiled* on the chalkboard. Have partners read each word and write it on an index card so that the *-ed* ending appears after a dotted line. Then have them turn the card over and write the word without the *-ed* ending. Invite volunteers to explain how the words *hiked* and *smiled* are spelled without the *-ed* ending. Then write *stop* and *care* on the chalkboard. Call on children to add *-ed* to each word, making sure either to double the final consonant or drop the final *e*.

▶ Linguistic

## ASSESS/CLOSE

**Identify More Base Words**

Use your observations from the Practice activity to determine if children need more reinforcement with *-ed* words with double consonants or dropped *-e* endings. Provide children with other *-ed* words such as *sipped, voted,* and *talked.* Have children circle the part of the word that they know and explain how each word changes when *-ed* is added.

| add | ed |
| hik | ed |
| smil | ed |

# Meeting Individual Needs for Vocabulary

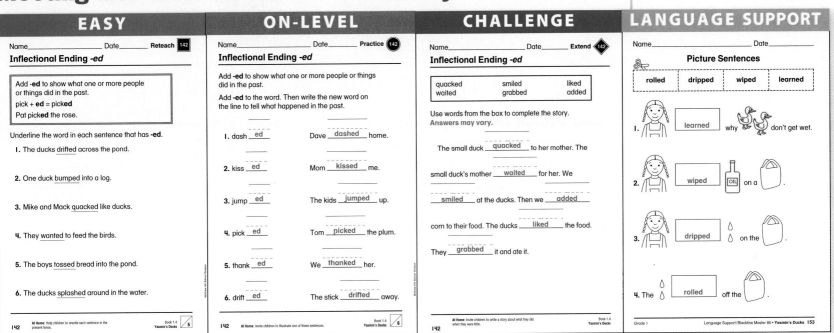

| EASY | ON-LEVEL | CHALLENGE | LANGUAGE SUPPORT |
| Reteach, 142 | Practice, 142 | Extend, 142 | Language Support, 153 |

65L

**GRAMMAR/SPELLING**
**CONNECTIONS**

See the 5-Day Grammar and Usage Plan on *Has* and *Have*, pages 65O–65P.

See the 5-Day Spelling Plan on Words with long *o: o-e* (silent *e* rule), pages 65Q–65R.

**TECHNOLOGY TIP**

Show children how to print an individual letter for each friend in the story.

# Persuasive Writing

## Prewrite

**WRITE A LETTER**  Present this writing assignment: Write a letter to your friends persuading them to make a duck mural. Put a personal note to each friend in your letter. Give reasons telling why it would be an exciting project.

**BRAINSTORM IDEAS**  Have children brainstorm ideas for how they can get their friends interested in making the mural. What can go on the mural? Are any of their friends really good at drawing? Are any of their friends really interested in ducks?

**Strategy: Make a Chart**  Have children make a chart telling what needs to be done to make a mural. Suggest the following:

- Write down each thing that needs to be done. Don't forget to list "buy materials" and "find a place to display the mural."

- Have children list a friend who they think would like to do each job.

- Have them list one or two things to persuade them to join in the activity.

## Draft

**USE THE CHART**  In their letters, children should write full sentences describing their idea for the mural. They should talk to each friend in a separate paragraph, and tell why that friend might want to do the project.

## Revise

**ELABORATING**  Have children use these questions as a revising checklist:

- Did I give each friend a good reason to join the project?

- What would be fun about making a mural?

- What things or animals could make my mural idea more interesting?

**GROUP**  Have children take turns trying to persuade classmates to make a mural. Have one child in each group list each reason given.

## Edit/Proofread

**CHECK FOR ERRORS**  Children should reread their letters for spelling, grammar, punctuation, and letter format.

## Publish

**SHARE THE LETTERS**  Children can "mail" their letters to four or five different classmates. Have each recipient give reasons why they will or will not join the project.

---

Maria Lopez
21 Elm St.
Somewhere, FL 00000
March 3, 20__

Dear Sharon, Kenny, Heather, and John,

    I think it will be fun if we make a mural for the lunchroom about ducks. We can draw a lot of kinds, and tell about what they eat. We can show where you could see them.
    Sharon, I hope you will want to draw the ducks. You are the best one at drawing. My mom said she would buy you new crayons.
    Kenny, I would like it if you write the sentences. I know how much you like to write.
    Heather, you know all about ducks. You can tell us everything.
    John, I would be so happy if you could plan this mural with me. Could you also help me go to buy all the things we need to make it?

Sincerely,
Maria

---

# Presentation Ideas

**SKETCH THE MURAL** Have children draw a sketch of the mural, showing the kinds of things they would like to see on it. Display their sketches in the school library.

▶**Viewing/Representing**

**PUT ON A SKIT** Have volunteers pretend that they're trying to persuade the leader of a Brownie or Cub Scout group to display their mural. Pick another volunteer to play the leader.

▶**Speaking/Listening**

Consider students' creative efforts, possibly adding a plus (+) for originality, wit, and imagination.

## Scoring Rubric

| Excellent | Good | Fair | Unsatisfactory |
|---|---|---|---|
| **4:** The writer<br>• makes a convincing proposal for a mural project.<br>• gives good reasons for each friend to participate.<br>• vividly describes the idea in full, clear sentences in letter form. | **3:** The writer<br>• clearly proposes a mural project.<br>• attempts to convince each friend to participate.<br>• uses full, clear sentences in letter form. | **2:** The writer<br>• attempts to propose a mural project.<br>• may not give each friend reasons to participate.<br>• may not follow through with a clear plan. | **1:** The writer<br>• may not grasp the idea to propose a project.<br>• may offer vague or unrelated reasons.<br>• may not use full sentences, letter form, or any organization of ideas. |

**0:** The writer leaves the page blank or fails to respond to the writing task. The student does not address the topic or simply paraphrases the prompt. The response is illegible or incoherent.

# Meeting Individual Needs for Writing

| EASY | ON-LEVEL | CHALLENGE |
|---|---|---|
| **Draw a Scene** Have children draw a scene of children making a mural. Ask them to write short sentences, telling what the children are doing. | **Write a Plan** Have children make believe that they have found friends to work on their mural project. Have them write, in full sentences, a detailed plan about what they need to do. | **Make a Journal Entry** Have children write about a project that they did with a friend or a family member. What was the project? Describe it. What did each person do? How did you feel while you were working? |

# 5 Day Grammar and Usage Plan

## LANGUAGE SUPPORT

Give children different objects, such as a book, a toy, a card, and a pen. Have children repeat as you say sentences such as, "Mark has a pen." Then ask children to say their own sentences such as, "I have a pen."

## DAILY LANGUAGE ACTIVITIES

Write the Daily Language Activities on the chalkboard each day or use **Transparency 17.** Have children correct the sentences orally, using the correct form of the verb *to have.*

### Day 1
**1.** Yasmin have a duck. has
**2.** Tim have a fish. has
**3.** Kate have a red truck. has

### Day 2
**1.** The girls has fun. have
**2.** They has cars. have
**3.** The children has pens. have

### Day 3
**1.** Ducks has wings. have
**2.** The lady have a hat. has
**3.** My parents has a lot of work. have

### Day 4
**1.** Miss Rome have a wish. has
**2.** The boys has toys. have
**3.** The truck have a hose. has

### Day 5
**1.** A fish have fins. has
**2.** We has many ducks. have
**3.** Yasmin have a new dress. has

---

**Daily Language Transparency 17**

---

## DAY 1 — Introduce the Concept

**Oral Warm-Up** Read aloud the following: *The cat has a mouse. The cats have a mouse.* Ask children to tell which words changed in the sentences. (cat, has; cats, have)

**Introduce *Has* and *Have*** Tell children that a *verb* is a word that shows action. Discuss with children:

### Has and Have

- The words *has* and *have* are verbs that tell about the present.

- The word *has* tells about one person, place, or thing.

Present the Daily Language Activity and have children correct the sentences orally. Then have children write a sentence using *has.*

 **WRITING** Assign the daily Writing Prompt on page 38C.

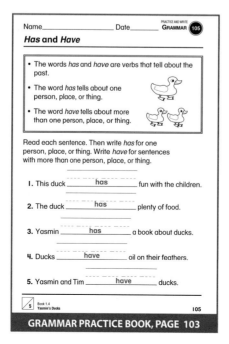

Name_____ Date_____ PRACTICE AND WRITE **GRAMMAR 105**

**Has and Have**

- The words *has* and *have* are verbs that tell about the past.
- The word *has* tells about one person, place, or thing.
- The word *have* tells about more than one person, place, or thing.

Read each sentence. Then write *has* for one person, place, or thing. Write *have* for sentences with more than one person, place, or thing.

**I.** This duck _____ **has** _____ fun with the children.

**2.** The duck _____ **has** _____ plenty of food.

**3.** Yasmin _____ **has** _____ a book about ducks.

**4.** Ducks _____ **have** _____ oil on their feathers.

**5.** Yasmin and Tim _____ **have** _____ ducks.

Book 1.4
Yasmin's Ducks                                          105

**GRAMMAR PRACTICE BOOK, PAGE 103**

---

## DAY 2 — Teach the Concept

**Review *Has*** Remind children that yesterday they learned about the word *has,* a verb that tells something in the present about one person, place, or thing. Write the following sentence on the chalkboard: *Meg has a new dress.* Ask children which word is a verb that tells about Meg. *(has)*

**Introduce *Have*** Read the following sentences aloud: *The boy has a big dog. The boys have a big dog.* Ask children to tell which words changed in the sentences. *(boy, has; boys, have)* Discuss with children:

### Have

- The word *have* tells about more than one person, place, or thing.

Present the Daily Language Activity. Have children correct the sentences orally. Then have children write a sentence using have.

 **WRITING** Assign the daily Writing Prompt on page 38C.

Name_____ Date_____ LEARN AND PRACTICE **GRAMMAR 104**

**Has and Have**

- The words *has* and *have* are verbs that tell about the present.
- The word *have* tells about more than one person, place, or thing.

Circle the verb that tells about more than one person, place, or thing.

**I.** The ducks have fun in the lake.
**2.** The child has ducks.
**3.** The children have many ducks.
**4.** Yasmin and Mack have water and oil.
**5.** The ducks have food.
**6.** The children have a good time.
**7.** The ducks have a home.
**8.** Yasmin has many ducks.

EXTENSION: Ask students to look around the classroom. Have them use the words *has* and *have* to write sentences about what they see.

104                                          Book 1.4
Yasmin's Ducks                                          8

**GRAMMAR PRACTICE BOOK, PAGE 104**

---

# Has and *Have*

**Learn from the Literature** Review *has* and *have* with children. Read the excerpt from the first sentence on page 54 of *Yasmin's Ducks*.

**These dresses have dots.**

Point out the word *have*. Ask why *have* is correct and not *has*. (*Have* tells about more than one thing.) Then write: *This dress _____ dots.* Ask children whether they would use *has* or *have* in this sentence and why. (*Has* because there is only one dress.)

**Use *Has* and *Have*** Present the Daily Language Activity and have children correct the sentences orally. Then have children write a sentence using *have*. Ask children to exchange papers with a partner. Have children rewrite their partners sentences, changing the verb from *have* to *has*. For example, *The girls have red shoes. The girl has red shoes.*

WRITING Assign the daily Writing Prompt on page 38D.

**Review *Has* and *Have*** Write the following sentence on the chalkboard: *The boys has a bat.* Ask children if the sentence is correct. (no) Why not? (The verb should be *have*.) Why? (Because *The boys* are more than one person) Correct the sentence on the chalkboard, then present the Daily Language Activity for Day 4.

**Mechanics and Usage** Before children begin the daily Writing Prompt on page 38D, review sentence punctuation. Display and discuss:

> **Sentence Punctuation**
> - Begin every sentence with a capital letter.
> - End every sentence with a period.
> - End every question with a question mark.

WRITING Assign the daily Writing Prompt on page 38D.

**Assess** Use the Daily Language Activity and page 107 of the **Grammar Practice Book** for assessment.

**Reteach** Help children write each rule about *has* and *have* on an index card. Have children write a sentence using *has* or *have*. Ask them to draw a picture to illustrate their sentences. Then have children attach the index card with the appropriate rule to the drawings.

Have children create a word wall with the pictures they have made, underlining *has* or *have* in each sentence.

Use page 108 of the **Grammar Practice Book** for additional reteaching.

WRITING Assign the daily Writing Prompt on page 38D.

---

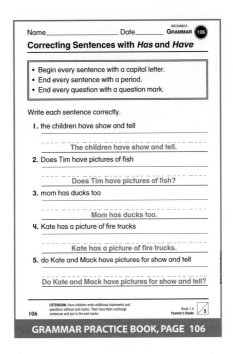

Name_____ Date_____ PRACTICE AND WRITE GRAMMAR 105

**Has and *Have***

- The words *has* and *have* are verbs that tell about the past.
- The word *has* tells about one person, place, or thing.
- The word *have* tells about more than one person, place, or thing.

Read each sentence. Then write *has* for one person, place, or thing. Write *have* for sentences with more than one person, place, or thing.

1. This duck _____has_____ fun with the children.

2. The duck _____has_____ plenty of food.

3. Yasmin _____has_____ a book about ducks.

4. Ducks _____have_____ oil on their feathers.

5. Yasmin and Tim _____have_____ ducks.

Book 1.4 Yasmin's Ducks 105

**GRAMMAR PRACTICE BOOK, PAGE 105**

---

Name_____ Date_____ MECHANICS GRAMMAR 106

**Correcting Sentences with *Has* and *Have***

- Begin every sentence with a capital letter.
- End every sentence with a period.
- End every question with a question mark.

Write each sentence correctly.

1. the children have show and tell

_____The children have show and tell._____

2. Does Tim have pictures of fish

_____Does Tim have pictures of fish?_____

3. mom has ducks too

_____Mom has ducks too._____

4. Kate has a picture of fire trucks

_____Kate has a picture of fire trucks._____

5. do Kate and Mack have pictures for show and tell

_____Do Kate and Mack have pictures for show and tell?_____

EXTENSION: Have children write additional statements and questions without end marks. Then have them exchange sentences and put in the end marks.

106 Book 1.4 Yasmin's Ducks 5

**GRAMMAR PRACTICE BOOK, PAGE 106**

---

Name_____ Date_____ TEST GRAMMAR 107

**Test**

Read each sentence. Circle the correct verb for each sentence.

1. Yasmin _____ a duck.
   (has)   have   do

2. Ducks _____ oil next to their tails.
   has   (have)   are

3. The duck _____ a friend.
   (has)   have   are

4. That duck _____ food.
   can   (has)   have

5. The ducks _____ fun.
   do   has   (have)

5 Book 1.4 Yasmin's Ducks 107

**GRAMMAR PRACTICE BOOK, PAGE 107**

**GRAMMAR PRACTICE BOOK, PAGE 108**

**65P**

# 5 Day Spelling Plan

To help children who have difficulty with the long *o* and the silent *e* rule, write the words *rope, nose, home,* and *hole* on the chalkboard. Pronounce each word slowly as you underline *o* and *e* in each word. Have children repeat the words after you.

## DICTATION SENTENCES

### Spelling Words

1. We came <u>home</u> after school.
2. I <u>hope</u> we win.
3. My cat can dig a <u>hole</u>.
4. She blew her <u>nose</u>.
5. The <u>rope</u> is in the shed.
6. <u>Those</u> pigs live on a farm.

### Challenge Words

7. He goes to <u>work</u> every morning.
8. We took the bus <u>because</u> it rained.
9. I can <u>buy</u> you that toy.
10. They want to have <u>some</u> cake.

## DAY 1 — Pretest

**Assess Prior Knowledge** Use the Dictation Sentences at left and **Spelling Practice Book** page 103 for the pretest. Allow children to correct their own papers. If children have trouble, have partners give each other a midweek test on Day 3.

|   Spelling Words   |         |   Challenge Words   |
|--------------------|---------|---------------------|
| 1. **home**        | 4. nose | 7. **work**         |
| 2. **hope**        | 5. rope | 8. **because**      |
| 3. hole            | 6. those| 9. **buy**          |
|                    |         | 10. **some**        |

*Note: Words in **dark type** are from the story.*

**Word Study** On page 104 of the **Spelling Practice Book** are word study steps and an at-home activity.

## DAY 2 — Explore the Pattern

**Sort and Spell Words** Say *hop* and *hope*. Ask children what sound they hear in each word. Write the words on the chalkboard and circle the *o-e* pattern as you repeat the word *hope*. Repeat with the following pairs: *not/note; mop/mope; rod/rode*.

Ask children to read aloud the six Spelling Words before sorting them according to the spelling pattern.

### Words ending with

| -ope | -ole | -ose  | -ome |
|------|------|-------|------|
| hope | hole | nose  | home |
| rope |      | those |      |

**Word Wall** As children read other stories and texts, have them look for new words with long vowel sounds that follow the silent *e* rule. Add them to a classroom word wall, underlining the vowel and the silent *e*.

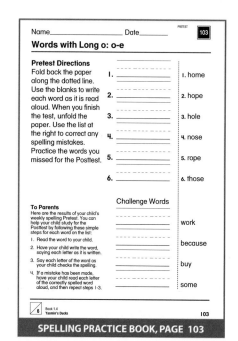

**SPELLING PRACTICE BOOK, PAGE 103**

**WORD STUDY STEPS AND ACTIVITY, PAGE 104**

**SPELLING PRACTICE BOOK, PAGE 105**

# Words with Long *o: o-e*

**Word Meaning: Riddles** Have children solve the riddle by answering with a Spelling Word.

1. This is in the middle of your face. nose

2. A doughnut has one of these in the middle. hole

3. This is the place where you live. home

4. When you wish for something, you do this. hope

5. This is used to tie things up. rope

6. This word means *that*, but for more than one. those

**Identify Spelling Patterns** Write this sentence on the chalkboard: *I hope to buy a new home.* Have a volunteer read it aloud. Ask children to tell which words have the spelling pattern *o-e* and which word is the Challenge Word. Then have children make up new sentences, using the Spelling and Challenge Words.

**Proofread Sentences** Write these sentences on the chalkboard, including the misspelled words. Ask children to proofread, circling incorrect spellings and writing the correct spellings. There are two errors in each sentence.

> I (hop) my mom is (hom). (hope, home)
>
> The (rop) is in the (hol). (rope, hole)

Have children create additional sentences with errors for partners to correct.

 Have children use as many Spelling Words as possible in the daily Writing Prompt on page 38D. Remind children to proofread their writing for errors in spelling, grammar, and punctuation.

**Assess Children's Knowledge** Use page 108 of the **Spelling Practice Book** or the Dictation Sentences on page 65Q for the posttest.

 **Personal Word List** If children have trouble with any words in the lesson, have them create a personal list of troublesome words in their journals. Have children write riddles for the Spelling Words.

Children should refer to their word lists during later writing activities.

---

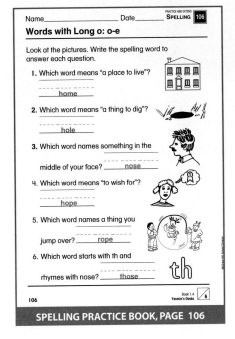

Name_____ Date_____ PRACTICE AND EXTEND **SPELLING** 106
**Words with Long o: o-e**

Look at the pictures. Write the spelling word to answer each question.

1. Which word means "a place to live"?
   _____ home

2. Which word means "a thing to dig"?
   _____ hole

3. Which word names something in the middle of your face? _____ nose

4. Which word means "to wish for"?
   _____ hope

5. Which word names a thing you jump over? _____ rope

6. Which word starts with th and rhymes with nose? _____ those

106    Book 1.4
Yasmin's Ducks    6

**SPELLING PRACTICE BOOK, PAGE 106**

---

Name_____ Date_____ PROOFREAD AND WRITE **SPELLING** 107
**Words with Long o: o-e**

Read the poem. There are six spelling mistakes. Circle the mistakes. Write the words correctly on the lines.

Look at that (hol).
It is (hom) to a mouse.
He packs it with (roep)
To make a house.
He adds thin sticks.
Can you see (hoze)?
I (hopp) we see him.
Look! There is his (noze)

1. _____ hole    2. _____ home

3. _____ rope    4. _____ those

5. _____ hope    6. _____ nose

Writing Activity
Write a story telling about an animal you like. Use three spelling words in your story.

6    Book 1.4
Greg's Mask    107

**SPELLING PRACTICE BOOK, PAGE 107**

---

Name_____ Date_____ POSTTEST **SPELLING** 108
**Words with Long o: o-e**

Look at the words in each set. One word in each set is spelled correctly. Use a pencil to color in the circle in front of that word. Before you begin, look at the sample sets of words. Sample A has been done for you. Do Sample B by yourself. When you are sure you know what to do, you may go on with the rest of the page.

**Sample A**
- (A) hose
- (B) hoze
- (C) hoose

**Sample B**
- (D) bitte
- (E) bite
- (F) byt

1. (A) home
   (B) hom
   (C) hoem

4. (D) hop
   (E) hope
   (F) hoope

2. (D) nos
   (E) nose
   (F) noze

5. (A) rope
   (B) rop
   (C) roope

3. (A) whol
   (B) hol
   (C) hole

6. (D) thoz
   (E) those
   (F) thos

108    Book 1.3
Yasmin's Ducks    6

**SPELLING PRACTICE BOOK, PAGE 108**

**65R**

# The Knee-High Man

**Selection Summary**  Sam, the Knee-High Man, wants to be something other than what he is. He solicits advice about how he can become bigger, until a wise owl teaches him about self-acceptance.

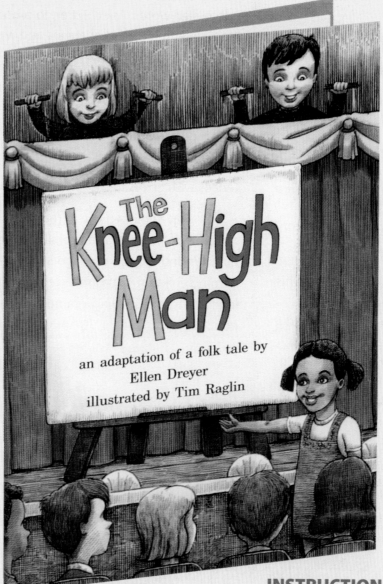

**Student Listening Library Audiocassette**

**INSTRUCTIONAL**
Pages 68–95

**About the Author**  Ellen Dreyer has always loved writing. She gets many ideas for her books from talking with children. Ms. Dreyer says it is important for writers to write down what they see and hear.

**About the Illustrator**  Tim Raglin illustrates children's books, magazines, and advertisements. Raglin especially likes to draw animals. He tells boys and girls, "If you like to draw, just keep practicing. Talent is just one small part, the rest is work."

# Resources for
# Meeting Individual Needs

**EASY**
Pages 95A, 95D

DECODABLE

**INDEPENDENT**
Pages 95B, 95D

🏠 *Take-Home version available*

**CHALLENGE**
Pages 95C, 95D

## LEVELED PRACTICE

**Reteach,** 143–150

blackline masters with reteaching
opportunities for each assessed skill

**Practice,** 143–150

workbook with Take-Home Stories and
practice opportunities for each assessed
skill and story comprehension

**Extend,** 143–150

blackline masters that offer challenge
activities for each assessed skill

## ADDITIONAL RESOURCES

- **Language Support Book** 154–162
- **Take-Home Story, Practice** pp. 144a–144b
- **Alternate Teaching Strategies** T64–T72

McGraw-Hill School
**TECHNOLOGY**

Phonics **CD-ROM** provides extra
phonics support.

*inter*NET
CONNECTION
Research & Inquiry ideas. Visit
**www.mhschool.com/reading.**

# Suggested Lesson Planner

 **Available on CD-Rom**

| READING AND LANGUAGE ARTS |  **DAY 1** *Focus on Reading and Skills* |  **DAY 2** *Read the Literature* |
|---|---|---|
| ● **Phonics Daily Routines** | Daily **Phonics** Routine: Segmenting, 68B <br><br>  **Phonics** CD-ROM | Daily **Phonics** Routines: Blending, 68C <br><br> **Phonics** CD-ROM |
| ● **Phonological Awareness** <br><br> ● **Phonics** *Long u* <br><br> ● **Comprehension** <br><br> ● **Vocabulary** <br><br> ● **Study Skills** <br><br> ● **Listening, Speaking, Viewing, Representing** | **Read** **Read Aloud and Motivate,** 66E <br> *Timimoto* <br><br> **Develop Phonological Awareness,** 66/67 <br> Long *u*: *u-e* <br> *Duck the Ant* <br><br> ☑ **Introduce Long *u*: *u-e*,** 68A-68B <br> **Reteach, Practice, Extend,** 143 <br> Phonics Workbook, 147–150 | **Build Background,** 68C <br> Develop Oral Language <br><br> **Vocabulary,** 68D <br><br> | carry | been | clean | <br> | done | far | | <br><br> **Vocabulary Cards** <br> **Teaching Chart 106** <br> **Reteach, Practice, Extend,** 144 <br><br> **Read** **Read the Selection,** 68–91 <br> Guided Reading <br> ☑ Long *u*: *u-e* <br> ☑ Cause and Effect <br><br> **Minilessons,** 73, 75, 77, 79, 89 <br><br> **Cultural Perspectives,** 72 |
| ● **Curriculum Connections** | **Link** Language Arts, 66E | **Link** Social Studies, 68C |
| ● **Writing** |  **Writing Prompt:** Write about the places you could go if you were very, very short. |  **Writing Prompt:** Write some dos-and-don'ts for growing. <br><br> **Journal Writing** <br> Quick-Write, 91 |
| ● **Grammar** | **Introduce the Concept:** *Go and Do,* 95O <br> Daily Language Activity: Use the correct form of *go* and *do* in sentences. <br><br> **Grammar Practice Book,** 109 | **Teach the Concept:** *Go and Do,* 95O <br> Daily Language Activity: Use the correct form of *go* and *do* in sentences. <br><br> **Grammar Practice Book,** 110 |
| ● **Spelling** *Long u* | **Pretest: Words with Long *u*: *u-e*,** 95Q <br><br> **Spelling Practice Book,** 109–110 | **Explore the Pattern: Words with Long *u*: *u-e*,** 95Q <br><br> **Spelling Practice Book,** 111 |

## Meeting Individual Needs

☑ = **Skill Assessed in Unit Test**

**Read EVERY DAY**

| | | |
|---|---|---|
| **DAY 3**  *Read the Literature* | **DAY 4**  *Build Skills* | **DAY 5**  *Build Skills* |

**DAY 3** — *Read the Literature*

Daily **Phonics** Routine:
Fluency, 93

**Phonics** CD-ROM

**Reread for Fluency,** 90

**Story Questions,** 92
Reteach, Practice, Extend, 145
**Story Activities,** 93

**Study Skill,** 94
☑ Charts
**Teaching Chart 107**
Reteach, Practice, Extend, 146

**Test Power,** 95

 **Read**

**Read the Leveled Books,**
Guided Reading
☑ Read Words with Long *u: u-e*
☑ Cause and Effect
☑ High-Frequency Words

 **Activity** Math, 76

 **Writing Prompt:** Write a letter to a friend about something silly you think he or she should do.

 **Journal Writing,** 95D

**Review and Practice:** *Go* and *Do*, 95P
Daily Language Activity: Use the correct form of *go* and *do* in sentences.

**Grammar Practice Book,** 111

**Practice and Extend: Words with Long *u: u-e*,** 95R

**Spelling Practice Book,** 112

---

**DAY 4** — *Build Skills*

Daily **Phonics** Routine:
Writing, 95F

**Phonics** CD-ROM

 **Read** Read the Leveled Books and Self-Selected Books

☑ **Review Long *u: u-e*,** 95E–95F
**Teaching Chart 108**
Reteach, Practice, Extend, 147
Language Support, 159
Phonics Workbook, 147–150

☑ **Review *u-e, o-e, i-e, a-e*,** 95G–95H
**Teaching Chart 109**
Reteach, Practice, Extend, 148
Language Support, 160
Phonics Workbook, 147–150

**Activity** Science, 80

 **Writing Prompt:** Name a place you went to. Write about what you did there.

**Persuasive Writing,** 95M
Prewrite, Draft

**Meeting Individual Needs for Writing,** 95N

**Practice and Write:** *Go* and *Do*, 95P
Daily Language Activity: Use the correct form of *go* and *do* in sentences.

**Grammar Practice Book,** 112

**Proofread and Write: Words with Long *u: u-e*,** 95R

**Spelling Practice Book,** 113

---

**DAY 5** — *Build Skills*

Daily **Phonics** Routine:
Letter Substitution, 95H

**Phonics** CD-ROM

 **Read** Read Self-Selected Books

☑ **Introduce Make Inferences,** 95–95J
**Teaching Chart 110**
Reteach, Practice, Extend, 149
Language Support, 161

☑ **Introduce Inflectional Endings -er, -est,** 95K–95L
**Teaching Chart 111**
Reteach, Practice, Extend, 150
Language Support, 162

**Listening, Speaking, Viewing, Representing,** 95N

**Minilessons,** 73, 75, 77, 79, 89

**Activity** Social Studies, 86

**Writing Prompt:** Write about a place you would like to go to when you get bigger.

**Persuasive Writing,** 95M
Revise, Edit, Proofread, Publish

**Assess and Reteach:** *Go* and *Do*, 95P
Daily Language Activity: Use the correct form of *go* and *do* in sentences.

**Grammar Practice Book,** 113, 114

**Assess and Reteach: Words with Long *u: u-e*,** 95R

**Spelling Practice Book,** 114

**66D**

**Language Arts**

# Read Aloud and Motivate

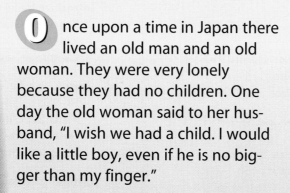

## Timimoto

retold by
Margaret H. Lippert

Once upon a time in Japan there lived an old man and an old woman. They were very lonely because they had no children. One day the old woman said to her husband, "I wish we had a child. I would like a little boy, even if he is no bigger than my finger."

That day as the old woman went to fetch water, she heard crying by the side of the path. She looked in the grass and there lay a tiny baby, only one inch long, wrapped in a red handkerchief.

The old woman was overjoyed. She took the baby home and showed him to her husband. "My wish has come true," she said. "Now we will never be lonely again." They named the baby Timimoto.

Timimoto grew up, but not very much. When he was five years old, he was as tall as his mother's thumb. At fifteen, he was only as tall as his mother's middle finger.

One morning Timimoto said, "I am going on a journey to see the world.

## Oral Comprehension

**LISTENING AND SPEAKING** Encourage children to think about cause-and-effect relationships by reading this story about a tiny Japanese boy. Ask children to think about things that happen in the story, and why those things happen. When you finish reading the story, ask, "Why did Timimoto leave his parents?" Then ask, "What happened when Timimoto stabbed the giant's tongue? Why did the town have a feast in Timimoto's honor?"

**Activity** Help children to make their own cartoon strip version of Timimoto's journey. Have children divide a piece of paper into six equal squares. In the first square, ask children to draw Timimoto in his boat. Remind them to include Timimoto's sword and paddle. In the other squares, have children include events from the journey.

▶ **Visual**

# Develop Phonological Awareness

**Anthology pages 66–67**

### Duke the Ant

Duke the ant is quite a dude.
He is very polite and never rude.
Duke the ant is small and cute.
He plays music on his new flute.
Duke the ant is always in tune!
He gave a concert just last June.
Duke can make a tone that's pure.
Duke the bug is cool, for sure!

66    67

## Objective: Listen for Long *u*

**RHYMING** Read "Duke the Ant." As you reread the poem, have children clap when they hear a word that rhymes with *mute*.

**Phonemic Awareness** **BLENDING** Write the spelling of each sound in *Duke* as you say it. Have children repeat after you. Explain that the final *-e* is silent, but tells you that the vowel sound is long like *Duke* instead of *duck*. Ask children to blend the sounds to read the word.

Repeat with **cute**.

**Phonemic Awareness** **SEGMENTING** Have children segment initial and final sounds.

- Say the word *cute*.
- Say *cute* again without the /t/
- Say *cute* again without the /c/.

Repeat with **tune** and **Duke**.

**66/67**

**OBJECTIVES**

Children will:

• identify long *u-e* words.

• blend and read long *u-e* words.

• review consonants.

---

**MATERIALS**

• letter and long *u* cards and word building boxes from the **Word Building Manipulative Cards**

## SPELLING/PHONICS CONNECTIONS

Words with long *u*: See the 5-Day Spelling Plan, pages 95Q–95R.

---

**TEACHING TIP**

**INSTRUCTIONAL** You may point out to children that the long *u* sound spelled *u-e* often makes slightly different long *u* sounds, as in the words *rude* and *mule*.

---

## Introduce Long *u: u-e*

> **TEACH**

**Identify the Letter *u* as the Symbol for /ū/**

Explain to children that they will learn to read words with the letters *u-e* where the letter *u* sounds like /ū/ and the *e* on the end is silent.

• Display the *u-e* letter card and say /ū/. Have children repeat.

$$\boxed{u \_ e}$$

**BLENDING Model and Guide Practice with Long *u-e* Words**

• Explain that many words with long *u* end in *e*.

• Point to the long *u* card and say /ū/. Remind children that the space between the letters *u* and *e* is a place for a consonant.

• Place the *t* letter card between the letters *u* and *e*. Blend the sounds together.

• Now place the *c* letter card before the *u t e*. Have children blend the sounds together to read *cute*.

**Use the Word in Context**

Use the word in context to reinforce its meaning. Example: *The little dog is so cute.*

**Repeat the Procedure**

Use the following words to continue modeling and guided practice with long *u*.

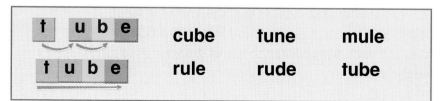

| | | |
|---|---|---|
| cube | tune | mule |
| rule | rude | tube |

## PRACTICE

**LETTER SUBSTITUTION**
Build Long *u* Words with Letter Cards

**PARTNERS**

Have children work in pairs. Build the word *mule* with letter cards and have one child in each pair do the same. Then ask the partner to replace the *m* with an *r* letter card. Ask children to read the new word. Have partners switch roles, and continue with the following word pairs: *tune/dune; use/fuse; pure/cure.*

## ASSESS/CLOSE

**Identify and Read Long *u* Words**

Observe children as they build words in the Practice activity. Then reread "*Duke and Ant*" and have children read two rhyming words with long *u*.

### ADDITIONAL PHONICS RESOURCES

**Phonics/ Phonemic Awareness Practice Book, pages 147–150**

**PHONICS KIT**
Hands-on Activities and Practice

McGraw-Hill School
**TECHNOLOGY**

**Phonics CD-ROM**
activities for practice with Blending and Segmenting

## Daily Routines

**DAY 1** **Segmenting** Distribute letter boxes. Say a long *u* word that follows the CVCe pattern aloud. Identify the pattern and have children write the letters in each box. (Use *cute, mule,* and *tube.*)

**DAY 2** **Blending** Use letter cards to create the -*ule* phonogram. Place the letter *r* before the phonogram and model how to blend the r with the -*ule* sound. Repeat with the letter *m.*

**DAY 3** **Fluency** Write on the chalkboard: *The mule is cute.* Ask children to blend sounds and read silently as you track print. Then, have them read aloud.

**DAY 4** **Writing** Write the word *duke* on chart paper and define the word. Ask children to write a sentence about a duke and draw a picture to illustrate it.

**DAY 5** **Letter Substitution** Using the letter and long *u* cards have pairs of children build the word *brute.* Then have them change letters to build *chute* and *flute.*

## Meeting Individual Needs for Phonics

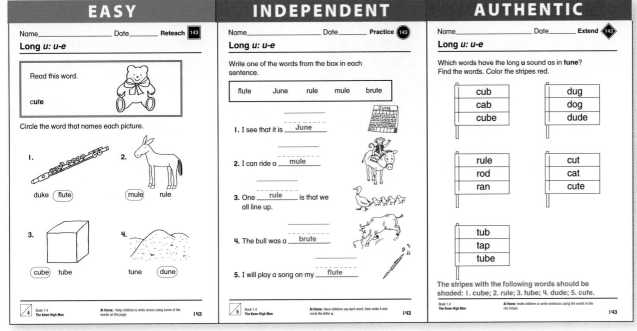

| EASY | INDEPENDENT | AUTHENTIC |
|---|---|---|

Reteach, 143      Practice, 143      Extend, 143

**PHONICS KIT**
HANDS-ON ACTIVITIES AND PRACTICE

**68B**

# Build Background

Social Studies

## Anthology and Leveled Books

## Evaluate Prior Knowledge

**CONCEPT: SELF-ACCEPTANCE** Display a picture of an elephant and a mouse. Ask which animal is big and which is small. Use the following activities to explore the concept of accepting being big and accepting being small.

**MAKE A STORY TABLE** Have the class work together to make a story table telling why it is good to be big and why it is good to be small. Then have children take turns naming some animals that fit into each category.

| Good to Be Big | Good to Be Small |
|---|---|
| strong (elephant) reach high (giraffe) | fit anywhere (bug) run fast (mouse) |

## Develop Oral Language

**CONNECT WORDS AND ACTIONS**

**ESL** Have children describe what it would be like to be a big animal and a small animal. Give directions such as:

- Jump like a frog.
- Roar like a lion.
- Make a sound like a small animal.

Prompt children to say what animal they are or what they are doing by asking:

- Who is jumping?
- What are you doing?
- What animal makes that noise?

▶ **Kinesthetic/Linguistic**

**DRAW AND LABEL A PICTURE** Invite children to fold a sheet of paper in half. On one side, have them draw a big animal doing something that it can do only because it is big; on the other side, a small animal doing something that it can do only because it is small. Have them label each animal.

# Vocabulary

## High-Frequency Words

**High-Frequency Words**

| carry | done |
| been | far |
| clean | |

**I Like Me**

If I'm feeling bad or mad or sad,
There's a song I sing to make me glad.
Hummmmmmmmm —
I like me.  I (clean) myself.
I (carry) myself near and (far).
I do things that I want (done)
I buy myself things for fun.
I wish you could have (been) born as me,
And know how grand being me can be.
Then you could sing this song and see
Why I like me!

**Teaching Chart 106**

**SPELLING/VOCABULARY CONNECTIONS**

The words *carry, been, clean, done* and *far* are Challenge Words. See page 95Q for Day 1 of the 5-Day Spelling Plan.

## Auditory

**LISTEN TO WORDS** Without displaying it, read aloud "I Like Me" on **Teaching Chart 106**. Ask children why they think the song might work to cheer them up when they're feeling bad. Is there anything else they do to make them feel good about themselves?

**RHYME HIGH-FREQUENCY WORDS** Have children aurally identify each high-frequency word using the following activity:

- Say aloud one of the high-frequency words. Read a line of the poem where that word appears.
- Ask children to find words that rhyme with that word. Then have them use the high-frequency word and a rhyming word in a few short lines about liking themselves. (NOTE: The lines don't have to rhyme.)
- Repeat this activity with each of the high-frequency words.

## Visual

**READ WORDS** Display "I Like Me" on **Teaching Chart 106**. Read the poem, tracking the print with your finger as you read. Then hold up vocabulary cards one at a time and have children circle the high-frequency words on the chart.  You may also have a volunteer read the introductory lines, and the whole class read the song part of the poem.

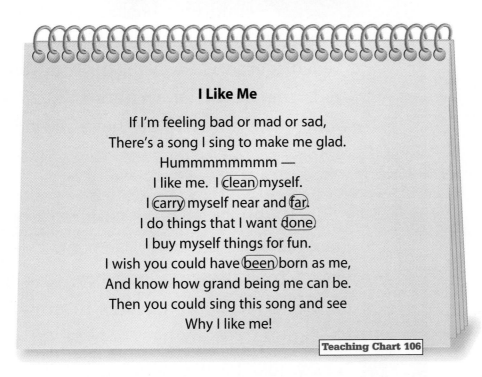

**Vocabulary Cards**

**WRITE A ME-STORY** Divide the class into groups of five children each.  Have each group write the five vocabulary words.  Then have them use their words to write sentences about liking themselves.

**ON-LEVEL**

Name_____ Date_____ Practice **144**

**High-Frequency Words**

Choose a word from the box to finish each sentence.

| carry | been | clean | done | far |

1. We will [c][l][e][a][n] the van.

2. We are not [f][a][r] from my home.

3. Is the cake [d][o][n][e] yet?

4. I have [b][e][e][n] on a ship.

5. I can [c][a][r][r][y] the pot on my head.

**At Home:** Have children draw pictures to show what the words *carry* and *clean* mean.

144    Book 1.4
The Knee-High Man

**Take-Home Story 144a
Reteach 144
Practice 144 • Extend 144**

# Guided Instruction

## Preview and Predict

Point to the name of the author and read it aloud. Then ask children to point to the name of the illustrator as you read it aloud. Point to the word *adaptation* and explain what it means. Then take a **picture walk** through the book, talking about the illustrations and the text format. Tell children that this is a play, and that each character has lines. Have children note the character name, color, and lines on each page. Then, ask what the story might be about:

- How big is Sam?
- Why is he unhappy?

Ask children to make predictions about the story. Chart children's predictions and read them aloud.

## Set Purposes

Ask children what they want to find out as they read the story.

- What do the animals tell Sam?
- What does Sam do?

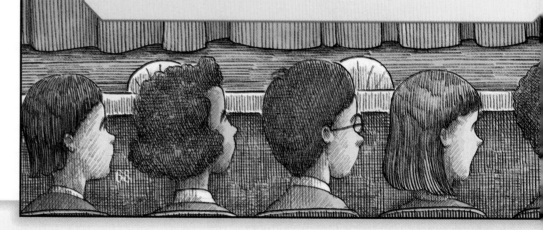

### Meet Ellen Dreyer

Ellen Dreyer has always loved writing. She has written many children's books. She gets her ideas from talking with children. Dreyer also teaches creative writing to children. She says it is important for writers to keep a notebook and write down what they see and hear.

### Meet Tim Raglin

Tim Raglin illustrates children's books, magazines, and advertisements. He spent a lot of time drawing as a boy, and later went to art school. Raglin likes to draw animals in human situations. He says, "If you like to draw, just keep practicing."

## Meeting Individual Needs · Grouping Suggestions for Strategic Reading

| EASY | ON-LEVEL | CHALLENGE |
|---|---|---|
| Track print as you read the story aloud. Invite children to read along with any familiar words or phrases. As you read, remind children how they can tell which character is speaking. | **Guided Reading** Ask children to read the story with you. Monitor any difficulties children may have while reading in order to determine which parts of the Guided Reading to emphasize. After reading the story aloud with children, have them reread it alone. See the rereading suggestions on page 90. | **Read Independently** Have children set purposes before they read. Remind them that as they read, visualizing the character who is speaking will help. Explain that in this play, the storyteller helps link the story ideas together. You may wish to have children read the story in small groups, each child taking the part of one character. |

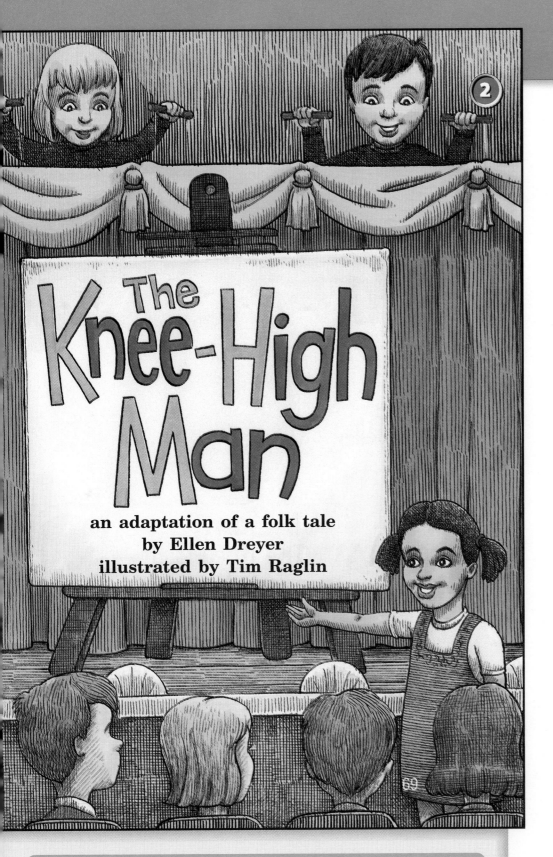

The Knee-High Man

an adaptation of a folk tale
by Ellen Dreyer
illustrated by Tim Raglin

# Guided Instruction

 **Long *u: u-e***

✓ **Cause and Effect**

**Strategic Reading** Explain to children that to help them understand the story, they can think about how one event causes another event to happen. Children will create a Story Comic Strip to focus on cause and effect.

**1** We are going to read *The Knee-High Man*. Let's look at the first picture on page 68. This is a picture of the author, Ellen Dreyer. Let's read about her. Now, point to the second picture. This is the illustrator, Tim Raglin. What does the illustrator say about drawing? *Concept of a Book: Author/Illustrator*

**2** Let's look at the picture on page 69. What do you see? (Answers will vary. Children should note the story title, the stage, the audience.) *Use Illustrations*

---

## TEACHING TIP

**INSTRUCTIONAL** The following chart indicates words from the story that children have learned to decode or high-frequency words that have been taught in previous lessons.

| Decodable | High-Frequency |
|-----------|----------------|
| brute | carry |
| June | been |
| Mule | clean |
| rule | done |
| sure | far |

---

## LANGUAGE SUPPORT

A blackline master for making the Story Comic Strip can be found in the **Language Support Book.**

You may want children to color in the pictures of Sam and his friends before they begin reading.

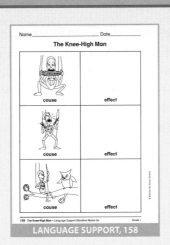

**LANGUAGE SUPPORT, 158**

# Guided Instruction

**(3)** This is the cast of characters in this play. How many people are there? (two) How many animals are there? (three) *Use Illustrations*

**(p/i) PHONOLOGICAL AWARENESS** Listen to the word *storyteller*. How many syllables are in that word? (four)

**(4)** Point to that mark in the middle of the word *Knee-High*. This is a hyphen. It connects the two words used to describe what kind of man Sam is. *Concepts of Print*

**(3)** The Players:

June
A Storyteller

Bob Bull

**(4)** Sam
The Knee-High Man

Kate Owl

Max Mule

70

---

**(p/i) PREVENTION/INTERVENTION**

**PHONOLOGICAL AWARENESS**
Say the word *book* aloud. Point out that this word has one syllable or part. Then say the word *story*. Ask children how many parts they hear in this word. (two) Say *book* and *story* again having children clap for each syllable they hear. Then say the word *story-teller* slowly. Have children clap out the syllables with you. Repeat this exercise with the words *biggest* and *wanted*.

June: Some folks grow big. Some folks stay
small. That's a rule of life. But Sam,
the Knee-High Man, wanted to be big. **7**
He just had to find out how to do it.

71

# Guided Instruction

**5** Why do you think Sam is called the
Knee-High Man? (because of his small
size) *Make Inferences*

**6** **Phonics** **LONG** *u: u-e* . . . *That's a*
. . . *I'm not sure what this word is. Let's*
blend the sounds of the letters together to
read it. r̲ u̲ l̲ (e) rule. *Blending*

**7** What does Sam want? (to be big)

# Guided Instruction

**8** **Phonics** **LONG u** *Max* . . . Who can read the next word with me? Remember to blend the sounds of the letters together. M  u  l (e) Mule. Now let's read the fourth word the same way. The *s* will sound a little like /sh/. s  u  r (e) sure. *Blending*

**8**

Sam: Max Mule is sure to know how I can get big like him. He will tell me how to grow.

72

# CULTURAL PERSPECTIVES

**CORN VARIETIES** Explain to children that corn is an important staple food that originated in this part of the world. The Native Americans in North and Central America cultivated many different types of corn. Because of this, corn now comes in many shapes, sizes, and colors.

**RESEARCH AND INQUIRY** Have children investigate the varieties of corn. Have them cut out pictures in magazines and seed catalogs of different types of corn and make a display. ▶ **Visual**

 inter**NET** **CONNECTION** For more information about vegetables, log on to *www.mhschool.com/reading*.

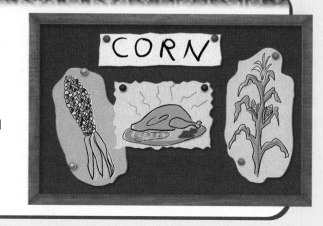

Max: What's up, Sam?

Sam: Max, you are so big! The bugs carry rope to get down from your back. How can I get big like you?

**9**

**10**

73

# Guided Instruction

**9** Look at the names *Max* and *Sam*. Who is asking a question? (both) What lets you know that a question is being asked? (question mark) *Concepts of Print*

**10** **CAUSE AND EFFECT** What does Sam want to know? (how to get big) Why does he ask Max Mule to help him? (because Max is big)

## Minilesson
### REVIEW
### Long o: *o-e*

Write *-ope* on the chalkboard. Then demonstrate how to blend the letter *r* with the remaining letters to read *rope*. Have children point out the consonant-vowel-consonant-*e* pattern of the word.

- Have children think of words that rhyme with *rope*. Make a list of the words on the chalkboard.

**Activity** Invite children to repeat the activity with *woke*.

**Phonics CD-ROM** Have children use the interactive phonics activities on the CD-ROM for more reinforcement with long *o* words.

# Guided Instruction

**11** Do you think Sam likes Max's idea? Why or why not? (Answers will vary.) *Make Inferences*

**CONCEPTS OF PRINT** Point to the sentences that Max says. Begin with the third sentence, and count the commas. How many commas are there? (five)

74

## Fluency

**READING WITH EXPRESSION** Have children guess what type of voice Max Mule might have. Then discuss how he might sound as he gives advice to Sam.

- Have children practice reading Max's sentences aloud.
- Remind them to experiment with expression and voice.
- Then have them read the section to their partners.

## PREVENTION/INTERVENTION

**CONCEPTS OF PRINT** Rewrite the sentences that Max says on chart paper. Invite volunteers to circle each comma. Remind children that a comma gives them a signal to pause when they are reading. Then have children point to the comma in Sam's sentence. Invite volunteers to read the sentence aloud, pausing at the comma.

Max: This is what you do. Pick lots of corn cobs. Clean them, eat them, and then run ten miles. Try that, Sam. In time, you will be big, just like me.

Sam: Thanks, Max. I sure will try.

75

# Guided Instruction

**12** What is the first thing that Sam must do? (pick lots of corn) What is the next thing? (clean them and eat them) What is the last thing Sam must do? (run ten miles) *Sequence of Events*

**13** What do you think will happen next? *Make Predictions*

## Minilesson
### REVIEW

### Context Clues

Point out to children that we can use words and pictures to understand new words.

- Have children point to the word *cobs* on page 75. Discuss how other words in the sentence, such as *corn* and *eat,* can help them understand the meaning. Connect the words *corn* and *cobs.*

- Ask children to describe a corn cob. Have them use the illustration on page 76 to help.

**Activity** Invite children to make a list of other vegetables and then name their parts.

# Guided Instruction

**14** June says that Sam *cleaned and then chomped on the corn cobs.* Show me how you clean corn. Now show me how you eat corn. *Pantomime*

**15** How does Sam feel? Show me with your face. *Nonverbal Response*

June: So Sam cleaned and then chomped on ten corn cobs. He ran ten miles, too. When he was done, his tummy hurt and his legs hurt. But he did not grow one inch. He just got mad, as mad as can be

**14**  **15**

## Cross Curricular: Math

**INCH BY INCH** Display a ruler marked in inches and talk about units of measurement. Then display some corn cobs of different lengths or corn cobs cut from construction paper. Demonstrate how to measure each one to the nearest inch and label each with the correct measurement.

Invite children to order the corn cobs from shortest to longest.

▶ **Kinesthetic/Logical**

Sam: What have I done? I ate that much. I ran that far. And I am still small!

17

77

# Guided Instruction

16 **CAUSE AND EFFECT** When one thing happens in a story, it often causes something else to happen. What happened after Sam ate the corn cobs? (His tummy and his legs hurt.) Let's draw a picture on our Story Comic Strip to show what happened. *Story Prop*

16

|  | |
|---|---|
| cause | effect |

17 Look at the punctuation on this page. What type of sentence is the first thing Sam says? (a question) What type of sentence is the last thing Sam says? (an exclamation) Let's read these sentences with feeling like Sam would say them. *Concepts of Print*

## Minilesson
### REVIEW

### High-Frequency Words

Write each of the following high-frequency words on index cards: *he, too, grow, one, small, be.* Distribute sets of cards to children.

Have pairs of children show each other the index cards in turn and practice reading them. Then have them find these words on pages 76–77.

**Activity** Give children a page from a newspaper or children's magazine. Ask them to circle any of these high-frequency words that they find.

**77**

# Guided Instruction

**18** What do you know about Sam so far? Do you think he will give up? (Answers will vary. Children should note that Sam wants something strongly and is trying hard to get it.) *Make Predictions*

**CONCEPTS OF PRINT** Read the last sentence with me. Why do you think Knee-High Man starts with capital letters? (because Sam's title is part of his name and names begin with capital letters)

**19** **Phonics** **LONG** *u: u-e* Who is narrating the story? Can you read her name? Let's blend the sounds of this person's name together. J u n (e) June. *Blending*

June: But Sam did not give up. No, not Sam, the Knee-High Man.

**19**

 **PREVENTION/INTERVENTION**

Ask children to point to the first word of each statement June makes, and tell why the words begin with capital letters. (They begin a sentence.) Then ask why *Sam* and *the Knee-High Man* begin with capital letters. Direct children by asking:

• What is this character's name?

• Does he have a special title that is part of his name?

• What do we call this type of word?

Point out to children that Sam's name and special title begin with capital letters because they are proper nouns. Then brainstorm a list of other proper nouns and invite volunteers to write the words on the chalkboard, making sure each one starts with a capital letter.

Sam:  Bob Bull is the biggest one I know. He is sure to know how I can get big like him. I will go see him. He will tell me what to do.

79

## LANGUAGE SUPPORT

**ESL** Display pictures of large animals of three different sizes, such as a large dog, a horse, and an elephant. Talk about the size of each animal. Then label them with *big, bigger, biggest.*

Select classroom objects to demonstrate small, smaller, smallest. Use comparative terms during the day to reinforce meaning: *Which cookie is bigger? Who has the shortest pencil?*

# Guided Instruction

**20** **Phonics** **LONG** *u: u-e* Look at the second sentence that Sam says. There's a long *u* word here we read earlier. Point to it now and read it with me. *(sure)* *Blending*

**21** What big animal do you see on this page? (a bull) Is he bigger than Sam? (yes) *Use Illustrations*

## Minilesson
### REVIEW
## Make Inferences

Tell children that an author and illustrator may not always say directly what is happening in a story. Let children know that they can use clues in words and pictures to understand how a story is being told. Ask:

- How do you know you are reading a play? (the stage, the audience, the dialogue)

- What are the children doing above the stage? (They are puppeteers. They are making the characters move.) How can you tell? (the strings)

- Who is June? (She is the storyteller. She is a real person who helps us link the story ideas together.)

**Activity** Invite children to pretend they are Sam. Have them read his lines and move as a marionette might move.

# Guided Instruction

**22** **CAUSE AND EFFECT** Let's look at our Story Comic Strips. What has Sam done so far? (asked Max Mule for advice and eaten lots of corn) Let's write what Sam is doing in our Story Comic Strips. *Story Prop*

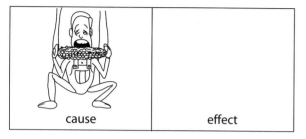

| | |
|---|---|
| cause | effect |

## 𝗦ELF-MONITORING

### STRATEGY

**SEARCH FOR CLUES** Using pictures can help a reader understand the story and the characters.

*MODEL* I don't understand what Sam means when he says that frogs think the bull's horns are tree branches. But if I look at the picture, I see small frogs sitting on the horns. The bull is so big, the frogs must think he is a tree.

Sam:   Bob Bull, you are so big. Frogs think your horns are tree branches. How can I get big like you?

80

## Activity

### Cross Curricular: Science

**FROGS** Invite children to find out about frogs. Explain that frogs are amphibians with long hind legs that help them jump. Frogs have thin, moist skin and are able to breathe through it. Have children investigate different kinds of frogs. Ask them to draw a frog and then label the parts of its body. ▶ **Visual/Linguistic**

**RESEARCH AND INQUIRY** Invite children to find out more about tree-peeper frogs.

**interNET CONNECTION** To find out more about amphibians, help children log on to **www.mhschool.com/reading**.

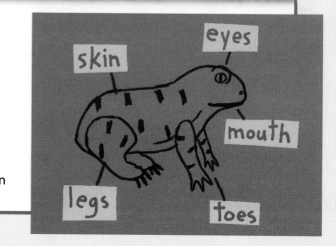

Bob: Well, Sam, this is what you do. Eat a lot of fine grass and yell and grunt a lot. Try that, Sam. In time, you will be a big old brute, just like me. **23**

81

# Guided Instruction

**23** **Phonics** **LONG** *u: u-e* There is a word on this page with the long *u* sound and silent *e*. Point to it. Now blend the sounds to read this word. Let's use what we know about -*ute*. b r u t (e) brute. *Blending*

**24** Let's look closely at the picture on this page. What does Bob Bull look like? (Answers will vary.) What is Bob Bull eating? (grass) Who is sitting on Bob Bull's horns? (two frogs) *Use Illustrations*

**24**

# Guided Instruction

25 What is Sam eating? (grass) Is there a large amount of grass or a small amount? (a large amount) *Use Illustrations*

June: Sam ate a peck of grass. He yelled and grunted till the sun set. When he was done, his tummy hurt and his throat hurt. But he did not grow one inch!

## LANGUAGE SUPPORT

**MULTIPLE-MEANING WORDS** Tell children that some words, like *peck,* have more than one meaning. Reread the first sentence together. Then reread Bob's advice on page 81. Help children use context clues by asking:

• How much grass did Sam eat?

• What do you think the word *peck* might mean in this sentence?

Show that the word *peck* is used as a term of measurement. It means "a large amount" (or eight dry quarts). Then ask children to give other meanings for the word *peck.*

Sam: What bad, bad luck! I ate that grass. I yelled and grunted. And I am still small!

83

# Guided Instruction

**26** **CAUSE AND EFFECT** What did Sam do? (He ate a lot of grass and made loud noises.) **What happened?** (His tummy and throat hurt, but he is still small.) Let's draw a picture on our Story Comic Strip to show what happened. *Story Prop*

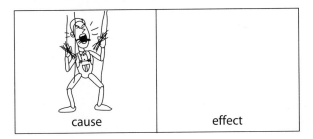

| | |
|---|---|
| cause | effect |

**26**

# Guided Instruction

**27** Who does Sam go to see next? (Kate Owl) *Sequence of Events*

**28** So Sam hasn't given up yet. What does that tell you about him? (He's brave, he tries hard, he's determined.) *Analyze Character*

June: But Sam did not give up. No, not Sam, the Knee-High Man. He went to see Kate Owl.

Sam: Kate Owl is very wise. She will tell me how I can get bigger, for sure.

85

# Guided Instruction

(29) Let's think about what we've already read. Every time Sam goes to see another friend, what does he ask? (how he can get big) So, what do you think Sam is going to ask Kate Owl? (Answers might vary.) *Make Predictions*

## LANGUAGE SUPPORT

**ESL** Write the words *for sure* on the chalkboard. Then read the second sentence on page 85 together. Talk about what the words mean in the sentence. Explain that some phrases are common expressions that people often use when they speak. Invite children to share other common expressions that they use and list them on the board.

# Guided Instruction

**29** **CAUSE AND EFFECT** What has happened in the story so far? (Sam wants to be bigger. He has eaten corn and grass, but he is still small.) Whom is he asking for help now? (Kate Owl) Let's write the owl's name on our Story Comic Strips. *Story Prop*

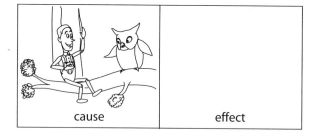

| | |
|---|---|
| cause | effect |

**30** Sam has tried several different things in trying to grow bigger. Has anything changed in his size? Let's look at the picture on this page. How do you think Sam must feel? (Answers will vary.) *Make Inferences*

Sam: Kate, you are wise. Tell me how I can get bigger. I have been trying my best.

Kate: Why do you want to be big, Sam?

Sam: If I am big, then I can win any fight.

86

## Activity

## Cross Curricular: Social Studies

**PEACEFUL SOLUTIONS** Read page 87 and talk about Sam's desire to win a fight. Brainstorm with children a list of problems or arguments they may have with their friends. Then make a list of peaceful ways to solve each problem. Help children focus by asking them what the outcome should be and then elicit ways to achieve that outcome. ▶ **Linguistic/Kinesthetic**

**interNET CONNECTION** Help children log on to sites about well-known peace movements and organizations at **www.mhschool.com/reading**.

### Peaceful Solutions
Apologize
Explain
Discuss the problem
Brainstorm solutions
Shake hands

Kate: Who has picked a fight with you?

Sam: No one.

Kate: Then you do not have to fight.
And you do not have to be big.

87

# Guided Instruction

**31** Point to the first question Kate asks Sam. How many commas are there? (one) Let's read it together correctly. *Concepts of Print*

**BLENDING WITH SHORT *i*** Tell children there are three words on the page that have the short i sound. Ask children to find the words. (*picked, with, big*)

---

## PREVENTION/INTERVENTION

**BLENDING WITH SHORT *i*** Write the following words on a piece of chart paper: *inch, with, pick, chin, snip.* Cover the consonants of each word with a self-stick note, so that only the short *i* shows. Have children tell you what sound the short *i* makes. (/i/)

Then, starting with the first word, have a volunteer pull off one of the self-stick notes and blend the letters together. Have another child pull off any remaining notes and blend all the letters together to read the word.

# Guided Instruction

**32** Ask children to describe what Sam is doing. (stretching tall and shading his eyes) **Why is he doing this?** (to see far away) *Use Illustrations*

**TEACHING TIP**

**INSTRUCTIONAL** Using pages 88–89, review the three types of sentences with children. Ask children to read the two statements on page 88, the question on page 89, and the exclamation on page 89 aloud. Remind them to change their expression and inflection for each type of sentence accordingly.

Sam: But if I am big, I can see far away. I can see far, just like you.

88

Kate: Can't you go up a tree to look far
      away?

Sam: Sure I can!

(33)

89

# Guided Instruction

**CONTRACTIONS** Point to the first word that Kate says. What does the apostrophe mean? (One or more letters have been taken out of the word.) Read it with me. (*can't*)

**33** What advice does Kate give Sam? (He doesn't have to fight anybody, and he can see far away just by climbing a tree.) Do you think Kate thinks Sam needs to be bigger? (no) *Critical Thinking*

## PREVENTION/INTERVENTION

**CONTRACTIONS** Write the word *can't* on the chalkboard. Invite children to read it with you. Then write the words *can not* below it. Ask children which letters were removed from *can not* and replaced by the apostrophe in *can't*. (the letters *n, o*) Ask children to use *can't* and then *can not* in the same sentence. Repeat with the contractions *didn't* and *wasn't*.

## Minilesson
### REVIEW

### Main Idea

Explain to children that the main idea tells what the story is about. Work together to write three sentences that tell the main idea of *The Knee-High Man*. Guide results by asking the following questions:

- What was Sam's problem?
- How did he try to solve the problem?
- What did he learn?

**Activity** Have children summarize the story orally. Record the sentences that describe the main idea.

# Guided Instruction

**(34) CAUSE AND EFFECT** Sam went up in the tree with Kate. What did he learn? (He was fine just as he is.) Let's draw a picture on our Story Comic Strip to show what happened. *Story Prop*

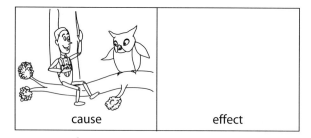

| cause | effect |

**RETELL THE STORY** Have groups of children retell the story, each taking the part of one of the characters. Have them use their Story Comic Strips to show how events caused other events to happen. Guide them to the conclusion by asking what Sam learned at the end of the story. *Story Prop/Summarize*

## STUDENT SELF-ASSESSMENT

Have children ask themselves the following questions to assess how they are reading:

- How did I use what I know about self-acceptance to help me understand the story?

- How did I use the pictures and words to help me understand what Sam learned?

- How did I use the pictures and the letters and sounds I know to help me read the words in the story?

### TRANSFERRING THE STRATEGIES

- How can I use these strategies to help me read other stories?

Kate: You see, Sam. You do not have to be bigger. You are just fine the way you are.

90

## REREADING FOR *Fluency*

**GROUP** Children who need fluency practice can read aloud in groups, each taking a character part.

**READING RATE** You may want to evaluate individual children's reading rates. Have the child read aloud from *The Knee-High Man* for one minute. When the minute is up, have the child place a self-stick note after the last word read. Then count the number of words the child has read.

Alternatively, you could assess small groups or the whole class together by having children count words and record their own scores.

A Running Record form provided in **Diagnostic/Placement Evaluation** will help you evaluate reading rate(s).

Sam: I think you are right, Kate.
Because if I were any bigger, I would
not be me. I would not be Sam,
the Knee-High Man!

91

# Guided Instruction

## Return to Predictions and Purposes

Reread children's predictions about the story. Ask if the story answered all of the questions they had before they read it. Discuss their predictions, noting which needed to be revised.

Have children discuss their Story Comic Strips. Did using the strips help children understand how one event led to another?

### INFORMAL ASSESSMENT

**HOW TO ASSESS**

**Phonics** LONG *u: u-e* Write the word *mule* on the chalkboard. Ask children to read the word. Then change the *m* to *r* and repeat.

**CAUSE AND EFFECT** Ask children to describe one cause and its effect from the story.

**FOLLOW UP**

**Phonics** LONG *u: u-e* Continue to model blending for long *u* words.

**CAUSE AND EFFECT** Turn to any page in *The Knee-High Man* and invite children to retell that part of the story. Discuss cause and effect as they relate to Sam's actions.

## LITERARY RESPONSE

**QUICK-WRITE** Have children draw in their journals a picture of someone who is too tall, and give that person a name such as Toby the Too-Tall Man.

**ORAL RESPONSE** Have children use their journal entries to discuss these questions:

• What did you draw?

• What advice would Sam have for someone who thinks he or she is too tall?

# Story Questions

Tell children that now they will read some questions about the story. Help children read the questions. Discuss possible answers.

**Answers:**

1. He told him to eat a lot of fine grass and yell and grunt a lot. *Literal/Details*

2. He only comes up to a person's knee. *Inferential/Characters*

3. Answers will vary. Accept appropriate responses. *Inferential/Characters*

4. Sam learned to accept himself the way he is. *Critical/Summarize*

5. Answers will vary. Accept appropriate responses. *Critical/Reading Across Texts*

**Help Sam** Help children read the directions in their anthologies. For a full writing process lesson related to Persuasive Writing, see pages 95M–95N.

## Story Questions & Activities

READ TOGETHER

1. What did Bob tell Sam to do?

2. Why is Sam called the Knee-High Man?

3. How did Kate help Sam?

4. Tell what you think Sam learned.

5. How is a play different from a story?

### Help Sam

Pretend you know Sam.
He asked you how to grow.
What would you tell him to do?
Write about it.

Eat good food.
Get rest.
Play.

## Meeting Individual Needs

| EASY | ON-LEVEL | CHALLENGE |
|---|---|---|

**EASY**

Name_____ Date_____ Reteach 145

Story Comprehension

Think about "The Knee-High Man." Fill in the chart. Then answer the questions.

| | Max Mule | Bob Bull |
|---|---|---|
| What to eat? | corn | grass |
| What to do? | run | yell |

1. What did Kate Owl think? Kate said that Sam did not have to be big.

2. Who gave Sam the best advice? Kate Owl

Book 1.4
The Knee-High Man
**At Home:** Have children draw pictures of Sam the Knee-High Man following one of the suggestions in the chart. 145

**ON-LEVEL**

Name_____ Date_____ Practice 145

Story Comprehension

Draw a line to connect the characters in "The Knee-High Man" to what they said.

1. June —— a. Yell and eat grass to be big like me.

2. Sam the Knee-High Man —— b. Sam did not grow an inch.

3. Bob Bull —— c. Eat a lot of corn and run ten miles to be like me.

4. Max Mule —— d. Will you tell me how I can grow?

5. Kate Owl —— e. You are fine just as you are.

Book 1.4
The Knee-High Man
**At Home:** Help children to list the order in which Sam visits the characters in the story (Max, Bob, and Kate). 145

**CHALLENGE**

Name_____ Date_____ Extend 145

Story Comprehension

Read the sentences. Write **T** if they are true. Write **F** if they are not. If the sentence is true, circle the name of the friend who said it.

| Sentence | T or F | Who Said it? |
|---|---|---|
| 1. Eat corn. | T | |
| 2. Run ten miles. | T | |
| 3. Drink juice. | F | |
| 4. Yell and grunt. | T | |
| 5. Go up a tree. | T | |

Book 1.4
The Knee-High Man
**At Home:** Have children act out the story of "The Knee-High Man." 145

Reteach, 145          Practice, 145          Extend, 145

**92**    *The Knee-High Man*

## Add to the Play

Work with your class.

Add two more animals to the play.

Make up things for them to say.

Then read the play aloud.

## Find Out More

"The Knee-High Man" is a folktale.

It teaches a lesson.

Find another folktale that teaches a lesson.

93

# Story Activities

### Add to the Play

**Materials:** chart paper

Read the directions aloud. Help children who have questions. Have the class discuss various animals they might add to the play. Are these animals small or big? What do the small animals say to the big animals? How do the big animals respond?

**PARTNERS** You may wish to have children work as partners to come up with more lines for the play. Then, have the partners read their lines aloud with expression.

### Find Out More

**RESEARCH AND INQUIRY** Again, read the directions aloud, and help children who have questions.

**ONE**

Point out that all cultures have folk tales and that such stories often teach a lesson. Explain that sometimes it's easier to teach something important by putting it in a story, rather than by just telling it to somebody. Then ask children if they have heard or read any folk tales that teach a lesson. Perhaps they can ask their parents or grandparents to tell them a tale that teaches a lesson. Have the children share the stories they have read or heard with the class.

*inter*NET **CONNECTION** To learn more about folk tales, have children log on to **www.mhschool.com/reading**.

DAILY **Phonics** ROUTINES

**DAY 3** **Fluency** Write on the chalkboard: *The mule is cute.* Ask children to blend sounds and read silently as you track print. Then, have them read aloud.

 **Phonics** CD-ROM

**F**ORMAL **A**SSESSMENT

After page 93, see the Selection Assessment Test.

# Study Skills

## CHARTS

### ✓ OBJECTIVES

Students will learn to use a chart to gather information.

**PREPARE**  Tell children that they will read a chart, a kind of list that shows what some of the characters in the play said.

**TEACH**  Display **Teaching Chart 107**. Have children read the sentences and the title of the chart. Read the lines together. Point to each animal and ask children to repeat what that character said to Sam.

**PRACTICE**  Then help children read the questions below the chart. Have them answer the questions.

**1.** Eat corn and run ten miles.

**2.** Bull

**ASSESS/CLOSE**  Have children tell how they would add their own advice for Sam to the chart.

# SKILLS

## Who Said What? Chart

This chart shows what the animals said to Sam.

| | | |
|---|---|---|
| | Mule | eat corn
run ten miles |
| | Bull | eat grass
yell and grunt |
| | Owl | don't do anything |

## Look at the Chart

**1** What did Mule say?

**2** Who told Sam to yell?

## Meeting Individual Needs

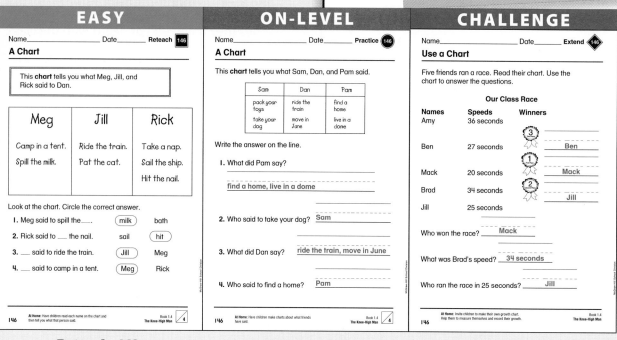

Reteach, 146        Practice, 146        Extend, 146

# TEST POWER

## What Is Polly Doing?

Polly put her toes out.

Polly put her legs out.

Polly put her fingers out.

Polly put her arms out.

Polly put her whole self out of bed.

The air was too cold.

So, Polly climbed back into her
warm bed.

---

Why did Polly climb back into her bed?

● The air was too cold.

○ She was sleepy.

Think about what the story tells you.

95

## Test Power

THE PRINCETON REVIEW

### Read the Page

Explain to children that you will be reading this story as a group. You will read the story, and they will follow in their books.

Request that children put pens, pencils, and markers away, since they will not be writing in their books.

### Discuss the Question

Discuss with children what constitutes an answer to a "why" question. Have them re-read the story, find the place where Polly goes back to bed, and put their fingers on the reason why she does so.

### Test-Tip

Always look back to the story to find the answer. The answer is always somewhere in the passage.

For The Princeton Review test preparation practice for **TerraNova, ITBS,** and **SAT-9,** visit the McGraw-Hill School Division Web site. See also McGraw-Hill's *Standardized Test Preparation Book.*

# Leveled Books

**ESL** Introduce vocabulary and concepts that may be unfamiliar. Then read the book together, stopping frequently to make sure students are following the story. Allow them to use gestures to answer. Afterwards, have students reread the story independently.

**Answers to Story Questions**

1. When he gets bigger.
2. He feels good and proud.
3. Answers will vary.
4. Will wants to do what grown-ups do. They won't let him. He wants to try something new. He decides to join the track team where he runs and wins a race. Everyone is happy in the end.
5. Like Sam, Will ends up happy just the way he is.

**Story Questions and Writing Activity**

1. When can Will play the flute?
2. How does Will feel after he runs?
3. When might Will run again?
4. Tell the story in your own words.
5. How is Will like Sam in *The Knee-High Man*?

**Make an Award**

Draw a ribbon shape on paper.
Color it in.
Write "Number 1" on it.
Cut it out and tape it to your shirt.
Hooray!

from *Fun Run*

## EASY

### Fun Run

☑ **Phonics** Long *u*: *u-e*
☑ **Cause and Effect**
☑ **High Frequency Words:** *carry, been, clean, done, far*

by Rachel Patrick
illustrated by Jane Sanders

# Guided Reading

**PREVIEW AND PREDICT** Discuss the concept of cause and effect as you take a **picture walk** up to page 8. Encourage children to predict what will happen in the story. Write their predictions on the chalkboard.

**SET PURPOSES** Have children write or draw why they want to read *Fun Run*. For example: *I want to find out what happens when Will races.*

**READ THE BOOK** Use questions like the following to guide children's reading, or to discuss after they have read the story independently.

**Pages 2–3:** What does Will want to do? (help clean) *High-Frequency Words*

**Pages 4–5:** Let's read to find out what Will wants to play. Help me blend the sounds of the letters together to read the word.
f  l  u  t(e)  **flut(e)**

**Pages 6–7:** Will's parents think he is too small to help clean or play the flute. How does that make him feel? (sad) *Phonics and Decoding*

**Pages 8–9:** Can you find a vocabulary word on these pages? *(carry)* *High-Frequency Words*

**Pages 10–16:** Why do you think Will won? (Answers will vary, including: he tried his best to have fun) *Cause and Effect*

**RETURN TO PREDICTIONS AND PURPOSES** Discuss children's predictions. Do they feel that some of the wrong predictions might have made a better story? Why? Did they find out what they wanted?

**LITERARY RESPONSE** You can use the following questions to gauge children's responses to the story:

- Do you think Will is too little to help his mom clean or to play the flute? Why or why not?

- Will is good at running. What are you good at?

Also see the questions and activities in *Fun Run*.

See the **Phonics** CD-ROM for practice with long *u*: *u-e*.

# Leveled Books

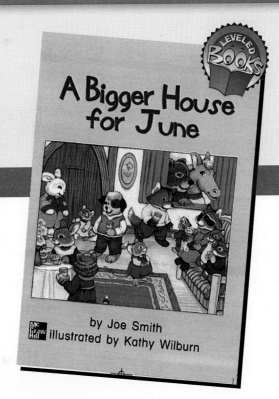

A Bigger House for June

by Joe Smith
illustrated by Kathy Wilburn

## INDEPENDENT

## A Bigger House for June

☑ **Phonics** Long *u*: *u-e*

☑ Cause and Effect

☑ High Frequency Words: *carry, been, clean, done, far*

# Guided Reading

**PREVIEW AND PREDICT** Have children read the title aloud and predict what the story will be about. Then take a **picture walk** up to page 7, incorporating the high-frequency words and focusing children's attention on cause and effect.

**SET PURPOSES** Have children write or draw why they want to read *A Bigger House for June*. For example: *I want to find out why June gets a bigger house.*

**READ THE BOOK** Use the following prompts as children read together or to discuss after they read independently:

**Pages 2–3:** What does June like to do? (clean) *High-Frequency Words*

**Pages 4–5:** Let's reread these pages. Raise your hand when you hear a word with the long *u* sound. (june, cube) *Phonics and Decoding*

**Pages 6–7:** Find and read a word on this page that has the long *u* sound. (mule) *Phonics and Decoding*

**Pages 8–11:** Why doesn't Jake's tune make June glad? (She is jealous of his home.) *Make Inferences*

**Pages 14–16:** What has happened to make June change her mind about her house? (It now looks cute; it is the right size for all her small friends) *Cause and Effect*

**RETURN TO PREDICTIONS AND PURPOSES** Review children's predictions and purposes. Were they surprised by what happened in the story? Did they find out what they wanted?

**LITERARY RESPONSE** The following questions will help focus children's responses:

• Would you tell a friend to read this story? Why or why not?

• Have you ever wanted something that someone else had? What happened?

Also see the questions and activities in *A Bigger House for June*.

See the **Phonics** CD-ROM for practice with long *u*: *u-e*.

**Answers to Story Questions**
1. Jim, the mule.
2. She doesn't like the shape and size.
3. Answers will vary.
4. No.
5. *Sam, the Knee-High Man*

**Story Questions and Writing Activity**
1. Which friend does June go to first?
2. Why doesn't June like her home?
3. What things does Jim carry on his back?
4. Do June's friends help her?
5. What's another story with a mule?

**Draw a Home**
Draw a picture of your home.
Write the name of your street near your home.
Put an **X** near your favorite room.
Share your picture with the class.

*from A Bigger House for June*

# Leveled Books

## AUTHENTIC

### Pete's Chicken

☑  **Phonics** Long *u: u-e*

☑ **Cause and Effect**

## Guided Reading

**PREVIEW AND PREDICT** Discuss illustrations up to page 20, making sure children understand the concept of cause and effect. Encourage children to predict what the story will be about. Have them write their ideas in their journals.

**Pages 1–15:** How does Pete feel about himself? (Good) How can you tell? (He looks happy and says good things about himself.) *Make Inferences*

**Pages 17–19:** Let's reread these pages. Raise your hand when you hear a word with long *u*. sound. (used) How is that sound spelled? (u-consonant-e) *Phonics and Decoding*

**Pages 20–27:** What is making Pete feel bad? (No one likes his chicken.) *Cause and Effect*

**Pages 28–31:** Why doesn't Pete want a kiss from his mom? (Answers will vary.) *Make Inferences*

**Pages 32–36:** What makes Pete change his mind about his chicken? (He realizes it is special because only he could make it.) *Make Inferences/Cause and Effect*

**RETURN TO PREDICTIONS AND PURPOSES** Ask children to share their predictions and purposes. Then discuss which predictions were close and why. Which purposes were met?

**LITERARY RESPONSE** Use the following questions to engage children in a discussion about the story:

- Why do you think that Pete draws a chicken that doesn't look like most chickens?

- Have you ever felt like Pete? When?

- Which illustration did you like the best? Why?

Also see story questions and activities in *Pete's Chicken*.

See the **Phonics** **CD-ROM** for practice with long *u: u-e*.

**Answers to Story Questions**

1. Black, orange, blue, red, purple, yellow, green.
2. Because they thought Pete's chicken was a turkey.
3. Answers will vary.
4. Pete is different. He draws a chicken of many colors. The class thought he drew a turkey. Pete took his chicken home. It was different. Just like Pete.
5. Answers will vary.

**Story Questions and Writing Activity**

1. What colors are in Pete's drawing?
2. Why do the children laugh at Pete?
3. What does the story tell you about being different?
4. Tell the story in your own words.
5. How is the story like *My Best Friend*?

**Make Up An Animal**

Think of an animal that no one has ever seen.

Draw a picture of it.

Write a few sentences describing it.

**from *Pete's Chicken***

## Activities
### Anthology and Leveled Books

## Connecting Texts

**CLASS DISCUSSION**

Lead a discussion of how the unit theme of Let's Find Out! applies to each of the stories. Have children construct a word web that describes what characters teach or what they learn from their own experiences or from others.

**CHARACTER WEB**

Have children create a web to compare the characters from their stories, their traits, and what they do.

**The Knee-High Man**
He decides he is big enough to do the things he wants to do.

**Fun Run**
He feels good because he had fun running.

**Let's Find Out!**

**A Bigger House for June?**
She feels good because her friends like her house.

**Pete's Chicken**
He feels better for having drawn the chicken.

## Viewing/Representing

**GROUP PRESENTATIONS** Divide the class into groups, one for each of the four books read in the lesson. (For *The Knee-High Man*, combine children of different reading levels.) Have each group create over-sized comic strips that show the book's main events. Encourage them to use speech balloons where appropriate. Invite groups to display their comic strips.

**AUDIENCE RESPONSE**
Give children time to view each groups' comic strip. Have them ask questions about what is happening in the frames and why.

## Research and Inquiry

**MORE ABOUT FEELINGS** Have children share their experiences when they felt happy, sad, and angry. Use the following questions to initiate discussion:

* Can you remember a time when you wanted something and you couldn't have it?

* Can you remember a time when someone told you that you were too small to do something?

* Can you remember a time when you were excited about doing something for the first time?

**interNET CONNECTION** Have children log onto **www.mhschool.com/reading** where they can access links to conflict resolution sites.

Children can write and draw what they learned in their journals.

JOURNAL

## Review Long *u*: *u-e*

---

**PREPARE**

**Listen for Long *u***  Read the following sentence aloud and have children raise their hands whenever they hear a word with the long *u* sound:

- Duke is a <u>cute</u> <u>mule</u> with long brown ears.

---

**TEACH**

**Review the Letters *u–e* as Symbols for /ū/**

- Tell children that they will review long *u* spelled *u* consonant *e*.
- Write *u–e* on the chalkboard. Have children say /u/ as you point to it.

**BLENDING Model and Guide Practice with Long *u* words**

- Display **Teaching Chart 108**. Tell children that there are five long *u*: *u–e* words hidden in the chart.
- Blend the first example for children, running your hand under the letters. Read the word *cute*. c  u  te   cute
- Repeat, having children read the word with you. Have a volunteer circle the word on the chart.

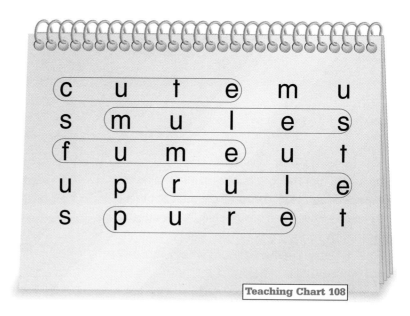

Teaching Chart 108

**Use the Word in Context**

- Use the word *cute* in a sentence. Example: *I have a cute, furry cat.*

**Repeat the Procedure**

- Have volunteers find and blend the remaining long *u*: *u–e* words in the chart and draw a circle around them.

**PRACTICE**

BLENDING
Build Long *u*
Words with
Letter Cards

PARTNERS

Write the following letter clusters on index cards: *ure, use, ule, une, ute*. Place them in a bag. Place the letter cards for *p, s, t, d, J, t, m, r, c, l* in a second bag. Have one child choose a letter cluster and blend the sounds aloud. Then have a second child choose consonants until a real word can be formed. Have pairs keep lists of the words they form.

▶ **Spatial/Kinesthetic**

 **J** une

**ASSESS/CLOSE**

Build and Read
Long *u* Words

To assess children's mastery of blending and reading long *u* words, observe them as they form words in the Practice activity. Ask each child to read two words aloud from the list.

## ADDITIONAL PHONICS RESOURCES

Phonics/Phonemic Awareness
Practice Book,
pages 147–150

McGraw-Hill School
**TECHNOLOGY**

 **CD-ROM**

activities for practice with
**Discriminating and Blending.**

DAY 4 **Writing** Write the word *duke* on chart paper and give the meaning of the word. Ask children to write a sentence about a duke and draw a picture to illustrate it.

 **CD-ROM**

## SELF–SELECTED Reading

Students may choose from following titles.

**ANTHOLOGY**

- *The Knee-High Man*

**LEVELED BOOKS**

- *Fun Run*
- *A Bigger House for June*
- *Pete's Chicken*

Bibliography, pages T92–T93

# Meeting Individual Needs for Phonics

| EASY | ON-LEVEL | CHALLENGE | LANGUAGE SUPPORT |
|---|---|---|---|
| Name_____ Date____ **Reteach** 189 | Name_____ Date____ **Practice** 189 | Name_____ Date____ **Extend** 189 | Name_____ Date____ |
| **Long o: o, oa, oe, ow** | **Long o: o, oa, oe, ow** | **Long o: o, oa, oe, ow** | **Long o Fun** |

**EASY — Reteach 189**

Read the words. What sound do you hear in each word?

cold    soap

goes    slow

Circle the word that completes the sentence. Then write the answer.

1. I ___hold___ the dog.
   (hold)   told   fold

2. I broke my ___toe___.
   hoe   (toe)   foe

3. We sail in the ___boat___.
   coat   (boat)   throat

4. The stream ___flows___ into the sea.
   rows   knows   (flows)

Book 1.5/Unit 1
**You Can't Smell a Flower with Your Ear!**   **At Home:** Help children practice the long o sound by writing four sentences to go with the words illustrated at the top of the page: cold, soap, goes, and slow.   **189**

**ON-LEVEL — Practice 189**

Write the word from the box to complete each sentence.

| slow | soap | open | cold | toe |

1. I wash with ___soap___.

2. Ice is ___cold___.

3. The bus was ___slow___.

4. Joe hurt his big ___toe___.

5. The chest was ___open___.

Book 1.5/Unit 1
**You Can't Smell a Flower with Your Ear!**   **At Home:** Help children to practice the long o sound by writing sentences using the words: show and float.   **189**

**CHALLENGE — Extend 189**

Read the clues. Circle the word that fits each clue.

You can wear me to keep warm. I am a (coat)/cat.

I am found on your foot. I am a (toe)/too.

I float on the water. I am a bat/(boat).

I can help you weed the garden. I am a (hoe)/how.

If something is on the ground, it is down/(low)/lot.

Think up clues for the words **boat** and **mow**. Write them on the lines.

_____

_____

_____

Book 1.5/Unit 1
**You Can't Smell a Flower with Your Ear!**   **At Home:** Make up a story! Ask children to think of an ending to this sentence: Once there was a slow . . . Take turns adding a line to the story.   **189**

**LANGUAGE SUPPORT**

**Long o Fun**

| o | oa | oe | ow | o | oa |
|---|---|---|---|---|---|
| oe | ow | o | oa | oe | ow |

| g | o | | kn | ow |
| h | o | me | pill | ow |
| m | o | st | sn | ow | ball |
| s | oa | p | g | oe | s |
| g | oa | t | pota | oe | s |
| b | oa | t | h | oe | |

204 You Can't Smell a Flower With Your Ear! • Language Support/Blackline Master 112   Grade 1

Reteach, 189     Practice, 189     Extend, 189    

**OBJECTIVES**

Children will:

- review long *u*: *u–e, o*: *o–e, i*: *i–e, a*: *a-e.*

- blend and read long *u, o, i,* and *a* words with silent *e.*

- review consonants and blends.

**MATERIALS**

- letter cards and long vowel cards from the **Word Building Manipulative Cards**

- **Teaching Chart 109**

---

**TEACHING TIP**

**INSTRUCTIONAL** Have children make up riddles for long *u, o, i,* and *a* words. Children can exchange and answer each other's riddles.

---

# Review *u-e, o-e, i-e, a-e*

**PREPARE**

**Identify the Letters *u–e, o–e, i–e, a–e* as the Symbols for Long *u, o, i, a***

Remind children that the letter *u* when followed by a consonant and silent *e* stands for /ū/. Write *u–e* on the chalkboard, saying its sound aloud. Have children say the sound as you point to the letter *u.* Repeat for long *o, i,* and *a.*

**Discriminate Among /ū/, /ō/, /ī/, and /ā/**

Slowly say the following sentence: *Jake and June like to jump rope.* Have children raise a hand when they hear a word with /ū/. Repeat for long *a, o,* and *i.*

**TEACH**

**BLENDING Model and Guide Practice in Matching Rhyming Words with Long *u, o, i, a***

- Display **Teaching Chart 109**. Explain that there are six pairs of rhyming words on the chart, but that they are all mixed up. Tell children that they will draw lines to connect the rhyming words.

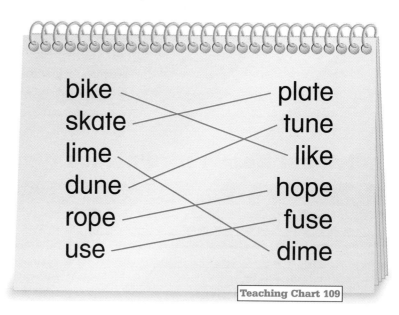

bike — plate
skate — tune
lime — like
dune — hope
rope — fuse
use — dime

Teaching Chart 109

- Blend the first word on the chart with children. b i k e  bike

- Then have volunteers blend and read aloud the words in the second column until they find the word that rhymes with *bike.*

- Have a volunteer read *bike* and *like* and draw a line to connect the two words.

**Use the Word in Context**

Have volunteers use the words in a sentence. For example: *I would like a red bike.*

**Repeat the Procedure**

Repeat the procedure until all the rhyming pairs have been connected.

## PRACTICE

**BLENDING**
**Build Long *u, o, i***
**and *a* Words**

**GROUP**

Have children work in small groups. Have each group use the letter cards and long vowel cards to build as many words as possible with long *u, o, i,* and *a*. Have groups choose two words for each vowel to put on a class bulletin board under *u, o, i,* or *a*. Have children then sort the words under each long vowel into groups of words that rhyme.

▶ **Linguistic/Kinesthetic**

## ASSESS/CLOSE

**Draw and Label**
**a Picture**

Use your observations from the Practice activity to determine if children need more reinforcement with long *u, o, i,* and *a* words. Have children choose a long vowel word and draw and label a picture of it.

## ADDITIONAL PHONICS RESOURCES

**Phonics/Phonemic Awareness**
**Practice Book,**
**pages 147–150**

McGraw-Hill School
**TECHNOLOGY**

 **CD-ROM**

**activities for practice with**
**Blending and Segmenting**

**DAY 5** **Letter Substitution**
Using the letter and long vowel cards, have pairs of children build the word *brute*. Then have them change letters to build *chute* and *flute*.

**Phonics CD-ROM**

## ALTERNATE TEACHING STRATEGY

**LONG VOWELS CVC*e***
**PATTERN**

For a different approach to teaching this skill, see pages T64, T68, and T69.

# Meeting Individual Needs for Phonics and Decoding

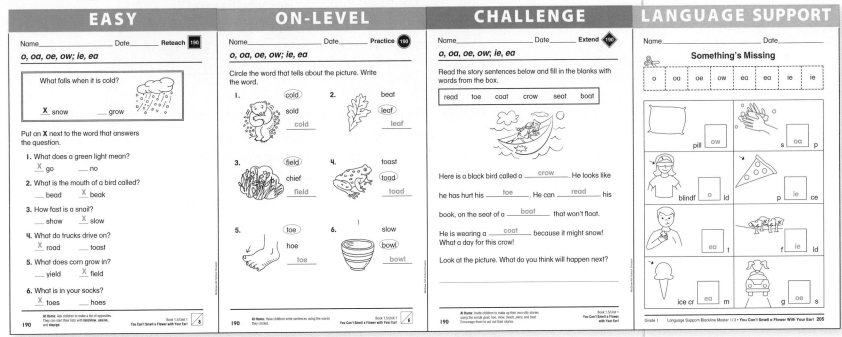

Reteach, 190          Practice, 190          Extend, 190          Language Support, 205

**95H**

**OBJECTIVES**

Children will learn how to make inferences.

.................................

**MATERIALS**
• **Teaching Chart 110**

---

**TEACHING TIP**

**INSTRUCTIONAL** Inferring is a subtle skill at which children excel may once they know what to look for. Use modeling to show children the kind of thinking they must do to make inferences.

---

## Review Make Inferences

**PREPARE**

**Introduce Make Inferences**   Tell children that they will learn how to make inferences to help them understand characters and story events better. Explain that they can use clues in the text and illustrations, as well their own experiences, to make a good guess, or inference.

**TEACH**

**Model Make Inferences**   Display **Teaching Chart 110**. Allow children to comment on the pictures. Then read the first sentence aloud.

The man has a <u>map</u>.
He is looking at the map.
He has a <u>confused</u> look on his face.
What could this mean?

The girl is on the bike.
The boy helps the girl.
Her bike has <u>training wheels</u>.
What could this mean?

Teaching Chart 110

*MODEL*   When I read, there are things that aren't always said, but that I can guess. I guess by looking at the pictures and reading what is on the page. When I guess it's called *making an inference*. In the first picture I see a man looking at a map. He looks confused and lost. From the picture and the sentences, I can guess that the man is probably lost. It looks like he is trying to find out where he is supposed to go.

Help children make additional inferences about the first picture. Example: The man is wearing a shirt and tie. Maybe he is going to a new job. Have them use picture clues and draw on their own experiences to make their inferences. Write their ideas in a list on the chalkboard.

## PRACTICE

**Make A List**

Divide children into groups. Have them make inferences about the second picture on **Teaching Chart 110.** Have them use picture and text clues to make a list of inferences. Encourage children to draw on their own experiences as well. Have groups present their lists to the class. ▶ **Linguistic/Interpersonal**

> she doesn't know how to push the pedals
>
> she doesn't know how to steer
>
> the boy is helping her
>
> she will learn how to ride her bike

## ASSESS/CLOSE

**Make Other Inferences**

Invite children to make inferences, based on the text and illustrations in other stories they have read. Create a new list for children's observations.

### ALTERNATE TEACHING STRATEGY

**MAKE INFERENCES**

For a different approach to teaching this skill, see page T70.

### LOOKING AHEAD

Children will apply this skill as they read the next selection, *Johnny Appleseed.*

# Meeting Individual Needs for Comprehension

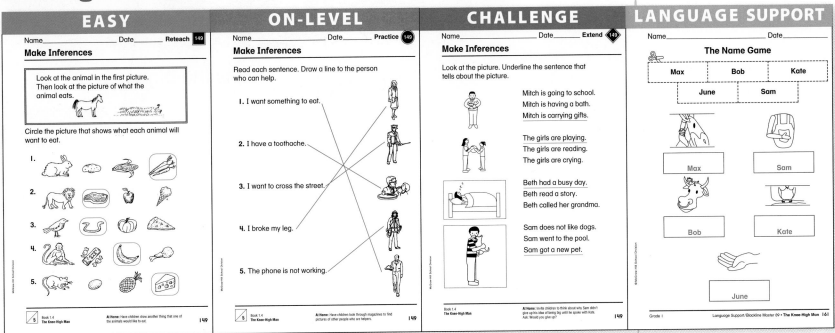

| | | | |
|---|---|---|---|
| **EASY** | **ON-LEVEL** | **CHALLENGE** | **LANGUAGE SUPPORT** |
| Reteach, 149 | Practice, 149 | Extend, 149 | Language Support, 161 |

**95J**

**OBJECTIVES**

Children will learn to read words with inflectional endings -er and -est including when the final consonant is doubled.

.................................................

**MATERIALS**
• **Teaching Chart 111**

# Introduce Inflectional Endings -er, -est

### PREPARE

**Make Comparisons**   On the chalkboard, draw three simple stick figures and write *big, bigger,* and *biggest* under the appropriate drawings. Elicit the words *big, bigger,* and *biggest* from children to describe the drawings.

### TEACH

**Identify Base Words and Endings**   Read the sentences on **Teaching Chart 111**. Point out the words *big, bigger,* and *biggest.* Model how understanding inflectional endings can help children read.

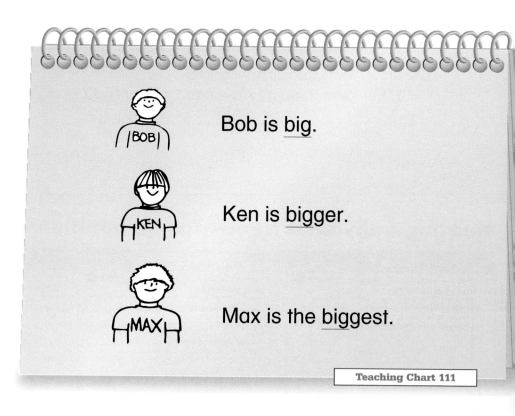

Bob is big.

Ken is bigger.

Max is the biggest.

Teaching Chart 111

*MODEL*  I can see in the three pictures that one boy is big, one is bigger, and one is the biggest. When I read the sentence *Ken is bigger,* I recognize the word *big.* I see that the last two letters of the word are -er. I know that sometimes when these letters are at the end of a word, it means *more.* So Ken is "more big", or *bigger* than Bob. I also notice that the -g is doubled when -er is added.

Repeat the procedure for the word *biggest.* Invite volunteers to underline the base word in each.

**Identify -er and -est Words**

GROUP

Write the following words on the chalkboard: *wetter, fastest, taller, saddest,* and *slower*. Have children identify the base word in each. Then create a three-column chart that shows the base words along with the inflectional endings. Call on children to identify the missing comparative word and write it in the proper column. Discuss whether or not the final letter is doubled.

| Base Word | -er | -est |
|---|---|---|
| wet | wetter | wettest |
| fast | faster | fastest |
| tall | taller | tallest |
| sad | sadder | saddest |
| slow | slower | slowest |

**ASSESS/CLOSE**

**Illustrate Comparatives**

Have partners choose one of the sets of words from the Practice activity. Invite them to illustrate the three words in the set and then label each picture.

ALTERNATE TEACHING
**STRATEGY**
..............................................
INFLECTIONAL ENDINGS
-er, -est

**For a different approach to teaching this skill, see page T71.**

# Meeting Individual Needs for Vocabulary

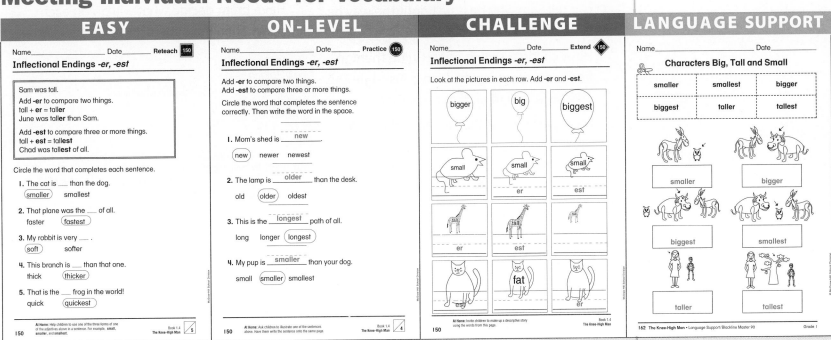

EASY
Reteach, 150

ON-LEVEL
Practice, 150

CHALLENGE
Extend, 150

LANGUAGE SUPPORT
Language Support, 162

**95L**

**GRAMMAR/SPELLING**
**CONNECTIONS**

See the 5-Day Grammar and Usage Plan on *Go* and *Do*, pages 95O–95P.

See the 5-Day Spelling Plan on Words with Long *u: u-e (silent e rule)*, pages 95Q–95R.

**TECHNOLOGY TIP**

Most word-processing programs have a "Help" function that shows how to indent. Encourage children to try setting different margins for their writing project.

# Persuasive Writing

## Prewrite

**WRITE A LETTER** Present this writing assignment: Write a letter to Sam the Knee-High Man, convincing him that he's fine the way he is. Give good reasons why Sam should not follow the animals' advice to get bigger.

**BRAINSTORM IDEAS** Have children brainstorm ideas for why the animals' advice is wrong for Sam. Have them discuss what they might tell Sam to prove that he's just right the way he is.

**Strategy: Play a Partner Game** Have children talk with a partner about Sam the Knee-High Man. Use this game to help children begin:

- One partner can play the part of Sam, and tell why he wants to be bigger.
- For each reason Sam gives for why he might like to be bigger, the other partner can tell Sam why he is just right the way he is.
- Have children switch roles. Guide them to find more reasons why Sam is just right the way he is, and to elaborate on them.
- Have partners list their ideas as they role-play.

## Draft

**USE THE LISTS** In their letters, have children write full sentences telling Sam why he is just right. They should imagine some of Sam's reasons for wanting to be bigger, and address them with ideas from their lists. Encourage them to write as if Sam is a real friend they want to help.

## Revise

**TAKING TIME OUT** Ask children to put their work aside and think about Sam again. Discuss with them some other things he might say. How would they answer those things? Make a board list of their ideas.

Have children trade letters with a partner. Have each partner pretend to be Sam and read their partner's letter. Are they convinced that they're fine the way they are, or do they still want to be bigger?

## Edit/Proofread

**CHECK FOR ERRORS** Children should reread their letters for spelling, grammar, punctuation, and letter format.

## Publish

**TURN THE LETTER INTO A BOOK** Help children turn their letters into a class book. Have them decide what will go on each page. Then have them illustrate their letters.

Max Golden
34 Oak Road
Old City, MA 00000
November 9, 20__

Dear Sam,
    I think you are just fine the way you are. You do not need to be bigger.
    You say you want to fight. But you do not like to fight. So it does not matter if you are big.
    You say that you do not want your friends to call you names. If someone calls you a name, that person is not your friend.
    You are lucky to be small. Your pants and your socks are easy to pack.

Sincerely,
Max Golden

## Presentation Ideas

**MAKE PUPPETS** Have children make a stick puppet of Sam and a stick puppet of themselves.

▶**Viewing/Representing**

**PUT ON A PUPPET SHOW** Have volunteers use their stick puppets to put on a puppet show about Sam. Have the children use puppets of themselves as characters telling Sam why he's fine the way he is.

▶**Speaking/Listening**

Consider students' creative efforts, possibly adding a plus (+) for originality, wit and imagination.

| Scoring Rubric | | | |
|---|---|---|---|
| **Excellent** | **Good** | **Fair** | **Unsatisfactory** |
| **4:** The writer<br>• makes an original, effective argument for Sam to be happy as he is.<br>• convincingly responds to each of Sam's worries.<br>• writes in full sentences, and may use sophisticated vocabulary. | **3:** The writer<br>• makes a solid argument for Sam to be happy as he is.<br>• attempts to answer Sam's worries.<br>• writes in clear, full sentences. | **2:** The writer<br>• attempts to help Sam feel better about his size.<br>• may not offer clear answers to Sam's worries.<br>• may not always use full sentences. | **1:** The writer<br>• may not grasp the task to persuade.<br>• may offer reasons that do not address Sam's worries.<br>• may not write in full sentences, or may present disorganized ideas. |

## Meeting Individual Needs for Writing

| EASY | ON-LEVEL | CHALLENGE |
|---|---|---|
| **Draw a Scene** Have children draw scenes featuring Sam the Knee-High Man in familiar settings: at a grocery store, in school, at the playground, and so on. Have them write one or two sentences about Sam's experiences in each place. | **Record a Dream** Have children write a description of a dream that Sam may have had. His height should play a part in the dream. | **Make a Journal Entry** Have children imagine a person named Pat the Mile-High Woman. Ask them to write a story about how she wishes she were smaller, and how she finds out that she is just right the way she is. |

# 5Day Grammar and Usage Plan

**ESL** To help children with irregular verbs, say, "Go to the front of the classroom." Then ask children what they just did. Guide them to respond, "We went to the front of the classroom."

## DAILY LANGUAGE ACTIVITIES

Write the Daily Language Activities on the chalkboard each day or use **Transparency 18**. Have children correct the sentences orally, using *go* or *do* in the past tense.

### Day 1

**1.** Sam goes over the hill yesterday. went
**2.** Max and June go to the shack before. went
**3.** Sam go to see Bob Bull early. went

### Day 2

**1.** Then Bob does what she asked. did
**2.** I do it last week. did
**3.** They do a lot of stuff early. did

### Day 3

**1.** Sam goes to Max first. went
**2.** Max and Bob do their best. did
**3.** Last week Sam goes up the tree. went

### Day 4

**1.** What does Sam do next? did
**2.** Finally, Sam goes to Kate Owl. went
**3.** Yesterday Kate does the math. did

### Day 5

**1.** Sam does a good job this morning. did
**2.** Then Sam and Max go for a walk. went
**3.** Later they go to the cliff. went

Daily Language Transparency 18

**950** *The Knee-High Man*

---

## DAY 1 — Introduce the Concept

**Oral Warm-Up** Ask children, "Where did you go yesterday after school?" Write their responses on the chalkboard, and circle the word *went* in each sentence.

**Introduce Go** Remind children that the past tense tells about an action that has already happened. Ask children how most past-tense verbs are formed. (add *-ed*) Explain that some verbs do not end with *-ed* in the past tense.

### Go

- The verb *go* has a special form to tell about the past.
- Use *go* or *goes* to tell about something that happens in the present.
- Use *went* to tell about something that happened in the past.

Present the Daily Language Activity and have students correct orally.

 **WRITING** Assign the daily Writing Prompt on page 66C.

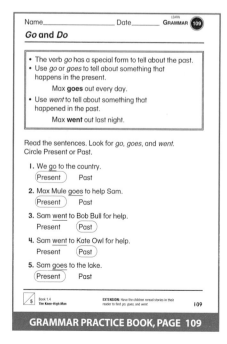

**GRAMMAR PRACTICE BOOK, PAGE 109**

---

## DAY 2 — Teach the Concept

**Review Go** Write this on the chalkboard: *Today I go to the zoo.* Then ask children to change the sentence to begin with *Yesterday.* (Yesterday, I went to the zoo.)

**Introduce Do** Write this on the chalkboard: *Today I do my best.* Then ask children to change the sentence to begin with *Yesterday.* (Yesterday I did my best.)

### Do

- The verb *do* has a special form to tell about the past.
- Use *do* or *does* to tell about something that happens in the present.
- Use *did* to tell about something that happened in the past

Present the Daily Language Activity. Then have children write two sentences, using *do* and *did*.

 **WRITING** Assign the daily Writing Prompt on page 66C.

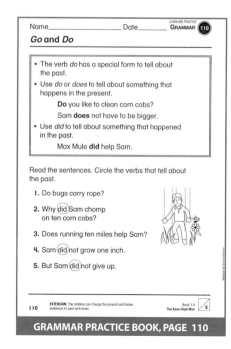

**GRAMMAR PRACTICE BOOK, PAGE 110**

# Go and Do

## DAY 3 — Review and Practice

**Learn from the Literature** Review *go* and *do* with children. Read the first and last sentences on page 85 of *The Knee-High Man.*

> **But Sam did not give up**
>
> **He went to see Kate Owl**

Emphasize *did* and *went* in the sentences. Then ask whether each sentence tells about the past or tells about now. (Both sentences tell about the past.)

**Use *Go* and *Do*** Present the Daily Language Activity and have children correct orally. Write the following sentences on the chalkboard: *Today I _____ to school. Yesterday we _____ to the park. Today I _____ some work. Yesterday they _____ a good job.* Ask children to fill in the sentences using the correct forms of *go* and *do.*

Present the Daily Language Activity and have children correct the sentences orally.

**WRITING** Assign the daily Writing Prompt on page 66D.

**GRAMMAR PRACTICE BOOK, PAGE 111**

## DAY 4 — Review and Practice

**Review *Go* and *Do*** Write the following sentence on the chalkboard: *Kate and Sam go to the hill yesterday.* Ask children if the sentence is correct. (no) Why not? (The verb should be *went.*) Why? (because it happened in the past) Correct the sentence on the chalkboard, then present the Daily Language Activity for Day 4.

**Mechanics and Usage** Before children begin the daily Writing Prompt on page 66D, review proper nouns. Display and discuss:

> **Proper Nouns**
>
> The special name of a person or place begins with a capital letter.

**WRITING** Assign the daily Writing Prompt on page 66D.

**GRAMMAR PRACTICE BOOK, PAGE 112**

## DAY 5 — Assess and Reteach

**Assess** Use the Daily Language Activity and page 113 of the **Grammar Practice Book** for assessment.

**Reteach** Write *Today* and *Yesterday* on the chalkboard. Then write the following sentences on paper strips: *The boys go to the store. We went to the store. She goes to the store. I do a good job. Pam does a good job. Nick and Jill did a good job.* Read the sentences aloud and ask whether each tells about the past or the present. Have children take turns placing the sentences under the appropriate column on the board.

Use page 114 of the **Grammar Practice Book** for additional reteaching.

**WRITING** Assign the daily Writing Prompt on page 66D.

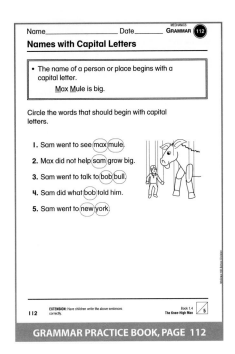

**GRAMMAR PRACTICE BOOK, PAGE 113**

GRAMMAR PRACTICE BOOK, PAGE 114

**95P**

# 5 Day Spelling Plan

## LANGUAGE SUPPORT

**ESL** The long *u* sound may be difficult for those children whose native language is not English. Say the following sentence, having children clap their hands when they hear the long *u*: *I can play the flute and tuba.*

## DICTATION SENTENCES

### Spelling Words

1. I do not like this <u>rule</u>.
2. What a <u>cute</u> cat you have!
3. The <u>mule</u> can work.
4. Look at that <u>tube</u>.
5. She likes this <u>tune</u>.
6. Do you have a <u>flute</u>?

### Challenge Words

7. Where have you <u>been</u>?
8. She can <u>clean</u> the dish.
9. This job is <u>done</u>.
10. We went <u>far</u> away.

---

## DAY 1 — Pretest

**Assess Prior Knowledge** Use the Dictation Sentences at left and **Spelling Practice Book**, page 109 for the pretest. Allow children to correct their own papers. If children have trouble, have partners give each other a midweek test on Day 3.

| Spelling Words | | Challenge Words |
|---|---|---|
| 1. r**ule** | 4. tube | 7. **been** |
| 2. cute | 5. tune | 8. **clean** |
| 3. mule | 6. flute | 9. **done** |
| | | 10. **far** |

*Note: Words in **dark type** are from the story.*

**Word Study** On page 110 of the **Spelling Practice Book** are word study steps and an at-home activity.

---

## DAY 2 — Explore the Pattern

**Sort and Spell Words** Say and write the words *cut* and *cute*. Ask children what vowel sound they hear in each word. (short *u*, long *u*) Circle the *e* at the end of *tube* and remind children that the silent *e* helps make the vowel sound long. Tell them that the words in this lesson have long *u* spelled *u*-consonant-*e*. Underline the letters *ube* in *tube*.

Ask children to read aloud the six spelling words before sorting them according to the spelling pattern.

| Words ending with | | | |
|---|---|---|---|
| -ule | -ute | -une | -ube |
| rule | cute | tune | tube |
| mule | flute | | |

**Word Wall** As children read other stories and texts, have them look for new words with long-vowel sounds that follow the silent *e* rule. Add them to a classroom word wall, underlining the vowel and the silent *e*.

---

### Spelling Practice Book, page 109

Name_____ Date_____ SPELLING **109**

**Words with Long u: u-e**

**Pretest Directions**
Here are the results of your child's
Fold back the paper along the dotted line. Use the blanks to write each word as it is read aloud. When you finish the test, unfold the paper. Use the list at the right to correct any spelling mistakes. Practice the words you missed for the Posttest.

1. _____ 1. rule
2. _____ 2. cute
3. _____ 3. mule
4. _____ 4. tube
5. _____ 5. tune
6. _____ 6. flute

**To Parents**
Here are the results of your child's weekly spelling Pretest. You can help your child study for the Posttest by following these simple steps for each word on the list:
1. Read the word to your child.
2. Have your child write the word, saying each letter as it is written.
3. Say each letter of the word as your child checks the spelling.
4. If a mistake has been made, have your child read each letter of the correctly spelled word aloud, and then repeat steps 1-3.

Challenge Words

_____ been
_____ clean
_____ done
_____ far

5 Book 1.4
The Knee-High Man      109

**SPELLING PRACTICE BOOK, PAGE 109**

**WORD STUDY STEPS AND ACTIVITY, PAGE 110**

---

### Spelling Practice Book, page 111

Name_____ Date_____ SPELLING **111**

**Words with Long u: u-e**

Look at the spelling words in the box.

| rule | cute | mule | tube | tune | flute |

Write the words that end with **ule**.

1. ___rule___      2. ___mule___

Write the words that end with **ute**.

3. ___cute___      4. ___flute___

Write the word that end with **une**.

5. ___tune___

Write the two letters that are found in every spelling word.

6. ___u___      7. ___e___

Make a new word by changing the r of rule to m.

8. ___mule___

6 Book 1.4
The Knee-High Man      111

**SPELLING PRACTICE BOOK, PAGE 111**

---

# Words with Long *u: u-e*

 **DAY 3 Practice and Extend**

**Word Meaning: Add -s** Remind children that we add -s to a noun to show that it names more than one. Ask children to add -s to the following spelling words and write sentences using the words: *rule, mule, tube, tune, flute.*

**Identify Spelling Patterns** Write this sentence on the chalkboard: *That mule is cute and clean.* Have a volunteer read it aloud. Ask children to tell which words have the spelling patterns -ule or -ute and which word is the Challenge Word. Repeat with the spelling patterns -une and -ube, using these sentences: *He was done with the tube. That tune has been played before.*

Then provide sentences with blanks for the Challenge Words and have students write and complete the sentences.

 **DAY 4 Proofread and Write**

**Proofread Sentences** Write these sentences on the chalkboard, including the misspelled words. Ask children to proofread, circling incorrect spellings and writing the correct spellings. There are two errors in each sentence.

> That is a cut mul. (cute, mule)
>
> Shall I play a tun on my flut? (tune, flute)

Have children create additional sentences with errors for partners to correct.

**WRITING** Have children use as many Spelling Words as possible in the daily Writing Prompt on page 66D. Remind children to proofread their writing for errors in spelling, grammar, and punctuation.

**DAY 5 Assess and Reteach**

**Assess Children's Knowledge** Use page 114 of the **Spelling Practice Book** or the Dictation Sentences on page 95Q for the posttest.

**Personal Word List** If children have trouble with any words in the lesson, have them add to their personal list of troublesome words in their journals. Have children draw a picture to illustrate each word.

Children should refer to their word lists during later writing activities.

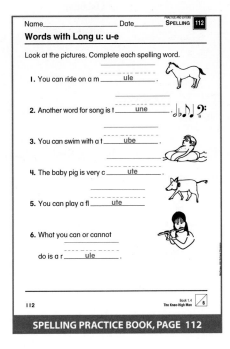

**SPELLING PRACTICE BOOK, PAGE 112**

**SPELLING PRACTICE BOOK, PAGE 113**

**SPELLING PRACTICE BOOK, PAGE 114**

**95R**

# Johnny Appleseed

**Selection Summary**   In this biography of John Chapman, known as Johnny Appleseed, children will read about one man's efforts to make Earth fruitful.  Johnny Appleseed shows people how to plant and cultivate apple seeds so that they can enjoy the fruit and beauty of the trees.  ❖ TEKS H 1.1:A,B,C

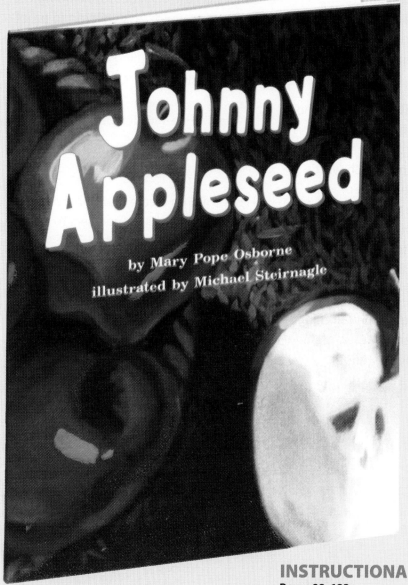

Johnny Appleseed
by Mary Pope Osborne
illustrated by Michael Steirnagle

**Student
Listening
Library
Audiocassette**

**INSTRUCTIONAL**
**Pages 98–123**

**About the Author**   When Mary Pope Osborne was little, she lived with her family on different army bases.  As an adult, she lived in Europe and traveled across Asia. Her travel experiences gave Ms. Osborne ideas for her writing.

**About the Illustrator**   Michael Steirnagle has illustrated children's books as well as advertisements. He often uses his two children, Matthew and Stacy, and his dog, Ralph, in his pictures.

# Resources for Meeting Individual Needs

**EASY**
Pages 123A, 123D

**INDEPENDENT**
Pages 123B, 123D

**AUTHENTIC**
Pages 123C, 123D

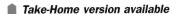 Take-Home version available

## LEVELED PRACTICE

**Reteach,** 151–158

blackline masters with reteaching opportunities for each assessed skill

**Practice,** 151–158

workbook with Take-Home Stories and practice opportunities for each assessed skill and story comprehension

**Extend,** 151–158

blackline masters that offer challenge activities for each assessed skill

## ADDITIONAL RESOURCES

- **Language Support Book** 163–171
- **Take-Home Story, Practice** pp. 152a–152b
- **Alternate Teaching Strategies** T64–T72

McGraw-Hill School

**TECHNOLOGY**

**Phonics CD-ROM** provides extra phonics support.

**interNET CONNECTION** Research & Inquiry ideas. Visit **www.mhschool.com/reading.**

 # Suggested Lesson Planner

 **Available on CD-ROM**

| READING AND LANGUAGE ARTS |  **DAY 1** *Focus on Reading and Skills* |  **DAY 2** *Read the Literature* |
|---|---|---|
| ● **Phonics Daily Routines** | Daily  **Routine:** **Substitution,** 98B <br><br>  **CD-ROM** | Daily  **Routines:** **Fluency,** 98C <br><br>  **CD-ROM** |
| ● **Phonological Awareness** <br><br> ● **Phonics** *Long a* <br><br> ● **Comprehension** <br><br> ● **Vocabulary** <br><br> ● **Study Skills** <br><br> ● **Listening, Speaking, Viewing, Representing** |  **Read Aloud and Motivate,** 96E <br> *The Great Big Enormous Turnip* <br><br> **Develop Phonological Awareness,** 96/97 <br> Long *a: ay, ai* <br> *The Gift* <br><br> ☑ **Introduce Long *a: ay, ai*,** 98A–98B <br> Reteach, Practice, Extend, 151 <br> Phonics Workbook, 151–154 | **Build Background,** 98C <br> Develop Oral Language <br><br> **Vocabulary,** 98D <br><br> | *how* | *light* | *little* | <br> | *live* | *pretty* | | <br> **Vocabulary Cards** <br> **Teaching Chart 112** <br> Reteach, Practice, Extend, 152 <br><br>  **Read the Selection,** 98–119 <br> Guided Reading <br> ☑ Long *a: ai, ay* <br> ☑ Make Inferences <br><br> **Minilessons,** 101, 105, 107, 109, 115, 117 <br><br> **Cultural Perspectives,** 100 |
| ● **Curriculum Connections** |  Language Arts, 96E | **Link** Science, 98C |
| ● **Writing** | **Writing Prompt:** Write a story about something Johnny Appleseed might always say. | **Writing Prompt:** Close your eyes and picture an apple. Write about what you see. <br><br> **Journal Writing** <br> Quick-Write, 119 |
| ● **Grammar** | **Introduce the Concept:** *See and Say*, 123O <br> Daily Language Activity: Use the correct form of *see* and *say* in sentences. <br><br> **Grammar Practice Book,** 115 | **Teach the Concept:** *See and Say*, 123O <br> Daily Language Activity: Use the correct form of *see* and *say* in sentences. <br><br> **Grammar Practice Book,** 116 |
| ● **Spelling** *Long a* | **Pretest: Words with Long *a: ai, ay*,** 123Q <br><br> **Spelling Practice Book,** 115–116 | **Explore the Pattern: Words with Long *a: ai, ay*,** 123Q <br><br> **Spelling Practice Book,** 117 |

**Meeting Individual Needs**

 ☑ = **Skill Assessed in Unit Test**

**Read EVERY DAY**

---

## DAY 3 — Read the Literature

**Daily**  **Routine:**
Segmenting, 121

 **CD-ROM**

**Reread for Fluency,** 118

**Story Questions,** 120
Reteach, Practice, Extend, 153
**Story Activities,** 121

**Study Skill,** 122
☑ Charts
**Teaching Chart 113**
Reteach, Practice, Extend, 154

 **Read**

**Read the Leveled Books,**
Guided Reading
☑ Words With Long a: ai, ay
☑ Make Inferences
☑ High-Frequency Words

**Activity** Art, 104

 **Writing Prompt:** Write a story about what two children say to each other after they see Johnny Appleseed.

 **Journal Writing,** 123D

**Review and Practice: See and Say,** 123P
Daily Language Activity: Use the correct form of see and say in sentences.

**Grammar Practice Book,** 117

**Practice and Extend: Words with Long a: ai, ay,** 123R

**Spelling Practice Book,** 118

---

## DAY 4 — Build Skills

**Daily**  **Routine:**
Writing, 123F

 **CD-ROM**

 **Read the Leveled Books and Self-Selected Books**

☑ **Review Long a: ay, ai,** 123E–123F
**Teaching Chart 114**
Reteach, Practice, Extend, 155
Language Support, 168
Phonics Workbook, 151–154

☑ **Review ai, ay; u-e, o-e,** 123G–123H
**Teaching Chart 115**
Reteach, Practice, Extend, 156
Language Support, 169
Phonics Workbook, 151–154

**Activity** Social Studies, 106

 **Writing Prompt:** Pretend you traveled with Johnny Appleseed. Write a letter to a friend telling about something you saw.

**Persuasive Writing,** 123M
Prewrite, Draft

**Meeting Individual Needs for Writing,** 123N

**Review and Practice: See and Say,** 123P
Daily Language Activity: Use the correct form of see and say in sentences.

**Grammar Practice Book,** 118

**Proofread and Write: Words with Long a: ai, ay,** 123R

**Spelling Practice Book,** 119

---

## DAY 5 — Build Skills

**Daily**  **Routine:**
Blending, 123H

 **CD-ROM**

 **Read Self-Selected Books**

☑ **Review Make Inferences,** 123I–123J
**Teaching Chart 116**
Reteach, Practice, Extend, 157
Language Support, 170

☑ **Review Inflectional Endings -er, -est,** 123K–123L
**Teaching Chart 117**
Reteach, Practice, Extend, 158
Language Support, 171

**Listening, Speaking, Viewing, Representing,** 123N

**Minilessons,** 105, 107, 109, 115, 117

**Activity** Math, 110

**Writing Prompt:** Pretend you are dreaming about Johnny Appleseed. Write about what you see in your dream.

**Persuasive Writing,** 123M
Revise, Edit, Proofread, Publish

**Assess and Reteach: See and Say,** 123P
Daily Language Activity: Use the correct form of see and say in sentences.

**Grammar Practice Book,** 119–120

**Assess and Reteach: Words with Long a: ai, ay,** 123R

**Spelling Practice Book,** 120

**Link**

**Language Arts**

# Read Aloud and Motivate

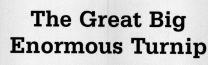

## The Great Big Enormous Turnip

a Russian folk tale
by Alexei Tolstoi

Once upon a time an old man planted a little turnip and said: "Grow, grow, little turnip, grow strong!"

And the turnip grew up sweet and strong and big and enormous.

Then, one day, the old man went to pull it up. He pulled and pulled again, but he could not pull it up. He pulled and pulled again, but he could not pull it up.

He called the old woman.
The old woman pulled the old man,

The old man pulled the turnip.
And they pulled and pulled again, but they could not pull it up.

So the old woman called her granddaughter.
The granddaughter pulled the old woman,
The old woman pulled the old man,
The old man pulled the turnip.

**Continued on pages T2-T5**

## Oral Comprehension

**LISTENING AND SPEAKING** Motivate children to make inferences by reading this Russian folk tale by Alexei Tolstoi. Ask children to picture the action as you read the story. When you are done, ask: Do you think the roots of the turnip were strong? What makes you think so?

**Activity** Have children work in small groups to illustrate the situation described in "The Great Big Enormous Turnip." On a large piece of poster board, have each group draw the people and animals working together to pull out the turnip. Group members should take turns adding an animal or person to the chain.

▶ **Visual**

# Develop Phonological Awareness

**Anthology pages 96-97**

### The Gift

I got a present in the mail.
It was sent from my pal Gail.
Gail mailed me a box of chalk.
I made five trees out on the walk.
I added apples and two blue jays,
And a big fat sun,
With lots of rays.

96    97

## Objective: Listen for Long *a*

**RHYMING** Read "The Gift." As you reread the poem, have children clap when they hear words that rhyme with *pail*. Repeat with *days*.

**Phonemic Awareness** **BLENDING** Write the spelling of each sound in *mail* as you say it. Have children repeat after you. Ask children to blend the sounds to read the word. Explain that *ai* makes the sound /a/.

Repeat with **Gail**. Then repeat with **jays** and **rays**, explaining that *ay* makes the sound /a/.

**Phonemic Awareness** **SEGMENTING** Have children segment initial and final sounds.

Use letter cards to build the word *mail*.

- Say the word *mail*.
  Take away the *m* card.
- Say *mail* without the letter *m*.
  Replace the *m* card. Take away the *l* card.
- Say *mail* without the letter *l*.

Repeat with **jays** and **rays**.

**96/97**

**OBJECTIVES**

Children will:

- identify long *a: ay, ai* words.

- blend and read long *a: ay, ai* words.

- review consonants and blends.

........................................

**MATERIALS**

- letter and vowel digraph cards and word building boxes from the **Word Building Manipulative Cards**

**SPELLING/PHONICS CONNECTIONS**

Words with long *a: ai, ay:* See the 5-Day Spelling Plan, pages 123Q–123R.

---

**TEACHING TIP**

**INSTRUCTIONAL** Point out to children that sometimes a sound can have more than one spelling. In this lesson, they will learn that long *a* can be spelled *ay* or *ai*. You may want to explain to children that only *ay* can appear at the very end of a word, as in *way*. The letters *ai* cannot appear at the end of a word.

---

## Introduce Long *a: ay, ai*

> **TEACH**

**Identify the Letters *ay, ai* as Symbols for the Sound /ā/**

Tell children they will learn to read words with the letters *ai* and *ay* that have the long *a* sound.

- Display the *ay* and *ai* letter cards and say /ā/.

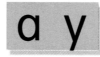 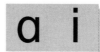

- Point to the *ay* card and have children repeat the sound after you. Do the same with the *ai* card.

**BLENDING Model and Guide Practice with Long *a: ay, ai* Words**

- Place the *w* letter card before the *ay* card.

- Point to the letters as you blend the sounds to read *way*.

- Have children read the word with you as you blend the sounds together.

- Repeat, using the *ai* letter card and adding a *t* at the end to show the word *wait*.

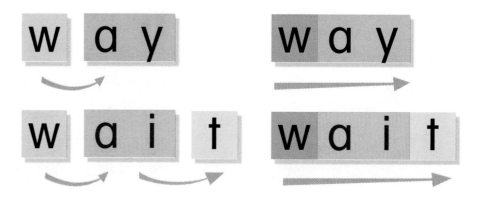

**Use the Words in Context**

Use the words in context to reinforce their meanings. Example: *Do you know the way to the park? I will wait for you there.* Then have children make up their own sentences using *way* and *wait*.

**Repeat the Procedure**

Use the following words to continue modeling and guided practice with long *a: ay*, and *ai*.

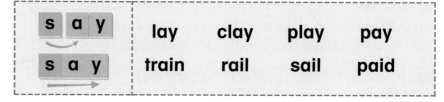

| | lay | clay | play | pay |
| | train | rail | sail | paid |

## PRACTICE

**LETTER SUBSTITUTION**
**Build Long *a*: *ay*, *ai* Words with Letter Cards**

**GROUP**

Start with the letter card for *ay* and build the word *pay*. Ask children to repeat each sound after you. Replace the *ay* card with an *ai* card and add the *d* letter card to show *paid*. Ask children to identify the new sound at the end of the word. (/d/) Build and read the word *paid* together. Use both words in context and have children build and read these words: *stay*, *play*, *gray*, *maid*, *pain*, and *sail*. ▶ **Linguistic/Kinesthetic**

## ASSESS/CLOSE

**Read and Write Long *a* Words**

To assess children's ability to blend and read long *a*: *ai*, *ay* words, observe them as they build and read the words from the Practice activity. Then have them turn to page 97 in their books. Read the poem aloud with them. Ask them to write one *ai* word and one *ay* word from the rhyme.

### ADDITIONAL PHONICS RESOURCES

**Phonics/Phonemic Awareness Practice Book, pages 151–154**

**PHONICS KIT**
Hands-on Activities and Practice

*McGraw-Hill School*
**TECHNOLOGY**

**Phonics CD-ROM**
activities for practice with Blending and Segmenting

## Meeting Individual Needs for Phonics

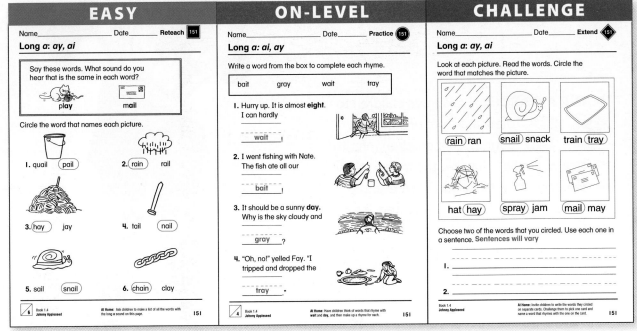

Reteach, 151      Practice, 151      Extend, 151

**PHONICS KIT**
HANDS-ON ACTIVITIES AND PRACTICE

**98B**

# Build Background

Science

## Anthology and Leveled Books

### Evaluate Prior Knowledge

**CONCEPT: TREES** Ask children to share what they know about trees. For example, talk about trees that lose their leaves in the fall versus trees that stay green all year. Ask children if they can name different kinds of trees. (maple, oak, pine, apple, cherry) Use the following activity to give children more information about trees.

**MAKE A WORD WEB FOR TREES** Ask children to create a word web to record the characteristics of a tree. For example: A tree starts from a seed. Some trees have leaves, others have needles. All trees have branches and roots. ▶ **Linguistic**

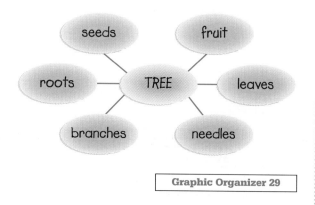

Graphic Organizer 29

**PLANT A GARDEN** Encourage children to draw a picture of a garden. Suggest that children refer to the tree web when drawing the trees in their garden. They might also add flowers and plants. Have each child write a sentence to describe his or her picture.

### Develop Oral Language

**CONNECT WORDS AND ACTIONS** Have children follow simple instructions to act out planting their gardens. Examples:

- Show how to plant seeds.
- Water the flowers.

Ask children to say what they are doing in the garden by asking:

- What are you doing?
- Why are you bending down?

▶ **Kinesthetic/Linguistic**

**DAILY Phonics ROUTINES**

**DAY 2** Fluency Write some sentences on the chalkboard and have children identify the long *a: ai, ay* words. Examples: *Wait* for the *rain* to go *away*. You *may play* with the *pail.*

Phonics CD-ROM

**LANGUAGE SUPPORT**

To build more background and help develop understanding and recognition of high-frequency words, see pages 163–166 in the Language Support Book.

# Vocabulary

## High-Frequency Words

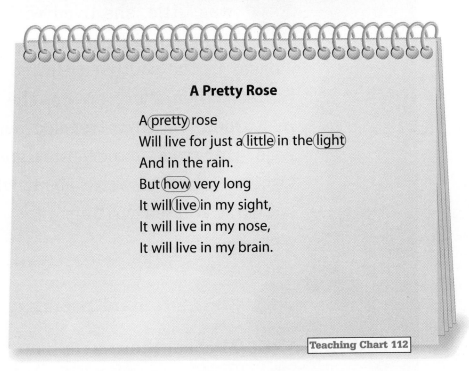

**A Pretty Rose**

A (pretty) rose
Will live for just a (little) in the (light)
And in the rain.
But (how) very long
It will (live) in my sight,
It will live in my nose,
It will live in my brain.

Teaching Chart 112

**SPELLING/VOCABULARY CONNECTIONS**
The words *how, light, little, live* and *pretty* are Challenge Words. See page 123Q for Day 1 of the 5-Day Spelling Plan.

## Auditory

**LISTEN TO WORDS** Without displaying it, read aloud "A Pretty Rose" on **Teaching Chart 112**. Ask children what they think the poem means. Is it only about a rose, or can it be about other things, too?

**LISTEN TO THE "MUSIC" OF HIGH-FREQUENCY WORDS** Tell children that not every poem rhymes or has a regular rhythm. But sometimes the words still sound like music.

- Read the first two lines of the poem. *Pretty* doesn't rhyme with *little*, but when you listen to them, they have some sounds in common that make them go nicely together.

- Say the words *live, little,* and *light*. What makes these words sound interesting together?

## Visual

**READ WORDS** Display "A Pretty Rose" on **Teaching Chart 112**. Read the poem, tracking the print with your finger as you read. Then hold up Vocabulary Cards one at a time and have children circle the high-frequency words on the chart.

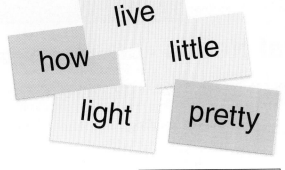

Vocabulary Cards

**WRITE POEMS** Have groups write the high-frequency words, and then write a poem using them. The poem doesn't have to rhyme or be in a regular rhythm, but it should sound "musical."

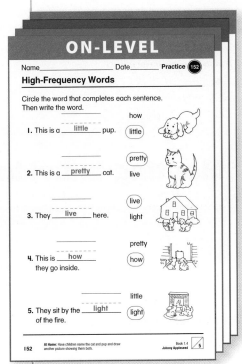

Take-Home Story 152a–152b
Reteach 152
Practice 152 • Extend 152

**98D**

# Guided Instruction

## Preview and Predict

Point to and read aloud the book title and names of the author and illustrator. Take a **picture walk** to discuss what children see, stopping at pages 102–103. Using words from the story, talk about each illustration.

- Where do you think this story takes place?
- What clues about the main character does the picture on pages 98–99 give?
- Do you think the story is going to be real or make believe?
- What is the story most likely about?

Children can record their predictions about the story and the characters in a predictions chart.

## Set Purposes

Ask children what they want to find out as they read the story. For example:

- Where does the man go?
- Why does he plant apple seeds?
- What happens to him?

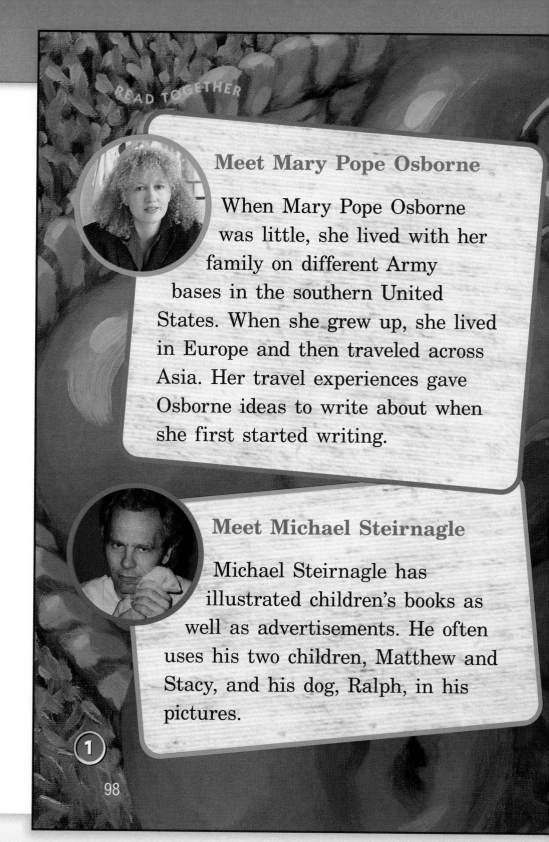

READ TOGETHER

### Meet Mary Pope Osborne

When Mary Pope Osborne was little, she lived with her family on different Army bases in the southern United States. When she grew up, she lived in Europe and then traveled across Asia. Her travel experiences gave Osborne ideas to write about when she first started writing.

### Meet Michael Steirnagle

Michael Steirnagle has illustrated children's books as well as advertisements. He often uses his two children, Matthew and Stacy, and his dog, Ralph, in his pictures.

1

98

# Meeting Individual Needs · Grouping Suggestions for Strategic Reading

| EASY | ON-LEVEL | CHALLENGE |
| --- | --- | --- |
| **Shared Reading** Read the story aloud as you track print and model directionality. Invite children to join in on repetitive words and phrases. Model the strategy of noticing characters' facial expressions and body language and of picture details that enable you to make inferences about story events. | **Guided Reading** Ask children to read the story with you. Monitor any difficulties in reading that the children have, in order to determine which prompts to emphasize. After reading the story with children, have them reread it, using the rereading options on page 118. | **Read Independently** Have children set purposes before they read. Remind them that they can make inferences about the story by noticing the characters' expressions, how they are dressed, and what's going on in the picture. After reading, have children retell the story. Children can use the questions on page 120 for a group discussion. |

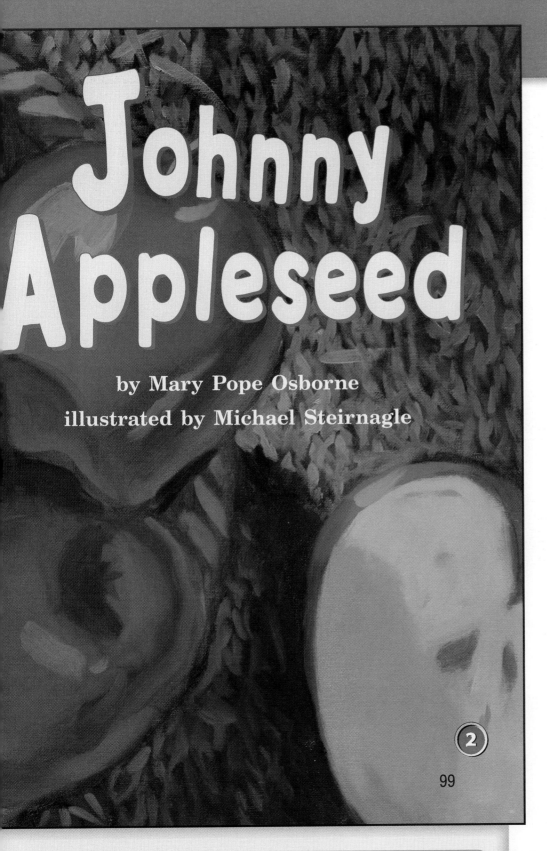

# Johnny Appleseed

by Mary Pope Osborne

illustrated by Michael Steirnagle

②

99

## LANGUAGE SUPPORT

A blackline master for the tree chart can be found in the **Language Support Book**. Whenever Johnny Appleseed helps someone new in the story, children can draw a picture of them inside one of the apples. As children make inferences about Johnny Appleseed, they can write their ideas in the tree trunk.

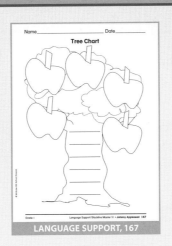

Name_____ Date_____
**Tree Chart**

Grade 1    Language Support/Blackline Master VI • *Johnny Appleseed*    167
**LANGUAGE SUPPORT, 167**

# Guided Instruction

 ☑ **Phonics** Long *a: ai, ay*

☑ **Make Inferences**

**Strategic Reading** Tell children that if they pay careful attention to details in the pictures that may not be mentioned in the words, it will help them understand more about the story. Explain that they will make and use a tree chart to keep track of the things that they learn about the kind of person Johnny Appleseed is.

**①** We are going to read *Johnny Appleseed* by Mary Pope Osborne. Let's read about her. What might have led Mary to want to write the story of this man's life? Now point to the second picture. This is Mike Steirnagle. Do you think Mike likes to draw trees? Why? *Concept of a Book: Author/Illustrator*

**②** **MAKE INFERENCES** Listen to the title of the story. What do you think the man in the story is famous for? (planting apple seeds)

> ## TEACHING **TIP**
>
> **INSTRUCTIONAL** The following chart indicates words from the story that children have learned to decode or high-frequency words that have been taught in previous lessons. As children read, observe any difficulties they may have.
>
> | Decodable | | High Frequency |
> |-----------|------|----------------|
> | day | rain | how |
> | gray | sail | light |
> | hail | say | little |
> | jay | stay | live |
> | may | wait | pretty |
> | quail | way | |

**99**

# Guided Instruction

**③ MAKE INFERENCES** Why do you think John Chapman was called Johnny Appleseed? (to show what he did) Who knows what a nickname is? (a special name that tells something about you)

**④** What do you think is the main idea of this story? (Johnny Appleseed's life)
*Main Idea*

100

## CULTURAL PERSPECTIVES

**APPLES** Point out that apples are used to make apple pie, an all-American food.

**RESEARCH AND INQUIRY** Have small groups choose another country and find out about a fruit that is popular there.

• What is the name of the fruit?

• What food is it used to make?

Have each group draw a picture of the fruit that they researched and write one sentence about their findings.

inter**NET**
**CONNECTION** Children can learn more about different fruits by visiting **www.mhschool.com/reading**.

Mangos are grown in Brazil

His name was John Chapman. **3**
But he was called Johnny Appleseed. **4**
This is his tale.

He dressed in rags and old sacks. **5**
He had no shoes. A tin pot was his hat.

101

# Guided Instruction

**PHONICS SHORT *e, i, a*** Read the last two sentences on page 101. Then find one short *e* word, three short *i* words, and four short *a* words. (*dressed; in, tin, his; rags, sacks, had, hat*) Model the sound of each letter and have children repeat after you.

**5** **MAKE INFERENCES** Why do you think Johnny Appleseed dressed the way he did? (It was what he had; he felt comfortable.)

## Minilesson

### REVIEW

## Context Clues

Remind children that they can find clues in both words and pictures to figure out the meaning of an unfamiliar word.

- Point to the word *tin* in the last sentence, and then read the sentence aloud.
- Ask children if there is another word in the sentence that can help them understand the meaning of *tin*. (pot)
- Ask if anyone knows what most pots are made of. (metal)
- Guide children to see that *tin* is a kind of metal that pots are made of. Have them confirm their guess by looking at the picture.

**Activity** Have children use the same steps to figure out the meaning of the word *rags*.

## PREVENTION/INTERVENTION

**PHONICS SHORT *e, i, a*** Children who are having trouble identifying the letters to be used for short vowel sounds will benefit from repeated exercises. Write a list of words with missing short vowels *a, i,* and *e*. Have children build the word with letter cards, placing one of the three vowels in the blank space. Ask children to read their words aloud and name the missing letter. Some words may lend themselves to more than one vowel. Examples: *sack/sick, quit, shed, mask, lift, west, stiff/staff, band/bend,* and *slant.*

**101**

# Guided Instruction

**6** **MAKE INFERENCES** How do you suppose Johnny got so many apple seeds? (Possible responses: He ate apples and kept the seeds. He bought them. They were given to him.)

**7** **MAKE INFERENCES** What is Johnny doing in the picture? (planting a seed) Let's put the information in our tree charts.

**8** Why is Johnny planting apple seeds? (He wants apple trees to grow.)
*Draw Conclusions*

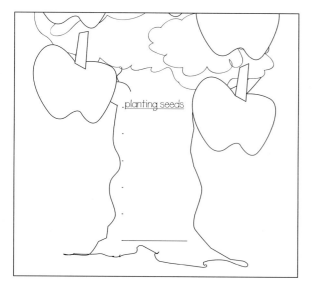

planting seeds

**6** Johnny knew a lot about plants and
**7** how to grow them. He had lots of
**8** apple seeds.

102

## Activity

# Cross Curricular: Science

**PLANT A SEED** Ask if anyone has grown plants from seeds before. Lead a discussion about how plants grow: the seed is planted in soil, then water and sunlight help the seed grow roots and leaves and grow into a plant. Ask children to identify plants they eat. (vegetables and fruits, nuts and seeds)

**Activity** Give each child a seed and a paper that has potting soil and a tiny hole in the bottom for drainage. Children will then gently press the seeds into the soil and lightly cover them with soil. Place cups in a sunny place and keep moist.
▶ **Kinesthetic**

One day, he packed his seeds and left home. He had a plan. He wanted to help the people who were going west. He wanted to help them plant apple trees.

**9**
**10**
**11**

103

# Guided Instruction

**9** **Phonics** **LONG *a: ay*** Let's read the first sentence. "One . . . hmm, what is the next word? Let's blend the sounds together and see: d ay day. *Blending*

**10** **MAKE INFERENCES** Who is the "he" in all these sentences? (Johnny) How do you know? (He's named on the previous page.)

**11** What is Johnny's plan? (to give seeds to people so they will plant lots of trees) Do you think he will succeed? *Make Predictions*

# Guided Instruction

**12** **Phonics** LONG *a: ai* Let's look at the second word here. (*sailed*) I'm going to blend the sounds of the letters together to read it. s ai l ed sailed *Blending*

**13** Do you see the mark at the end of the first sentence? Who knows what it means? (to say the sentence with feeling) There are other marks before the word *Quick!* and at the end of *Plant my apple seeds!* Does anyone know what these marks mean? (someone is saying something) *Concepts of Print*

**12** He sailed down the river on a raft.

**13** "Quick! Plant my apple seeds!" he said to those who were on the banks.

104

## Activity

### Cross Curricular: Art

**COLOR THEORY** Show children a color wheel and explain how many colors can be created from red, yellow, and blue—the primary colors. Demonstrate how to make green by mixing blue and yellow. Make purple from red and blue. Mix the purple and green together to make black.

Have children make pink by mixing a small amount of red with a lot of white.

**Activity** Children can use sponges to sponge-paint pink apple blossoms on black tree trunks. They may wish to mix green and paint grass and leaves on their trees.

▶ **Visual/Kinesthetic**

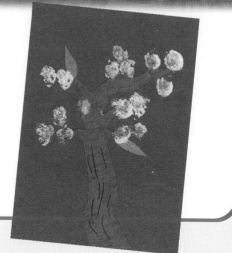

"They will give you pretty, pink buds (14) in May! In the fall, you can make pies (15) and jam!"

105

# Guided Instruction

(14) **MAKE INFERENCES** What are the people on the river banks doing? (waving good-bye to Johnny) Do you think he helped them? How? (Yes, he gave them seeds for apples.) What kind of person do you think Johnny is? (helpful, kind) Let's include a drawing of the people in our tree chart.

(15) Why do you think the people won't have pies and jam until fall? (There won't be apples until the trees grow.) *Critical Thinking*

**CONCEPTS OF PRINT** Why is the word *May* written with a capital *M*? (name of month)

## Minilesson
### REVIEW
### Vowels

You can use a calendar and the names of the months to review short and long vowels.

- Review the short and long vowel sounds and make a column for each on a chart.
- Display a calendar and read the names of the months slowly.
- Ask children to raise hands if they hear a short or long *a, e, i, o,* or *u.*

**Activity** Children can work in small groups to practice long and short vowel sounds. Ask them to practice saying the months aloud.

**Phonics CD-ROM** Have children use the interactive phonics activities on the Phonics Fun CD-ROM for vowel review.

## PREVENTION/INTERVENTION

**CONCEPTS OF PRINT** Review capitalization with children: the first letter of a sentence or a proper name is capitalized. Say some proper and some common nouns and ask children to raise their hands when they hear a word that always starts with a capital letter. Examples could include names of children in the class, days of the week, months of the year, cities, and countries.

# Guided Instruction

**16** What is happening here? Why does Johnny want the people to plant the seeds? (so that more apple trees will grow) *Analyze Character and Plot*

**17** Why are the farmers using mules instead of tractors to plant their crops? (The story takes place before tractors were invented.) *Critical Thinking*

As Johnny went west, he passed women in sun hats and men with mules. **16** "Take them and plant them!" he said. **17** And he gave them seeds.

106

## Activity

### Cross Curricular: Social Studies

**FAMILY FARMING** Explain that long ago many families raised their own food and sold any extra to buy other things. Families had fruit orchards or dairy farms. Have children draw a picture showing what they would have grown if they had lived in that time period.

**RESEARCH AND INQUIRY** Give children books and magazines about family farming in the 19th and early 20th centuries. ▶ **Linguistic/Visual**

 **interNET CONNECTION** For more information on farming go to **www.mhschool.com/reading.**

"Where is your home?" they asked him. He just smiled and went on his way. **18**

107

# Guided Instruction

**18** **MAKE INFERENCES** Why did Johnny Appleseed just smile and go on his way? (He didn't really have a home. He just traveled from place to place.)

## Minilesson

### REVIEW

### Setting

Remind children that they can tell the time of the day or the season by looking at the pictures and reading the words.

- Ask children to tell what season they think it is. How do they know?
- Remind children that they can use the pictures and words to tell where a story is taking place.
- Have children suggest things they know of can guess abut where and when the story takes place. (Examples: farmland, the country, long ago, daytime.)

**Activity** Have children draw pictures that illustrate a season. Ask them to include "clues," such as snow or trees with leaves. Display the pictures and invite children to guess the season.

## LANGUAGE SUPPORT

**ESL** Children may have trouble distinguishing the names of the four directions: east, west, north, and south. Use a globe or map to show children where they are. Then show where they would go if they went north, east, south, and west. Write the four direction words and display them in the classroom so you can refer to them often.

Have children practice their sense of direction. Say the words *east, west, north,* and *south* as children stand up and face the appropriate direction.

**107**

# Guided Instruction

**19** 🅟honics LONG *a:,ai* Do you see two words with the long *a* sound in the first sentence? What are they? Let's blend the sounds together to read each one:
r ai n  rain   h ai l  hail  *Blending*

**20** 🅟honics LONG *a: ay* Let's read the second sentence. Which word has a long *a* sound? *(stayed)* Write the word on the board and underline the letters that make the long *a* sound. *(stayed)*

**P/i** LONG *a: a-e* WORDS  Can you find a long *a* word that does not have *ai* or *ay*? *(caves)* Model blending this word, having the children repeat the sounds after you.

## Ⓢelf-Monitoring

### STRATEGY

**SEARCH FOR CLUES** Go back through the story and look for clues to help you remember what has happened so far.

- Why did Johnny leave home?
- What did he take with him?
- Where did he go?
- What did he find along the way?

**19**
**20** In rain and hail, mist and fog, he kept on. He stayed in sheds with hens and chicks. He camped in caves with bats.

108

**P/i** PREVENTION/INTERVENTION

**LONG *a: a-e* WORDS** Read the last sentence on page 108. Explain that *caves* is a long *a-e* word, even though it ends in *s* rather than *e*. The *s* shows more than one cave. The root word is *cave*.

Review the long *a: a-e* rule by showing children word cards and modeling as

you read the words aloud. Identify which words show long *a: a-e*. Examples: *cap, cape, man, mane, rat,* and *rate*. Remind children that the *e* at the end is silent, and it makes the *a* say its name.

But he was not sad. **21**
He always had a big smile. **22**
"What a pretty day this is,"
he would say. "Life is very good!"

109

# Guided Instruction

**21** Let's look at page 108. Where is Johnny? (a cave) Think about what Johnny has done in the story so far. What do you think he will do next?(visit more places, plant more seeds) *Make Predictions*

**22** **MAKE INFERENCES** Look at the picture of Johnny on page 108 and compare it to the one on page 109. How is Johnny's expression different? (He seems sad and lonely on one page, and smiling and happy in the other.) Why do you think that is? (On page 108, it's dark and he is in a cave with bats. But on page 109, it's a sunny, pretty day.)

## Minilesson

### REVIEW

### Character

Remind children that they can tell about a character in a story by looking at the pictures and reading the words.

- Ask children to describe the kind of person Johnny Appleseed is.
- Have them indicate words and pictures in the story that led them to make these statements.
- Ask if they would like to have known Johnny Appleseed, and ask them to tell why.

**Activity** Ask children to think of someone they like and describe him or her.

## LANGUAGE SUPPORT

**ESL** The word *pretty* is pronounced more like a short *i* word than a short *e* word. Help children become comfortable reading this word by talking about things they think are pretty. Write the sentence below on the chalkboard. Ask each child to repeat this sentence and fill in the blank: "I think _____ is (are) pretty."

# Guided Instruction

**23** Why do you think Johnny might just fling seeds one day and dig holes another day? (Possible responses: he dug holes where he could; he flung seeds only when it was windy) *Critical Thinking*

**23** Some days, he stopped to dig holes and dropped in the seeds. But some days, he just flung them to the wind.

110

## TEACHING TIP

**INSTRUCTIONAL** Help children understand the differences between the words *some, all* and *none* by doing simple math activities with the counters. Example: Use 10 counters and two cups. Put some counters in each cup. Ask children to tell what they see, using the word *some*. Put all the counters in one cup and show both cups. (all) Now empty both cups and ask children how many counters there are. (none)

## Activity

### Cross Curricular: Math

**ESTIMATION** Put sticks of chalk or pencils in a cup and ask children to guess if there are "more than or fewer than five."

**Activity** Give pairs of children 10 counters and a small paper cup. The counters are apple seeds and the cups are holes. Children take turns deciding how many

"seeds" to "put in a hole" and how many to "fling to the wind" (put on the desk top). The partner guesses how many are in each place, then children count to check.

▶ Logical

"Do not take them," he would tell the blue jays. "Wait for the trees to grow. **24** As they get bigger, you can [live] in **25** their branches."

111

# Guided Instruction

**24** **MAKE INFERENCES** What is Johnny doing on this page? (talking to the bird) How is he helping the birds? (He's telling them to wait and not eat the seeds so they'll have a home.) Let's draw a picture of the birds in one of the apples on our tree chart.

**25** What is the main idea this picture illustrates? (Johnny doesn't want the birds to eat the seeds; he wants the seeds to grow into apple trees.) *Main Idea*

**p/i** **TRACKING PRINT** How many sentences do you see on this page? (three)

## TEACHING TIP

**INSTRUCTIONAL** Review with children the use of quotation marks and commas. Ask which marks show that someone is speaking. (quotation marks) Ask children to identify the commas and read the sentences so that listeners can identify where there is a pause. Remind children that commas set parts of a sentence off from each other.

**p/i** PREVENTION/INTERVENTION

**TRACKING PRINT** Ask children to put a self-stick note on the first word of each sentence. (Do, Wait, As) Ask children to read with you as you read the page aloud. Pause briefly at the commas, longer after a period. Reread, and have children raise their hand- seach time you begin a sentence.

**111**

# Guided Instruction

**26** **MAKE INFERENCES** Let's read these two pages and look at the illustrations. What does Johnny do to show that's a good man? (He helped animals.) Let's put that information in our chart.

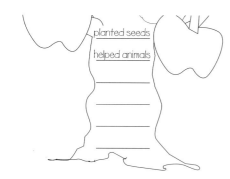

planted seeds

helped animals

**27** **Phonics** **LONG *a: ai, ay*** Point to and read aloud the word that shows a long *ai*. (quail) Now point to and read aloud the word that shows long *ay*. (gray) What other long *a* word with a long *a* sound do you see on the page? (saved)

**p/i** **CONCEPTS OF PRINT** Why does the word *quail's* end in this mark and the letter *s*? (shows the wing belongs to the quail)

## Fluency

### READD WITH EXPRESSION

**ONE** Try echo reading one-on-one with a child who has demonstrated difficulty with fluent reading.

- Read one sentence of the text aloud with appropriate intonation and phrasing.
- Then ask a volunteer to imitate this oral reading model.
- Continue and repeat until the child can imitate more than one sentence at a time.

**26** Johnny was a good man.

**27** One time, he mended a quail's wing.

**28** Then he saved a gray wolf from a trap.

112

**p/i** **PREVENTION/INTERVENTION**

**CONCEPTS OF PRINT** Have children use the possessive to talk about items in the classroom and to whom or what they belong. Point to and identify, for example: Jack's shirt, Maria's desk, the teacher's hair. Write *Jack's shirt* on the board. Ask children to tell why you added the apostrophe mark and letter *s* at the end. (to show something belongs to a person, animal, or thing) Invite children to identify and use the possessive in sentences.

One day, he found an old horse.
He fed him and gave him a bath.

113

# Guided Instruction

**28** Tell the order in which the things pictured on page 112 happened. What clues are in the words? (He mended the wing, then he saved the wolf.) *Sequence of Events*

**29** **MAKE INFERENCES** How do you think the horse felt after Johnny gave him a bath and fed him? Why do you think this? (The horse probably felt better. Maybe it hadn't had food or a bath in awhile.) Let's include all the animals we've seen Johnny help in our tree chart.

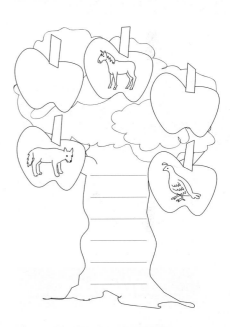

**113**

# Guided Instruction

 Were you surprised that Johnny kept the horse and wolf as pets? Why or why not? (Possible answers: Yes, because Johnny usually traveled alone; because a wolf is a wild animal.) *Confirm Predictions*

## Fluency

### GROUP READING

 Model tracking print and rereading to achieve fluency.

- Point to and read aloud each word in the first sentence, running your hand beneath the word as you read it.

- Pause briefly at every comma, longer at the end of a sentence.

- Have children repeat this process with you, pointing to each word as they read.

- Repeat the group reading. Ask children to listen to and compare the sounds of the words *horse* and *stores*.

**30** Now with his pets, he went to place after place. He visited mills and shops.

114

"I bring little seeds to grow into big trees!" he said with a big smile. His eyes flashed with light as he explained how to plant them.

**31**

**1**

115

# Guided Instruction

**31** **MAKE INFERENCES** How do you think Johnny feels if he's smiling and his eyes flashed with light? (He was excited.) What was he excited about? (planting seeds that would grow into trees)

**32** **MAKE INFERENCES** Where are the people in the picture on these pages? (in a store) Why do you think Johnny is visiting them? (Possible answers: he may be asking them to sell seeds; he may be buying food and supplies)

## Minilesson
### REVIEW
## Cause and Effect

Remind children that they can figure what is happening in a story by thinking about how the characters relate to one another.

- Have children talk about the people in the picture.
- Ask: Who is talking? Who is listening?
- Encourage them to notice the effect Johnny's words seem to be having on the people listening.
- What do people will do after listening to Johnny?

**Activity** Tell children that one person's words or actions may cause something to happen. Play "Simon Says" or "Mother May I". Point out the cause (What Simon or Mother say) and the effect (children move).

## LANGUAGE SUPPORT

**ESL** Read aloud the first sentence on page 115. Talk with children about how a seed becomes a tree. Brainstorm different parts of a tree and talk about where those parts are on a tree. Then have children curl into balls and pretend to be little seeds. Give directional phrases to help them grow such as: "Your roots are growing, stretch out your legs;" "Your branches are growing, stretch your arms to the sky."

**115**

# Guided Instruction

**33** What is happening in the picture on these pages? (Johnny is having dinner with a family.) Do you think the family feels comfortable having Johnny in their home? Why or why not? (Yes, because they're talking and smiling.) *Use Illustrations*

**34** Why did some people not trust Johnny? (He was different.) Why would this make people not like him? (They were afraid of him and his different ways.) *Critical Thinking*

Some people did not trust Johnny. **33**
He did not live the way they did. **34**
But most people liked him.
They would ask him into their homes.

116

## Visual Literacy

### VIEWING AND REPRESENTING

Pretend that you are a neighbor of the family and have stopped by to visit.

- Where would you be standing or sitting in the room?

- What would you have to eat?

- Talk about how the artist makes the room on pages 116–117 seem cozy and friendly? (He uses bright colors; the people sit closely around a table; they are smiling.)

▶ **Visual**

## LANGUAGE SUPPORT

**ESL** Have children read the second sentence on the page. Children may be confused about the word *live*, which can be either a long *i-e* word or a short *i* word, as it is here. Explain that some words look just alike but sound different depending on their meaning. Use the words in context: *Chad is going to live in Texas. Pinocchio wanted to be a real live boy. Tina and Lil live near the airport. I saw a live wolf in the national park.* Invite children to make up sentences using the two words.

He would tell them about his trip west. **35**
They would give him some ham and
cake. Then he would rest.

117

# Guided Instruction

**35** Johnny tells the family about his travels. Do you think Johnny will also tell the family about how to plant apple seeds? (Probably, because he's shared this information with all the other people he's met.) *Make Predictions*

## Minilesson

### REVIEW

## Summarize

Remind children that summarizing means telling only a story's main parts and leaving out the details. When they summarize they should include the main idea, the most important events, and how the story ends. Ask children:

- Would you tell how Johnny dressed?
- Would you tell about the pretty pink blossoms?
- Would you tell about Johnny's trip west?
- Would you tell about apple seeds?

**Activity** Have children orally summarize the story. Help them keep to the main idea and most important events. Write the summary on chart paper and invite children to draw pictures to display with it.

# Guided Instruction

**(36) MAKE INFERENCES** Let's reread the last sentence on page 119. What do you think it means that Johnny had *given a gift that would live on?* (The trees will keep growing and will produce more apples, which will produce more trees.) Let's include that in our tree chart.

planted seeds

helped animals

gave the gift
of many trees

**RETELL THE STORY** Have children sit in a circle to retell the story. They can use the ideas and pictures in their tree charts to help them remember what they have learned. *Summarize*

When the sun came up, he was on his way. He waved and flung his seeds to the wind.

118

## REREADING FOR *Fluency*

**GROUP** Children who need fluency practice can read aloud as they listen to the story being read.

**READING RATE** Evaluate individual children's reading rates. Have the child read aloud from *Johnny Appleseed* for one minute. Then have the child place a self-stick note after the last word read. Count how many words the child has read. Alternatively, you could assess small groups or the whole class together by having children count words and record their own scores.

A Running Record form provided in **Diagnostic/Placement Evaluation** will help you evaluate reading rate(s).

When Johnny died, he was missed a lot. But his trees got bigger and bigger. He had given a gift that would live on. **36**

119

# Guided Instruction

## Return to Predictions and Purposes

Reread and discuss children's predictions about the story. Ask how their predictions turned out, and if their questions got answered.

Have children talk about using the word web. Did it help them remember things about the people and events in the story?

### INFORMAL ASSESSMENT

**HOW TO ASSESS**

**LONG *a: ai, ay*** Have children turn to pages 108–109 and read all the long *a: ai, ay* words. (*rain, hail, stayed, always, day, say*)

**MAKE INFERENCES** Ask children to describe the feelings of Johnny Appleseed and other characters in the story. (when Johnny left another town to travel, when the people waved good-bye)

**FOLLOW UP**

**LONG *a: ai, ay*** Continue to model blending the sounds and distinguishing *ai* and *ay* words for children who are having difficulty.

**MAKE INFERENCES** Invite children who are having difficulty making inferences to use the story illustrations to help them.

## LITERARY RESPONSE

**QUICK-WRITE** Have children list in their journals some parts of the story they found interesting. They can use the word web or ask for help with difficult words.

**ORAL RESPONSE** Have children use their journal entries to discuss these questions:

- What was Johnny's gift?
- Why did he make this journey?
- Why do you think people missed him after he died?
- If you could do anything you wanted to do someday when you are grown up, what would it be? Draw a picture to show what you would like to do someday.

**119**

# Story Questions

Tell children that now they will read some questions about the story. Help children read the questions. Discuss possible answers.

**Answers:**

1. He went west. *Literal*

2. He gave them apple seeds to plant. *Make Inferences*

3. because he thought life was very good *Inferential/ Character*

4. Answers will vary. Accept appropriate summaries. *Critical/Summarize*

5. Answers will vary. Accept appropriate examples. *Critical/ Reading Across Texts*

**Picture It!** Help children read the directions in their anthologies. Have them discuss different foods that are made with apples. Examples: apple pie, applesauce, apple juice.

## Story Questions & Activities

READ TOGETHER

1 Where did Johnny go?

2 How did Johnny help people?

3 Why did Johnny always smile?

4 Tell about Johnny's life in your own words.

5 What other book have you read about a real person?

## Picture It!

Think of a food made with apples.
Draw a picture of it.
Write about it.

I like hot apple pie with ice cream.

## Meeting Individual Needs

### EASY

Name_____ Date_____ Reteach **153**

**Story Comprehension**

Think about "Johnny Appleseed." Write one thing Johnny did that matches each word. Answers may vary.

Kind ⟶
He mended a quail's wing;
he saved a wolf from a trap.

Happy ⟶
He always had a big smile;
he was not sad.

Poor ⟶
He dressed in rags and
old sacks; he had no shoes.

Helpful ⟶
He helped people by planting
apple trees.

Book 1.4
Johnny Appleseed

At Home: Have children draw a picture of Johnny Appleseed being kind or helpful. 153

**Reteach, 153**

### ON-LEVEL

Name_____ Date_____ Practice **153**

**Story Comprehension**

Circle the pictures that tell what happened in "Johnny Appleseed."

1. Johnny Appleseed planted _____.

2. Johnny Appleseed sailed on a _____.

3. Johnny Appleseed slept with _____.

4. Johnny Appleseed had _____ as pets.

5. Johnny Appleseed ate at a _____.

6. Johnny Appleseed's _____ grew big.

Book 1.4
Johnny Appleseed

At Home: Have children tell what each picture shows. 153

**Practice, 153**

### CHALLENGE

Name_____ Date_____ Extend **153**

**Story Comprehension**

How did Johnny Appleseed help others? Complete each sentence. Sample answers are given.

He wore a tin **pot** on his head.

One time he **mended a quail's wing**

He saved **a gray wolf** from a trap.

He fed **an old horse hay**

He planted **apple trees**

Book 1.4
Johnny Appleseed

At Home: Invite children to think about how they help others. Encourage children to list how they helped others yesterday. 153

**Extend, 153**

# Have an Apple Party!

There are many kinds of apples.
Bring in your favorite kind of apple.
Look at all the apples.
Taste them.
Talk about how they are alike
and different.

## Find Out More

Find out about another good American.
Tell what the person did for our country.

121

# Story Activities

## Have an Apple Party!

**Materials:** different varieties of apples

 **ONE** Read the directions aloud. Help children who have questions. Have the children discuss the kinds of apples they know.
It might be a good idea if you bring in samples of unusual varieties of apples.

## Find Out More

**RESEARCH AND INQUIRY** Again, read the directions aloud and help children **PARTNERS** who have questions.

Show children the biography section of the library and explain that biographies tell true stories about people. Help each pair choose one.

inter**NET** CONNECTION Have children log on to ***www.mhschool.com/reading***, where they can access sites about famous Americans.

## ASSESSMENT

See the Selection Assessment Test for book 1.4.

DAILY  ROUTINES

**DAY 3** **Segmenting** Give children word building boxes and say long *a: ay* words. Have children listen to the sounds in the word and write the letter(s) for each sound in the appropriate box.

*Phonics* **CD-ROM**

**121**

# Study Skills

## APPLE TREE CHART

BJECTIVES

Children will read a chart to learn how an apple tree grows.

Remind children that they have just read a story about a man who plants apple trees. Tell them that now they will read a chart, a kind of picture with words, to learn more about apple trees.

Have children read the phrases and the title of the chart with you. Then invite children to explain each phrase. Help children read the questions below the chart, encouraging them to identify the phrases that answer each question.

# Study SKILLS

READ TOGETHER

## Apple Tree Chart

This chart tells how an apple tree grows.

Plant the Seed

Water the Seed

Let It Grow

Pick Apples

## Look at the Chart

**1** What do you do first to grow an apple tree?

**2** What helps the apple tree grow?

## Meeting Individual Needs

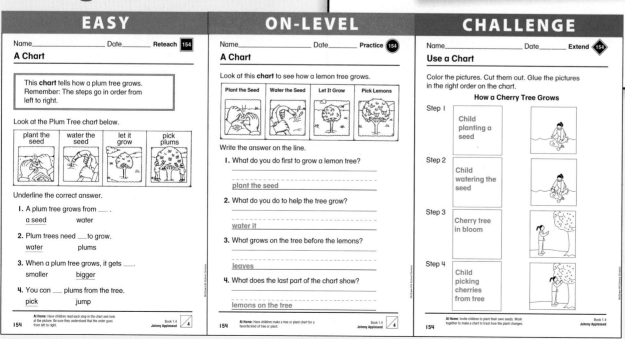

Reteach, 154

Practice, 154

Extend, 154

# TEST POWER

## A Trip to the Barn

It was early in the evening.
Farmer Joe wanted corn for dinner.
He had put the corn in the big red barn.
Farmer Joe put on his boots and walked
out to the barn.
He picked out three ears of corn.
"One, two, three," Farmer Joe counted.
"I can't wait to eat dinner," he said happily.
Then Farmer Joe took the corn
back to the house.

What will Farmer
Joe do with the corn?

Read the story again to help answer the question.

● Eat it
○ Feed it to the pigs

123

# Test Power

## Read the Page

Explain to children that you will be reading this story as a group. You will read the story, and they will follow in their books.

Request that children put pens, pencils, and markers away, since they will not be writing in their books.

## Discuss the Question

Have children reread the last line of the story. Ask them what farmer Joe is doing at the end of the story. Then ask them what he will probably do with the corn.

## Test-Tip

The answer to the question is always in the story—all you have to do is read carefully to find it.

For The Princeton Review test preparation practice for **TerraNova, ITBS,** and **SAT-9,** visit the McGraw-Hill School Division Web site. See also McGraw-Hill's *Standardized Test Preparation Book.*

# Leveled Books

## EASY

### Fall Is Fun!

☑ **Phonics** Long *a: ai, ay*

☑ **Make Inferences**

☑ **High Frequency Words:** *how, light, little, live, pretty*

by Joe Smith
illustrated by Selina Alko

## LANGUAGE SUPPORT

**ESL** Before reading, invite children to share any knowledge they have about harvesting. Then preview the story, paying special attention to the vocabulary words. Read the book together and then encourage children to read it independently.

**Answers to Story Questions**

1. Is it cleaned and then put into bags. Some of the fruit goes into cans.
2. Pumpkin pie
3. Answers will vary: at the supermarket or grocery store.
4. Pick fruit, cut grains, go for a hike.
5. Answers may vary: *Johnny Appleseed.*

**Story Questions and Writing Activity**

1. Where does fruit go after it is picked?
2. What kind of pie will the pumpkins make?
3. Where can you buy fruit in cans?
4. What are the three things to do in the fall?
5. What other story that you read had apples in it?

**What Kind of Apples**

Go to the store with an adult.

Write down the names of the three apples.

Draw a picture of the apple under its name.

## Guided Reading

**PREVIEW AND PREDICT** Incorporate the high-frequency words as you take a **picture walk** up to page 5. Invite children to predict what else will happen on the farm. Chart their ideas.

**SET PURPOSES** Ask children to write or draw what they hope to learn in *Fall is Fun!* For example: *I want to know what happens to the pumpkins.*

**READ THE BOOK** You can use questions like the following to help guide children as you read the story together or after they have read it **independently.**

**Pages 2–3:** What word does the girl use to describe where she lives? (pretty) What happens as the days get shorter? (There is less light.) *High-Frequency Words*

**Pages 4–5:** Raise your hands when you hear a word with the long *a* sound. (grain, days) What two different ways is the long *a* sound spelled in these words? (*ai, ay*) *Phonics and Decoding*

**Pages 6–7:** What other kinds of things do you think a baker might bake? *Make Inferences*

**Page 8–11:** Look at the word *m-a-y.* Model: I don't know how to read this word. But I know that *m* makes the /m/ sound, and the letters *ay* can make the long *a* sound. If I blend the two sounds together, I get m a y , *may. High-Frequency Words*

**Pages 12–13:** What happens after the fruit is picked? (It's cleaned, drained, and put into bags or cans.) *Make Inferences*

**Page 14–16:** How do you think the children in these pictures feel? Why? Answers will vary. *Make Inferences*

**RETURN TO PREDICTIONS AND PURPOSES** Have children compare their predictions with what actually happened on the farm.

**LITERARY RESPONSES** If you could visit a farm, what would you enjoy doing the most?

Also see the story questions and writing activity in *Fall is Fun!*

# Leveled Books

## INDEPENDENT

### The Land

☑ **Phonics** Long *a: ai, ay*

☑ Make Inferences

☑ High-Frequency Words:
*how, light, little, live, pretty*

# Guided Reading

**PREVIEW AND PREDICT** As you take a **picture walk** through page 5, help children use inference skills and high-frequency vocabulary to predict what will happen.

**SET PURPOSES** Children can write or draw what they want to learn by reading *The Land*. For example: *I want to learn what kind of plants will grow on the land.*

**READ THE BOOK** Use questions like the following while children are reading or after they have read independently:

**Pages 2–3:** When is this part of the story happening—now or a long time ago? How can you tell? (Long ago; the children's dress) *Make Inferences*

**Pages 4–5:** Let's look for words with the long *a* sound spelled *ai*. (frail, rain) *Phonics and Decoding*

**Pages 6–7:** Where did the plants come from? (The seeds that were in the wind, the animals) *Make Inferences*

**Page 9:** Read the second sentence. What word helps you to know what light means? (sun.) *High-Frequency Words*

**Pages 12–13:** What happened to the smaller plants that needed a lot of sun? (They died.) *Make Inferences*

**Page 16:** Is this part of the story happening now, or long ago? (now) How can you tell? (children's dress) *Make Inferences*

**RETURN TO PREDICTIONS AND PURPOSES** Ask children to read their predictions and purposes aloud. Were they close in predicting what would happen?

**LITERARY RESPONSES** Discuss with children the following questions:

• How does the land in this story change?

• Have you ever seen a place change? How?

Also see the story questions and activity in the story, *The Land*.

**Answers to Story Questions**

1. Playing
2. The wind blew it.
3. Answers will vary.
4. Ray and Gail played on the land. They moved away. Seeds landed on the land and grew into plants and trees. Time went by, and bigger trees grew and took over the land. Now children hike on the land.
5. Both stories have trees in them.

**Story Questions and Writing Activity**

1. What are Ray and Gail doing on the land?
2. How did the seed get to the land?
3. Where did Ray and Gail move to?
4. Tell the story in your own words.
5. How are this story and *Johnny Appleseed* alike?

**Go On A Hike**

Find woods near your home.

Ask an adult to take you there.

Look around.

What kinds of things do you see?

Draw a picture about your hike.

*from The Land*

# Leveled Books

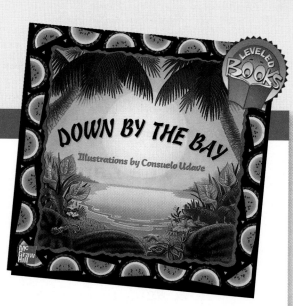

## AUTHENTIC

### Down By The Bay

- ☑  **Phonics** Long *a: ai, ay*
- ☑ **Make Inferences**

**ESL** Determine if children are familiar with the musical version of *Down by the Bay*. Then encourage children to use both the illustrations and rhymes to figure out unfamiliar words. After children are comfortable with the vocabulary and concepts, have them read the book independently.

**Answers to Story Questions**

1. Row a boat.
2. Make-believe
3. Answers will vary.
4. The story is about animals doing strange things down by the bay.
5. Both stories are about animals that someone thinks they see.

**Story Questions and Writing Activity**

1. What does the goat do?
2. Is this story real or make-believe?
3. What other funny animals might you see down by the bay?
4. What is this story about?
5. How is this story like *Walking Through the Jungle*?

**Make a Rhyme**

Make up a funny rhyme about an animal.

Draw a picture to go with the rhyme.

Share your picture with your class.

*from Down By The Bay*

# Guided Reading

**PREVIEW AND PREDICT** Take a **picture walk** up to page 10. Invite children to predict what other animals they might meet in the story. Have them record their ideas.

**READ THE BOOK** Use the following questions to guide children's reading or to ask after they have read the story **independently.**

**Pages 4–5:** What's the first word on this page that has the long *a* sound? *(bay)* What's the other word with the long *a* sound? *(say)* Which letters in both words make the long *a* sound? *(ay)* *Phonics and Decoding*

**Pages 7–10:** Where does the narrator call home? (the bay) Why can't the narrator go back to his home? (because of what the mother will say) *Plot*

**Pages 19–20:** Where did the dragon get the watermelons? (The dragon picked them down by the bay.) *Make Inferences*

**Pages 27–30:** Where did the dragon get the boat? (It was the goat's boat.) Why do you think he is in it alone? (Answers will vary.) *Make Inferences*

**RETURN TO PREDICTIONS AND PURPOSES** Ask children to read aloud their predictions. Were any of their animals in the story? Were they surprised by the ending?

**LITERARY RESPONSE** Have children discuss questions like the following:

- Which illustration did you like the best?
- Why? What part did you think was the funniest?

If you could add another verse to this song, what would it be?

Also see the story questions and activity in *Down By The Bay*.

See the **Phonics** CD-ROM for practice using long *a* words.

# Activities

## Anthology and Leveled Books

## Connecting Texts

**SETTING CHARTS**
Write the story titles on a chart. Discuss the different settings in the books, including what grows and what happens in each setting. Write the children's ideas in the charts. Afterwards, have children discuss what is the same and what is different about the books.

|  | Johnny Appleseed | Fall is Fun! | The Land | Down By The Bay |
|---|---|---|---|---|
| Setting | • Outdoors<br>• Out West | • Outdoors<br>• A farm | • Outdoors<br>• A field | • Outdoors<br>• A bay |
| What Grows | • Apple trees | • Pumpkins, grain, apples | • All different kinds of plants, including shrubs, grass and trees | • Watermelons |
| What Happens | • Johnny spreads apple seeds. Trees grow. | • Many different crops are harvested. | • Different things grow and change the land | • A lot of animals do silly things and then the dragon picks the watermelon |

## Viewing/Representing

**GROUP PRESENTATIONS** Divide the class into groups, one for each of the four books read in the lesson. (For *Johnny Appleseed,* combine children of different reading levels.) Provide the groups with old magazines, posterboard, art materials, seeds, twigs, and other natural objects. Have children make collages to represent their books. Afterwards, have each group display and explain their collages.

**AUDIENCE RESPONSE**
Encourage children to discuss and compare the contents of the various colleges.

## Research and Inquiry

**MORE ABOUT PLANTS** Have children ask themselves: What else would I like to know about plants and how they grow? Then help them to do the following:

• Look at books to find out more about plants.

• Take a nature walk and observe different plant close up.

• Grow plants in the classroom.

 Have children log on to the publisher's website for links to pages about plants.

 Children can write or draw what they learned in their journals.

## TESTED OBJECTIVES

Children will:

- review long *a: ay* and *ai*.
- blend and read words with long *a: ay* and *ai*.
- review consonants and blends

---

### MATERIALS

- **Teaching Chart 114**
- letter and vowel digraph cards from the **Word Building Manipulative Cards**

### SPELLING/PHONICS CONNECTIONS

Words with long *a: ay, ai:* See the 5-Day Spelling Plan, pages 133Q–133R.

---

### LANGUAGE SUPPORT

If children are having trouble hearing long *a*, give them a list of words and have them pick one or two and draw pictures of them in their journals. Examples: *mail, nail, tail, rain, bay, hay, train.*

### ALTERNATE TEACHING STRATEGY

**REVIEW LONG *a***

For a different approach to teaching this skill, see page T72.

---

# Review Long *a: ay, ai*

### PREPARE

**Listen for Long *a: ay, ai***

Read the following sentence aloud and ask children to clap when they hear a word with the long *a* sound spelled *ay* or *ai*.

- A ray of light showed on the rail.

### TEACH

**Review the Letters *ay, ai* as Spellings for Long *a***

- Tell children that they will review the letters *ay* and *ai* and the sound they make. Say /ā/. Ask children to repeat after you and write the letter combinations that stand for /ā/ as they say it.

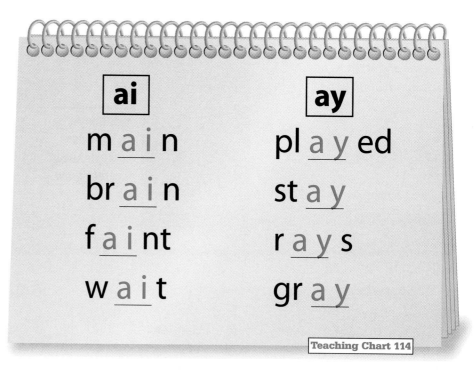

ai — m a i n, br a i n, f a i nt, w a i t

ay — pl a y ed, st a y, r a y s, gr a y

Teaching Chart 114

**BLENDING Model and Guide Practice with Long *a* Words**

- Display **Teaching Chart 114.** Point to the *ai* and *ay* at the top of the two columns.

- Write the letters *ai* in *raise* and *ay* in *played*. Track the letters with your hand and ask children to blend and read each word with you.

- Repeat, and ask children to read the words independently.

**Use the Word in Context**

- Invite volunteers to use each word in a sentence. Example: *Please raise your hand. We played a game.*

**Repeat the Procedure**

- Continue, asking volunteers to fill in the missing letters to complete the /ā/ words on the chart.

## PRACTICE

**BLENDING**
**Build Long *a: ay, ai* Words with Letter Cards**

PARTNERS

Children work in pairs. Give one child in each pair the *ay* letter card and give the partner the *ai* letter card. Ask them to choose other letter cards and build two words with their cards. Then have them exchange *ay* and *ai* cards and repeat the activity. Have them keep a list of the words they make.

## ASSESS/CLOSE

**Read and Use Long *a: ai, ay* Words in Sentences**

To assess children's mastery of blending and reading long *a: ai, ay* words, check the words they build in the Practice activity. Ask them to read some of the words from their lists. Then have them use the words in sentences.

### ADDITIONAL PHONICS RESOURCES

McGraw-Hill School
**TECHNOLOGY**

**Phonics/Phonemic Awareness Practice Books pages 155–158**

**Phonics CD-ROM**
activities for practice with **Blending and Segmenting**

DAILY **Phonics** ROUTINES

**DAY 4**
**Writing** Have children write long *a: ay* or *ai* words to complete rhymes. Examples: If it starts to rain, let's take the _____ (train). If you stay, we can _____ (play).

**Phonics** CD-ROM

## SELF-SELECTED Reading

Children may choose from the following titles.

**ANTHOLOGY**

- *Johnny Appleseed*

**LEVELED BOOKS**

- *Fall is Fun!*
- *The Land*
- *Down by the Bay*

Bibliography, pages T92–T93

# Meeting Individual Needs for Phonics

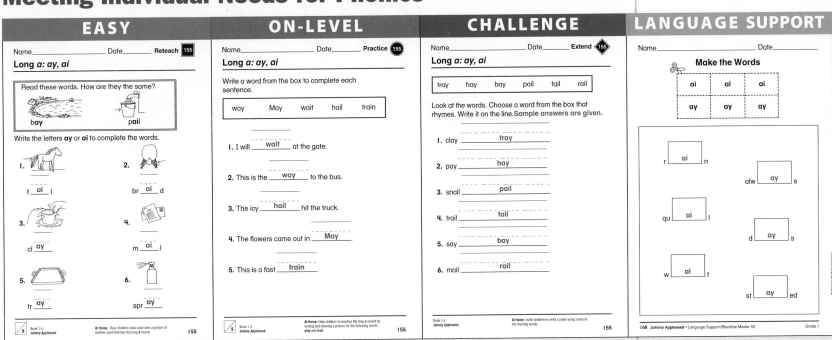

| EASY | ON-LEVEL | CHALLENGE | LANGUAGE SUPPORT |
|---|---|---|---|
| Reteach, 155 | Practice, 155 | Extend, 155 | Language Support, 168 |

## OBJECTIVES

**Children will:**

- review long *a: ai* and *ay.*
- blend and read long *a: ai* and *ay* words.
- review long *u: u-e* and long *o: o-e* words.

........................................

## MATERIALS

- **Teaching Chart 115**
- word building boxes from the **Word Building Manipulative Cards**

# Review *ai, ay; u-e, o-e*

**PREPARE**

**Identify the Letters *ai* and *ay* as Symbols for /ā/**

Identify the letters *ai* and *ay* as symbols for /ā/. Remind children that the letters *ai* and *ay* stand for the sound /ā/. Write the letters *ai* and *ay* on the chalkboard and say their sounds aloud.

**Discriminate Among *ai, ay; u-e,* and *o-e* Words**

Write the following words on the chalkboard: *main, rope, cute, tray.* Ask volunteers to read the words and identify the long vowel sound in each word.

**TEACH**

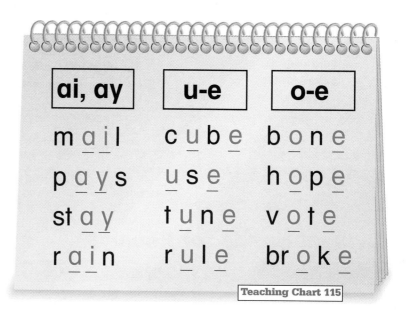

Teaching Chart 115

**BLENDING**
**Model and Guide Practice with Long *a: ai, ay, u-e,* and *o-e* Words**

- Display **Teaching Chart 115.** Point to the *ai, ay, u-e,* and *o-e* at the top of the three columns.
- Point to the first example on the chart and ask children which letters at the top of the column will make a word.
- Write the letters *ai* in the blanks and have children repeat after you as you blend the sounds and read the word *mail.*

**Use the Word in Context**

- Have children use the word in a sentence to reinforce its meaning. Example: *Please mail this letter.*

**Repeat the Procedure**

- Continue until the chart is complete, asking volunteers to fill in the blanks with *ai, ay, u-e,* or *o-e* to make words.

## PRACTICE

**BLENDING**
**Build and Sort ai, ay; u-e, o-e**

GROUP

Have children work in small groups. Ask them to build *ai, ay, u-e,* and *o-e* words using word building boxes. Have each group read their words and choose one word for each vowel combination to write on chart paper.

▶ **Linguistic/Visual**

## ASSESS/CLOSE

**Write a Story Using *ai, ay, u-e,* and *o-e* words**

Some children may need more reinforcement with *ai, ay, u-e* and *o-e* words. Have them write a short story (two to four sentences) using words displayed on the chart that the class created in the Practice activity. Continue to determine whether children need more practice with long vowels.

### ADDITIONAL PHONICS RESOURCES

McGraw-Hill School
**TECHNOLOGY**

**Phonics CD-ROM**

**Phonics/Phonemic Awareness Practice Book pages 153–158**

activities for practice with **Building and Sorting**

DAILY **Phonics** ROUTINES

**DAY 5**
**Blending** Write the spelling of each sound in *brain* as you say it. Have children repeat after you. Ask children to blend the sounds to read the word. Repeat with *raise, mail, tray, bay, clay.*

**Phonics CD-ROM**

## ALTERNATE TEACHING STRATEGY
..............................

**PHONICS: LONG** *a: ai, ay*
For a different approach to teaching this skill, see page T72.

---

# Meeting Individual Needs for Phonics

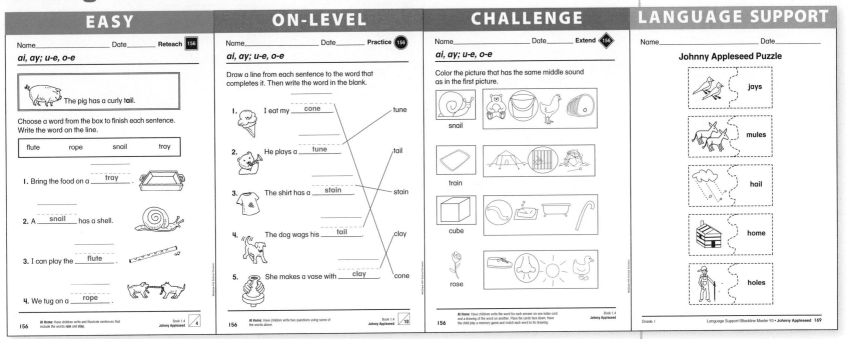

| EASY | ON-LEVEL | CHALLENGE | LANGUAGE SUPPORT |
|---|---|---|---|
| Reteach, 156 | Practice, 156 | Extend, 156 | Language Support, 169 |

**OBJECTIVES**

Children will make inferences based on words, pictures and what they already know.

......................................

**MATERIALS**

- **Teaching Chart 116**

---

**TEACHING TIP**

**MANAGEMENT** Find a few picture books without any text. Have students divide into groups to look at the pictures. Ask them to tell the story by discussing the pictures.

---

## Review Make Inferences

> **PREPARE**

**Introduce the Concept**

Tell children they can figure out things in a story by thinking about what they see in the pictures and about the words they read. They can also use what they already know to help them understand a story better. Explain that when readers use these clues they are making inferences.

> **TEACH**

**Make Inferences Using Words and Pictures**

Display **Teaching Chart 116**. Encourage children to look carefully at the pictures and think about the words as they read them.

It is too much!
The plant is sick.
It has too much water.

Joe wants a apple.
The tree is too tall.
Joe must get help.

My team is the best!
I feel great!
We won!

Teaching Chart 116

*MODEL* I can tell how the girl with the watering can is feeling by looking at her expression. She looks sad. I think she is sad because the plant does not look healthy. I see water around the plant, and I read the words *It is too much!* So I can figure out that the plant has been given too much water.

Ask children to help figure out the other pictures on the chart using picture and word clues. Have volunteers write a sentence with the class' inference for each example on **Teaching Chart 116**. Sample answers are given.

## PRACTICE

**Make Inferences Using Words and Pictures**

**PARTNERS**

Provide pairs of children with books and magazines and have them select a picture. Encourage partners to discuss what they can tell about the picture by looking at people's expressions and/or what they are doing with their bodies. They can think about their own experiences as well. Then have each pair write a few sentences that tell about their picture. Invite volunteers to share their sentences with the rest of the class. Encourage them to explain what clues they used to decide what the picture was about.

▶ **Visual/Linguistic**

## ASSESS/CLOSE

**Create Pictures and Captions**

Form small groups. Ask children to draw a picture that tells a story—a picture in which something is happening. Then have groups trade pictures, and let each group create a caption for another group's picture. Discuss with the groups how correct their inferences were.

### ALTERNATE TEACHING STRATEGY

**MAKE INFERENCES**
For a different approach to teaching this skill, see page T70.

**LOOKING AHEAD**
Children will apply this skill as they read the next selection, *Ring! Ring! Ring! Put Out the Fire!*

# Meeting Individual Needs for Comprehension

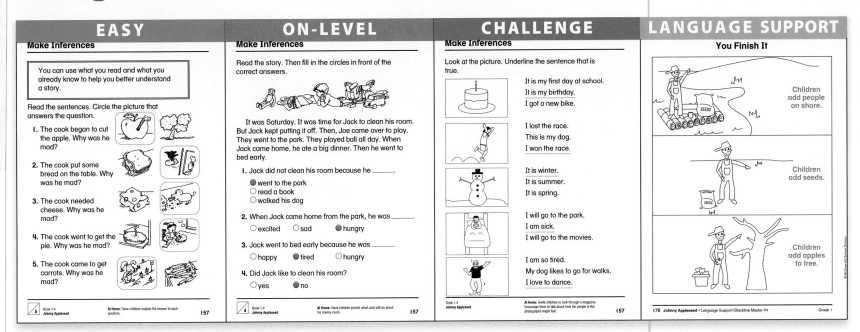

| EASY | ON-LEVEL | CHALLENGE | LANGUAGE SUPPORT |
|---|---|---|---|
| Reteach, 157 | Practice, 157 | Extend, 157 | Language Support, 170 |

OBJECTIVES

Children will read words with the comparative endings -er and -est.

**MATERIALS**

- **Teaching Chart 117**
- index cards

---

**TEACHING TIP**

**INSTRUCTIONAL** Point out to the class that the -er ending is used when comparing two objects, while -est words are used when comparing three or more. Ask questions to illustrate this: *Who has the bigger chair, Ted or the teacher? Who is the tallest person in the room?*

---

# Review Inflectional Endings -er, -est

**PREPARE**

**Introduce the Concept** Write the word *fast* on the chalkboard. Ask a volunteer to clap his or her hands. Tell the class that the volunteer is clapping fast. Then have another volunteer clap faster. Elicit that the second volunteer is clapping faster. Then begin clapping even faster. Ask children to describe how you are clapping compared to the others. *(fastest)*

**TEACH**

**Identify Base Words** Track the first sentence on **Teaching Chart 117** as you read it with children: *Whose hair is longer?* Point to the word *longer* and ask children if they recognize part of the word. *(long)* Then model the skill.

Whose hair is longer? Which boy is the tallest?

Which bird is shorter? Who has the cleanest shirt?

Teaching Chart 117

**MODEL** I know the word *long.* I can see the last two letters of the word are *-er.* I know that sometimes when these two letters appear together at the end of a word it means "more." The word is *longer,* which means "more long."

Repeat for the other three sentences. Invite volunteers to underline the base words, and to point to the pictures that answer the questions.

## PRACTICE

**Read -er, -est**

PARTNERS

Write the words *thicker, cleanest, darkest, lighter, longer,* and *smartest* on the chalkboard. Have children read the words, identifying the base word in each. On blank index cards, have children write each word so that the ending *-er* or *-est* appears after a dotted line. Put the cards in a pile. Have each pair of children draw a card. One partner reads the word and the other uses the word in a sentence..

▶ **Linguistic/Visual**

## ASSESS/CLOSE

**Use the Words in Context**

Invite pairs of children to make up stories using the index cards in the Practice activity. Have children tell their stories to the class or to act them out. Have them call on classmates to identify the base words.

### ALTERNATE TEACHING STRATEGY

Inflectional
**ENDINGS-*er*, -*est***

For a different approach to teaching this skill, see page T71.

# Meeting Individual Needs for Vocabulary

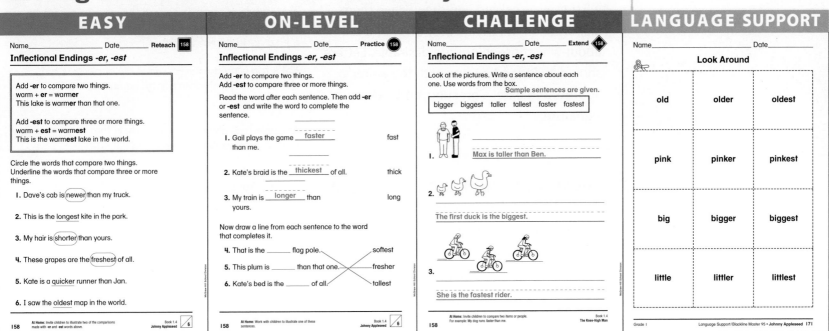

**Reteach, 158**          **Practice, 158**          **Extend, 158**          Language Support, 171

**123L**

# Persuasive Writing

## Prewrite

**WRITE A LETTER** Present this writing assignment: Pretend you are Johnny. Write a letter to a settler friend convincing him or her to plant apple seeds. Give good reasons, and use descriptive language.

**BRAINSTORM IDEAS** Have children brainstorm ideas about what apple trees are good for. Encourage them to "think" with their tongues and noses and eyes.

**Strategy: Visualize and Draw** Have children draw different things an apple tree might be good for. Suggest the following:

- Think of what you can do with apples.
- Think of what a house looks like with a pretty tree in front of it.

## Draft

**USE THE DRAWING** In their letters, have children write full sentences that refer to what they visualized and drew. Have them elaborate on the things they drew and tell about why those things are desirable. Letters should include a heading with the writer's address and date, a greeting, and a closing signature.

## Revise

**CREATING A CHECKLIST** Ask children if they remembered to put in all the reasons why an apple tree would be good to have. Suggest they create a checklist showing:

- foods to make with apples.
- why a tree looks and feels good.
- other things that would be nice about having a tree.

**GROUP** Have children pretend they're settlers. Have them read each other's letters and talk about which ideas they like.

## Edit/Proofread

**CHECK FOR ERRORS** Children should reread their letters for spelling, grammar, punctuation, and letter format.

## Publish

**SHARE THE LETTERS** Children can "mail" their letters to one another. Encourage the recipients to tell the writers why they did or did not decide to plant apple trees.

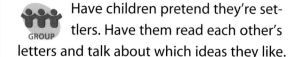

> Johnny Appleseed
> Somewhere in the West
> USA
> May 5, 20___
>
> Dear Bob,
>
> Here are some apple seeds. I hope you will plant trees.
>
> Apple trees are good because they give us apples to eat. You can also use apples to make pie and jam and even a good drink.
>
> If it's too hot, you can go under the apple tree for shade. And the children can go up and down the tree for fun.
>
> An apple tree always looks pretty in the yard. It is nice to look at to make you feel good when you are sad.
>
> Your Friend,
> Johnny Appleseed

## Presentation Ideas

**MAKE AN APPLE TREE** Have children cut out the trunk of a tree from dark paper. They can then tape or glue on branches using a lighter paper. Finally, have them paste colorful leaves and apples on the branches.

▶ **Viewing/Representing**

**TALK ABOUT APPLES** Have children imagine that they meet a Martian, who has never seen or tasted an apple before.

Encourage them to describe an apple to their new acquaintance.

▶ **Speaking/Listening**

Consider students' creative efforts, possibly adding a plus (+) for originality, wit, and imagination.

### Scoring Rubric

| Excellent | Good | Fair | Unsatisfactory |
|---|---|---|---|
| **4:** The writer<br>• clearly writes in full sentences and uses vivid descriptions.<br>• gives several convincing reasons why apple trees would be good to have.<br>• goes beyond the material in the story, improvising original ideas. | **3:** The writer<br>• writes in full sentences, and attempts some description.<br>• gives some good reasons why apple trees would be good to have.<br>• effectively uses much of the material from the story. | **2:** The writer<br>• may not always use full sentences, or may not attempt to describe.<br>• gives only one or two reasons why apple trees would be good to have<br>• may not effectively use material from the story. | **1:** The writer<br>• may not always use full sentences.<br>• may not grasp the task to persuade.<br>• may not respond to material from the story |

**0:** The writer leaves the page blank or fails to respond to the writing task. The student does not address the topic or simply paraphrases the prompt. The response is illegible or incoherent.

## Meeting Individual Needs for Writing

### EASY

**Draw Contrasting Scenes** Ask children to draw a picture of a settlement without apple trees, and then another one of the same settlement with apple trees. Have them write a few simple sentences under the second picture telling why the settlement is better off with its trees.

### ON-LEVEL

**Write a Handbook** Have children write a simple handbook for people who have new apple trees. The handbook should tell the people what they can do with their trees.

### CHALLENGE

**Make a Journal Entry** Have children make up an adventure that Johnny Appleseed has while he's walking through the West giving out his apple seeds. Apples, apple trees, or apple seeds should be featured prominently in the adventure.

**COMMUNICATION TIPS**

**VIEWING** Have children close their eyes and visualize what a tree looks like. How are the branches attached? How are the leaves attached? Where do the flowers or the fruit go?

**SPEAKING** Encourage the children to speak slowly and clearly. Martians don't understand English very well!

**LANGUAGE SUPPORT**

**ESL** ESL children may have trouble coming up with the names of foods made from apples. Have them work with a fluent partner to describe a special fruit tree from their own culture.

**PORTFOLIO** Invite children to include their letters from Johnny Appleseed in their portfolios.

# 5 Day Grammar and Usage Plan

**ESL** Point to an object in the classroom and say, "I see a chair. I see a desk." Then ask, "What did I see?" Guide children to respond, "You saw a chair. You saw a desk."

## DAILY LANGUAGE ACTIVITIES

Write the Daily Language Activities on the chalkboard each day or use **Transparency 4**. Have children correct the sentences orally, using the past tense of *see* or *say*.

### Day 1

**1.** Johnny sees the tree yesterday. saw

**2.** Before, he sees a bird. saw

**3.** Johnny sees the town later. saw

### Day 2

**1.** Last week Johnny says, "Plant this." said

**2.** Later, he says, "I have a plan." said

**3.** After, he says, "Life is good!" said

### Day 3

**1.** Last night they see the river. saw

**2.** The men say they took the seeds. said

**3.** Finally Johnny sees the sun. saw

### Day 4

**1.** Yesterday I say hello to Johnny. said

**2.** We see him early. saw

**3.** Last night Johnny says, "Seeds grow into trees." said

### Day 5

**1.** Last year Johnny sees an old horse. saw

**2.** Later, Johnny says good-bye. said

**3.** I see Johnny this morning. saw

*Daily Language Transparency 4*

---

## DAY 1 — Introduce the Concept

**Oral Warm-Up** Ask children, "Yesterday, what did you see?" Write children's responses on the chalkboard and circle the word *saw* in each sentence.

**Introduce See** Remind children that a verb is a word that shows action. Discuss with children:

> ### See
> - The verb *see* has a special form to tell about the past.
> - Use *see* or *sees* to tell about something that happens in the present.
> - Use *saw* to tell about something that happened in the past.

Present the Daily Language Activity and have children correct the sentences orally. Then have them write their own sentences using *see* and *saw*.

 **WRITING** Assign the daily Writing Prompt on page 96C.

---

Name_____ Date_____ LEARN AND PRACTICE **GRAMMAR** 116

**See and Say**

- The verb *say* has a special form to tell about the past.
- Use *say* and *says* to tell about the present.
- Use *said* to tell about something that happened in the past.
  I **say** something.    He **said** something.

Write the underlined verb so that it tells about the past.

I. Johnny says the ham was good.    said

2. He says he would rest.    said

3. He says the sun was up.    said

4. He says "I'm Johnny."    said

5. They say, "Hello, Johnny."    said

116    Book 1.4 Johnny Appleseed    5

**GRAMMAR PRACTICE BOOK, PAGE 116**

---

## DAY 2 — Teach the Concept

**Review See** Write on the chalkboard: *Meg sees a cat.* Then ask children to change the sentence to begin with *Yesterday.* (*Yesterday Meg saw a cat.*)

**Introduce Say** Read aloud the following sentence: *Today Pam says yes.* Then ask children to change the sentence to begin with *Yesterday.* (*Yesterday Pam said yes.*)

> ### Say
> - The verb *say* has a special form to tell about the past.
> - Use *say* or *says* to tell about something that happens in the present.
> - Use *said* to tell about something that happened in the past.

Present the Daily Language Activity. Then have children write their own sentences, using *say* and *said*.

 **WRITING** Assign the daily Writing Prompt on page 96C.

---

Name_____ Date_____ PRACTICE AND WRITE **GRAMMAR** 117

**See and Say**

- Use *see* or *sees* to tell about the present.
  We **see** pink flowers.
- Use *saw* to tell about something that happened in the past.
  We **saw** pink buds.

Circle the word that makes each sentence tell about the past.

1. Johnny (saw, see, sees) a wolf in a trap.

2. One day, he (saw, see, sees) an old horse.

3. People (saw, see, sees) his pets.

Circle the word that makes each sentence tell about the present.

4. Johnny (saw, see, sees) many plants.

5. He could (saw, see, sees) rain.

6. He (saw, see, sees) many people.

6    Book 1.4 Johnny Appleseed    EXTENSION: Have the children write present or past tense sentences about seeing apples.    117

**GRAMMAR PRACTICE BOOK, PAGE 117**

---

# See and *Say*

## DAY 3 — Review and Practice

**Learn from the Literature** Review *see* and *say* with children. Read the following sentence from page 104 of *Johnny Appleseed*:

> **"Quick! Plant my apple seeds," he said to those who were on the banks.**

Emphasize the word *said*. Ask children whether the sentence tells about the past or tells about the present. (tells about the past)

**Use *See* and *Say*** Present the Daily Language Activity and have children correct orally.

Ask children to write sentences using *see* and *say*. Then have children exchange papers with partners and rewrite the sentences, beginning them with *Yesterday*. For example: *I see a van. Yesterday I saw a van.*

 **WRITING** Assign the daily Writing Prompt on page 96D.

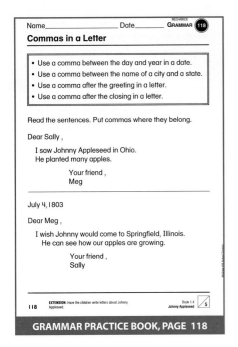

**GRAMMAR PRACTICE BOOK, PAGE 118**

## DAY 4 — Review and Practice

**Review *See* and *Say*** Write the following sentence on the chalkboard: *Yesterday Johnny sees an apple tree.* Ask children if the sentence is correct. (no) Why not? (The verb should be *saw*.) Why? (because it happened in the past) Correct the sentence on the chalkboard, then present the Daily Language Activity for Day 4.

**Mechanics and Usage** Before children begin the daily Writing Prompt on page 96D, review commas. Display and discuss:

### Commas

- Use a comma between the day and year in a date.
- Use a comma between the name of a city and a state.
- Use a comma after the greeting in a letter.
- Use a comma after the closing in a letter.

 **WRITING** Assign the daily Writing Prompt on page 96D.

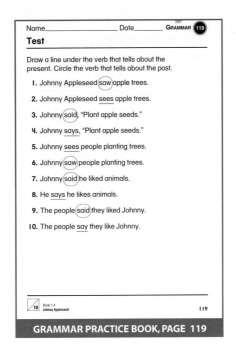

**GRAMMAR PRACTICE BOOK, PAGE 119**

## DAY 5 — Assess and Reteach

**Assess** Use the Daily Language Activity and page 120 of the **Grammar Practice Book** for assessment.

**Reteach** Write *Today* and *Yesterday* on the chalkboard. Then write the following sentences on paper strips: *I saw a big dog. She sees the movie. The boys saw the bike. We say yes. He gave a speech. Nick said nothing.* Read the sentences aloud and ask whether each tells about the past or the present. Have children take turns placing the sentences under the appropriate column on the board.

Have children create a classroom word wall with sentences using *say* and *see*.

Use page 121 of the **Grammar Practice Book** for additional reteaching.

 **WRITING** Assign the daily Writing Prompt on page 96D.

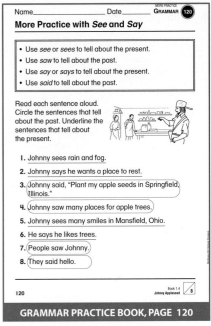

**GRAMMAR PRACTICE BOOK, PAGE 120**

**GRAMMAR PRACTICE BOOK, PAGE 121**

**123P**

# 5 Day Spelling Plan

## LANGUAGE SUPPORT

**ESL** Children whose native language is not English may have difficulty with long *a*. In Spanish, for instance, the sound for long *a* is represented by the vowel *e*. For those children who do have difficulty, present the following sentence. Read it with the children, then have them come to the chalkboard and underline *ai* and *ay* in the long *a* words: *I must wait for the rain to stop before I can play today.*

## DICTATION SENTENCES

### Spelling Words

1. I have a hat for the rain.
2. Can you wait for me?
3. Is this the way to go?
4. Do you know what day it is?
5. What could you say?
6. That cat has a small tail.

### Challenge Words

7. How big you are!
8. The sun gives us light.
9. Where do you live?
10. What a pretty dress that is!

---

## DAY 1 — Pretest

**Assess Prior Knowledge** Use the Dictation Sentences at left and **Spelling Practice Book** page 115 for the pretest. Allow children to correct their own papers. If children have trouble, have partners give each other a midweek test on Day 3.

| Spelling Words | | Challenge Words |
|---|---|---|
| 1. **rain** | 4. **day** | 7. **how** |
| 2. **wait** | 5. say | 8. **light** |
| 3. **way** | 6. tail | 9. **live** |
| | | 10. **pretty** |

*Note: Words in **dark type** are from the story.*

**Word Study** On page 116 of the **Spelling Practice Book** are word study steps and an at-home activity.

---

## DAY 2 — Explore the Pattern

**Sort and Spell Words** Say the words *way* and *rain*. Ask children what vowel sound they hear in each word. (long *a*) Write the words on the chalkboard and circle the letters that spell long *a*.

| Words with long *a* spelled | |
|---|---|
| ***ay*** | ***ai*** |
| way | rain |
| day | wait |
| say | tail |

**Word Wall** As children read other stories and texts, have them look for new words with long *a* spelled *ay* or *ai*. Add them to a classroom word wall, underlining the *ay* or *ai* in each word.

---

*(Spelling Practice Book worksheet, page 115)*

Name_____ Date_____ PRETEST SPELLING **115**

**Words with Long a: ai, ay**

**Pretest Directions**
Fold back the paper along the dotted line. Use the blanks to write each word as it is read aloud. When you finish the test, unfold the paper. Use the list at the right to correct any spelling mistakes. Practice the words you missed for the Posttest.

1. _____ 1. rain
2. _____ 2. wait
3. _____ 3. way
4. _____ 4. day
5. _____ 5. say
6. _____ 6. tail

**To Parents**
Here are the results of your child's weekly spelling Pretest. You can help your child study for the Posttest by following these simple steps for each word on the list:
1. Read the word to your child.
2. Have your child write the word, saying each letter as it is written.
3. Have your child check the spelling. If the word is not spelled correctly, have your child read each letter of the correctly spelled word aloud, and then repeat steps 1-3.

Challenge Words
_____ how
_____ light
_____ live
_____ pretty

Book 1.4
Johnny Appleseed    115

**SPELLING PRACTICE BOOK, PAGE 115**

WORD STUDY STEPS AND ACTIVITY, PAGE 116

---

*(Spelling Practice Book worksheet, page 117)*

Name_____ Date_____ EXPLORE THE PATTERN SPELLING **117**

**Words with Long a : ai-ay**

Read the words. Circle the letters that are the same in each set of words.

1. rain    tail    wait
2. day    say    way

Write the letters that complete each spelling word.

3. r___ai___n    4. w___ai___
5. w___ay___    6. d___ay___
7. s___ay___    8. t___ai___l

Read the rhyme. Circle the words that have the long a sound as in may.

I wait in the rain on a school day,
Hoping the bus will come my way.

Write the words you circled that have the long a spelled ay.

9. __day__    10. __way__

Write the words you circled that have the long a spelled ai.

11. __wait__    12. __rain__

Book 1.4
Johnny Appleseed    117

**SPELLING PRACTICE BOOK, PAGE 117**

# Words with Long *a: ai, ay*

**Word Meaning: Synonyms** Remind children that synonyms are words that mean the same, or nearly the same, thing. For example, *big* and *large* are synonyms. Ask children to think of a synonym for *say*. *(tell)* Then remind children that synonyms for some words are given in the Glossary. Have children look up the words *bag, jars,* and *rocket* in the Glossary and find their synonyms. Have children match the following synonyms:

| rock | also |
|------|------|
| little | stone |
| too | small |

(rock/stone; little/small; too/also)

**Identify Spelling Patterns** Write this sentence on the chalkboard: *How long will we wait for the rain?* Have a volunteer read it aloud. Ask children to tell which words have the spelling pattern *ai* and which is the Challenge Word. Repeat with the spelling pattern *ay* using these sentences: *This is the way to live. The cat had a pretty tail.* Then have children write sentences using the Challenge Words.

**Proofread Sentences** Write these sentences on the chalkboard, including the misspelled words. Ask children to proofread, circling incorrect spellings and writing the correct spellings. There are two errors in each sentence.

> Did you (sae) you like the (rane?) (say, rain)
>
> I cannot (wate) for that (dai.) (wait, day)
>
> That cat's (tayl) is (wai) too big. (tail, way)

Have students create additional sentences with errors for partners to correct.

 Have students use as many Spelling Words as possible in **WRITING** the daily Writing Prompt on page 96D. Remind students to proofread their writing for errors in spelling, grammar, and punctuation.

**Assess Children's Knowledge** Use page 120 of the **Spelling Practice Book** or the Dictation Sentences on page 123Q for the posttest.

**Personal Word List** If children have trouble with any words in the lesson, have them add them to a personal list of troublesome words in their journals. Have children write a sentence using as many of the Spelling Words as they can.

Children should refer to their word lists during later writing activities.

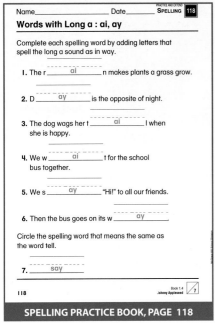

---

**SPELLING PRACTICE BOOK, PAGE 118**

Name_____ Date_____ SPELLING 118
**Words with Long a : ai, ay**

Complete each spelling word by adding letters that spell the long a sound as in way.

1. The r___ai___n makes plants a grass grow.

2. D___ay___ is the opposite of night.

3. The dog wags her t___ai___l when she is happy.

4. We w___ai___t for the school bus together.

5. We s___ay___ "Hi!" to all our friends.

6. Then the bus goes on its w___ay___

Circle the spelling word that means the same as the word tell.

7. ___say___

---

**SPELLING PRACTICE BOOK, PAGE 119**

Name_____ Date_____ SPELLING 119
**Words with Long a: ai, ay**

Read the poem. There are five spelling mistakes. Circle the mistakes. Write the words correctly on the lines.

Johnny Appleseed spent each (dae)
Giving apple seeds away.
"Plant these seeds," he would (sai)
"And apple trees will line your (wey)
Plant these seeds, Jack and Jane,
And then just (wate) for the (raine)."

1. ___day___  2. ___say___
3. ___way___  4. ___wait___
5. ___rain___

Johnny planted apples. What would you plant? Write a poem or story. Use three spelling words.

---

**SPELLING PRACTICE BOOK, PAGE 120**

Name_____ Date_____ SPELLING 120
**Words with Long a: ai, ay**

Look at the words in each set. One word in each set is spelled correctly. Use a pencil to color in the circle in front of that word. Before you begin, look at the sample sets of words. Sample A has been done for you. Do Sample B by yourself. When you are sure you know what to do, you may go on with the rest of the page.

| Sample A | Sample B |
|----------|----------|
| (A) nail | (D) rool |
| (B) nale | (E) rule |
| (C) nayl | (F) roul |

| 1. (A) say | 4. (D) dae |
| (B) sae | (E) daye |
| (C) saye | (F) day |

| 2. (D) wate | 5. (A) raine |
| (E) wayt | (B) rain |
| (F) wait | (C) rayn |

| 3. (A) way | 6. (D) tayl |
| (B) waye | (E) tail |
| (C) wae | (F) taile |

**123R**

# Ring! Ring! Ring! Put Out the Fire!

**Selection Summary** Children will be reading about firefighters and the work they do. They will learn about fire trucks, ladders, hoses, and water pumps.

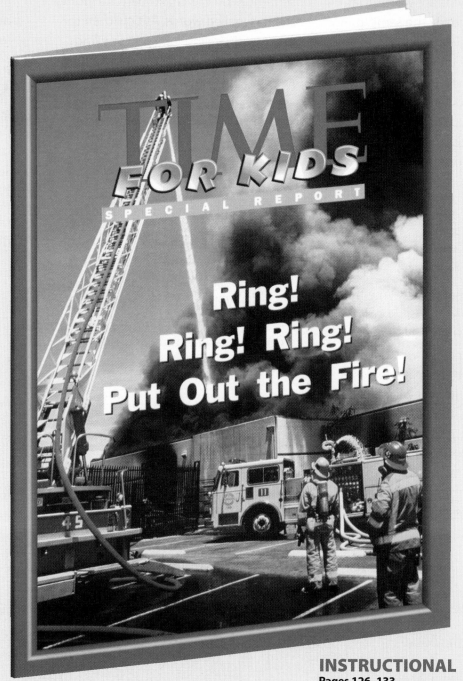

**Student Listening Library Audiocassette**

**INSTRUCTIONAL**
Pages 126–133

# Resources for Meeting Individual Needs

## LEVELED BOOKS

### EASY
**Pages 133A, 133D**

`DECODABLE`

### INDEPENDENT
**Pages 133B, 133D**

🏠 *Take-Home version available*

### AUTHENTIC
**Pages 133C, 133D**

## LEVELED PRACTICE

**Reteach, 159–166**

blackline masters with reteaching
opportunities for each assessed skill

**Practice, 159–166**

workbook with Take-Home Stories and
practice opportunities for each assessed
skill and story comprehension

**Extend, 159–166**

blackline masters that offer challenge
activities for each assessed skill

## ADDITIONAL RESOURCES

- **Language Support Book** 172–180
- **Take-Home Story, Practice** pp. 160a–160b
- **Alternate Teaching Strategies** T64–T72

McGraw-Hill School
**TECHNOLOGY**

**Phonics CD-ROM** provides extra
phonics support.

**interNET CONNECTION** Research & Inquiry ideas. Visit
***www.mhschool.com/reading.***

# Suggested Lesson Planner

  **Available on CD-ROM**

| READING AND LANGUAGE ARTS |  DAY **1** *Focus on Reading and Skills* | DAY **2** *Read the Literature* |
|---|---|---|
| ● **Phonics** *Daily Routines* | Daily  Routine: **Segmenting,** 126B <br><br>  **CD-ROM** | Daily  Routines: **Blending,** 126C <br><br>  **CD-ROM** |
| ● **Phonological Awareness** <br><br> ● **Phonics** *Review* <br><br> ● **Comprehension** <br><br> ● **Vocabulary** <br><br> ● **Study Skills** <br><br> ● **Listening, Speaking, Viewing, Representing** |  **Read Aloud and Motivate,** 124E <br>*The Brave Ones* <br><br> **Develop Phonological Awareness,** 124/125 <br> Review <br> *Fire Pups* <br><br>  **Review** *ai, ay; u-e, o-e, i-e, a-e,* 126A–126B <br> **Teaching Chart 118** <br> **Reteach, Practice, Extend,** 159 <br> Phonics Workbook, 155–158 | **Build Background,** 126C <br> Develop Oral Language <br><br> **Vocabulary,** 126D <br><br> | **always**  **work**  **clean** <br> **done**  **how** | <br> **Vocabulary Cards** <br> **Teaching Chart 119** <br> **Reteach, Practice, Extend,** 160 <br><br>  **Read the Selection,** 126–129 <br> Guided Reading <br> ☑ Cumulative Review <br> ☑ Make Inferences |
| ● **Curriculum Connections** |  Language Arts, 124E |  Science, 126C |
| ● **Writing** |  **Writing Prompt:** Write some rules about fires. |  **Writing Prompt:** Write about the difference between a fire truck and a bus. Why can't a bus help put out a fire? <br><br> 📓 **Journal Writing** <br> Quick-Write, 129 |
| ● **Grammar** | **Introduce the Concept: More Contractions with** *Not,* 133O <br> Daily Language Activity: Write contractions correctly. <br> **Grammar Practice Book,** 121 | **Teach the Concept: More Contractions with** *Not,* 133O <br> Daily Language Activity: Write contractions correctly. <br> **Grammar Practice Book,** 122 |
| ● **Spelling** *Words from Social Studies* | **Pretest: Words from Social Studies,** 133Q <br><br> **Spelling Practice Book,** 121, 122 | **Explore the Pattern: Words from Social Studies,** 133Q <br><br> **Spelling Practice Book,** 123 |

**DAY 3** *Read the Literature*

**DAY 4** *Build Skills*

**DAY 5** *Build and Review Skills*

---

Daily  Routine:
Fluency, 131

 CD-ROM

Daily  Routine:
Writing, 133F

 CD-ROM

Daily Phonics Routine:
Letter Substitution, 133H

Phonics CD-ROM

---

**Reread for Fluency,** 128

**Story Questions,** 130
Reteach, Practice, Extend, 161

**Story Activities,** 131

**Study Skill,** 132
☑ **Charts**
**Teaching Chart 121**
Reteach, Practice, Extend, 162

**Test Power,** 133

**Read the Leveled Books,**
Guided Reading
☑ Cumulative Review
☑ Make Inferences
☑ High-Frequency Words

 **Read Self-Selected Books**

☑ **Review Cause and Effect,** 133E–133F
**Teaching Chart 121**
Reteach, Practice, Extend, 163
Language Support, 177

☑ **Review Make Inferences,** 133G–133H
**Teaching Chart 122**
Reteach, Practice, Extend, 164
Language Support, 178

 **Read Self-Selected Books**

☑ **Review Inflectional Endings -ed, -s, -es,** 133–133J
**Teaching Chart 123**
Reteach, Practice, Extend, 165
Language Support, 179

☑ **Review Inflectional Endings -er, est,** 133K–133L
**Teaching Chart 124**
Reteach, Practice, Extend, 166
Language Support, 180

**Listening, Speaking, Viewing, Representing,** 133N

---

 **Writing Prompt:** Write about some things we wouldn't be able to do without fire.

**Journal Writing,** 133D

 **Writing Prompt:** Write a funny story about a fire fighter who can't slide down the pole in the fire house.

**Persuasive Writing,** 133M
Prewrite , Draft

**Meeting Individual Needs for Writing,** 133N

**Writing Prompt:** Write a letter to an aunt or uncle who isn't careful about fire. Tell them what you think.

**Persuasive Writing,** 133M
Revise, Edit, Proofread, Publish

---

**Review and Practice: More Contractions with *Not*,** 133P
Daily Language Activity: Write contractions correctly.

**Grammar Practice Book,** 123

**Review and Practice: More Contractions with *Not*,** 133P
Daily Language Activity: Write contractions correctly.

**Grammar Practice Book,** 124

**Assess and Reteach: More Contractions with *Not*,** 133P
Daily Language Activity: Write contractions correctly.

**Grammar Practice Book,** 125, 126

---

**Practice and Extend: Words from Social Studies,** 133R

**Spelling Practice Book,** 124

**Proofread and Write: Words from Social Studies,** 133R

**Spelling Practice Book,** 125

**Assess and Reteach: Words from Social Studies,** 133R

**Spelling Practice Book,** 126

**Language Arts**

# Read Aloud and Motivate

## The Brave Ones

a poem by
Eloise Greenfield

We hear the bell clanging

we come in a hurry

we come with our ladders and hoses

our hoses

we come in a hurry

to fight the fire

the furious fire

to smother the smoke

the smoke

we don't have much time

we climb, we spray

we are the brave ones who save

who save

we are the brave ones who save

## Oral Comprehension

**LISTENING AND SPEAKING** Motivate children to think about why a poet repeats words and phrases by reading this poem about firefighters. Ask children to listen for words, word pairs, and sentences that are repeated as you read the poem. When you are done, ask, "What are some words that are repeated during the poem?" Then point out repeated word pairs and phrases such as *we come in a hurry*, *the smoke*, and *we are the brave ones who save*. Ask children why the poet might have repeated those words.

**Activity** Ask children to act out the situation described in "The Brave Ones." When you ring a bell, volunteers will pretend to be firefighters responding to the fire. Ask children to mime driving to the fire, climbing, and spraying water.

▶ **Kinesthetic/Auditory**

# Develop **Phonological Awareness**

**Anthology pages 124-125**

### Fire Pup

I'm a little fire pup. My name is Spot.
You can ask for me when things get
   very hot.

If you see a fire and if you need
   a water hose,
I'll use my fast fire truck and bring you
   one of those.

Is there a trail of smoke or a bit
   of flame?
Anytime day or night, just yell out
   my name!

124    125

## Objective: Listen for Long *a, i,* and *o*

**RHYMING**  Read the "Fire Pup." As you reread the poem, have children clap when they hear words that rhyme with *tame*.
Repeat with **close**.

**Phonemic Awareness**  **BLENDING**  Write the spelling of each sound in *fire* as you say it. Have children repeat after you. Ask children to blend the sounds to read the word.

Repeat with **name, trail, smoke,** and **those.**

**Phonemic Awareness**  **SEGMENTING**  Have children segment initial and final sounds.

• Say the word *trail*.
• Say *trail* again without the /l/.
• Say *trail* again without the /tr/.

Repeat with **flame, hose,** and **fire.**

**124/125**

**Build Skills**

**PHONICS AND DECODING**

## Review *ai, ay;* *u-e, o-e, i-e, a-e*

### OBJECTIVES

**Children will:**

- review long u: *u-e;* o: *o-e;* i: *i-e;* a: *a-e;* a: *ai, ay* words.
- blend and read long u: *u-e;* o: *o-e;* i: *i-e;* a: *a-e;* a: *ai, ay* words.

.....................................

### MATERIALS

- **Teaching Chart 116**
- letter cards and word building boxes from the **Word Building Manipulative Cards**
- index cards

### SPELLING/PHONICS CONNECTIONS

Words with long u: *u-e;* o: *o-e;* i: *i-e;* a: *a-e;* a: *ai, ay*: See the 5-Day Spelling Plan, pages 133Q–133R.

### ALTERNATE TEACHING STRATEGY

**PHONICS: LONG *u, o, i, a.***
For a different approach to teaching these skills, see pages T64, T68, T69, and T72.

---

### TEACHING TIP

**INSTRUCTIONAL** Point out to children that the long *a* sound can be spelled three ways: *ai, ay, and a-e.*

---

**126A** *Put Out the Fire*

---

**PREPARE**

**Identify the Patterns *u-e, o-e, i-e, a-e,* and *ai, ay* as Symbols for /ū/, /ō/, /ī/, and /ā/.**

Remind children that they have learned to read words with the vowel-consonant-silent *e* pattern for long *u, o, i,* and *a*. They have also learned that *ai* and *ay* make the long *a* sound. Display the letter cards for the long vowels, and ask children to make each long vowel sound as you point to the card.

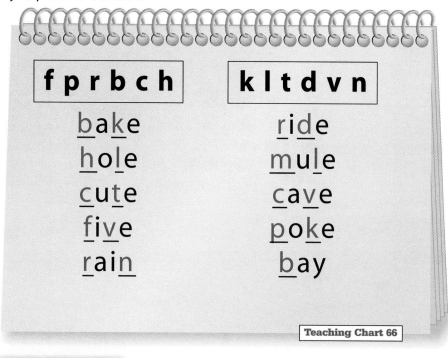

Teaching Chart 66

**TEACH**

**BLENDING Model and Guide Practice with *u-e, o-e, i-e, a-e, ai, ay***

- Display **Teaching Chart 116**. Run your hand under the letters *a-e* in the first item and say the sound /ā/.
- Write the letter *k* in the blank space between the letters *a-e*. Write the letter *b* in the first blank space. Blend all the sounds together to say the word *bake*. b͝ake → bake Explain to children that they can build long *u, o, i,* and *a* words by choosing a letter from the second letter bank to fit between the letters *u-e, o-e, i-e,* and *a-e*, and then choosing a letter from the first letter bank to complete the word.

**Use the Words in Context**

Have children use the word in a sentence to reinforce its meaning. Example: *I like to bake cakes.*

**Repeat the Procedure**

Repeat the procedure with the remaining words on the chart.

## PRACTICE

**LETTER SUBSTITUTION**
**Build Long** *u: u-e;*
*o: o-e; i: i-e; a: a-e;*
*a: ai, ay* **Words**

**PARTNERS**

Build the word *rate*, asking children to repeat after you. Change the word to *late* by replacing the *r* with *l*. Next, ask pairs of children to build and write the following words: *pure; cure; time; lime; main; may; rode; code.* ▶ **Linguistic/Kinesthetic**

## ASSESS/CLOSE

**Build and Read**
**Long** *u: u-e; o: o-e;*
*i: i-e; a: a-e; a: ai,*
*ay* **Words**

To assess children's ability to blend and read CVCe and double-vowel pattern words, observe children as they build words in the Practice activity. Ask children to read the words they have written.

## ADDITIONAL PHONICS RESOURCES

**Phonics/Phonemic Awareness Practice Book pages 155–158**

*McGraw-Hill School* **TECHNOLOGY**

**PHONICS KIT** Hands-on Activities and Practice

**Phonics CD-ROM** activities for practice with Blending and Segmenting

## Daily Routines

**DAY 1 Segmenting** Distribute word building boxes. Say a CVCe pattern word aloud. Have children write the spelling of each sound in the appropriate box. (Use *bake, nine, rope, fuse*.)

**DAY 2 Blending** Write the spelling of each sound in *fire* as you say it. Have children repeat after you, blending the sounds to read the word. Repeat with *tire* and *wire*.

**DAY 3 Fluency** Write a list of long *u: u-e; o: o-e; i: i-e; a: a-e; a: ai, ay* words. Point to each word, asking children to blend the sounds silently. Ask a volunteer to read each word.

**DAY 4 Writing** Have children choose two CVCe pattern or double-vowel pattern words and create a rhyming couplet with the words. Children can illustrate their rhymes.

**DAY 5 Letter Substitution** Using letter and long-vowel cards, have pairs of children build *rule*. Taking turns, one child is to change a letter to build a new word, asking the partner to read it.

# Meeting Individual Needs for Phonics

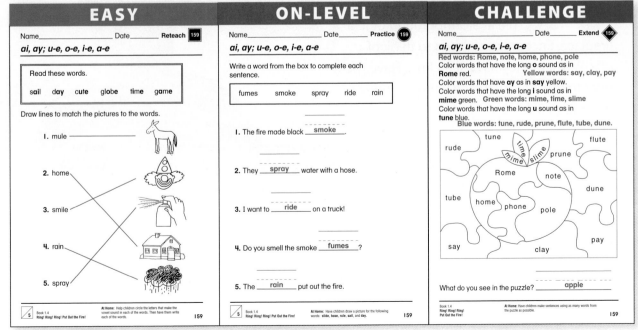

Reteach, 159     Practice, 159     Extend, 159

**PHONICS KIT** HANDS-ON ACTIVITIES AND PRACTICE

# Build Background

**Social Studies**

## Evaluate Prior Knowledge

**CONCEPT: FIRE** Ask children to share what they know about fire. Have them talk about any experiences they may have had, such as building a fire at a campground or in a fireplace; or seeing firefighters put out a fire. Use the following activities if children need more information about fire.

**MAKE A WORD WEB FOR FIRE** Work with children to create a word web to record various words associated with fire.

▶ **Linguistic**

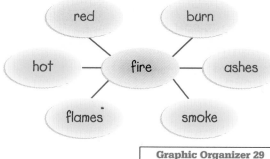

red • burn
hot • fire • ashes
flames • smoke

Graphic Organizer 29

**DRAW FIRE** Have children draw a scene in which there is fire, for example at a campground or in a fireplace. Encourage children to think of places where they have seen fires. Have them refer to the word web and write a sentence describing fire.

ONE   WRITING

## Develop Oral Language

**CONNECT WORDS AND ACTIONS** Write the following words on the board: *pop, hiss, crackle, roar.* Say these words aloud as you point to them. Explain to children that flames of a fire often make these sounds.

**ESL**

Then divide children into four groups and give each group one of the fire sounds. Tell children they will play a game called "Dancing Flames." As you call out each sound, the appropriate group will say the sound. ▶ **Auditory**

The flames are hot.

# Vocabulary

## High-Frequency Words

*Fire! Fire!*

Fire! Fire! Ring! Ring! Ring!

Get the fire truck.  Ding! Ding! Ding!

There is (work) that must be (done.)

W (always) run, run, run!

The fire is hot and the smoke is thick.

This is (how) we get there quick.

Out of the way! (Here) comes the hose.

Today we can't (clean.)

The flames rose and rose.

Pump that pump! Spray that spray!

Make the fire go away!

**Teaching Chart 118**

### SPELLING/VOCABULARY CONNECTIONS

The words *clean, always, work, done,* and *how* are Challenge Words.  See page 133Q for Day 1 of the 5-Day Spelling Plan.

## Auditory

**LISTEN TO WORDS**  Without displaying it, read aloud "Fire! Fire!" on **Teaching Chart 118.** Ask children if they were able to hear the noise and yelling at the fire. It wasn't always clear who was yelling, was it?  Have any of them ever seen a fire truck in action at a fire?  What did the firefighters do?  Was the scene noisy?

**RING FOR HIGH-FREQUENCY WORDS** Have children aurally identify each high-frequency word using the following activity:

- Say aloud each high-frequency word, and have the children repeat it.

- Tell children that they should make believe the poem is on fire. To put out the fire, they can say "Ring!" every time you come to one of the vocabulary words, and then say the word. Read the poem again, pausing at each Vocabulary Word.

## Visual

**READ WORDS**  Display "Fire! Fire!" on **Teaching Chart 118.** Read the poem, tracking the print with your finger as you read. Then hold up Vocabulary Cards one at a time and have children circle the high-frequency words on the chart.  Have volunteers read the poem, as they pretend they're really at a fire.

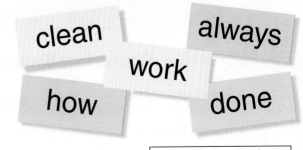

**Vocabulary Cards**

**MATCH WORDS**  Pair children and supply two sets of cards. Have one partner display a Vocabulary Card while the other reads the word and displays a matching card. Then children can think of a sentence using that word, and write it.

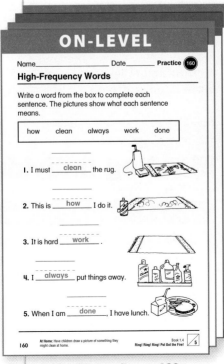

**ON-LEVEL**

Name_____ Date_____ Practice (160)

**High-Frequency Words**

Write a word from the box to complete each sentence. The pictures show what each sentence means.

| how | clean | always | work | done |

1. I must ____clean____ the rug.

2. This is ____how____ I do it.

3. It is hard ____work____ .

4. I ____always____ put things away.

5. When I am ____done____ , I have lunch.

At Home: Have children draw a picture of something they might clean at home.

160    Book 1.4    Ring! Ring! Ring! Put Out the Fire!    5

Take-Home Story 160a
Reteach 160
Practice 160 • Extend 160

**126D**

# Guided Instruction

### Preview and Predict

Ask children to look at the picture on the title page. Discuss how the photo might give clues about the story.

- What might this story be about?
- Where might it take place?
- Will the story be real or make believe? How can you tell? (Real, because the people and the scenes look like something you might see happen.)

Next, take a **picture walk** through the story. Have children pay attention to the details of the photos, such as what the firetrucks look like and what the firefighters are wearing. Have children make predictions about the story. Chart their predictions and read them aloud.

### Set Purposes

Ask children what they want to find out as they read the story. For example:

- What kind of work do firefighters do?
- Why do firefighters need to rush?

TIME FOR KIDS
SPECIAL REPORT

Ring! Ring! Ring! Put Out the Fire!

126

# Meeting Individual Needs · Grouping Suggestions for Strategic Reading

### EASY

**Shared Reading** Read the story aloud as you track print and model directionality. Invite children to chime in when they see words they know. As you read each page, discuss the photos.

### ON-LEVEL

**Guided Reading** Ask children to read the story with you. Monitor any difficulties children may have in order to determine which numbered prompts to use. Model strategies using prompts as you read the story together. After reading the story with children, have children reread it. See the rereading suggestions on page 128.

### CHALLENGE

**Read Independently** Have children set purposes before they read. Remind children that as they read, noticing words they know can help them understand the story. Children can also use the questions on page 130 for a group discussion.

15 LADDER

Boston
15

BILL STORMONT/THE STOCK MARKET

BOB DAEMMRICH/STOCK BOSTON

TIME
FOR KIDS

How do firefighters do their work? They must ride in a big, red fire truck to get to the fire. The big, red fire truck has lots of things that are used to put out fires. The ladder helps the firefighter get to the hot flames. The engine pumps water through the long fire hose. The fire hose sprays it on the fire.

127

# Guided Instruction

☑ **Phonics** *ai, ay; u-e, o-e, i-e, a-e*

☑ **Make Inferences**

**Strategic Reading** Tell children they will use a flow chart to help them record what they learn from the story. The chart will also help them connect the story to the real world. *Graphic Organizer*

**①** **MAKE INFERENCES** Let's look at the three photos on page 127. What do you see in each photo? (a fire truck, firefighters on a ladder, a fire hose pumping water) What do these photos tell us about the work firefighters do? (They ride in a truck. The use ladders and hoses.) *Graphic Organizer*

**②** **Phonics** *ai, ay; u-e, o-e, i-e, a-e*
Let's find and read long *i* words on this page. Remember that the *e* is silent. (ride, fire) Now let's read the long *a* words. (flames spray) What is different about these words? (The long *a* in *flames* is spelled with a silent *e*, and *sprays* is spelled with *ay*) How about long *o* words? (hose) *Blending*

---

## TEACHING TIP

**INSTRUCTIONAL** The following chart indicates words from the story with the target phonics elements that children have learned to decode and high-frequency words that have been taught in previous lessons.

| Decodable | | High-Frequency | |
|---|---|---|---|
| brave | ride | how | clean |
| day | slide | always | done |
| fire(s) | smoke | work | |
| flames | sprays | | |
| fumes | used | | |

---

## LANGUAGE SUPPORT

A graphic transparency organizer for making a flowchart can be found in the **Language Support Book**. As children make inferences about firefighting, they add their ideas to the flowchart.

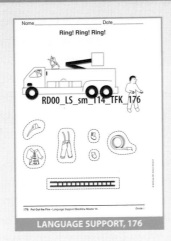

Name_____ Date_____
**Ring! Ring! Ring!**

RD00_LS_sm_114_TFK_176

176 Put Out the Fire • Language Support/Blackline Master 16    Grade 1

**LANGUAGE SUPPORT, 176**

**127**

# Guided Instruction

**3** **MAKE INFERENCES** Now let's look at the two photos on this page. What are the firefighters wearing over their faces? (masks) Why do they need to wear masks? (Responses may vary; for example, to protect themselves, to keep the smoke away, to stay safe.) Let's add this information to our story charts about firefighters: They have masks. The masks keep out smoke and flames. *Graphic Organizer*

**4** **Phonics** *u-e* Let's read the last sentence on this page: *"The firefighters have masks to stay safe and keep out smoke and… hmm, I'm not sure what this word is. Let's blend the sounds together and read it."* f u m(e) s fumes *Blending*

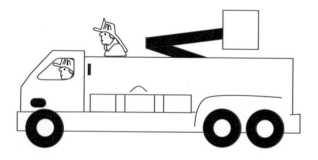

**ORGANIZE INFORMATION** Ask volunteers to tell what they learned about firefighters and the work they do. Then have children summarize their ideas in a statement about firefighters. *Summarize*

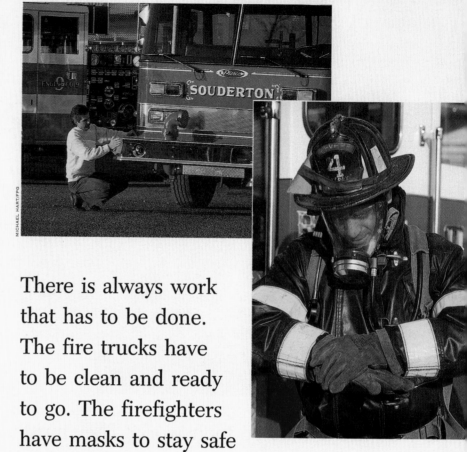

MICHAEL HART/FPG

There is always work that has to be done. The fire trucks have to be clean and ready to go. The firefighters have masks to stay safe and keep out smoke and fumes.

**FIND OUT MORE**
Visit our website:
**www.mhschool.com/tfk**

*inter***NET**
**CONNECTION**

128

## REREADING FOR *Fluency*

**PARTNERS** Children who need fluency practice can read with a partner. Ask children to read aloud, alternating sentences. Remind children to track print as they read and to be aware of punctuation marks.

**READING RATE** You may want to evaluate individual children's reading rates. Have the child read aloud from *Ring! Ring! Ring! Put Out the Fire!* for one minute. When the minute is up, have

the child place a self-stick note after the last word read. Then count the number of words the child has read.

Alternatively, you could assess small groups or the whole class together by having children count words and record their own scores.

A Running Record form provided in **Diagnostic/Placement Evaluation** will help you to evaluate reading rate(s).

Ring! Ring! Ring! Ring! Ring! The fire bell rings, and the firefighters run! They slide down the long pole and put on fire gear. They rush, rush, rush to put out the fire. They can put out the biggest fires. They are very fast! Don't you think they are brave? Would you want to put out big fires one day?

A story from the editors of *TIME FOR KIDS*.

129

# Guided Instruction

**⑤ MAKE INFERENCES** How do you think the firefighters know there is a fire? (They hear the fire bell ringing.) Do you think the firefighters need to work slowly or quickly? (They need to work quickly.) Why do you think they need to work quickly? (Answers will vary.) Let's add this information to our flow-chart.

## Return to Predictions and Purposes

Reread children's predictions about the story. Discuss these predictions, noting which need to be revised. Then ask the children if the story answered the questions they had before they read.

### INFORMAL ASSESSMENT

**HOW TO ASSESS**

**Phonics** *ai, ay; u-e, o-e, i-e, a-e*
Write the following words on the chalkboard and ask children to read them aloud: *rain, day, fumes, pole, slide, safe*.

**MAKE INFERENCES** Ask children how they think firefighters feel about the work they do.

**FOLLOW UP**

**Phonics** *ai, ay; u-e, o-e, i-e, a-e*
Continue to model the blending of sounds in long vowel words for children who are having difficulty.

**MAKE INFERENCES** Children who are having difficulty can look at the pictures in the story and use the flow charts to make more inferences about firefighters.

## LITERARY RESPONSE

**QUICK-WRITE** Have children write a short letter to a firefighter about what they do.

**ORAL RESPONSE** Have children use their letters for discussion:

• Why is it important for firefighters to wear special uniforms and hats?

• Why do fire trucks have sirens?

• What kinds of jobs need to be done inside a fire house?

**RESEARCH AND INQUIRY** Have children find out other facts about firefighters to share with the class.

**interNET CONNECTION** For more information or activities on this topic go to **www.mhschool.com/reading.**

**129**

# Story Questions

Help children read the questions. Discuss possible answers:

**Answers:**

1. The engine pumps water through the fire hose. *Literal*

2. The fire truck's sirens will blow and bells will ring. *Inferential/Make Inferences*

3. Firefighters lift heavy equipment and sometimes they carry people and animals to rescue them. *Inferential/Make Inferences*

4. Firefighters put out fires and keep the trucks and hoses clean and safe. *Critical/Summarize*

5. Firefighters wear heavy gear; vets do not. Firefighters use ladders and hoses; vets use medical equipment. *Critical/Reading Across Texts*

**Write a Description** For a full writing lesson related to persuasive writing, see pages 133M–133N.

## Story Questions & Activities

*READ TOGETHER*

1. What pumps water through the fire hose?

2. How can you tell if a fire truck is going to a fire?

3. Why must firefighters be strong?

4. Tell about the work a firefighter does.

5. What are some differences between the work of a firefighter and the work of a vet?

## Write a Speech

Write a speech persuading others to be careful in case of fire. Give the speech.

## Meeting Individual Needs

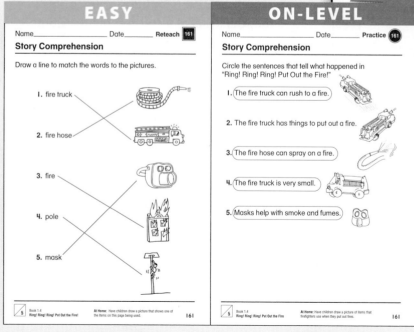

| EASY | ON-LEVEL | CHALLENGE |
|------|----------|-----------|

**Reteach, 161**   **Practice, 161**   **Extend, 161**

**130**   *Ring! Ring! Ring! Put Out the Fire!*

## Make a Fire Safety Badge

Make yourself a fire safety badge.
Color it and cut it out.
Wear it on your shirt.

I know how to keep safe from fire.

I know how to keep safe from fire.

I know how to keep safe from fire.

## Find Out More

Find out the best way to exit from school and your home in case of a fire.

131

---

# Story Activities

### Make a Fire Safety Badge

**Materials:** cutouts of safety badges (made of oaktag or poster board), paints and paint-brushes, or felt-tipped markers

Read the directions aloud. Help children who have questions. First, ask children if they have ever seen firefighters at work. Invite children to talk about what they saw. Was a building in their neighborhood on fire? Did the children hear sirens and bells? What were the firefighters wearing?

**ONE** Have children design and color their own fire safety badges. When they are finished, children can wear them on their shirts.

### Find Out More

**RESEARCH AND INQUIRY** Divide children into pairs and ask them to find out more about fire safety. Have partners find out the best way to exit from the school and their homes in case of a fire. Have each pair report its findings.

**interNET CONNECTION** To access Web sites on firefighters go to ***www.mhschool.com/reading***.

---

**FORMAL ASSESSMENT**

See the Selection and Unit Assessment Tests for Book 4.

---

**DAILY Phonics ROUTINES**

**DAY 3** **Fluency** Write a list of long *u: u-e; o: o-e; i: i-e; a: a-e; a: ai, ay* words. Point to each word, asking children to blend the sounds silently. Ask a volunteer to read each word.

Phonics CD-ROM

# Study Skills

## CHARTS

### ✓ OBJECTIVES

Children will learn to read a tally chart to count votes.

Remind children that they have just read a story about the job of a firefighter. Tell them that now they will think about different kinds of jobs, and talk about what some children want to do when they grow up.

Display **Teaching Chart 120**. Have children read the title of the tally chart. Then invite children to describe what they notice about the chart, such as the illustrations and the column with the number of votes. Together read the words using picture clues. Point to each face and ask children to name the job. Have them explain what each person does. Then help children read the questions below the tally chart, encouraging them to identify the labels that answer each question.

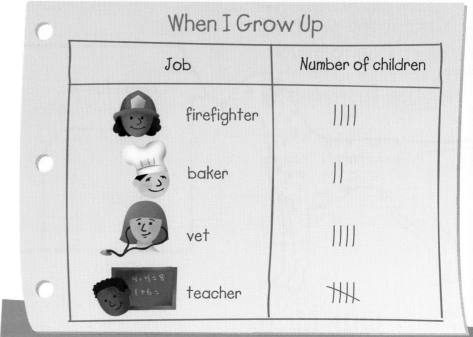

# STUDY SKILLS

## Vote and Tally

Children voted on what they want to be when they grow up. This tally shows their votes.

### When I Grow Up

| Job | Number of children |
|-----|--------------------|
| firefighter | \|\|\|\| |
| baker | \|\| |
| vet | \|\|\|\| |
| teacher | ₪₪₪ |

## Look at the Tally

1 How many children want to be vets?

2 Which job did the most children want to do?

## Meeting Individual Needs

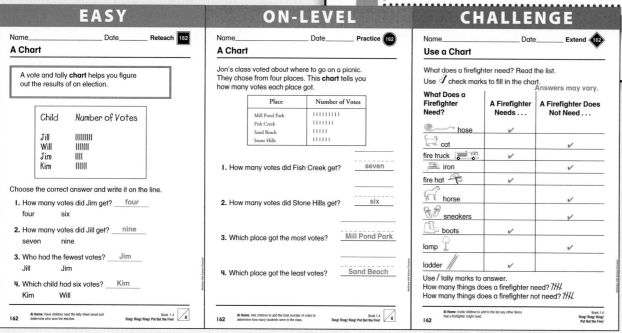

**EASY** — Reteach, 162

**ON-LEVEL** — Practice, 162

**CHALLENGE** — Extend, 162

# TEST POWER

## The Fireplace

The man came in from outside.
He shook the snow off his boots.
He had a bundle of wood in his arms.
He put some wood on the fire.
Then he put the fire screen in front.
The fire in the fireplace was warm.
It warmed the man's toes.
The man sat down in his chair.
He rocked forward and backward.
His cat came and sat on his lap.
Then they took a little nap together.

What time of year is it
in this story?
○ Summer
● Winter

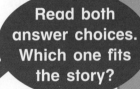

Read both
answer choices.
Which one fits
the story?

133

## Test Power

THE PRINCETON REVIEW

### Read the Page

Explain to children that you will be reading this story as a group. You will read the story, and they will follow in their books.

Request that children put pens, pencils, and markers away, since they will not be writing in their books.

### Discuss the Question

Discuss with children the kinds of things that might indicate the season. If it's very warm, it is probably summer. If it's snowing, it is probably winter.

### Test-Tip

Sometimes you can use the answer choices to help you locate the answer in the passage. Look at each choice and see which one is better.

**EASY**
**DECODABLE**

- Review long *u: u-e,* long *o: o-e,* long *i: i-e,* long *a: a-e,* long *a: ai, ay.*

✓ **Comprehension**

- Review cause and effect.
- Review make inferences.

Answers will vary. Have children cite examples from the story to suppport their answers.

---

**EASY**

**Story Questions for Selected Reading**

1. Who is the main character in the story?

2. Which illustrations did you like best? Why?

3. How was the story problem solved?

4. If you could be a character in the story, who would you be? Why?

5. Did you like the story? Why or why not?

**Draw a Picture**

Draw a picture for the selected story.

---

# Self-Selected Reading
# Leveled Books

## EASY

**UNIT SKILLS REVIEW**

✓

✓ **Comprehension**

Help children self-select an Easy Book to read and apply phonics and comprehension skills.

## Guided Reading

**PREVIEW AND PREDICT** Discuss the illustrations in the beginning of the book. As you take the **picture walk**, have children predict what the story will be about. List their ideas.

**SET PURPOSES** Have children write or draw why they want to read the book. Have them share their purposes.

**READ THE BOOK** Use the following items to guide children's reading, or to discuss after they have read the story independently. Model blending and other phonics and decoding strategies for children who need help.

Let's look at the pictures. Where does this story take place? *Use Illustrations*

Can you find a word in the story with the long *a* sound spelled *ai, ay* or *a-e*? Let's say the word aloud. *Phonics and Decoding*

What happens at the end of the story? *Summarize*

**RETURN TO PREDICTIONS AND PURPOSES** Discuss children's predictions. Ask which were close to the book contents and why. Have children review their purposes for reading. Did they find out what they wanted to know?

**LITERARY RESPONSE** Have children discuss questions such as the following:

- Which part of the book was most interesting?

- What might be another good title for the book?

 **CD-ROM**

# Self-Selected Reading
# Leveled Books

## INDEPENDENT

### UNIT SKILLS REVIEW

☑  **Phonics**

☑ **Comprehension**

Help children self-select an Independent Book to read and apply phonics and comprehension skills.

## Guided Reading

**PREVIEW AND PREDICT** Discuss the illustrations in the beginning of the book. As you take the **picture walk**, have children predict what the story will be about. List their ideas.

**SET PURPOSES** Have children write or draw why they want to read the book. Have them share their purposes.

**READ THE BOOK** Use the following items to guide children's reading, or to discuss after they have read the story independently. Model blending and other phonics and decoding strategies for children who need help.

Can you find a word in the story with the long *a* sound spelled *ai*, *ay*, or *a-e* ? Let's say the word aloud. *Phonics and Decoding*

Do you think this story is real or make believe? *Distinguish Between Fantasy and Reality*

Think about the story. Has something similar happened to you? *Make Inferences*

**RETURN TO PREDICTIONS AND PURPOSES** Discuss children's predictions. Ask which were close to the book's contents and why. Have children review their purposes for reading. Did they find out what they wanted to know?

**LITERARY RESPONSE** Have children discuss questions such as the following:

- Which part of the book was most interesting?

- What might be another good title for the book?

 **CD-ROM**

## INDEPENDENT
**DECODABLE**

☑  **Phonics**

- Review long *u: u-e*, long *o: o-e*, long *i: i-e*, long *a: a-e*, long *a: ai, ay*.

☑ **Comprehension**

- Review cause and effect.

- Review make inferences.

Answers will vary. Have children cite examples from the story to suppport their answers.

## INDEPENDENT

### Story Questions for Selected Reading

1. Where does this story take place?

2. Did the story teach you anything new? What?

3. Did you like the ending? Why or why not?

4. What caused the main event to happen?

5. How is the main character like you? How is he or she different?

**Draw a Picture**

Draw a picture for the selected story.

**133B**

# Presentation Ideas

**MAKE A FIRE PREVENTION CHART**
Have children make a chart of fire prevention tips. The chart should be pictures only, with *X*'s through them. Ask them to think of scenes that illustrate the things people shouldn't do, and to draw them.
▶ **Viewing/Representing**

**ACT OUT A TV NEWS FIRE REPORT**
Ask volunteers to put on a play about a fire scene. Pick a child to be the television news reporter. The reporter should interview fire fighters, owners of a house on fire, and bystanders. ▶ **Speaking/Listening**

Consider students' creative efforts, possibly adding a plus(+) for originality, wit, and imagination.

## Scoring Rubric

| Excellent | Good | Fair | Unsatisfactory |
|---|---|---|---|
| **4:** The writer<br>• presents full sentences.<br>• effectively organizes ideas, in a strong persuasive voice.<br>• provides many vivid details drawn from real life. | **3:** The writer<br>• presents full sentences.<br>• presents clear, well-organized persuasive points.<br>• provide some details drawn from real life. | **2:** The writer<br>• may not always use full sentences.<br>• may show trouble with organizing ideas.<br>• provides few or vague details. | **1:** The writer<br>• may not grasp the task to persuade.<br>• may not use full sentences.<br>• may present vague or irrelevant ideas and details. |

**0:** The writer leaves the page blank or fails to respond to the writing task. The student does not address the topic or simply paraphrases the prompt. The response is illegible or incoherent.

# Meeting Individual Needs for Writing

| EASY | ON-LEVEL | CHALLENGE |
|---|---|---|
| **Draw a Fire Scene** Have children pretend that they are present at the scene of a fire. Have them draw what they see. Then have them write a few sentences describing their drawings. | **Write a Description of a Fire Scene** Ask children to pretend that they are present at the scene of a fire. Have them describe what they see, using as many details as they can. | **Make a Journal Entry** Have children imagine that they are the owners of a house on fire. Have them write a story about how the fire got started, what they did when they realized their house was on fire, what the firefighters did, and what happened after the fire was put out. |

## LANGUAGE SUPPORT

**ESL** Write *was not, were not, do not, did not* on the board. Then erase the *o* in each word, add an apostrophe, and form the contractions *wasn't, weren't, don't,* and *didn't.* Have children repeat each word as you pronounce it.

## DAILY LANGUAGE ACTIVITIES

Write the Daily Language Activities on the chalkboard each day or use **Transparency 20.** Have students correct the sentences orally.

### Day 1
1. The men werent there yet. weren't
2. The ladder wasnt short. wasn't
3. We werent here. weren't

### Day 2
1. Jim didnt start the fire. didn't
2. Dont put that out! Don't
3. The hoses weren't in the truck. weren't

### Day 3
1. The fire wasnt going out. wasn't
2. The trucks werent clean. weren't
3. The men didnt have their masks. didn't

### Day 4
1. I dont want to go. don't
2. The smoke wasnt thick. wasn't
3. Pam and Tom werent sad. weren't

### Day 5
1. The men werent quick. weren't
2. The bell wasnt loud. wasn't
3. Dont go out there! Don't

**Daily Language Transparency 20**

---

## DAY 1 — Introduce the Concept

**Oral Warm-Up** Read these two sentences aloud: *I did not go to school. I didn't go to school.* Ask children if these sentences mean the same thing.

**Introduce Contractions** Review with children that using a contraction is like saying two words at once.

### Contractions

- A **contraction** is a short form of two words.

- An **apostrophe** (') takes the place of the letters that are left out.

Write the following on the chalkboard: *was + not = wasn't; were + not = weren't.*

Present the Daily Language Activity and have students correct orally. Then have students write their own sentences using *wasn't* and *weren't.*

**WRITING** Assign the daily Writing Prompt on page 124C.

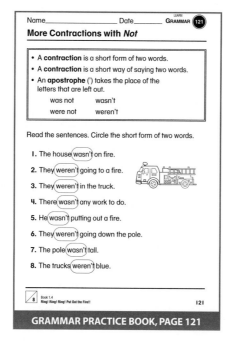

**GRAMMAR PRACTICE BOOK, PAGE 121**

---

## DAY 2 — Teach the Concept

**Review Contractions** Remind children that a contraction is a short form of two words. Ask children to change the underlined words into contractions in the following sentences: *It was not a big cat. We were not sad.*

**Introduce More Contractions** Explain to children that they can make contractions out of other words. Write the following on the chalkboard: *do + not = don't; did + not = didn't.*

Present the Daily Language Activity and have children correct orally. Then have children write their own sentences, using *don't* and *didn't.*

**WRITING** Assign the daily Writing Prompt on page 124C.

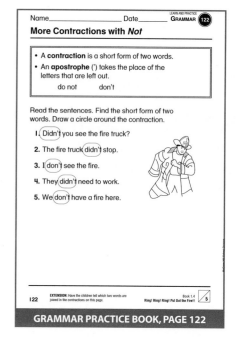

**GRAMMAR PRACTICE BOOK, PAGE 122**

---

# Contractions with *Not*

## DAY 3 — Review and Practice

**Learn from the Literature** Review contractions with *not*. Read aloud the second-to-last sentence on page 129 of *Put Out the Fire!*

> **Don't you think they are brave?**

Ask children which word is a contraction. (*Don't*) Then ask what two words make up the contraction. (*Do not*)

**Use Contractions with *Not*** Present the Daily Language Activity and have children correct orally.

Write these sentences on the board: *I was happy. Mom and Dad were coming. They did have a ball. They do like cake.* Have children add *not* to each sentence and then make contractions.

 **WRITING** Assign the daily Writing Prompt on page 124D.

## DAY 4 — Review and Practice

**Review Contractions** Write *wasn't, weren't, didn't,* and *don't* on the chalkboard. Have children take turns saying which two words make up each contraction. Have them use the words orally in a sentence. Then present the Daily language Activity for Day 4.

**Mechanics and Usage** Review the use of apostrophes in contractions with *not*.

> **Apostrophes**
> * Use an **apostrophe** in place of an *o* in contractions with *not*.

 **WRITING** Assign the daily Writing Prompt on page 124C.

## DAY 5 — Assess and Reteach

**Assess** Use the Daily Language Activity and page 125 of the **Grammar Practice Book** for assessment.

Reteach Have children write from dictation the four contractions studied this week. Then have them write a simple sentence for each contraction. If they'd like, they can write the contraction in a different color pencil. Have children create a word wall with two columns: in the first column, a list of words (*was, were, do,* and *did*) followed by not; in the second column, a list of contractions.

 **WRITING** Assign the daily Writing Prompt on page 124D.

---

### Grammar Practice Book, Page 123

Name_____ Date_____ PRACTICE AND WRITE GRAMMAR 123

**More Contractions with *Not***

* A **contraction** is a short form of two words.
* An **apostrophe** (') takes the place of the letters that are left out.

| | |
|---|---|
| was not | wasn't |
| were not | weren't |
| do not | don't |
| did not | didn't |

Read the sentences. Circle the two words that make the contraction in each sentence.

1. The firefighters don't always need masks.
   (do not)  was not  did not
2. The firefighters weren't on their way.
   (were not)  was not  do not
3. They didn't rush away.
   (did not)  was not  do not
4. They didn't go down the pole.
   (did not)  was not  do not
5. That wasn't the ladder.
   (was not)  did not  do not

Book 1.4 Ring! Ring! Put Out the Fire!  EXTENSION: The children can think of sentences about fire prevention that include these contractions.  123

**GRAMMAR PRACTICE BOOK, PAGE 123**

### Grammar Practice Book, Page 124

Name_____ Date_____ MECHANICS GRAMMAR 124

**More Contractions with *Not***

* A **contraction** is a short form of two words.
* Use an **apostrophe** (') in place of *o* in a contraction with *not*.
   was not    wasn't

On the lines, write the contractions for the words in ( ).

1. (Do not) ___Don't___ stop, the firefighters are on the way.
2. (Does not) ___Doesn't___ the fireman work fast?
3. The fireman (was not) ___wasn't___ in the fire truck.
4. They (were not) ___weren't___ in the fire truck.
5. The firefighters (were not) ___weren't___ working.

124  EXTENSION: The children can identify the two words that are put together to make each contraction.  Book 1.4 Ring! Ring! Put Out the Fire!  5

**GRAMMAR PRACTICE BOOK, PAGE 124**

### Grammar Practice Book, Page 125

Name_____ Date_____ TEST GRAMMAR 125

**Test**

Write the contraction for the underlined words.

1. The house <u>was not</u> on fire.
   ___wasn't___
2. The men <u>did not</u> rush.
   ___didn't___
3. <u>Do not</u> go near the fire.
   ___Don't___
4. They <u>were not</u> at home.
   ___weren't___
5. She <u>did not</u> see the truck.
   ___didn't___

5 Book 1.4 Ring! Ring! Put Out the Fire!  125

**GRAMMAR PRACTICE BOOK, PAGE 125**

**GRAMMAR PRACTICE BOOK, PAGE 126**

# 5 Day Spelling Plan

## DICTATION SENTENCES

### Spelling Words

1. Here comes the fire truck.
2. I see the smoke.
3. I have the bell.
4. The man went down the pole.
5. Can I make it ring?
6. She is very brave.

### Challenge Words

7. We will clean the truck.
8. I always wait for my dad.
9. He can work at home.
10. Are you done?

---

## DAY 1 — Pretest

**Assess Prior Knowledge** Use the Dictation Sentences at left and **Spelling Practice Book** page 121 for the pretest. Allow children to correct their own papers. If children have trouble, have partners give each other a midweek test on Day 3.

| Spelling Words | | Challenge Words |
|---|---|---|
| 1. **truck** | 4. **pole** | 7. **clean** |
| 2. **smoke** | 5. **ring** | 8. **always** |
| 3. **bell** | 6. **brave** | 9. **work** |
| | | 10. **done** |

*Note: Words in **dark type** are from the story.*

**Word Study** On page 122 of the **Spelling Practice Book** are word study steps and an at-home activity.

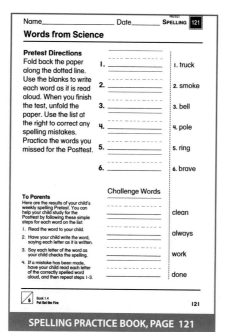

**SPELLING PRACTICE BOOK, PAGE 121**

**WORD STUDY STEPS AND ACTIVITY, PAGE 122**

---

## DAY 2 — Explore the Pattern

**Sort and Spell Words** Say *sock* and *smoke*. Ask children what vowel sound they hear in each word. Discuss with children how each vowel (*a, e, i, o,* and *u*) can have a short sound and a long sound.

Ask children to read aloud the six Spelling Words before sorting them into words with short-vowel sounds and words with long-vowel sounds.

| Short Vowels | Long Vowels |
|---|---|
| truck | smoke |
| bell | pole |
| ring | brave |

**Word Wall** As children read other stories and texts, have them look for new words with short- or long- vowel sounds. Add them to a classroom word wall, underlining the letters in the word that make the long- or short- vowel sound.

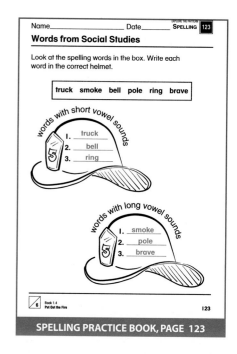

**SPELLING PRACTICE BOOK, PAGE 123**

---

# Words from Social Studies

## DAY 3 — Practice and Extend

**Word Meaning: Definitions** Have children match each definition below with a Spelling Word.

> **Sound a bell makes** (ring)
>
> **Not afraid** (brave)
>
> **Something that comes from fire** (smoke)
>
> **Bigger than a car** (truck)
>
> **Something to slide down** (pole)
>
> **Something that makes a ringing sound** (bell)

**Identify Spelling Patterns** Write the following on the board: *We always keep the truck clean. You can ring the bell when the work is done.* Have volunteers read aloud and tell which are the Spelling Words and Challenge Words. Then have children use Spelling and Challenge Words in a sentence.

## DAY 4 — Proofread and Write

**Proofread Sentences** Write these sentences on the chalkboard, including the misspelled words. Ask children to proofread, circling incorrect spellings and writing the correct spellings. There are two spelling errors in each sentence.

> The ⟨braev⟩ man sat on the ⟨truk⟩. (brave, truck)
>
> The ⟨bel⟩ rang, and we saw ⟨smok⟩. (bell, smoke)
>
> ⟨Rign⟩ the bell and go down the ⟨pol⟩. (ring, pole)

 Have children use as many Spelling Words as possible in the daily Writing Prompt on page 124D. Remind children to proofread their writing for errors in spelling, grammar, and punctuation.

## DAY 5 — Assess

**Assess Childrens' Knowledge** Use page 126 of the **Spelling Practice Book** or the Dictation Sentences on page 133Q for the posttest.

**Personal Word List** If children have trouble with any words in the lesson, have them add to their personal list of troublesome words in their journals. Have children draw pictures of each Spelling Word and label it.

Children should refer to their word lists during later writing activities.

---

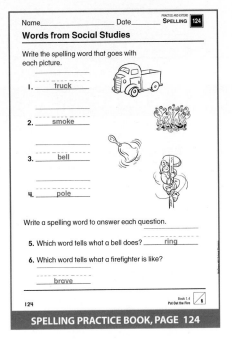

SPELLING PRACTICE BOOK, PAGE 124

SPELLING PRACTICE BOOK, PAGE 125

SPELLING PRACTICE BOOK, PAGE 126

**133R**

# Wrap Up the Theme

134

## Let's Find Out!
**Looking for answers is an adventure.**

**REVIEW THE THEME** Remind children that all of the selections in this unit relate to the theme Let's Find Out! What were some of the answers that the characters found? Were children surprised by any of the adventures or answers. Ask children to name other stories or movies they know that also fit the theme of Let's Find Out!

**READ THE POEM** Read "Who Lived in a Shoe" by Beatrix Potter aloud to children. After reading, discuss how the poem connects to the theme of Let's Find Out! What story is the poet writing about? What is the poet trying to figure out? Reread the poem, having children chime in with you.

**STUDENT LISTENING LIBRARY AUDIOCASSETTES**

**MAKE CONNECTIONS** Have children work in small groups to brainstorm a list of ways that the stories, poems, and the *Time for Kids* magazine article relate to the theme Let's Find Out!

Groups can then compare their lists as they share them with the class.

## LOOKING AT GENRE

Have children review *Yasmin's Ducks* and *The Knee-High Man*. What makes *Yasmin's Ducks* an informational science story? What makes *The Knee-High Man* a play?

Help children list the key characteristics of each literary form or genre. Encourage children to give other examples of informational stories and plays.

| INFORMATIONAL SCIENCE STORY *Yasmin's Ducks* | PLAY *The Knee-High Man* |
|---|---|
| • Characters and story are made up. <br> • Story gives true facts about a science topic (*ducks*). | • Has parts for different characters. <br> • Every sentence is spoken by a character. <br> • You could act it out yourself. |

# Who Lived in a Shoe?

You know that old woman
Who lived in a shoe?
She had so many children
She didn't know what to do?

I think if she lived in
A little shoe-house
That little old lady was
Surely a mouse!

*by Beatrix Potter*

135

## LEARNING ABOUT POETRY

**Literary Devices: Rhyme** Read the poem aloud, having children listen for words that rhyme. Reread the poem, having children echo the last word in each line. Have volunteers give pairs of rhyming words from the poem. *(shoe, do; house, mouse)*

**Response Activity.** Have children draw a picture based on the poem. Encourage them to think about how big a real shoe is, and how many mice could fit in it.

# Research *and Inquiry*

**Complete the Theme Project**
GROUP Have children work in teams to complete their group project. Remind children that the information that they have gathered on their place to explore can be presented in any creative way. For example, they might enjoy making an illustrated map of their place. Encourage children to share tasks so that each member of the team can contribute to the project.

**Make a Classroom Presentation**
Have teams take turns presenting their projects. Be sure to include time for questions from the audience.

**Draw Conclusions** Have children draw conclusions about what they learned from researching, preparing, and sharing their projects. Was the Resource chart they made helpful? Was using the internet helpful? What other resources did they use? What conclusions have children reached about their topic? Finally, ask children if the project has changed their opinion about the place they want to explore. What conclusions can they draw from this?

**Ask More Questions** What additional questions do children now have about their place to explore? Do children have questions about other places? You might encourage the teams to continue their research and prepare another presentation.

**135**

# Persuasive Writing

**CONNECT TO LITERATURE** Have a class discussion about "The Shopping List." Invite children to comment on how each person tried to help Mike remember the missing item from his list. Ask children what suggestions they would have made to help him remember.

Dear Mrs. Nevins,

　　If we want to make the world a better place, we can start in our own town. Teachers and parents can help us to help others. There are children right here who do not have enough to eat. We can have hot lunches for them at school. If they need clothes or toys, we can collect things to give away. I think we can all help to make a difference.

Sincerely,

Yannek Leiderman

# Prewrite

**PURPOSE & AUDIENCE** Children will write persuasive letters to a parent or teacher. They can present arguments to support an activity they would like to do, or an outing to a place they would like to see.

**STRATEGY: BRAINSTORM** Have children brainstorm ideas about how to make the world a better place—especially for children. Make a list on the chalkboard of children's remarks for reflection later.

Use **Writing Process Transparency 4A** to model a Persuasive Writing organizer.

---

### PERSUASIVE WRITING FEATURES

A good argument:

- Explains how you feel about something in order to persuade, or talks the reader into agreeing with you.

- Gives facts that support how you feel about the topic.

- Gives the facts in an organized way.

---

### TEACHING TIP

**ORGANIZATION** Have children start to organize details of their persuasive arguments. Have them make lists of their opinions. Instruct them to back up each opinion with a fact. If you focus the assignment on a specific topic for the whole class, provide them with books and children's periodicals to help them research their ideas.

**PREWRITE** TRANSPARENCY

**What I Want to Do:**
Let's Visit the Aquarium

**Reason:** there are different animals to see

**Explanation:** it's the only place you can see them up close

**Reason:** we can learn a lot about sea animals

**Explanation:** you can see how they eat, swim, and play together

# Draft

**STRATEGY: DEVELOP A MAIN IDEA** Encourage children to begin with an opening sentence clearly stating their position. From there, guide them to write freely, without self-editing for punctuation or spelling. Give concrete examples of how to support their opinions with facts and details.

Use **Writing Process Transparency 4B** to model a first draft.

**LANGUAGE CONTROL** Have children review *do* and *did,* and *go* and *went*. Instruct them to write practice sentences relating to their topic. For example: *I want to do a finger painting. I did a finger painting. We want to go to the museum. We went to the museum.* They can save the exercise in their writing portfolios.

---

***DRAFT* TRANSPARENCY**

Woods Elementary
543 High Street
Long City, Idaho 99999
April 7, 1999

We want to visit the Aquarium on monday. they have a jellyfish show there. We dont want to miss it. Sea otters play tricks in the water. Keepers feed the seals.

  our class can learn a lot at the aquarium. The aquarium is a good place to see.

       sincerely,

       *Nora Ruiz*

McGraw-Hill School Division

Book 1.4: Persuasive Narrative / Drafting 1B

# Revise

Have a class discussion on how to make children's persuasive letters more effective. Ask children to comment on what their audience would find convincing about their arguments. Challenge them to come up with more ideas and facts to persuade the reader to agree.

**STRATEGY: ELABORATION** Have children examine their work for changes that will enhance their arguments. Use the following questions to inspire the revision process:

- Do my words clearly say how I feel?

- Does the letter sound like the way I naturally talk?

- What else could I say to back up my feelings? Do I need to add more facts?

Use **Writing Process Transparency 4C** for classroom discussion on the revision process. Ask children to comment on how revisions may have improved this writing sample.

**REVISE TRANSPARENCY**

Woods Elementary
543 High Street
Long City, Idaho 99999
April 7, 1999

Dear Ms. Adams

Monterey Bay
We want to visit the Aquarium on

monday. they have a jellyfish show
They also have sharks.
there. We dont want to miss it. Sea
We can watch the
otters play tricks in the water. Keepers

feed the seals.

Monterey Bay
our class can learn a lot at the
It's an interesting
aquarium. The aquarium is a good

place to see.

sincerely,

Nora Ruiz

McGraw-Hill School Division

Book 1.4 • Persuasive Narrative • Revising 1C

135D

# Persuasive Writing

## GRAMMAR/SPELLING CONNECTIONS

See the 5-Day Grammar and Usage Plan on verbs, on pages 370–37P, 650–65P, 950–95P, and 1230–123P, 1330–133P.

See the 5-Day Spelling Plans, pages 37Q–37R, 65Q–65R, 95Q–95R, 123Q–123R, and 133Q–133R.

# Edit/Proofread

After children finish revising their texts, have them proofread for final corrections and additions.

### GRAMMAR, MECHANICS, USAGE

- Begin sentences with a capital letter and end them with a period.
- Begin names of people or special places with a capital letter .
- Use an apostrophe in place of the *o* when *not* is joined with another word.
- Begin the names of days and months with a capital letter.

# Publish

**SEND THE LETTERS** Help children to correctly address and stamp their letters for mailing. They can decorate the envelope backs with colorful stickers.

Use **Writing Process Transparency 4D** as a proofreading model and **Writing Process Transparency 4E** as a model to discuss presentation ideas for their writing.

---

### PROOFREAD TRANSPARENCY

Woods Elementary
543 High Street
Long City, Idaho 99999
April 7, 1999

Dear Ms. Adams,

¶ We want to visit the Aquarium on

monday. they have a jellyfish show

there. We dont want to miss it. Sea

They also have sharks.

We can watch the

otters play tricks in the water. Keepers

feed the seals.

Monterey Bay

our class can learn a lot at the

It's an interesting

aquarium. The aquarium is a good

place to see.

sincerely,

Nora Ruiz

Book 1-4 Persuasive Narrative / Proofreading 1D

---

### PUBLISH TRANSPARENCY

Woods Elementary
543 High Street
Long City, Idaho 99999
April 7, 1999

Dear Ms. Adams,

We want to visit the Monterey Bay Aquarium on Monday. They have a jellyfish show there. We don't want to miss it. They also have sharks. Sea otters play tricks in the water. We can watch the keepers feed the seals.

Our class can learn a lot at the Monterey Bay Aquarium. It's an interesting place to see.

Sincerely,

Nora Ruiz

Book 1-4 Persuasive Narrative / Publishing 1E

# Presentation Ideas

**DISPLAY THE LETTERS** Make a board display of the letters, and give children a chance to see others' work. Children may wish to read their letters aloud to classmates. ▶ **Representing/Speaking**

**HAVE A DISCUSSION** Ask children to comment on which letters were the most effective and why. ▶ **Viewing/Speaking**

## Assessment

**SCORING RUBRIC** When using the rubric, please consider children's creative efforts, possibly adding a plus (+) for originality, wit, and imagination.

## Scoring Rubric

| **4** Excellent | **3** Good | **2** Fair | **1** Unsatisfactory |
|---|---|---|---|
| **Ideas & Content** crafts a convincing argument, with a full set of supporting details and ideas; holds the reader's attention throughout. | **Ideas & Content** crafts a solid argument, with details that show an understanding of the topic; holds the reader's interest | **Ideas & Content** has some control of the persuasive argument, but may not offer adequate details; may not keep the reader's attention. | **Ideas & Content** does not successfully argue a position; it is hard to tell what the writer thinks or feels about the topic; ideas and details are not connected, and may not fit the arguement. |
| **Organization** careful strategy moves the reader logically through the argument; has a strong beginning and ending. | **Organization** presents a capable strategy; reader can follow the logic from beginning to end; ideas and details fit where they are placed. | **Organization** tries to structure an argument, but has trouble sequencing information; may lose control of topic after stating the main idea; beginning or ending may be missing or underdeveloped. | **Organization** extreme lack of structure makes the text difficult to follow; points of the argument may be disordered; no clear beginning and ending. |
| **Voice** states a personal message, with potential to influence the reader; writer's deep involvement with the topic enlivens the argument. | **Voice** shows who is behind the words; personal message matches the writing purpose and reaches out to convince the reader. | **Voice** states the main argument, with some hint of who is behind the words; writer may seem personally uninvolved with the argument and the audience. | **Voice** is not involved in the topic; lacks a purpose and interaction with a reader. |
| **Word Choice** thoughtfully uses words to communicate clear opinions and details; advanced vocabulary helps to create a convincing tone. | **Word Choice** uses a variety of words that fit the message; may experiment with new words or use familiar words in a fresh way. | **Word Choice** gets the message across, but experiments with few new words; some words may not fit the topic or the audience. | **Word Choice** does not use words that express an opinion or attempt to convince a reader; some words may take away from the meaning; words do not fit, or are overused. |
| **Sentence Fluency** fluid sentences flow naturally; a variety of beginnings, lengths, and patterns adds interest to the argument. | **Sentence Fluency** sentences make sense and are easy to follow and read aloud; lengths and patterns vary, and fit together well. | **Sentence Fluency** sentences are understandable, but may be incomplete or awkward; some of the writing is difficult to follow or read aloud. | **Sentence Fluency** uses incomplete or confusing sentences; does not understand how words and sentences fit together; writing is hard to read aloud. |
| **Conventions** has skills in most writing conventions; proper use of the rules of English enhances clarity of the arguement; editing is largely unnecessary. | **Conventions** uses a variety of conventions correctly; some editing may be needed; errors are few and do not interfere with understanding the argument. | **Conventions** makes frequent mistakes which may interfere with a smooth reading of the text; extensive need for editing and revision. | **Conventions** has repeated errors in spelling, word choice, punctuation and usage; reader has a hard time getting through the text. |

**0:** This piece is either blank, or fails to respond to the writing task. The topic is not addressed, or the student simply paraphrases the prompt. The response may be illegible or incoherent.

## VOCABULARY

Have partners write all the vocabulary words from one selection on pieces of paper, and place the pieces in a bag. Taking turns, have each partner pull a word from the bag and make up a riddle for it. The other partner must try to answer the riddle.

### Unit Review

**The Shopping List**

| after | blue | who |
| always | were | |

**Yasmin's Ducks**

| work | buy | some |
| because | found | |

**The Knee-High Man**

| carry | clean | far |
| been | done | |

**Johnny Appleseed**

| how | little | pretty |
| light | live | |

**Ring! Ring! Ring! Put Out the Fire!**

| always | clean | how |
| work | done | |

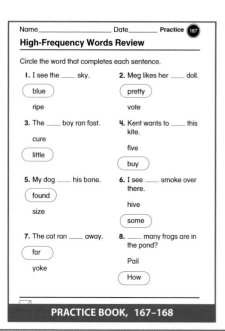

Name_____ Date_____ Practice 167

**High-Frequency Words Review**

Circle the word that completes each sentence.

1. I see the ____ sky.
   - (blue)
   - ripe

2. Meg likes her ____ doll.
   - (pretty)
   - vote

3. The ____ boy ran fast.
   - cure
   - (little)

4. Kent wants to ____ this kite.
   - five
   - (buy)

5. My dog ____ his bone.
   - (found)
   - size

6. I see ____ smoke over there.
   - hive
   - (some)

7. The cat ran ____ away.
   - (far)
   - yoke

8. ____ many frogs are in the pond?
   - Pail
   - (How)

**PRACTICE BOOK, 167–168**

## GRAMMAR

Write some sentences on the chalkboard leaving a blank space for the following verbs to be filled in by the children: *was, were, has, have, go, do* (past tense), *see, say* (past tense). Call on volunteers to come to the chalkboard to supply the correct form of each verb.

### Unit Review

**The Shopping List**
*Was* and *Were*

**Yasmin's Ducks**
*Has* and *Have*

**The Knee-High Man**
*Go* and *Do*

**Johnny Appleseed**
*See* and *Say*

**Ring! Ring! Ring! Put Out the Fire!**
More Contractions with *Not*

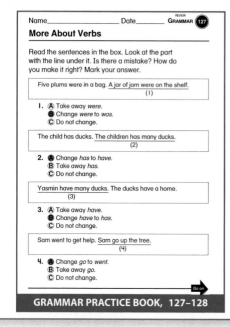

Name_____ Date_____ REVIEW GRAMMAR 127

**More About Verbs**

Read the sentences in the box. Look at the part with the line under it. Is there a mistake? How do you make it right? Mark your answer.

Five plums were in a bag. A jar of jam were on the shelf.
(1)

1. (A) Take away *were*.
   (B) Change *were* to *was*.
   (C) Do not change.

The child has ducks. The children has many ducks.
(2)

2. (A) Change *has* to *have*.
   (B) Take away *has*.
   (C) Do not change.

Yasmin have many ducks. The ducks have a home.
(3)

3. (A) Take away *have*.
   (B) Change *have* to *has*.
   (C) Do not change.

Sam went to get help. Sam go up the tree.
(4)

4. (A) Change *go* to *went*.
   (B) Take away *go*.
   (C) Do not change.

Go on →

**GRAMMAR PRACTICE BOOK, 127–128**

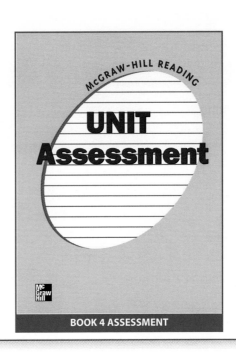

Assign spelling words from two different selections to partners. Have each partner write his or her words in scrambled form on a sheet of paper. Then have partners exchange papers and try to unscramble the spelling words as fast as they can.

### Unit Review

**Long i**
smile
white
hide

**Long a**
rain
day
tail

**Long o**
home
hope
nose

**Social Studies Words**
truck
smoke
ring

**Long u**
rule
cute
tube

---

Name_____ Date_____ UNIT TEST SPELLING **127**

**Book 1.4 Unit Review Test**

Read each sentence. If an underlined word is spelled wrong, fill in the circle that goes with that word. If no word is spelled wrong, fill in the circle below NONE.

Read Sample A, and do Sample B.

A. The twigs will drope in the snow.
A  B  C
A. Ⓐ Ⓑ Ⓒ Ⓓ NONE

B. When was the class tripe.
E  F  G
B. Ⓔ Ⓕ ● Ⓗ NONE

1. That dog has a white nose and taile.
A  B  C
1. Ⓐ Ⓑ ● Ⓓ NONE

2. I hope to fill the tuube with white seeds.
E  F  G
2. Ⓔ ● Ⓖ Ⓗ NONE

3. The baby at home has a cute pink noize.
A  B  C
3. Ⓐ Ⓑ ● Ⓓ NONE

4. Do not hide your smyle in the smoke.
E  F  G
4. Ⓔ ● Ⓖ Ⓗ NONE

5. I hope it will not raine on that day.
A  B  C
5. Ⓐ ● Ⓒ Ⓓ NONE

6. He will hope to find a ring at hom.
E  F  G
6. Ⓔ Ⓕ ● Ⓗ NONE

Book 1.4

**SPELLING PRACTICE BOOK, 127–128**

---

### Phonics and Decoding
☑ Long *i: i-e*
☑ Long *o: o-e*
☑ Long *u: u-e*
☑ Long *a: ay, ai*

### Comprehension
☑ Cause and Effect
☑ Make Inferences

### Vocabulary Strategies
☑ Inflectional Endings *-s, -es*
☑ Inflectional Ending *-ed*
☑ Inflectional Endings *-er, -est*

### Study Skills
☑ Charts

### Writing
Persuasive Writing

---

McGRAW-HILL READING

**UNIT Assessment**

McGraw Hill

**BOOK 4 ASSESSMENT**

# Assessment
# Follow-Up

Use the results of the informal and formal assessment opportunities in the unit to help you make decisions about future instruction.

| SKILLS AND STRATEGIES | Reteaching Blackline Masters | Alternate Teaching Strategies |
|---|---|---|
| **Phonics and Decoding** | | |
| Long *i: i-e* | 127, 131, 132, 140, 148, 159 | T64 |
| Long *o: o-e* | 135, 139, 140, 148, 156, 159 | T68 |
| Long *u: u-e* | 143, 147, 148, 156, 159 | T70 |
| Long *a: ay, ai* | 151, 155, 156, 159 | T72 |
| **Comprehension** | | |
| Cause and Effect | 133, 141, 163 | T66 |
| Make Inferences | 149, 157, 164 | T70 |
| **Vocabulary Strategies** | | |
| Inflectional Endings *-s, -es, -ed* | 134, 142, 165 | T65, T67 |
| Inflectional Endings *-er, -est* | 150, 158, 166 | T66 |
| **Study Skills** | | |
| Charts | 130, 138, 146, 154, 162 | T65 |

| | Alternate Writing Project–Easy | Unit Writing Process Lesson |
|---|---|---|
| **Writing** | | |
| Persuasive Writing | 37N, 65N, 95N, 123N, 133N | 135A–135F |

**McGraw-Hill School**
**TECHNOLOGY**

 **Phonics** **CD-ROM** provides extra phonics support.

 **inter NET**
**CONNECTION** Research & Inquiry ideas. Visit **www.mhschool.com/reading.**

# Glossary

Introduce children to the Glossary by inviting them to look through the pages, describing and discussing what they see there.

Explain that the Glossary will help them find out the meanings of words. Explain that the **Glossary** is a special kind of dictionary just for words from the selections in this book. You will probably want to give a simple definition of *dictionary*, such as: "a book that shows how words are spelled and what they mean."

Point out that words in a glossary, like words in a dictionary, are listed in **alphabetical order.** Explain that in this glossary, not all the letters of the alphabet are represented.

Point out the **entry words.** Ask children to note that each entry word is printed in heavy black type and that it appears on a line by itself. Also point out that each entry word is used in a sentence and is illustrated in a picture. Mention that there are two sentences for some of the words; in such cases, the second sentence includes a word that has the same meaning as the entry word. Also mention that each picture helps to make the meaning of the accompanying word clearer.

Give children time to study the Glossary and discover what information it includes.

# Glossary

This glossary can help you to find out the meanings of words in this book that you may not know.

The words are listed in alphabetical order. There is a picture and a simple sentence for each word. You can use the picture and sentence to help you understand the meaning of each word.

## Sample Entry

Main Entry | Sample Sentence

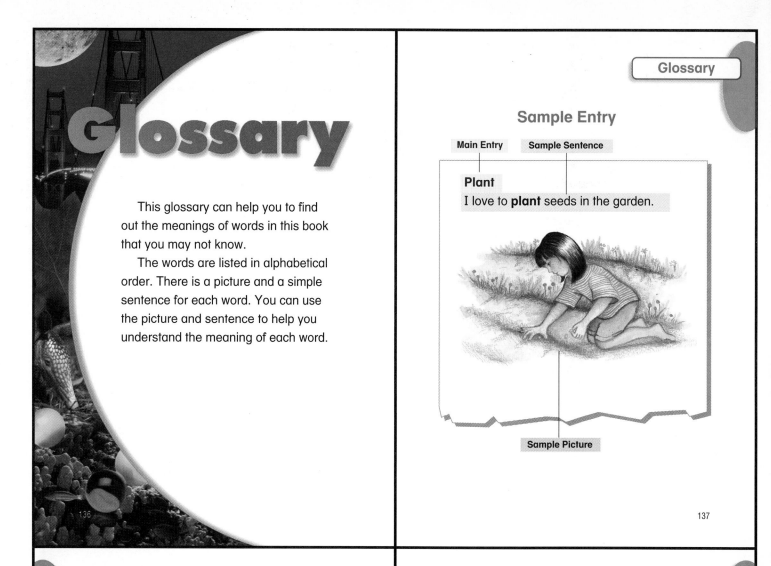

**Plant**
I love to **plant** seeds in the garden.

Sample Picture

**Apple**
An **apple** is a fruit.

**Bag**
Tim put the potatoes in the **bag**.
Another word for **bag** is *sack*.

**Corn**
I love to eat **corn** on the cob.

**Ducks**
**Ducks** are birds that swim in ponds.

### Grapes

**Grapes** grow on a grapevine.

### Hose

Water in the **hose** will help put out the fire.

140

### Jars

The **jars** are filled with jelly.
*Bottles* is another word for **jars.**

### Ladder

The **ladder** helps the fireman put out the fire.

141

### Plant

I love to **plant** seeds in the garden.

### Pole

The **pole** helps firefighters get to the fire quickly.

142

### Rocket

The **rocket** travels to outer space.
Another word for **rocket** is *spaceship.*

### Smoke

The **smoke** is coming from the burning building.

143

**G3**

# ACKNOWLEDGMENTS

*The publisher gratefully acknowledges permission to reprint the following copyrighted material:*

"To the Top" by Sandra Liatsos. Copyright ©1992 by Sandra Liatsos. Used by premission of Marian Reiner for the author.

"Who Lived in a Shoe?" by Beatrix Potter from SING A SONG OF POPCORN. Copyright © 1988 by Scholastic Inc. Reprinted by permission of Scholastic Inc.

**Illustration**
Steve Johnson, Lou Francher, 6–7; Michele Noiset, 8–9; Shirley Beckes, 10–33, 34tl; Daniel Del Valle, 34br, 62br, 120b; Rita Lascaro, 35tr, 36, 64, 94, 122; Ken Bowser, 37, 123; Nancy Davis, 38–39; Dominic Catalano, 40–61, 62tl; Bernard Adnet, 65, 133; Doreen Gay–Kassel, 66–67; Tim Raglin, 68–93; Eldon Doty, 95; Kathleen O'Malley, 96–97; Michael Steirnagle, 98–119, 120tl; Darcia Labrosse, 124–125; Nancy Tobin, 132; Yuri Salzman, 134–5; George Thompson, 138; Peter Fasolino, 140–141; Holly Jones, 142–143.

**Photography**
40: b. Nick Cantalano/Courtesy of Dominic Catalano.  68: T. Courtesy of Ms. Ellen Dryer.  98: b. Courtesy of Michael Steirnagle. 138: t. .  139: b. Image Bank/Alvis Upitis.  t. Corbis/Philip Gould; 140: t. The Stock Market/(c) Bo Zaunders.  141: b. Corbis/George Hall.  142: b. FPG international/(c) Ron Rovtar.  143: t. Image Bank.

# Contents

## General Store
**Rachel Field**

Someday I'm going to have a store
With a tinkly bell hung over the door,
With real glass cases and counters wide
And drawers all spilly with things inside.
There'll be a little of everything:
Bolts of calico; balls of string;
Jars of peppermint; tins of tea;
Pots and kettles and crockery;
Seeds in packets; scissors bright;
Kegs of sugar, brown and white;
Sarsaparilla for picnic lunches,
Bananas and rubber boots in bunches.
I'll fix the window and dust each shelf,
And take the money in all myself,
It will be my store and I will say:
"What can I do for you today?"

## Drawing Ducks
**Constance Levy**

I'm really good at drawing ducks
I make them very yellow
I always make them following
the leader in a row
I always make them walking left—
and then I wonder *where they go*!

I give each one an orange bill
Each eye I dot just so . . .
and then they look at me so hard
it makes me wonder
*what they know*!

# Timimoto

**retold by Margaret H. Lippert**

Once upon a time in Japan there lived an old man and an old woman. They were very lonely because they had no children. One day the old woman said to her husband, "I wish we had a child. I would like a little boy, even if he is no bigger than my finger."

That day as the old woman went to fetch water, she heard crying by the side of the path. She looked in the grass and there lay a tiny baby, only one inch long, wrapped in a red handkerchief.

The old woman was overjoyed. She took the baby home and showed him to her husband. "My wish has come true," she said. "Now we will never be lonely again." They named the baby Timimoto.

Timimoto grew up, but not very much. When he was five years old, he was as tall as his mother's thumb. At fifteen, he was only as tall as his mother's middle finger.

One morning Timimoto said, "I am going on a journey to see the world. Do not worry about me, for I will return safely." His parents were sad, but they did not want to stop him. They knew he would not be happy unless they let him go. "You will need a sword," said his mother. She took a sewing needle, slid it into a piece of straw, and tied it to his belt. "Use this to defend yourself against danger," she said.

His father got a rice bowl from the cupboard and carried it down to the river. He gave a chopstick to his son and said, "Now you have a boat and a paddle." Timimoto climbed into his boat and paddled happily down the river. His parents waved until he disappeared behind a bend.

Suddenly Timimoto felt something slap him across his back. Turning quickly, he saw a huge green frog behind his boat. The frog's long tongue lashed out at him again.

Timimoto ducked. He pushed the chopstick as hard as he could against the giant frog's jaw. The frog tumbled over in the water and dived out of sight. Timimoto turned his boat and paddled across the river.

Near the other shore the wind blew stronger. The waves got higher and higher. One wave broke over the bowl and almost turned it upside-down. Timimoto paddled as hard as he could toward the shore. It was getting late, and he did not want to spend the night on the water.

Just ahead he saw a dock. Beyond the dock was a town. He tied up his little boat and climbed onto the dock. The dock was crowded with people rushing to town. Timimoto walked along the dock with them, taking care to stay out of the way of their huge feet.

At the end of the dock, Timimoto could see a road crowded with carts, all going to town. To keep from being run over, Timimoto climbed up onto the wheel of a cart and rode there. When the cart stopped he hopped down. "Thank you," he called up to the driver.

The driver looked all around, then he looked down by his feet. "Ho, little one, you must be new in town," he said. "Don't you know that a terrible giant comes out when the sun sets?" The driver hurried away, and Timimoto saw that all the people were going into their houses.

Soon the streets were empty. The sun went down. Timimoto heard the earth rumble. He looked up and saw a huge giant with red eyes and sharp teeth standing over him. Strong fingers closed around him and lifted him into the air.

"AH-AH! A tender little morsel!" roared the giant. He popped Timimoto into his mouth. Timimoto drew his sword and stabbed the giant's tongue. "AGGGGH!" screamed the giant, and Timimoto leaped from his open mouth to the ground.

The giant ran screaming into the forest. Timimoto heard cheering all around him. People poured from their houses into the street. "You have defeated the giant!" they shouted. All night long they feasted and danced in his honor. When the sun came up everyone went down to the dock. Timimoto untied his little boat, climbed in, and headed home.

## The Great Big Enormous Turnip

**a Russian Folktale**
**retold by Alexei Tolstoi**

Once upon a time an old man planted a little turnip and said: "Grow, grow, little turnip, grow strong!"

And the turnip grew up sweet and strong and big and enormous.

Then, one day, the old man went to pull it up. He pulled and pulled again, but he could not pull it up.

He called the old woman.

The old woman pulled the old man,

The old man pulled the turnip.

And they pulled and pulled again, but they could not pull it up.

So the old woman called her granddaughter.

The granddaughter pulled the old woman,

The old woman pulled the old man,

The old man pulled the turnip.

And they pulled and pulled again, but they could not pull it up.

The granddaughter called the black dog,

The black dog pulled the granddaughter,

The granddaughter pulled the old woman,

The old woman pulled the old man,

The old man pulled the turnip.

And they pulled and pulled again, but they could not pull it up.

The black dog called the cat,

The cat pulled the black dog,

The black dog pulled the granddaughter,

The granddaughter pulled the old woman,

The old woman pulled the old man,

The old man pulled the turnip.

And they pulled and pulled again, but they could not pull it up.

The cat called the mouse.

The mouse pulled the cat,

The cat pulled the dog,

The dog pulled the granddaughter,

The granddaughter pulled the old woman,

The old woman pulled the old man,

The old man pulled the turnip.

And they pulled and pulled again, and up came the turnip at last.

## The Brave Ones
**Eloise Greenfield**

We hear the bell clanging
we come in a hurry
we come with our ladders and hoses
our hoses
we come in a hurry
to fight the fire
the furious fire
to smother the smoke
the smoke
we don't have much time
we climb, we spray
we are the brave ones who save
who save
we are the brave ones who save

## Annotated Workbooks

---

Name_____ Date_____ **Practice** 127

### Long *i: i-e*

Use the words in the box to answer the riddles.

| five | smile | time | rice | ripe |
|------|-------|------|------|------|

1. Six is after me. What am I? ___five___

2. You do this with your lips. What am I? ___smile___

3. A good plum is this way. What am I? ___ripe___

4. A clock tells you about me. What am I? ___time___

5. You can eat me. What am I? ___rice___

Book 1.4
The Shopping List

**At Home:** Have children make up sentences using each of the words in the box.

127

---

Name_____ Date_____ **Practice** 128

### High-Frequency Words

Write the word from the box that completes each sentence.

| after | always | blue | were | who |
|-------|--------|------|------|-----|

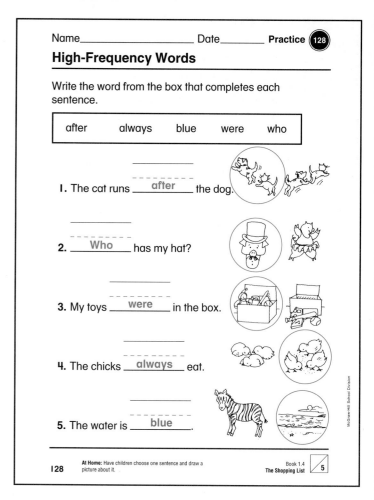

1. The cat runs ___after___ the dog.

2. ___Who___ has my hat?

3. My toys ___were___ in the box.

4. The chicks ___always___ eat.

5. The water is ___blue___.

128

**At Home:** Have children choose one sentence and draw a picture about it.

Book 1.4
The Shopping List

5

---

The Wish Fish

Then the man wished for a kite. So the fish tied the man and his wife to the kite. Soon they were up in the sky.
"Now I have my wish!" said the fish. "They are gone."

**At Home:** Have children draw a picture that illustrates the story.

128a

---

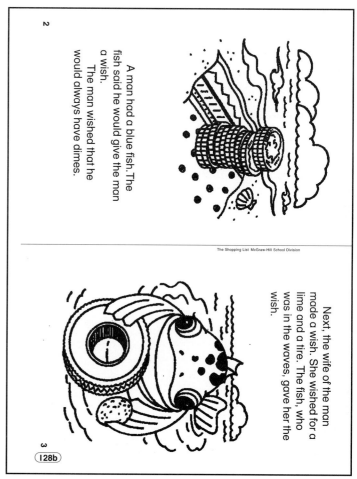

A man had a blue fish. The fish said he would give the man a wish.
The man wished that he would always have dimes.

Next, the wife of the man made a wish. She wished for a lime and a tire. The fish, who was in the waves, gave her the wish.

128b

---

# The Shopping List • PRACTICE

## Story Comprehension

Think about what happened in "The Shopping List."
Write **T** if the sentence is **true**. Write **F** if the
sentence is **false**.

1. ___T___ Mike has a list.

2. ___F___ His dad drives a bus.

3. ___T___ Dad wants to know what Mike forgot.

4. ___T___ Dad hunts and hunts.

5. ___T___ Fran and Ann try to help Mike.

6. ___T___ At last, Miss Lin gives up.

7. ___F___ Mike gets sad and goes away.

8. ___T___ Mom wants Mike to tell Dad it is time to eat.

---

## A Chart

Look at the **chart**.

| What You Buy in a Hardware Store | |
| --- | --- |
| Kitchen | Workshop |
| pot | pipe |
| cups | lock |
| forks | file |
| cake pan | nails |
| plates | pump |
| | clamp |

Write the correct answer on the line.

1. Which things are for the workshop?

   _____

   **pipe, lock, file, nails, pump, clamp**

2. Which things are for the kitchen?

   _____

   **pot, cups, forks, cake pan, plates**

3. Name something you use to eat with.

   _____

   **fork**

4. What is something you might hit with a hammer?

   _____

   **nails**

---

## Long *i*: *i-e*

Write the words in each group that have the same
middle sound as in h**i**d**e**.

1. bike    nine    take

   __bike__    __nine__    _____

2. lime    pine    cane

   __lime__    __pine__    _____

3. late    slide    kite

   _____    __slide__    __kite__

4. write    wide    wade

   __write__    __wide__    _____

5. tire    ride    tale

   __tire__    __ride__    _____

---

## *i-e, a-e*

Circle the word that completes the sentence.
Then write it on the line.

1. They ___bite___ the chunk.

   (bite)    fake    wade

2. He locks the ___gate___.

   shame    (gate)    tale

3. Fish swim in the ___lake___.

   bake    late    (lake)

4. We see a bee ___hive___.

   (hive)    rake    size

5. The clock ___wakes___ me up.

   (wakes)    trade    line

**T7**

# The Shopping List • PRACTICE

## Cause and Effect

Look at the picture. Underline the sentence that tells what will probably happen.

1. He rides on a pony.

   He goes inside the house.

2. She fixes the tire.

   She rides to school.

3. She goes outside.

   She goes to bed.

4. The rain comes in.

   The sun comes out.

5. The tree has no leaves.

   The tree has many leaves.

5 Book 1.4 The Shopping List

At Home: Have children tell the cause and the effect in each situation.

133

## Inflectional Endings -s, -es

Add **-s** or **-es** to tell what only one person or thing does.

When a word ends in **e** or most consonants, add **-s**. When a word ends in **sh, ch, x,** or **ss**, add **-es**.

Circle the word that completes each sentence. Then write the word on the line.

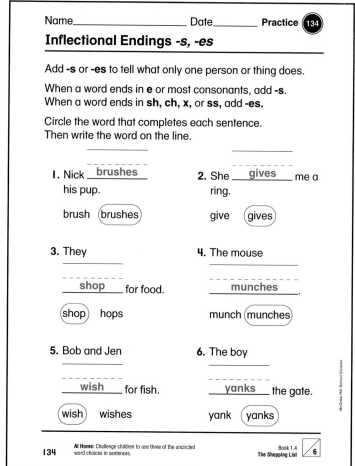

1. Nick _____brushes_____ his pup.

   brush (brushes)

2. She _____gives_____ me a ring.

   give (gives)

3. They

   _____shop_____ for food.

   (shop) hops

4. The mouse

   _____munches_____.

   munch (munches)

5. Bob and Jen

   _____wish_____ for fish.

   (wish) wishes

6. The boy

   _____yanks_____ the gate.

   yank (yanks)

134

At Home: Challenge children to use three of the uncircled word choices in sentences.

Book 1.4 The Shopping List 6

# The Shopping List • RETEACH

## Long *i*: *i-e*

> Read the sentence.
> Would you **like** to **bite** a **lime**?

Circle the word that completes the sentence.
Then write the word.

1. I _____ smile _____ when I am glad.

   (smile)   bite   gripe

2. He wants to _____ write _____ a letter.

   (write)   wide   live

3. I like her _____ white _____ dress.

   mile   drive   (white)

4. My cat had _____ five _____ kittens.

   rice   bride   (five)

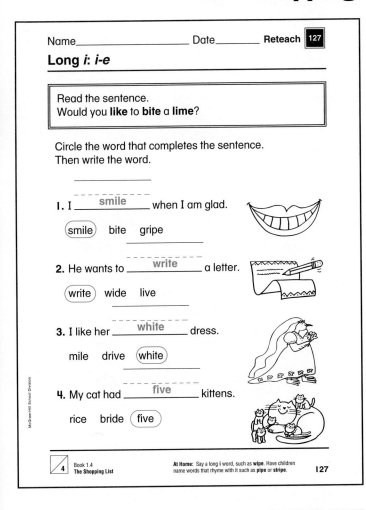

---

## High-Frequency Words

Write the word in each sentence that is taken from the box.

| always | after | blue | were | who |
| --- | --- | --- | --- | --- |

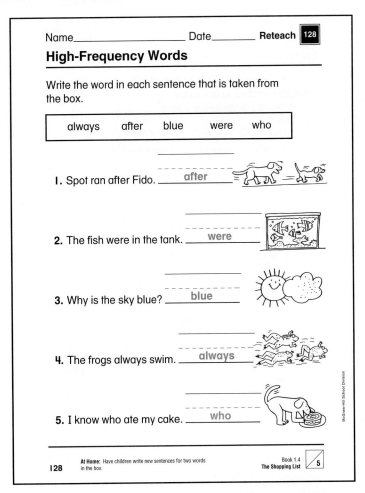

1. Spot ran after Fido. _____ after _____

2. The fish were in the tank. _____ were _____

3. Why is the sky blue? _____ blue _____

4. The frogs always swim. _____ always _____

5. I know who ate my cake. _____ who _____

---

## Story Comprehension

Think about "The Shopping List." Fill in the chart below.

**First:** Mike goes to the store with a

shopping list.

**Then:** Mike can't remember one thing he had to get.

**Next:** Miss Lin, Fran, and Ann try to help Mike.

**Finally:** Mike remembers what is not on the list.

Mom wants Dad to come home with Mike.

---

## A Chart

> This **chart** tells you which things are food and which are not.

| FOOD | | NON-FOOD | |
| --- | --- | --- | --- |
| jam | cake | lamp | drum |
| ham | grapes | box | crib |
| milk | fish | tent | lock |
| celery | dill | mask | hat |

Circle the word that completes each sentence.

1. A box ( is  (is not) ) a food.

2. Milk is a ( (food)  non-food ).

3. Two non-foods are the tent and the ( jam  (mask) ).

4. Two foods are ham and ( tent  (fish) ).

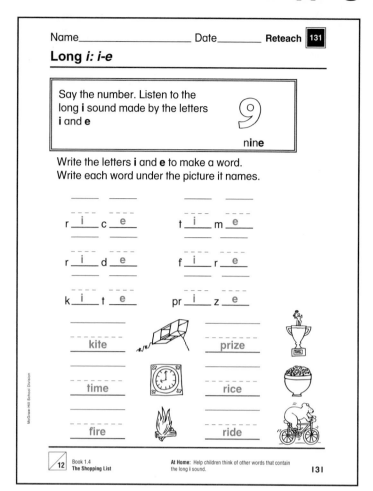

Name_____ Date_____ **Reteach** 131

## Long *i*: *i-e*

Say the number. Listen to the
long **i** sound made by the letters
**i** and **e**

9

nine

Write the letters **i** and **e** to make a word.
Write each word under the picture it names.

r__i__ c __e__          t __i__ m __e__

r __i__ d __e__          f __i__ r __e__

k __i__ t __e__          pr __i__ z __e__

kite                    prize

time                    rice

fire                    ride

12
Book 1.4
**The Shopping List**
**At Home:** Help children think of other words that contain
the long **i** sound.
131

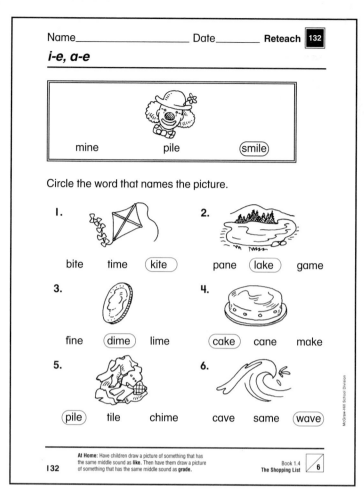

Name_____ Date_____ **Reteach** 132

## *i-e*, *a-e*

mine          pile          (smile)

Circle the word that names the picture.

1.                          2.

bite    time    (kite)      pane    (lake)    game

3.                          4.

fine    (dime)    lime      (cake)    cane    make

5.                          6.

(pile)    tile    chime      cave    same    (wave)

**At Home:** Have children draw a picture of something that has
the same middle sound as **like**. Then have them draw a picture
132    of something that has the same middle sound as **grade**.
Book 1.4
**The Shopping List**
6

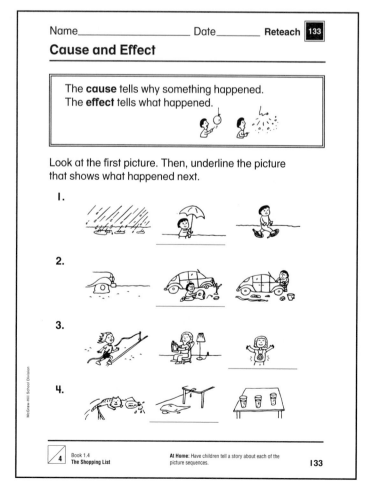

Name_____ Date_____ **Reteach** 133

## Cause and Effect

The **cause** tells why something happened.
The **effect** tells what happened.

Look at the first picture. Then, underline the picture
that shows what happened next.

1.

2.

3.

4.

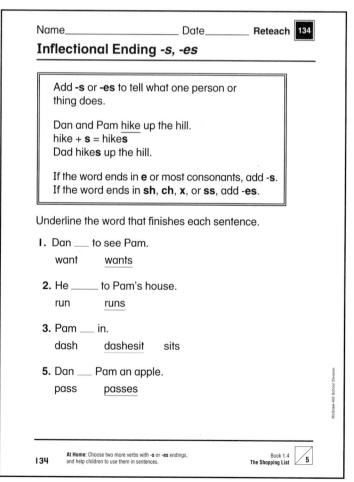

Name_____ Date_____ **Reteach** 134

## Inflectional Ending *-s*, *-es*

Add **-s** or **-es** to tell what one person or
thing does.

Dan and Pam hike up the hill.
hike + **s** = hike**s**
Dad hike**s** up the hill.

If the word ends in **e** or most consonants, add -**s**.
If the word ends in **sh**, **ch**, **x**, or **ss**, add -**es**.

Underline the word that finishes each sentence.

1. Dan ___ to see Pam.
   want        wants

2. He _____ to Pam's house.
   run         runs

3. Pam ___ in.
   dash    dashesit    sits

5. Dan ___ Pam an apple.
   pass        passes

134    **At Home:** Choose two more verbs with **-s** or **-es** endings,
and help children to use them in sentences.
Book 1.4
**The Shopping List**
5

# The Shopping List • EXTEND

## Long *i*: *i-e*

Read the words in the box. Find them in the puzzle.
Circle them.

| like | white | ride | ripe | Mike | nice | smile |

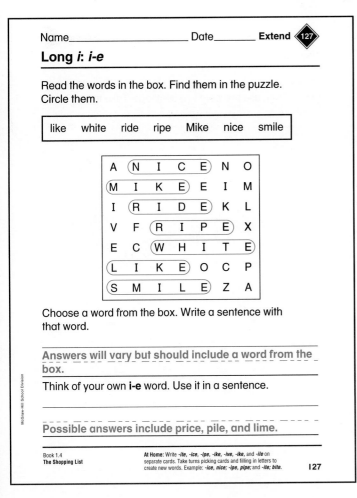

Choose a word from the box. Write a sentence with that word.

_____

_Answers will vary but should include a word from the box._

Think of your own **i-e** word. Use it in a sentence.

_____

_Possible answers include price, pile, and lime._

Book 1.4
The Shopping List

**At Home:** Write *-ite, -ice, -ipe, -ike, -ive, -ike,* and *-ile* on separate cards. Take turns picking cards and filling in letters to create new words. Example: *-ice, nice; -ipe, pipe;* and *-ile; bite.*

127

## High-Frequency Words

| after | always | blue | were | who |

Write the word from the box that completes each sentence. Then write a sentence using the word that is left.

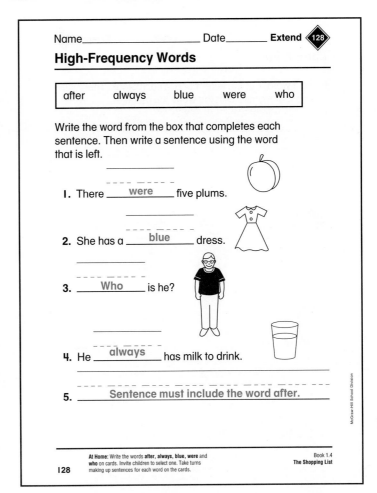

_____

1. There ___were___ five plums.

_____

2. She has a ___blue___ dress.

_____

3. ___Who___ is he?

_____

4. He ___always___ has milk to drink.

_____

5. _Sentence must include the word after._

128

**At Home:** Write the words **after, always, blue, were** and **who** on cards. Invite children to select one. Take turns making up sentences for each word on the cards.

Book 1.4
The Shopping List

## Story Comprehension

What do you put on a shopping list? Look at the pictures. Make a list of things to buy. Then add more things. Draw a picture, too.

**SHOPPING LIST**

cake

milk

grapes

Book 1.4
The Shopping List

**At Home:** Invite children to identify the fruits and vegetables and their colors. Make a shopping list together.

129

## Use a Chart

Fill in the chart.

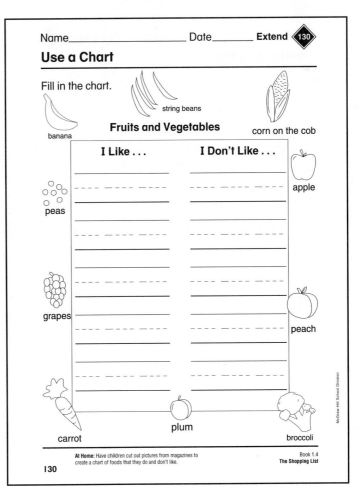

**Fruits and Vegetables**

| I Like . . . | I Don't Like . . . |
| --- | --- |
| | |

130

**At Home:** Have children cut out pictures from magazines to create a chart of foods that they do and don't like.

Book 1.4
The Shopping List

**T11**

# The Shopping List • EXTEND

## Long *i: i-e*

Make a word. Put the letter **i** or **e** in each blank. Then write a word that rhymes with the word you made.

Sample answers are given.

| Word | Rhyming Words |
|------|---------------|

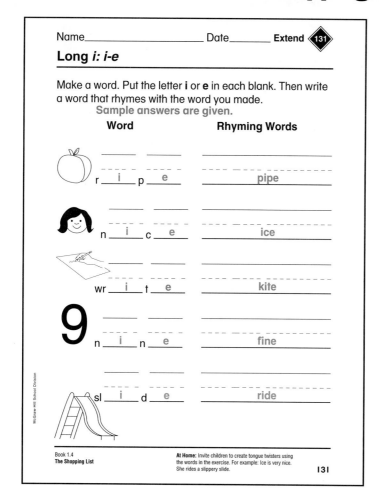

r _i_ p _e_     pipe

n _i_ c _e_     ice

wr _i_ t _e_     kite

**9**   n _i_ n _e_     fine

sl _i_ d _e_     ride

**At Home:** Invite children to create tongue twisters using the words in the exercise. For example: Ice is very nice. She rides a slippery slide.

131

---

## *i-e, a-e*

Play a word game with a friend. Move one space. Read the word. Then use the word in a sentence. Take turns. Get to the end!

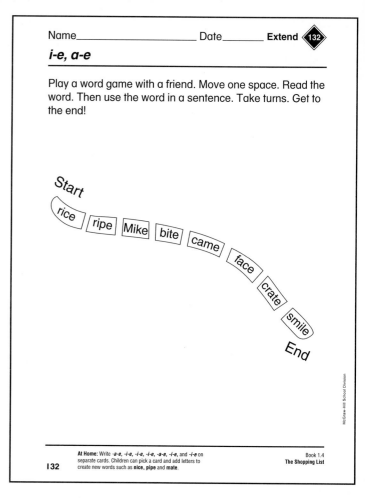

Start — rice — ripe — Mike — bite — came — face — crate — smile — End

**At Home:** Write -a-e, -i-e, -i-e, -i-e, -a-e, -i-e, and -i-e on separate cards. Children can pick a card and add letters to create new words such as **nice, pipe** and **mate**.

132

---

## Cause and Effect

Draw a picture of what could happen next.

**At Home:** Ask children what happens when: 1) they are late for school, 2) they go to bed too late at night, 3) they're hungry.

133

---

## Inflectional Endings *-s, -es*

Choose one of the two words. Use it in a sentence. Circle the word you used.   Sample answers are given.

**can   cans**

I will buy a can of soup.

**grape   grapes**

Here are the red grapes.

**muffin   muffins**

I like corn muffins.

**plum   plums**

Plums taste good.

Look at the picture. Write a sentence about it. Use one of the words in the box.

**duck   ducks**

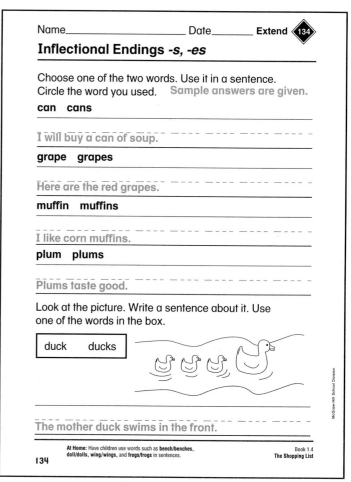

The mother duck swims in the front.

**At Home:** Have children use words such as **bench/benches, doll/dolls, wing/wings,** and **frogs/frogs** in sentences.

134

---

**T12**   *Annotated Workbooks*

# The Shopping List • GRAMMAR

## *Was* and *Were*

- The words *was* and *were* are verbs that tell about the past.
- The word *was* tells about one person, place, or thing.

    Mike **was** in his Dad's store

Read the sentences. Write *was* in each sentence.

1. Dad _____was_____ happy.

2. Mike _____was_____ in the store.

3. No one _____was_____ home.

4. Miss Lin _____was_____ with Mike.

5. The store _____was_____ full of people.

5 | Book 1.4
The Shopping List

EXTENSION: Ask students to use the words *was* and *were* to write sentences about what they did yesterday.

97

## *Was* and *Were*

- The words *was* and *were* are verbs that tell about the past.
- The word *was* tells about one person, place, or thing.
- The word *were* tells about more than one person, place, or thing.

    Gran and Ann **were** in the store.

Read the sentence about each picture.
Circle the verb for more than one person, place, or thing.

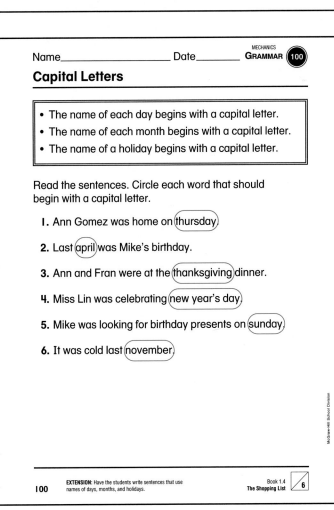

1. Mom and Dad (were) happy.

2. The jam and rice (were) for supper.

3. Mike and Dad (were) smiling.

4. The five plums (were) in a bag.

5. Grapes (were) on the list.

98

EXTENSION: Have the children think of sentences about shopping for groceries. The sentences should be about more than one person, place, or thing.

Book 1.4
The Shopping List | 5

## *Was* and *Were*

- The words *was* and *were* are verbs that tell about the past.
- The word *was* tells about one person, place, or thing.

    Mike **was** smiling.

- The word *were* tells about more than one person, place, or thing.

    Fran and Ann **were** smiling.

Read the sentences. Write *was* for one person, place, or thing. Write *were* for more than one person, place, or thing.

1. Mike _____was_____ in the store.

2. Fran _____was_____ in the store.

3. Fran and Ann _____were_____ there.

4. Tin cans and glass jars _____were_____ on the shelves.

5. Fran and Ann _____were_____ trying to help.

5 | Book 1.4
The Shopping List

EXTENSION: Have the children change the sentences with one person, place, or thing to sentences with more than one.

99

## Capital Letters

- The name of each day begins with a capital letter.
- The name of each month begins with a capital letter.
- The name of a holiday begins with a capital letter.

Read the sentences. Circle each word that should begin with a capital letter.

1. Ann Gomez was home on (thursday)

2. Last (april) was Mike's birthday.

3. Ann and Fran were at the (thanksgiving) dinner.

4. Miss Lin was celebrating (new year's day)

5. Mike was looking for birthday presents on (sunday)

6. It was cold last (november)

100

EXTENSION: Have the students write sentences that use names of days, months, and holidays.

Book 1.4
The Shopping List | 6

# The Shopping List • GRAMMAR

**Test**

Circle *was* or *were* to complete each sentence.

1. Mike _____ was _____ glad to see Mom.
   (was)   were

2. Miss Lin and Dad _____ were _____ helping.
   was   (were)

3. Ann and Fran _____ were _____ helping.
   was   (were)

4. There _____ was _____ something else to get.
   (was)   were

5. It _____ was _____ not milk.
   (was)   were

**More Practice With *Was* and *Were***

- The words *was* and *were* are verbs that tell about the past.
- The word *was* tells about one person, place, or thing.
- The word *were* tells about more than one person, place, or thing.

Read each sentence. Write *was* or *were* in the blank. Color the pictures. The sentences tell you how.

1. The grapes _____ were _____ green.
   Color them purple.

2. The can _____ was _____ tan.
   Color it red.

3. The boxes _____ were _____ yellow.
   Color them blue.

4. The ducks _____ were _____ white.
   Color them yellow.

# The Shopping List • SPELLING

## Words with Long i : i-e

**Pretest Directions**

Fold back the paper along the dotted line. Use the blanks to write each word as it is read aloud. When you finish the test, unfold the paper. Use the list at the right to correct any spelling mistakes. Practice the words you missed for the Posttest.

1. _____
2. _____
3. _____
4. _____
5. _____
6. _____

1. smile
2. white
3. wide
4. while
5. bite
6. hide

**To Parents**

Here are the results of your child's weekly spelling Pretest. You can help your child study for the Posttest by following these simple steps for each word on the list:

1. Read the word to your child.
2. Have your child write the word, saying each letter as it is written.
3. Say each letter of the word as your child checks the spelling.
4. If a mistake has been made, have your child read each letter of the correctly spelled word aloud, and then repeat steps 1-3.

**Challenge Words**

after

blue

were

who

Book 1.4
5  The Shopping List          97

---

## Words with Long *i*: *i-e*

**Using the Word Study Steps**

1. LOOK at the word.
2. SAY the word aloud.
3. STUDY the letters in the word.
4. WRITE the word.
5. CHECK the word. Did you spell the word right? If not, go back to step 1.

**Spelling Tip**

When there is a long vowel sound at the beginning or in the middle of a one-syllable word, it usually has two vowels.

wi**d**e

**X the Word**

In each row, put an X on the word that does not belong.

| 1. | smile | pile | ~~win~~ |
| 2. | white | ~~pat~~ | red |
| 3. | wide | ~~dig~~ | tide |
| 4. | hot | cold | ~~while~~ |
| 5. | bite | ~~back~~ | kite |
| 6. | ~~lake~~ | hide | ride |

**To Parents or Helpers:**

Using the Word Study Steps above as your child comes across any new words will help him or her spell well. Review the steps as you both go over this week's spelling words.

Go over the Spelling Tip with your child. Help your child write new one-syllable words that have a long vowel sound at the beginning or in the middle and have two vowels.

Help your complete the spelling activity.

Book 1. 4
98          Shopping List  6

---

## Words with Long i : i-e

Look at the spelling words in the box.

| smile | white | wide | while | bite | hide |

Write the two letters that are found in every spelling word.

1. ___i___
2. ___e___

Write the words that end with ite.

3. ___white___
4. ___bite___

Write the words that end with ile.

5. ___smile___
6. ___while___

Write the words that end with ide.

7. ___wide___
8. ___hide___

Book 1.4
8  The Shopping List          99

---

## Words with Long i : i-e

Look at the pictures. Complete each spelling word by adding ite, ile, or ide.

1. My pal Dina always has a big

   sm ___ile___ on her face.

2. Her teeth are wh ___ite___ .

3. Her grin is very w ___ide___ .

4. The dog will not

   b ___ite___ your hand.

5. He will wag his tail wh ___ile___ you pet him.

6. Sometimes he likes to

   h ___ide___ in his doghouse.

Book 1.4
100          The Shopping List  6

**T15**

# The Shopping List • SPELLING

## Words with Long i : i-e

Finding Mistakes
Read the poem. There are six spelling mistakes.
Circle the mistakes. Write the words correctly on
the lines.

A tent that is (whide)
Is a good place to (hyd)
All the (whyle,)
I sit and (smil.)
I take a (bitte)
Of cake so (wite)

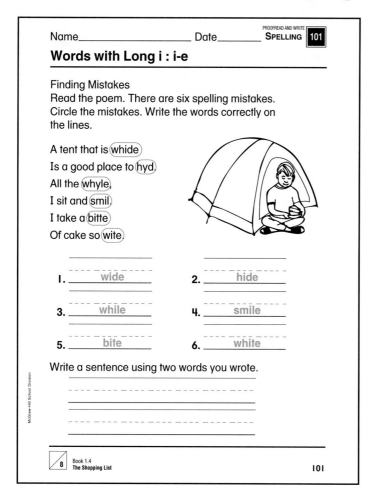

1. _____wide_____   2. _____hide_____
3. _____while_____   4. _____smile_____
5. _____bite_____   6. _____white_____

Write a sentence using two words you wrote.
_____
_____
_____

---

## Words with Long i : i-e

Look at the words in each set. One word in each
set is spelled correctly. Use a pencil to color in the
circle in front of that word. Before you begin, look at
the sample sets of words. Sample A has been
done for you. Do Sample B by yourself. When you
are sure you know what to do, you may go on with
the rest of the page.

Sample A
(A) side
(B) sid
(C) sidde

Sample B
(D) lak
(E) lacke
(F) lake

1. (A) byt
   (B) biet
   (C) bite

4. (D) hyde
   (E) heid
   (F) hide

2. (D) while
   (E) wile
   (F) whyl

5. (A) smyl
   (B) smile
   (C) smil

3. (A) wid
   (B) wide
   (C) wyde

6. (D) wite
   (E) white
   (F) whyte

## Practice 135

Name_____ Date_____ Practice **135**

### Long *o: o-e*

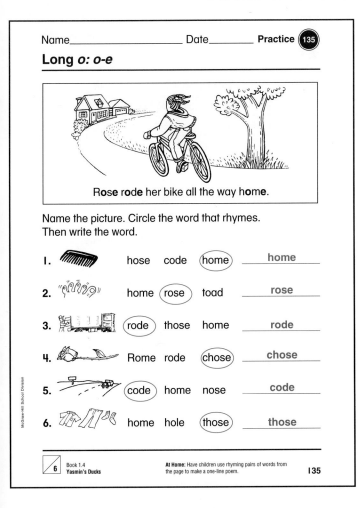

**R**ose r**o**de her bike all the way h**o**me.

Name the picture. Circle the word that rhymes.
Then write the word.

1. hose    code    (home)    ___home___

2. home    (rose)    toad    ___rose___

3. (rode)    those    home    ___rode___

4. Rome    rode    (chose)    ___chose___

5. (code)    home    nose    ___code___

6. home    hole    (those)    ___those___

Book 1.4
**Yasmin's Ducks**    6

**At Home:** Have children use rhyming pairs of words from the page to make a one-line poem.    135

## Practice 136

Name_____ Date_____ Practice **136**

### High-Frequency Words

Write the words from the box to finish the sentences.

| some | found | work | because | buy |

1. Dad went to ___work___.

2. We ___found___ our cat.

3. I will ___buy___ it at the store.

4. Jane is sad ___because___ she lost her ball.

5. Pam wants ___some___ chips.

136    **At Home:** Have children draw a picture to go along with one of the sentences.    Book 1.4
**Yasmin's Ducks**    5

---

Jake Gets Work

Now Jake has found a job. He puts out fires. And he is good at it. Now Jake can buy things. He has a home in Rome!

**At Home:** Invite children to talk about what jobs they would like to have when they are older.

4    136a

---

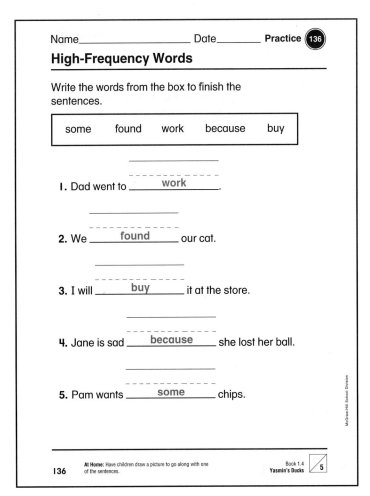

2

One day Jake went to work. But there was no work for him. Jake said. "I can go fast. I have a hose." Jake said. "I can go fast. I have a hose, I have to work. I want to buy some things."

NO WORK TODAY!

Yasmin's Ducks  McGraw-Hill School Division

Jake went in his truck to Rome. "There must be work here because it is big." said Jake.
At the woods near Rome, Jake saw smoke. He drove close. It was a fire. He got his hose. He put out the fire.

3    136b

# Yasmin's Ducks • PRACTICE

## Story Comprehension

Think about "Yasmin's Ducks." Finish each
sentence by circling the picture that tells the answer.

1. Yasmin likes to draw ___.

    a.                          b.

2. Yasmin saw ducks in a ___.

    a.                          b.

3. Ducks stay dry by ___.

    a.                          b.

4. Ducks can dive in a ___.

    a.                          b.

5. The ducks can't eat when the lake is ___.

    a.                          b.

---

## A Chart

Look at the tally **chart** below.

| What Pets Do You Like Best? | | | |
|---|---|---|---|
| Mice | IIIIII | Rats | IIIII |
| Cats | IIIIIIII | Birds | IIII |
| Dogs | IIIIII | Fish | IIIII |

This chart shows some children's favorite pets.
Count the marks next to each item. Then you will
know which pets the children like best.

Write the correct word to complete each sentence.

1. The favorite pet of most of the children is a ___cat___.

2. ___Five___ children like rats best.

3. Mice and dogs each have ___six___ tally marks.

4. Birds have ___four___ tally marks.

---

## Long *o: o-e*

Circle the picture in each box that has the long **o**
sound as in j**o**ke. Then write the word from the list
that tells what the picture shows.

| phone | rope | globe | cone |
|---|---|---|---|

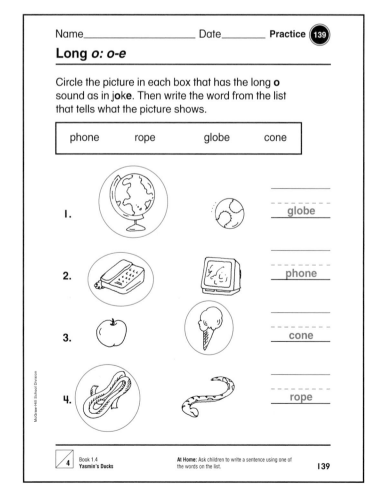

1. _____ globe

2. _____ phone

3. _____ cone

4. _____ rope

---

## *o-e, i-e, a-e*

Look at the picture. Complete each word by writing
**a**, **i**, or **o** in the blank.

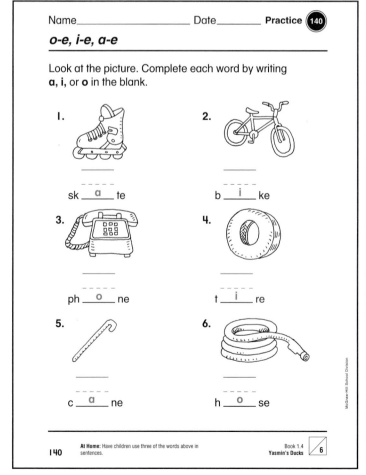

1. sk __a__ te

2. b __i__ ke

3. ph __o__ ne

4. t __i__ re

5. c __a__ ne

6. h __o__ se

---

**T18**  *Annotated Workbooks*

# Yasmin's Ducks • PRACTICE

## Cause and Effect

Look at each picture. It shows what happened.
Underline the sentence that tells why it happened.

|  Effect | Cause |
| --- | --- |

1.  Grandma lives near us.
    <u>Grandma lives far away.</u>
    Grandma came to see us.

2.  Dad rides the bike.
    Dad will go away.
    <u>Dad needs some help.</u>

3.  They are looking for a cat.
    <u>The girl wants a new ball.</u>
    Mother wants a green hat.

4.  <u>The dog wants the bone.</u>
    The dog will go away.
    The dog hit its nose.

4 / Book 1.4
Yasmin's Ducks

**At Home:** Challenge children to think of a sentence for each effect picture.

141

---

## Inflectional Ending -ed

Add **-ed** to show what one or more people or things did in the past.

Add **-ed** to the word. Then write the new word on the line to tell what happened in the past.

1. dash __ed__          Dave __dashed__ home.

2. kiss __ed__          Mom __kissed__ me.

3. jump __ed__          The kids __jumped__ up.

4. pick __ed__          Tom __picked__ the plum.

5. thank __ed__          We __thanked__ her.

6. drift __ed__          The stick __drifted__ away.

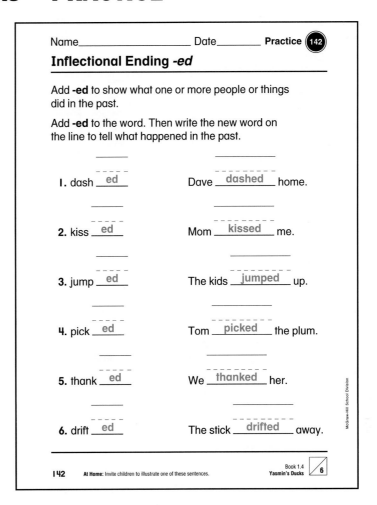

142    **At Home:** Invite children to illustrate one of these sentences.

Book 1.4
Yasmin's Ducks / 6

# Yasmin's Ducks • RETEACH

## Long *o* spelled *o-e*

| cone | smoke | bone |
|------|-------|------|

Circle the word that tells about the picture.

1. Is this a (home) or a **dome**?

2. Is this a **hose** or a (rose)?

3. Is this a (joke) or a **poke**?

4. Is this a **stone** or a (stove)?

5. Is this a (nose) or a **note**?

5 | Book 1.4
**Yasmin's Ducks**

At Home: Have children draw pictures of the long o words that are not circled (**dome, hose, poke, stone, note**). Have them write the word next to the picture.

135

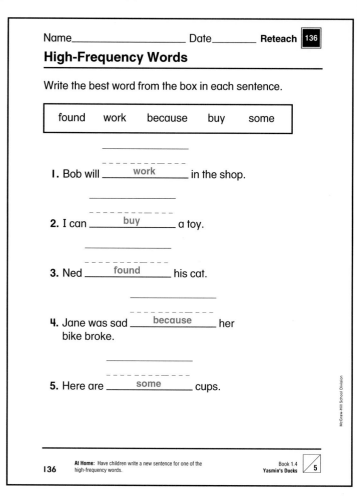

## High-Frequency Words

Write the best word from the box in each sentence.

| found | work | because | buy | some |
|-------|------|---------|-----|------|

1. Bob will _____work_____ in the shop.

2. I can _____buy_____ a toy.

3. Ned _____found_____ his cat.

4. Jane was sad _____because_____ her bike broke.

5. Here are _____some_____ cups.

136 | At Home: Have children write a new sentence for one of the high-frequency words.

Book 1.4
**Yasmin's Ducks** | 5

## Story Comprehension

Draw a line from the children to their pictures.

1. Tim

2. Kate

3. Mack

4. Yasmin

4 | Book 1.4
**Yasmin's Ducks**

At Home: Ask children to draw and label a picture of something they like.

137

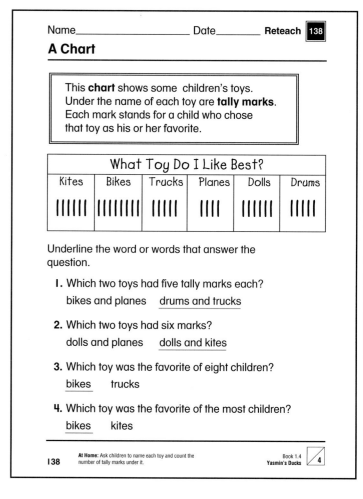

## A Chart

This **chart** shows some children's toys. Under the name of each toy are **tally marks**. Each mark stands for a child who chose that toy as his or her favorite.

| What Toy Do I Like Best? | | | | | |
|-------|-------|--------|--------|-------|-------|
| Kites | Bikes | Trucks | Planes | Dolls | Drums |
| ||||| | |||||||| | ||||| | |||| | |||||| | ||||| |

Underline the word or words that answer the question.

1. Which two toys had five tally marks each?
   bikes and planes     <u>drums and trucks</u>

2. Which two toys had six marks?
   dolls and planes     <u>dolls and kites</u>

3. Which toy was the favorite of eight children?
   <u>bikes</u>     trucks

4. Which toy was the favorite of the most children?
   <u>bikes</u>     kites

138 | At Home: Ask children to name each toy and count the number of tally marks under it.

Book 1.4
**Yasmin's Ducks** | 4

# Yasmin's Ducks • RETEACH

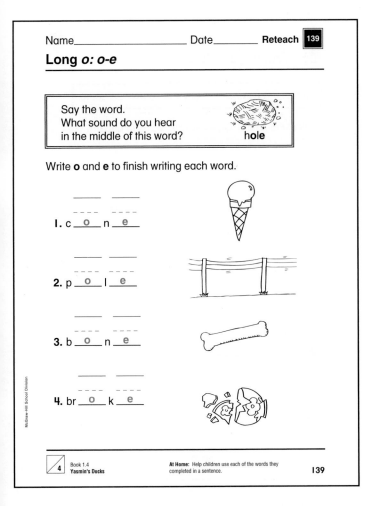

## Long *o*: *o-e*

Say the word.
What sound do you hear
in the middle of this word?

**hole**

Write **o** and **e** to finish writing each word.

1. c __o__ n __e__

2. p __o__ l __e__

3. b __o__ n __e__

4. br __o__ k __e__

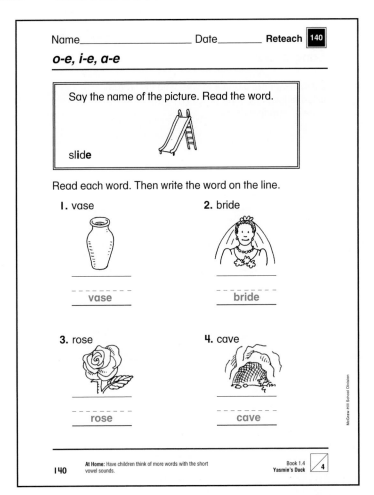

## *o-e, i-e, a-e*

Say the name of the picture. Read the word.

sl**ide**

Read each word. Then write the word on the line.

1. vase

vase

2. bride

bride

3. rose

rose

4. cave

cave

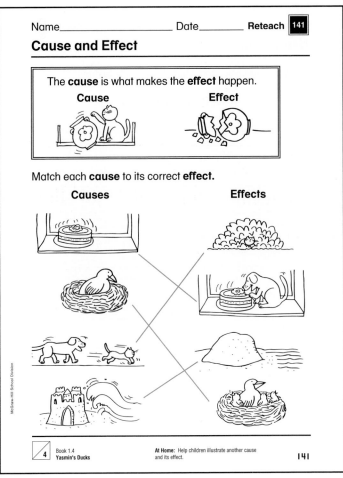

## Cause and Effect

The **cause** is what makes the **effect** happen.

**Cause**

**Effect**

Match each **cause** to its correct **effect**.

**Causes**    **Effects**

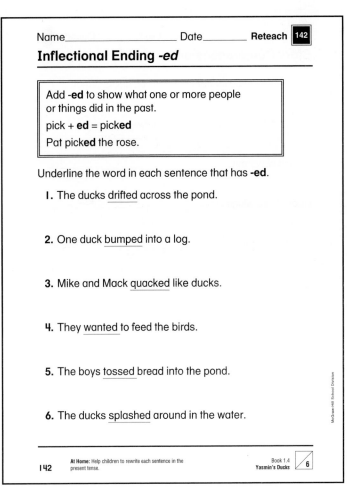

## Inflectional Ending *-ed*

Add **-ed** to show what one or more people
or things did in the past.
pick + **ed** = pick**ed**
Pat pick**ed** the rose.

Underline the word in each sentence that has **-ed**.

1. The ducks drifted across the pond.

2. One duck bumped into a log.

3. Mike and Mack quacked like ducks.

4. They wanted to feed the birds.

5. The boys tossed bread into the pond.

6. The ducks splashed around in the water.

# Yasmin's Ducks • EXTEND

## Long o: o-e

Fill in the letters **o** and **e** to complete the words listed below. Read the word. Write the word. Then write a word that rhymes.

1. h__o__ m __e__

_____ dome _____

2. h__o__ p __e__

_____ cope _____

3. j__o__ k __e__

_____ poke _____

4. h__o__ s __e__

_____ nose _____

5. n__o__ t __e__

_____ vote _____

Book 1.4
**Yasmin's Ducks**

At Home: Invite children to create a poem with the words on this page and share it with others.

135

## High-Frequency Words

| work | because | buy | found | some |
|------|---------|-----|-------|------|

Look at the letters. Cross out the words **in** and **on**. Then read the words that are left.

~~ON~~ ~~IN~~ WORK ~~IN~~ ~~ON~~ ~~IN~~ BECAUSE ~~IN~~ ~~IN~~
BUY ~~ON~~ ~~IN~~ FOUND ~~ON~~ ~~IN~~ ~~ON~~ ~~IN~~ SOME

Choose two of the words. Write a sentence for each one. Sentences will vary.

1. _____

2. _____

136

Book 1.4
**Yasmin's Ducks**

At Home: Invite children to write a sentence about something they have found and then something they would like to buy.

## Story Comprehension

Yasmin learned a lot from her book on ducks. What did you learn?

Read each sentence. Write **Yes** or **No.**

Oil and water mix. — No

Ducks have wings. — Yes

Ducks can't swim. — No

Ducks don't get wet. — Yes

A duck wipes oil on its body. — Yes

Kids do not get wet in rain. — No

Ducks go south in the fall for food. — Yes

Book 1.4
**Yasmin's Ducks**

At Home: Invite children to correct the incorrect facts. Have them rewrite the statements so that they are true.

137

## Use a Chart

Take a class vote. Find what children like to draw.

**What Do You Like to Draw?**

Look at the chart. What do children like to draw best?

Answer should be based on the chart.

138

Book 1.4
**Yasmin's Ducks**

At Home: Ask children other questions about the chart they made, such as: How many children chose [object] to draw?

# Yasmin's Ducks • EXTEND

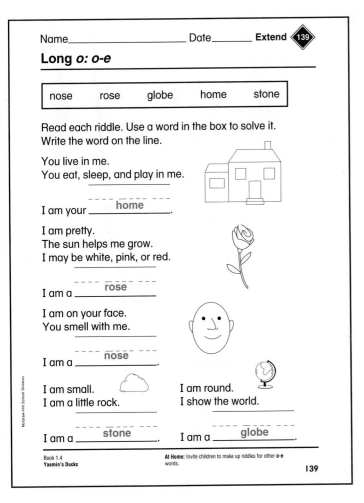

## Long o: o-e

| nose | rose | globe | home | stone |

Read each riddle. Use a word in the box to solve it.
Write the word on the line.

You live in me.
You eat, sleep, and play in me.

I am your ___home___ .

I am pretty.
The sun helps me grow.
I may be white, pink, or red.

I am a ___rose___

I am on your face.
You smell with me.

I am a ___nose___

I am small.
I am a little rock.

I am round.
I show the world.

I am a ___stone___ . I am a ___globe___ .

Book 1.4
Yasmin's Ducks

At Home: Invite children to make up riddles for other o-e words.

139

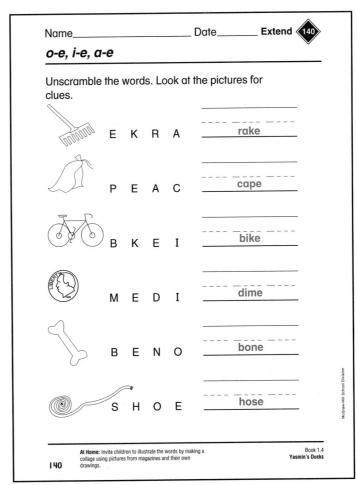

## o-e, i-e, a-e

Unscramble the words. Look at the pictures for clues.

E K R A _____ ___rake___

P E A C _____ ___cape___

B K E I _____ ___bike___

M E D I _____ ___dime___

B E N O _____ ___bone___

S H O E _____ ___hose___

At Home: Invite children to illustrate the words by making a collage using pictures from magazines and their own drawings.

140

Book 1.4
Yasmin's Ducks

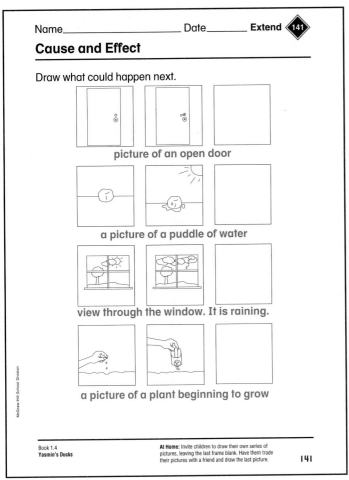

## Cause and Effect

Draw what could happen next.

picture of an open door

a picture of a puddle of water

view through the window. It is raining.

a picture of a plant beginning to grow

Book 1.4
Yasmin's Ducks

At Home: Invite children to draw their own series of pictures, leaving the last frame blank. Have them trade their pictures with a friend and draw the last picture.

141

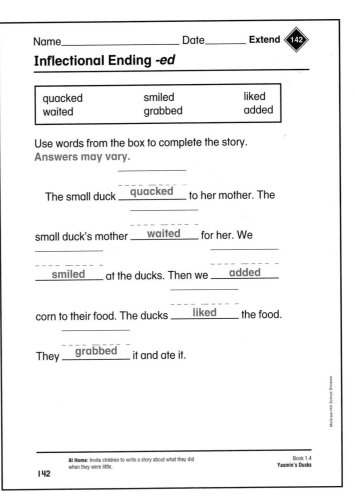

## Inflectional Ending -ed

| quacked | smiled | liked |
| waited | grabbed | added |

Use words from the box to complete the story.
**Answers may vary.**

The small duck ___quacked___ to her mother. The

small duck's mother ___waited___ for her. We

___smiled___ at the ducks. Then we ___added___

corn to their food. The ducks ___liked___ the food.

They ___grabbed___ it and ate it.

At Home: Invite children to write a story about what they did when they were little.

142

Book 1.4
Yasmin's Ducks

**T23**

# Yasmin's Ducks • GRAMMAR

## *Has* and *Have*

- The words *has* and *have* are verbs that tell about the present.
- The word *has* tells about one person, place, or thing.

Yasmin has the best ducks.

Yasmin is one person.

The verb is *has*.

Draw a line under the verb for one person, place, or thing in each sentence.

1. Tim (has) pictures of fish.

2. Kate (has) trucks.

3. One truck (has) four wheels.

4. The duck (has) feathers.

5. The lake (has) ducks.

5 Book 1.4
Yasmin's Ducks

EXTENSION: Have children make up sentences with one person, place, or thing, and *has* as the verb.

103

## *Has* and *Have*

- The words *has* and *have* are verbs that tell about the present.
- The word *have* tells about more than one person, place, or thing.

Circle the verb that tells about more than one person, place, or thing.

1. The ducks (have) fun in the lake.

2. The child has ducks.

3. The children (have) many ducks.

4. Yasmin and Mack (have) water and oil.

5. The ducks (have) food.

6. The children (have) a good time.

7. The ducks (have) a home.

8. Yasmin has many ducks.

104

EXTENSION: Ask students to look around the classroom. Have them use the words *has* and *have* to write sentences about what they see.

Book 1.4
Yasmin's Ducks 8

## *Has* and *Have*

- The words *has* and *have* are verbs that tell about the past.
- The word *has* tells about one person, place, or thing.
- The word *have* tells about more than one person, place, or thing.

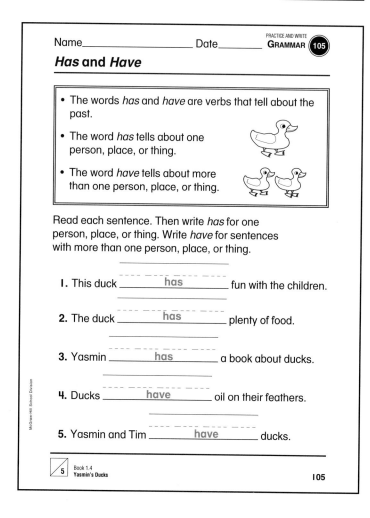

Read each sentence. Then write *has* for one person, place, or thing. Write *have* for sentences with more than one person, place, or thing.

1. This duck _____has_____ fun with the children.

2. The duck _____has_____ plenty of food.

3. Yasmin _____has_____ a book about ducks.

4. Ducks _____have_____ oil on their feathers.

5. Yasmin and Tim _____have_____ ducks.

## Correcting Sentences with *Has* and *Have*

- Begin every sentence with a capital letter.
- End every sentence with a period.
- End every question with a question mark.

Write each sentence correctly.

1. the children have show and tell

       The children have show and tell.

2. Does Tim have pictures of fish

       Does Tim have pictures of fish?

3. mom has ducks too

       Mom has ducks too.

4. Kate has a picture of fire trucks

       Kate has a picture of fire trucks.

5. do Kate and Mack have pictures for show and tell

       Do Kate and Mack have pictures for show and tell?

106

EXTENSION: Have children write additional statements and questions without end marks. Then have them exchange sentences and put in the end marks.

Book 1.4
Yasmin's Ducks 5

# Yasmin's Ducks • GRAMMAR

## Test

Read each sentence. Circle the correct verb for each sentence.

1. Yasmin _____ a duck.

   (has)    have    do

2. Ducks _____ oil next to their tails.

   has    (have)    are

3. The duck _____ a friend.

   (has)    have    are

4. That duck _____ food.

   can    (has)    have

5. The ducks _____ fun.

   do    has    (have)

## More Practice with *Has* and *Have*

- The words *has* and *have* are verbs that tell about the present.
- The word *has* tells about one person, place, or thing.
- The word *have* tells about more than one person, place, or thing.

Read each sentence aloud. Write the sentences to make them correct.

1. Yasmin have three ducks.

   **Yasmin has three ducks.**

2. Yasmin's ducks has fun.

   **Yasmin's ducks have fun.**

3. Pets has fun with us.

   **Pets have fun with us.**

4. Mack have a pup.

   **Mack has a pup.**

5. Ducks has a home.

   **Ducks have a home.**

# Yasmin's Ducks • SPELLING

Name_____ Date_____

## Words with Long o: o-e

### Pretest Directions

Fold back the paper along the dotted line. Use the blanks to write each word as it is read aloud. When you finish the test, unfold the paper. Use the list at the right to correct any spelling mistakes. Practice the words you missed for the Posttest.

1. _____
2. _____
3. _____
4. _____
5. _____
6. _____

1. home
2. hope
3. hole
4. nose
5. rope
6. those

### To Parents

Here are the results of your child's weekly spelling Pretest. You can help your child study for the Posttest by following these simple steps for each word on the list:

1. Read the word to your child.
2. Have your child write the word, saying each letter as it is written.
3. Say each letter of the word as your child checks the spelling.
4. If a mistake has been made, have your child read each letter of the correctly spelled word aloud, and then repeat steps 1-3.

Challenge Words
_____
_____ work
_____
_____ because
_____
_____ buy
_____
_____ some

6 Book 1.4
Yasmin's Ducks
103

---

Name_____ Date_____

## Words with Long o : o-e

### Using the Word Study Steps

1. LOOK at the word.
2. SAY the word aloud.
3. STUDY the letters in the word.
4. WRITE the word.
5. CHECK the word.
   Did you spell the word right? If not, go back to step 1.

**Spelling Tip**

Use beginnings and endings of words you can spell to help you spell new words.

then + nose = those

### Crossword Puzzle

Write the spelling word that best fits each sentence. Put the spelling words in the boxes that start with the same number.

**Across**
1. I ___ you will come.
2. ___ pots are hot!
5. I like to jump ___.

**Down**
1. I go ___ on the bus.
3. I have a ___ in my sock.
4. My ___ is on my face.

**To Parents or Helpers:**
Using the Word Study Steps above as your child comes across any new words will help him or her spell well. Review the steps as you both go over this week's spelling words.
Go over the Spelling Tip with your child. Help your child write new words that use beginnings and endings of words he or she can spell.
Help your child complete the spelling activity.

104
Book 1.4
Yasmin's Ducks 6

---

Name_____ Date_____

## Words with Long o: o-e

Look at the spelling words in the box.

| home | hope | hole | nose | rope | those |

Write the words that end with ope.

1. hope        2. rope

Write the words that end with ose.

3. nose        4. those

Write the word that ends with ome.

5. home

Write the word that ends with ole.

6. hole

All of these words have an **o** and a final **e**.

7. Which letter says its name? o

8. Which letter is silent? e

8 Book 1.4
Yasmin's Ducks
105

---

Name_____ Date_____

## Words with Long o: o-e

Look at the pictures. Write the spelling word to answer each question.

1. Which word means "a place to live"?
   home

2. Which word means "a thing to dig"?
   hole

3. Which word names something in the middle of your face? nose

4. Which word means "to wish for"?
   hope

5. Which word names a thing you jump over? rope

6. Which word starts with th and rhymes with nose? those

106
Book 1.4
Yasmin's Ducks 6

---

**T26** Annotated Workbooks

# Yasmin's Ducks • SPELLING

## Words with Long o: o-e

Read the poem. There are six spelling mistakes.
Circle the mistakes. Write the words correctly on the lines.

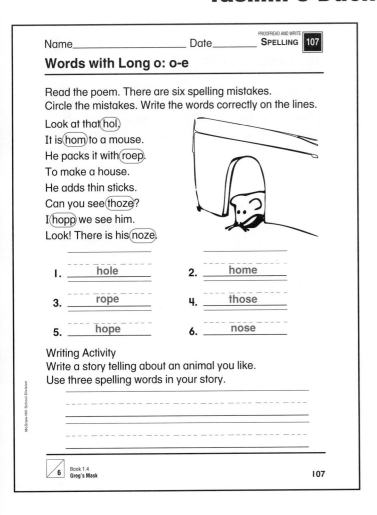

Look at that (hol.)
It is (hom) to a mouse.
He packs it with (roep).
To make a house.
He adds thin sticks.
Can you see (thoze)?
I (hopp) we see him.
Look! There is his (noze).

1. ___hole___    2. ___home___

3. ___rope___    4. ___those___

5. ___hope___    6. ___nose___

Writing Activity
Write a story telling about an animal you like.
Use three spelling words in your story.

_____

_ _ _ _ _ _ _ _ _ _ _ _ _ _ _ _ _ _

_____

---

## Words with Long o: o-e

Look at the words in each set. One word in each
set is spelled correctly. Use a pencil to color in the
circle in front of that word. Before you begin, look at
the sample sets of words. Sample A has been done
for you. Do Sample B by yourself. When you are
sure you know what to do, you may go on with the
rest of the page.

**Sample A**
Ⓐ hose
Ⓑ hoze
Ⓒ hoose

**Sample B**
Ⓓ bitte
Ⓔ bite
Ⓕ byt

1. Ⓐ home
Ⓑ hom
Ⓒ hoem

4. Ⓓ hop
Ⓔ hope
Ⓕ hoope

2. Ⓓ nos
Ⓔ nose
Ⓕ noze

5. Ⓐ rope
Ⓑ rop
Ⓒ roope

3. Ⓐ whol
Ⓑ hol
Ⓒ hole

6. Ⓓ thoz
Ⓔ those
Ⓕ thos

**T27**

# The Knee-High Man • PRACTICE

## Long *u*: *u-e*

Write one of the words from the box in each sentence.

| flute | June | rule | mule | brute |
|---|---|---|---|---|

1. I see that it is __June__.

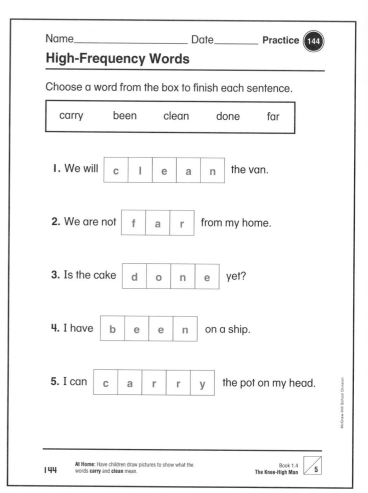

2. I can ride a __mule__.

3. One __rule__ is that we all line up.

4. The bull was a __brute__.

5. I will play a song on my __flute__.

**At Home:** Have children say each word, then write it and circle the letter **u**.
143

---

## High-Frequency Words

Choose a word from the box to finish each sentence.

| carry | been | clean | done | far |
|---|---|---|---|---|

1. We will [c][l][e][a][n] the van.

2. We are not [f][a][r] from my home.

3. Is the cake [d][o][n][e] yet?

4. I have [b][e][e][n] on a ship.

5. I can [c][a][r][r][y] the pot on my head.

**At Home:** Have children draw pictures to show what the words **carry** and **clean** mean.
Book 1.4 The Knee-High Man | 5

---

## June Rules

"Can I rule June?" asked Max. "No, I cannot!" He still had far to go. But not on June. She was in her shed.

**At Home:** Encourage children to talk about different kinds of transportation. What is good about each kind? What may be difficult?

144a

---

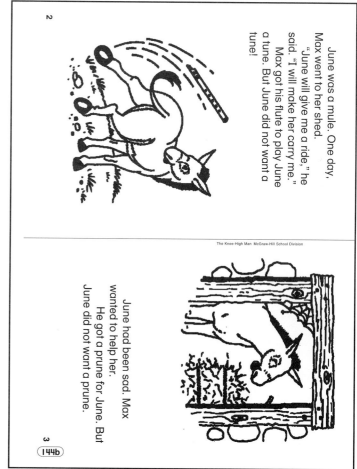

2

June was a mule. One day, Max went to her shed. "June will give me a ride," he said. "I will make her carry me." Max got his flute to play June a tune. But June did not want a tune!

The Knee-High Man McGraw-Hill School Division

3

June had been sad. Max wanted to help her. He got a prune for June. But June did not want a prune.

144b

---

# The Knee-High Man • PRACTICE

## Story Comprehension

Draw a line to connect the characters in "The Knee-High Man" to what they said.

1. June

2. Sam the Knee-High Man

3. Bob Bull

4. Max Mule

5. Kate Owl

a. Yell and eat grass to be big like me.

b. Sam did not grow an inch.

c. Eat a lot of corn and run ten miles to be like me.

d. Will you tell me how I can grow?

e. You are fine just as you are.

## A Chart

This **chart** tells you what Sam, Dan, and Pam said.

| Sam | Dan | Pam |
|---|---|---|
| pack your toys | ride the train | find a home |
| take your dog | move in June | live in a dome |

Write the answer on the line.

1. What did Pam say?

___find a home, live in a dome___

2. Who said to take your dog? ___Sam___

3. What did Dan say? ___ride the train, move in June___

4. Who said to find a home? ___Pam___

## Long *u: u-e*

Look at each picture. Write the word from the box that answers each question.

| dune | mule | tune | cube |
|---|---|---|---|

1. I look like a horse. What am I?

___mule___
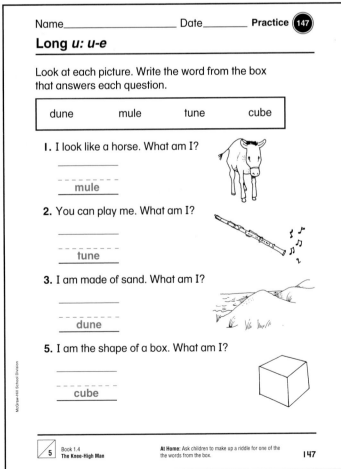

2. You can play me. What am I?

___tune___

3. I am made of sand. What am I?

___dune___

5. I am the shape of a box. What am I?

___cube___

## *u-e, o-e, i-e, a-e*

Read each clue. Circle the answer. Then write the word on the line.

1. Dogs eat me. What am I?

(bone)   bike   stone

I am a ___bone___.

2. You stop a bike with me. What am I?

bake   broke   (brake)

I am a ___brake___.

3. I am on a happy face. What am I?

mile   (smile)   slope

I am a ___smile___.

4. You swim with me. What am I?

(tube)   poke   cube

I am a ___tube___.

# The Knee-High Man • PRACTICE

**Make Inferences**

Read each sentence. Draw a line to the person who can help.

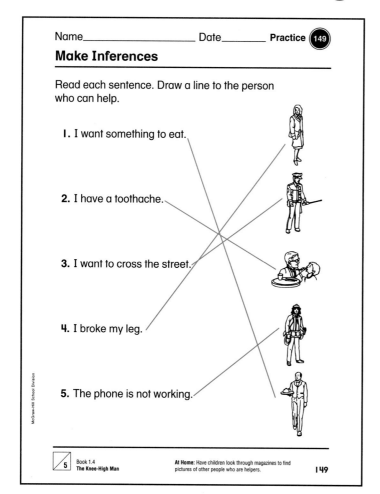

1. I want something to eat.

2. I have a toothache.

3. I want to cross the street.

4. I broke my leg.

5. The phone is not working.

**Inflectional Endings -er, -est**

Add **-er** to compare two things.
Add **-est** to compare three or more things.

Circle the word that completes the sentence correctly. Then write the word in the space.

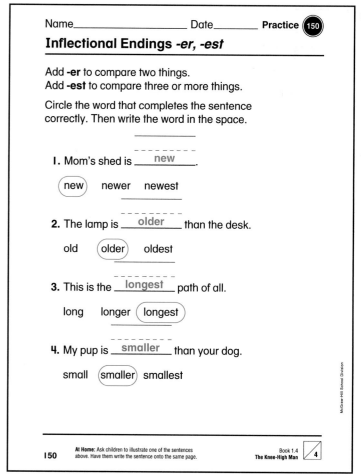

1. Mom's shed is ____new____.

   (new)   newer   newest

2. The lamp is ____older____ than the desk.

   old   (older)   oldest

3. This is the ____longest____ path of all.

   long   longer   (longest)

4. My pup is ____smaller____ than your dog.

   small   (smaller)   smallest

# The Knee-High Man • RETEACH

## Worksheet 143

Name_____ Date_____ Reteach **143**

### Long *u: u-e*

Read this word.

cute

Circle the word that names each picture.

1. duke (flute)

2. (mule) rule

3. (cube) tube

4. tune (dune)

4 Book 1.4
The Knee-High Man

**At Home:** Help children to write verses using some of the words on the page.

143

## Worksheet 144

Name_____ Date_____ Reteach **144**

### High-Frequency Words

Write the correct word to complete each sentence.

| done | clean | far | carry | been |
|------|-------|-----|-------|------|

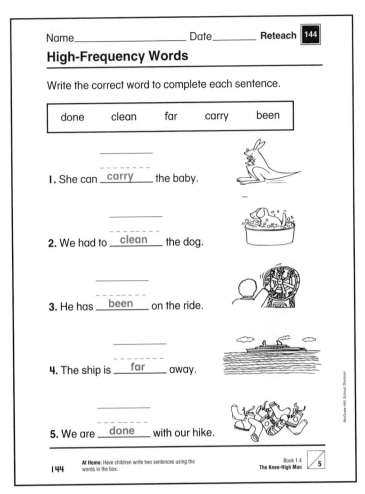

1. She can __carry__ the baby.

2. We had to __clean__ the dog.

3. He has __been__ on the ride.

4. The ship is __far__ away.

5. We are __done__ with our hike.

144 **At Home:** Have children write two sentences using the words in the box.

Book 1.4
The Knee-High Man 5

## Worksheet 145

Name_____ Date_____ Reteach **145**

### Story Comprehension

Think about "The Knee-High Man." Fill in the chart. Then answer the questions.

| | Max Mule | Bob Bull |
|---|----------|----------|
| What to eat? | corn | grass |
| What to do? | run | yell |

1. What did Kate Owl think? __Kate said that Sam did__

__not have to be big.__

2. Who gave Sam the best advice? __Kate Owl__

6 Book 1.4
The Knee-High Man

**At Home:** Have children draw pictures of Sam the Knee-High Man following one of the suggestions in the chart.

145

## Worksheet 146

Name_____ Date_____ Reteach **146**

### A Chart

This **chart** tells you what Meg, Jill, and Rick said to Dan.

| Meg | Jill | Rick |
|-----|------|------|
| Camp in a tent. | Ride the train. | Take a nap. |
| Spill the milk. | Pat the cat. | Sail the ship. |
| | | Hit the nail. |

Look at the chart. Circle the correct answer.

1. Meg said to spill the___. (milk) bath

2. Rick said to ___ the nail. sail (hit)

3. ___ said to ride the train. (Jill) Meg

4. ___ said to camp in a tent. (Meg) Rick

146 **At Home:** Have children read each name on the chart and then tell you what that person said.

Book 1.4
The Knee-High Man 4

# The Knee-High Man • RETEACH

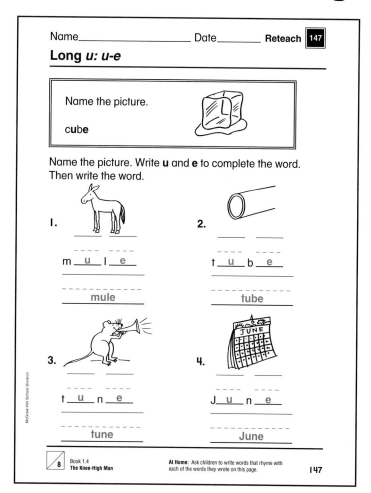

Name_____ Date_____ **Reteach** `147`

## Long *u: u-e*

Name the picture.

cub**e**

Name the picture. Write **u** and **e** to complete the word.
Then write the word.

1. m _u_ l _e_

mule

2. t _u_ b _e_

tube

3. t _u_ n _e_

tune

4. J _u_ n _e_

June

At Home: Ask children to write words that rhyme with
each of the words they wrote on this page.

Book 1.4
The Knee-High Man

8

147

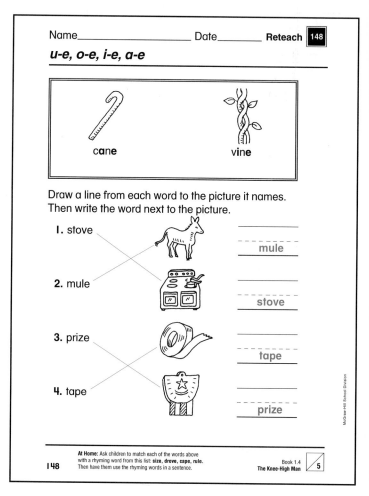

Name_____ Date_____ **Reteach** `148`

## *u-e, o-e, i-e, a-e*

can**e**          vin**e**

Draw a line from each word to the picture it names.
Then write the word next to the picture.

1. stove

mule

2. mule

stove

3. prize

tape

4. tape

prize

At Home: Ask children to match each of the words above
with a rhyming word from this list: **size, drove, cape, rule.**
Then have them use the rhyming words in a sentence.

148

Book 1.4
The Knee-High Man

5

Name_____ Date_____ **Reteach** `149`

## Make Inferences

Look at the animal in the first picture.
Then look at the picture of what the
animal eats.

Circle the picture that shows what each animal will
want to eat.

1.
2.
3.
4.
5.

At Home: Have children draw another thing that one of
the animals would like to eat.

Book 1.4
The Knee-High Man

5

149

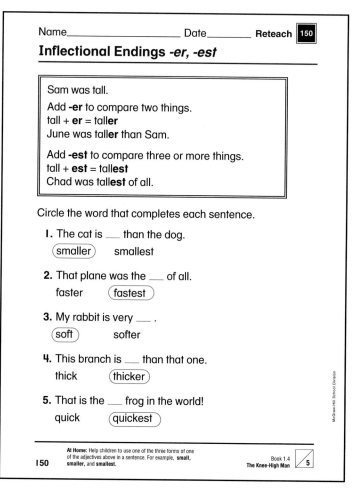

Name_____ Date_____ **Reteach** `150`

## Inflectional Endings *-er, -est*

Sam was tall.

Add **-er** to compare two things.
tall + **er** = tall**er**
June was tall**er** than Sam.

Add **-est** to compare three or more things.
tall + **est** = tall**est**
Chad was tall**est** of all.

Circle the word that completes each sentence.

1. The cat is ___ than the dog.
   (smaller)   smallest

2. That plane was the ___ of all.
   faster   (fastest)

3. My rabbit is very ___ .
   (soft)   softer

4. This branch is ___ than that one.
   thick   (thicker)

5. That is the ___ frog in the world!
   quick   (quickest)

At Home: Help children to use one of the three forms of one
of the adjectives above in a sentence. For example, **small,
smaller,** and **smallest.**

150

Book 1.4
The Knee-High Man

5

# The Knee-High Man • EXTEND

## Long *u: u-e*

Which words have the long **u** sound as in **tune**?
Find the words. Color the stripes red.

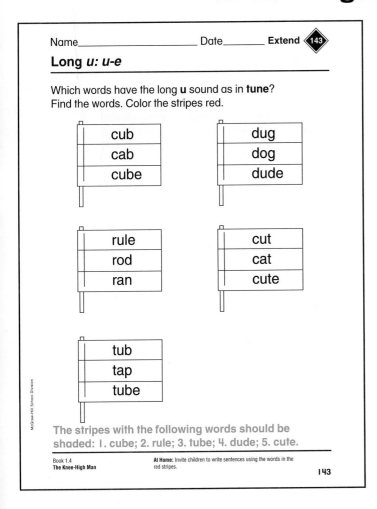

| | |
|---|---|
| cub | dug |
| cab | dog |
| cube | dude |

| | |
|---|---|
| rule | cut |
| rod | cat |
| ran | cute |

| |
|---|
| tub |
| tap |
| tube |

The stripes with the following words should be
shaded: 1. cube; 2. rule; 3. tube; 4. dude; 5. cute.

Book 1.4
The Knee-High Man

At Home: Invite children to write sentences using the words in the
red stripes.

143

---

## High-Frequency Words

| carry | been | clean | done | far |
|---|---|---|---|---|

Write the word from the box that completes each
sentence.

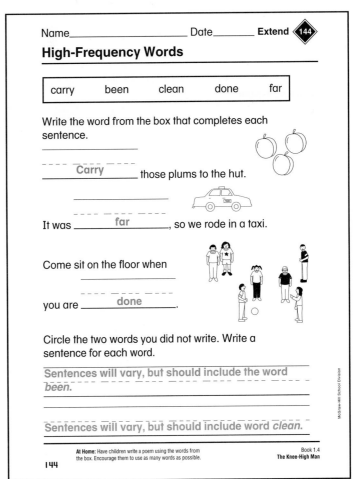

_____

_____ **Carry** _____ those plums to the hut.

_____

It was _____ **far** _____, so we rode in a taxi.

Come sit on the floor when

_____

you are _____ **done** _____.

Circle the two words you did not write. Write a
sentence for each word.

Sentences will vary, but should include the word
been.

_____

Sentences will vary, but should include word *clean*.

At Home: Have children write a poem using the words from
the box. Encourage them to use as many words as possible.

Book 1.4
The Knee-High Man

144

---

## Story Comprehension

Read the sentences. Write **T** if they are true. Write
**F** if they are not. If the sentence is true, circle the
name of the friend who said it.

| Sentence | T or F | Who Said it? |
|---|---|---|
| 1. Eat corn. | T | |
| 2. Run ten miles. | T | |
| 3. Drink juice. | F | |
| 4. Yell and grunt. | T | |
| 5. Go up a tree. | T | |

Book 1.4
The Knee-High Man

At Home: Have children act out the story of "The Knee-
High Man."

145

---

## Use a Chart

Five friends ran a race. Read their chart. Use the
chart to answer the questions.

### Our Class Race

| Names | Speeds | Winners |
|---|---|---|
| Amy | 36 seconds | |
| Ben | 27 seconds | 3 Third Place — Ben |
| Mack | 20 seconds | 1 First Place — Mack |
| Brad | 34 seconds | 2 Second Place — Jill |
| Jill | 25 seconds | |

Who won the race? _____ **Mack** _____

What was Brad's speed? _____ **34 seconds**

Who ran the race in 25 seconds? _____ **Jill**

At Home: Invite children to make their own growth chart.
Help them to measure themselves and record their growth.

Book 1.4
The Knee-High Man

146

## Page 147

Name_____ Date_____ Extend ◆147

### Long *u: u-e*

Color the pictures whose names have the long **u** sound as in **cube**.

shade the pictures of the mule, and the flute.

Write a word that has the long u sound as in **cube**.

Possible words: rule, tune, cute, dune, rude, prune, fume, June

Book 1.4
The Knee-High Man

At Home: Have children make a word search game using the **long** *u: u-e* words from this page.

147

## Page 148

Name_____ Date_____ Extend ◆148

### *u-e, o-e, i-e, a-e*

Read the words.
Color the leaves with the long **u** sound as in **cube** brown.
Color the leaves with the long **o** sound as in **rose** red.
Color the leaves with the long **i** sound as **bike** green.
Color the leaves with the long **a** sound as in **cake** yellow.

**Start**

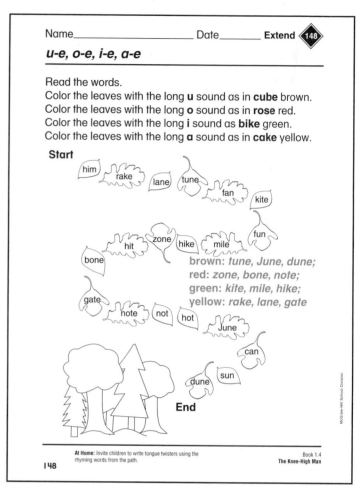

him, rake, lane, tune, fan, kite, hit, zone, hike, mile, fun, bone, gate, note, not, hot, June, can, dune, sun

brown: *tune, June, dune;*
red: *zone, bone, note;*
green: *kite, mile, hike;*
yellow: *rake, lane, gate*

**End**

At Home: Invite children to write tongue twisters using the rhyming words from the path.

Book 1.4
The Knee-High Man

148

## Page 149

Name_____ Date_____ Extend ◆149

### Make Inferences

Look at the picture. Underline the sentence that tells about the picture.

Mitch is going to school.
Mitch is having a bath.
Mitch is carrying gifts.

The girls are playing.
The girls are reading.
The girls are crying.

Beth had a busy day.
Beth read a story.
Beth called her grandma.

Sam does not like dogs.
Sam went to the pool.
Sam got a new pet.

Book 1.4
The Knee-High Man

At Home: Invite children to think about why Sam didn't give up his idea of being big until he spoke with Kate. Ask: Would you give up?

149

## Page 150

Name_____ Date_____ Extend ◆150

### Inflectional Endings *-er, -est*

Look at the pictures in each row. Add **-er** and **-est**.

bigger — big — biggest

small — small ___ er — small ___ est

tall ___ er — tall ___ est — tall

fat ___ est — fat — ___ er

At Home: Invite children to make up a descriptive story using the words from this page.

Book 1.4
The Knee-High Man

150

## Page 109

LEARN
GRAMMAR 109

Name_____ Date_____

### *Go* and *Do*

- The verb *go* has a special form to tell about the past.
- Use *go* or *goes* to tell about something that happens in the present.

    Max **goes** out every day.
- Use *went* to tell about something that happened in the past.

    Max **went** out last night.

Read the sentences. Look for *go*, *goes*, and *went*. Circle Present or Past.

1. We go to the country.
   (Present)    Past

2. Max Mule goes to help Sam.
   (Present)    Past

3. Sam went to Bob Bull for help.
   Present    (Past)

4. Sam went to Kate Owl for help.
   Present    (Past)

5. Sam goes to the lake.
   (Present)    Past

## Page 110

LEARN AND PRACTICE
GRAMMAR 110

Name_____ Date_____

### *Go* and *Do*

- The verb *do* has a special form to tell about the past.
- Use *do* or *does* to tell about something that happens in the present.

    **Do** you like to clean corn cobs?

    Sam **does** not have to be bigger.
- Use *did* to tell about something that happened in the past.

    Max Mule **did** help Sam.

Read the sentences. Circle the verbs that tell about the past.

1. Do bugs carry rope?

2. Why (did) Sam chomp on ten corn cobs?

3. Does running ten miles help Sam?

4. Sam (did) not grow one inch.

5. But Sam (did) not give up.

## Page 111

PRACTICE AND WRITE
GRAMMAR 111

Name_____ Date_____

### *Go* and *Do*

- The verb *go* has a special form to tell about the past.
- Use *went* to tell about something that happened in the past.

    Sam *went* to see Bob the Bull.
- The verb *do* has a special form to tell about the past.
- Use *did* to tell about something that happened in the past.

    Why *did* Sam want to be big?

Read the sentences. Write the verbs that tell about the past.

1. How _____did_____ Kate Owl help Sam?    (do did)

2. Who _____did_____ Sam have to fight?    (do did)

3. He _____went_____ to see Kate Owl.    (go went)

4. Why _____did_____ Sam want to be big?    (do did)

5. Sam _____went_____ up a tree to look.    (go went)

## Page 112

MECHANICS
GRAMMAR 112

Name_____ Date_____

### Names with Capital Letters

- The name of a person or place begins with a capital letter.

    Max Mule is big.

Circle the words that should begin with capital letters.

1. Sam went to see (max) (mule).

2. Max did not help (sam) grow big.

3. Sam went to talk to (bob) (bull).

4. Sam did what (bob) told him.

5. Sam went to (new) (york).

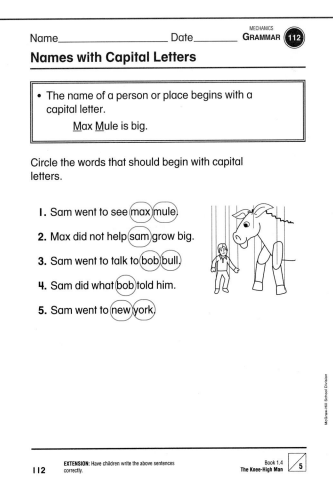

# The Knee-High Man • GRAMMAR

**Test**

Draw a line under each verb that tells about the present. Circle each verb that tells about the past.

1. Sam (went) up the tree.

2. Sam does not get help.

3. Kate and Owl (did) help.

4. Kate and Owl do the work.

5. Sam goes to the tree.

6. Sam (went) to get help.

7. Why do you go there?

8. Why (did) Sam go up a tree?

9. Sam goes to see Bob the Bull.

10. Sam (went) to see Bob the Bull.

**More Practice with *Go* and *Do***

- Use *go* or *goes* to tell about the present.
- Use *went* to tell about the past.
- Use *do* or *does* to tell about the present.
- Use *did* to tell about the past.

Look at Picture 1. Read the sentences next to it. Circle the sentences about the past.

1. (Sam went to get help.)

2. Sam does things to get big.

3. (Sam did not want to fight.)

4. (Sam went to Kate the Owl.)

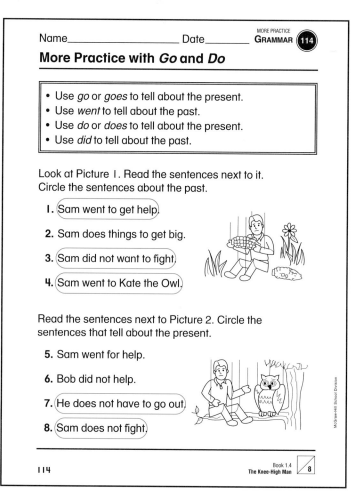

Read the sentences next to Picture 2. Circle the sentences that tell about the present.

5. Sam went for help.

6. Bob did not help.

7. (He does not have to go out.)

8. (Sam does not fight.)

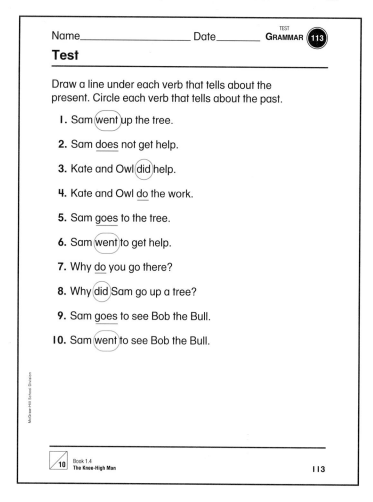

# The Knee-High Man • SPELLING

## Words with Long *u* : *u-e*

### Pretest Directions

Fold back the paper along the dotted line. Use the blanks to write each word as it is read aloud. When you finish the test, unfold the paper. Use the list at the right to correct any spelling mistakes. Practice the words you missed for the Posttest.

1. _____    1. rule

2. _____    2. cute

3. _____    3. mule

4. _____    4. tube

5. _____    5. tune

6. _____    6. flute

**Challenge Words**

_____ been

_____ clean

_____ done

_____ far

### To Parents

Here are the results of your child's weekly spelling Pretest. You can help your child study for the Posttest by following these simple steps for each word on the list:

1. Read the word to your child.

2. Have your child write the word, saying each letter as it is written.

3. Say each letter of the word as your child checks the spelling.

4. If a mistake has been made, have your child read each letter of the correctly spelled word aloud, and then repeat steps 1-3.

---

## Words with Long *u* : *u-e*

### Using the Word Study Steps

1. LOOK at the word.

2. SAY the word aloud.

3. STUDY the letters in the word.

4. WRITE the word.

5. CHECK the word. Did you spell the word right? If not, go back to step 1.

**Spelling Tip**

When there is a long vowel sound at the beginning or in the middle of a one-syllable word, it usually has two vowels.

tune   flute

### Find and Circle

Where are the spelling words?

p d (r u l e) k (c u t e)
s (m u l e) i (t u b e) o
(t u n e) q (f l u t e) g

### To Parents or Helpers:

Using the Word Study Steps above as your child comes across any new words will help him or her spell well. Review the steps as you both go over this week's spelling words.

Go over the Spelling Tip with your child. Help your child write new one-syllable words that have a long vowel sound at the beginning or in the middle and have two vowels.

Help your child find and circle the spelling words in the puzzle.

---

## Words with Long u: *u-e*

Look at the spelling words in the box.

| rule   cute   mule   tube   tune   flute |
|---|

Write the words that end with **ule**.

1. rule    2. mule

Write the words that end with **ute**.

3. cute    4. flute

Write the word that end with **une**.

5. tune

Write the two letters that are found in every spelling word.

6. u    7. e

Make a new word by changing the r of rule to m.

8. mule

---

## Words with Long u: *u-e*

Look at the pictures. Complete each spelling word.

1. You can ride on a m_____ule_____ .

2. Another word for song is t_____une_____ .

3. You can swim with a t_____ube_____ .

4. The baby pig is very c_____ute_____ .

5. You can play a fl_____ute_____ .

6. What you can or cannot do is a r_____ule_____ .

**T37**

Name_____ Date_____

## Words with Long u: u-e

**Finding Mistakes**
Read the story. There are five spelling mistakes.
Circle the mistakes. Write the words correctly on the lines.

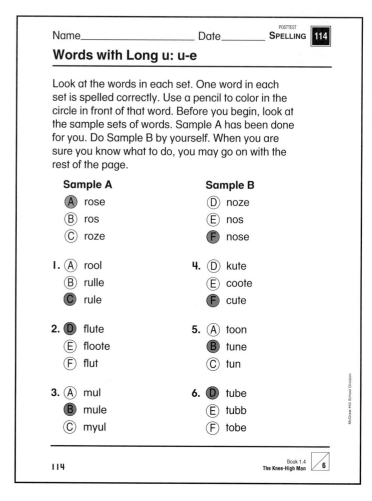

In June, Will and I go to a camp in the woods. We
ride on (muls) up and down the hills. We swim in the
lake with (toobs.) We learn to play a (toon) on a (flut.)
We take care of (kute) hens, chicks and ducks.
Camp is fun. We want to go back soon.

1. ____mules____   2. ____tubes____   3. ____tune____

4. ____flute____   5. ____cute____

**Writing Activity**
Your school has rules. Write about a rule in your
school. Tell why it is a good rule.
Use two spelling words in your story.

_____

_____

_____

---

Name_____ Date_____

## Words with Long u: u-e

Look at the words in each set. One word in each
set is spelled correctly. Use a pencil to color in the
circle in front of that word. Before you begin, look at
the sample sets of words. Sample A has been done
for you. Do Sample B by yourself. When you are
sure you know what to do, you may go on with the
rest of the page.

**Sample A**          **Sample B**
(A) rose           (D) noze
(B) ros            (E) nos
(C) roze           (F) nose

1. (A) rool        4. (D) kute
   (B) rulle          (E) coote
   (C) rule           (F) cute

2. (D) flute       5. (A) toon
   (E) floote         (B) tune
   (F) flut           (C) tun

3. (A) mul         6. (D) tube
   (B) mule           (E) tubb
   (C) myul           (F) tobe

# Johnny Appleseed • PRACTICE

## Long *a: ai, ay*

Write a word from the box to complete each rhyme.

| bait | gray | wait | tray |
|------|------|------|------|

**1.** Hurry up. It is almost **eight**.
I can hardly

_____

_____ **wait** _____ !

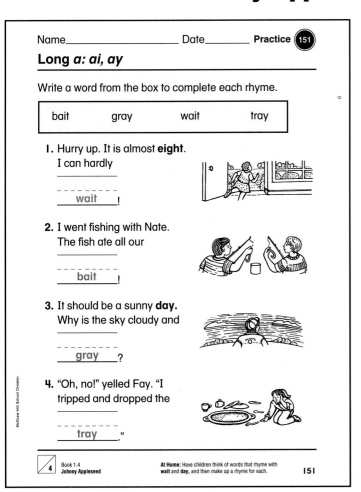

**2.** I went fishing with Nate.
The fish ate all our

_____

_____ **bait** _____ !

**3.** It should be a sunny **day**.
Why is the sky cloudy and

_____

_____ **gray** _____ ?

**4.** "Oh, no!" yelled Fay. "I
tripped and dropped the

_____

_____ **tray** _____ ."

Book 1.4
**Johnny Appleseed**

**At Home:** Have children think of words that rhyme with
**wait** and **day**, and then make up a rhyme for each.

151

---

## High-Frequency Words

Circle the word that completes each sentence.
Then write the word.

**1.** This is a ___ **little** ___ pup.

how
(little)

**2.** This is a ___ **pretty** ___ cat.

(pretty)
live

**3.** They ___ **live** ___ here.

(live)
light

**4.** This is ___ **how** ___
they go inside.

pretty
(how)

**5.** They sit by the ___ **light** ___
of the fire.

little
(light)

152

**At Home:** Have children name the cat and pup and draw
another picture showing them both.

Book 1.4
**Johnny Appleseed**
5

---

## Gail the Train Nail

"How do you do?" said Gail to
the man. "Can I stay on your
train?"
"Can my light stay on you?"
said the man.
"Yes!" said Gail.
And the nail was safe from
the rain.

**At Home:** Encourage children to talk about why the nail
in this story might not have done well in the rain. What
are some other things that should not be in the rain?

4

152a

---

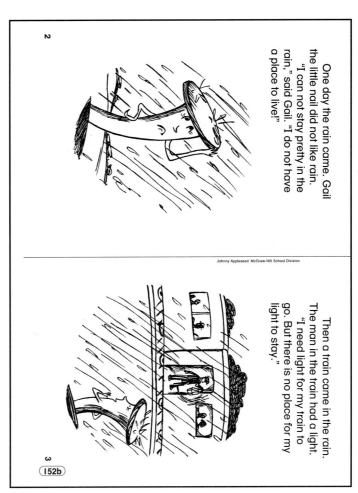

2

One day the rain came. Gail
the little nail did not like rain.
"I can not stay pretty in the
rain," said Gail. "I do not have
a place to live!"

Johnny Appleseed  McGraw-Hill School Division

Then a train came in the rain.
The man in the train had a light.
"I need light for my train to
go. But there is no place for my
light to stay."

3

152b

T39

# Johnny Appleseed • PRACTICE

Name_____ Date_____ Practice 153

**Story Comprehension**

Circle the pictures that tell what happened in "Johnny Appleseed."

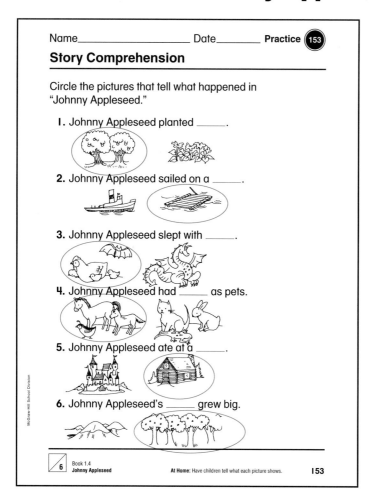

1. Johnny Appleseed planted _____.

2. Johnny Appleseed sailed on a _____.

3. Johnny Appleseed slept with _____.

4. Johnny Appleseed had _____ as pets.

5. Johnny Appleseed ate at a _____.

6. Johnny Appleseed's _____ grew big.

---

Name_____ Date_____ Practice 154

**A Chart**

Look at this **chart** to see how a lemon tree grows.

| Plant the Seed | Water the Seed | Let It Grow | Pick Lemons |
|---|---|---|---|
| | | | |

Write the answer on the line.

1. What do you do first to grow a lemon tree?

   _____
   plant the seed

2. What do you do to help the tree grow?

   _____
   water it

3. What grows on the tree before the lemons?

   _____
   leaves

4. What does the last part of the chart show?

   _____
   lemons on the tree

---

Name_____ Date_____ Practice 155

**Long *a: ay, ai***

Write a word from the box to complete each sentence.

| way | May | wait | hail | train |
|---|---|---|---|---|

1. I will ___wait___ at the gate.

2. This is the ___way___ to the bus.

3. The icy ___hail___ hit the truck.

4. The flowers came out in ___May___.

5. This is a fast ___train___.

---

Name_____ Date_____ Practice 156

***ai, ay; u-e, o-e***

Draw a line from each sentence to the word that completes it. Then write the word in the blank.

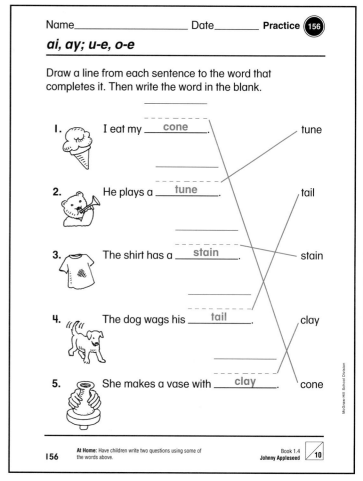

1. I eat my ___cone___.                    tune

2. He plays a ___tune___.                   tail

3. The shirt has a ___stain___.             stain

4. The dog wags his ___tail___.             clay

5. She makes a vase with ___clay___.        cone

# Johnny Appleseed • PRACTICE

## Make Inferences

Read the story. Then fill in the circles in front of the correct answers.

It was Saturday. It was time for Jack to clean his room. But Jack kept putting it off. Then, Joe came over to play. They went to the park. They played ball all day. When Jack came home, he ate a big dinner. Then he went to bed early.

1. Jack did not clean his room because he _____.
   - ● went to the park
   - ○ read a book
   - ○ walked his dog

2. When Jack came home from the park, he was _____.
   - ○ excited    ○ sad    ● hungry

3. Jack went to bed early because he was _____.
   - ○ happy    ● tired    ○ hungry

4. Did Jack like to clean his room?
   - ○ yes    ● no

At Home: Have children predict what Jack will do about his messy room.

## Inflectional Endings -er, -est

Add **-er** to compare two things.
Add **-est** to compare three or more things.

Read the word after each sentence. Then add **-er** or **-est** and write the word to complete the sentence.

1. Gail plays the game _____faster_____ than me.     fast

2. Kate's braid is the _____thickest_____ of all.     thick

3. My train is _____longer_____ than yours.     long

Now draw a line from each sentence to the word that completes it.

4. That is the _____ flag pole.     softest

5. This plum is _____ than that one.     fresher

6. Kate's bed is the _____ of all.     tallest

At Home: Work with children to illustrate one of these sentences.

# Johnny Appleseed • RETEACH

Name_____ Date_____ **Reteach** 151

## Long *a*: *ay, ai*

Say these words. What sound do you hear that is the same in each word?

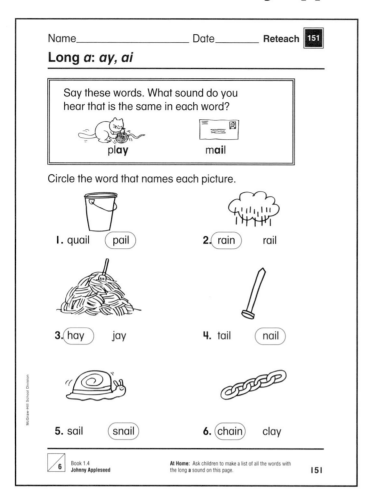

play          mail

Circle the word that names each picture.

1. quail  (pail)      2. (rain)  rail

3. (hay)  jay          4. tail  (nail)

5. sail  (snail)       6. (chain)  clay

---

Name_____ Date_____ **Reteach** 152

## High-Frequency Words

Complete each sentence with the correct word from the box.

| how | light | little | live | pretty |
|-----|-------|--------|------|--------|

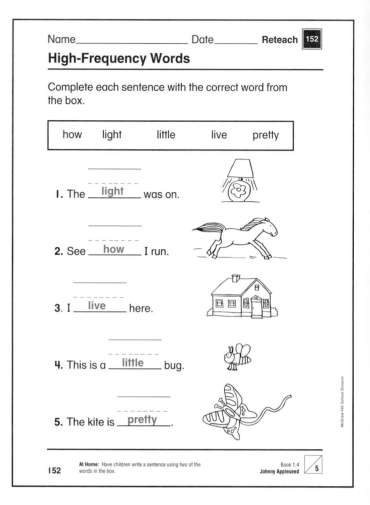

1. The __light__ was on.

2. See __how__ I run.

3. I __live__ here.

4. This is a __little__ bug.

5. The kite is __pretty__.

---

Name_____ Date_____ **Reteach** 153

## Story Comprehension

Think about "Johnny Appleseed." Write one thing Johnny did that matches each word. **Answers may vary.**

Kind  ⟶  He mended a quail's wing; he saved a wolf from a trap.

Happy  ⟶  He always had a big smile; he was not sad.

Poor  ⟶  He dressed in rags and old sacks; he had no shoes.

Helpful  ⟶  He helped people by planting apple trees.

---

Name_____ Date_____ **Reteach** 154

## A Chart

This **chart** tells how a plum tree grows. Remember: The steps go in order from left to right.

Look at the Plum Tree chart below.

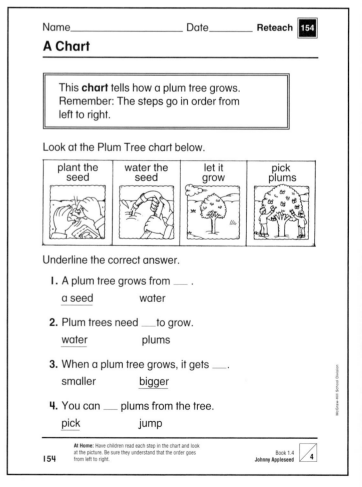

| plant the seed | water the seed | let it grow | pick plums |
|----------------|----------------|-------------|------------|

Underline the correct answer.

1. A plum tree grows from ___ .
   a seed          water

2. Plum trees need ___ to grow.
   water          plums

3. When a plum tree grows, it gets ___.
   smaller        bigger

4. You can ___ plums from the tree.
   pick          jump

---

# Johnny Appleseed • RETEACH

## Reteach 155

Name_____ Date_____ **Reteach** 155

### Long *a*: *ay*, *ai*

Read these words. How are they the same?

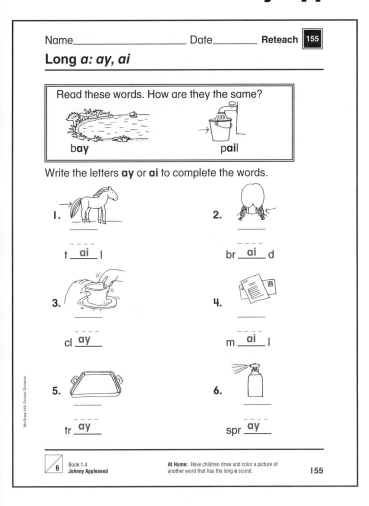

b**ay**            p**ai**l

Write the letters **ay** or **ai** to complete the words.

1. t __ai__ l

2. br __ai__ d

3. cl __ay__

4. m __ai__ l

5. tr __ay__

6. spr __ay__

At Home: Have children draw and color a picture of another word that has the long **a** sound.

155

## Reteach 156

Name_____ Date_____ **Reteach** 156

### *ai*, *ay*; *u-e*, *o-e*

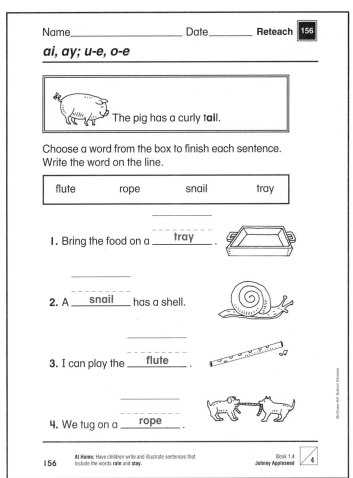

The pig has a curly t**ai**l.

Choose a word from the box to finish each sentence. Write the word on the line.

| flute | rope | snail | tray |

1. Bring the food on a ___**tray**___ .

2. A ___**snail**___ has a shell.

3. I can play the ___**flute**___ .

4. We tug on a ___**rope**___ .

At Home: Have children write and illustrate sentences that include the words **rain** and **stay**.

Book 1.4
Johnny Appleseed  4

## Reteach 157

Name_____ Date_____ **Reteach** 157

### Make Inferences

You can use what you read and what you already know to help you better understand a story.

Read the sentences. Circle the picture that answers the question.

1. The cook began to cut the apple. Why was he mad?

2. The cook put some bread on the table. Why was he mad?

3. The cook needed cheese. Why was he mad?

4. The cook went to get the pie. Why was he mad?

5. The cook came to get carrots. Why was he mad?

At Home: Have children explain the answer to each question.

157

## Reteach 158

Name_____ Date_____ **Reteach** 158

### Inflectional Endings *-er*, *-est*

Add **-er** to compare two things.
warm + **er** = warm**er**
This lake is warm**er** than that one.

Add **-est** to compare three or more things.
warm + **est** = warm**est**
This is the warm**est** lake in the world.

Circle the words that compare two things. Underline the words that compare three or more things.

1. Dave's cab is (newer) than my truck.

2. This is the longest kite in the park.

3. My hair is (shorter) than yours.

4. These grapes are the (freshest) of all.

5. Kate is a quicker runner than Jan.

6. I saw the oldest map in the world.

At Home: Invite children to illustrate two of the comparisons made with **-er** and **-est** words above.

Book 1.4
Johnny Appleseed  6

# Johnny Appleseed • EXTEND

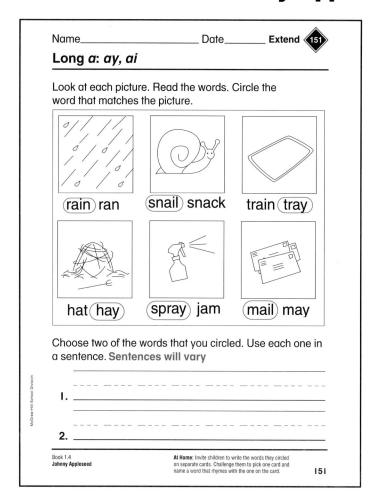

Name_____ Date_____ Extend 151

## Long *a*: *ay, ai*

Look at each picture. Read the words. Circle the word that matches the picture.

(rain) ran    (snail) snack    train (tray)

hat (hay)    (spray) jam    (mail) may

Choose two of the words that you circled. Use each one in a sentence. **Sentences will vary**

1. _____

_____

2. _____

Book 1.4
**Johnny Appleseed**

At Home: Invite children to write the words they circled on separate cards. Challenge them to pick one card and name a word that rhymes with the one on the card.

151

---

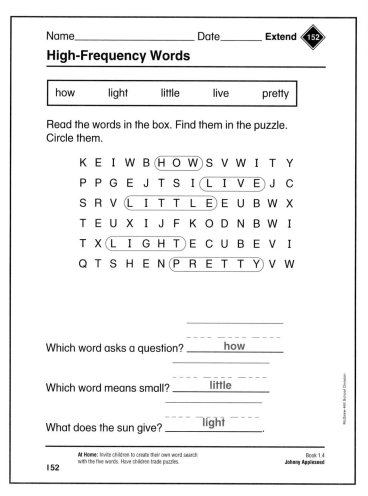

Name_____ Date_____ Extend 152

## High-Frequency Words

| how | light | little | live | pretty |

Read the words in the box. Find them in the puzzle. Circle them.

```
K E I W B (H O W) S V W I T Y
P P G E J T S I (L I V E) J C
S R V (L I T T L E) E U B W X
T E U X I J F K O D N B W I
T X (L I G H T) E C U B E V I
Q T S H E N (P R E T T Y) V W
```

Which word asks a question? _____ how _____

Which word means small? _____ little _____

What does the sun give? _____ light _____ .

At Home: Invite children to create their own word search with the five words. Have children trade puzzles.

152

Book 1.4
**Johnny Appleseed**

---

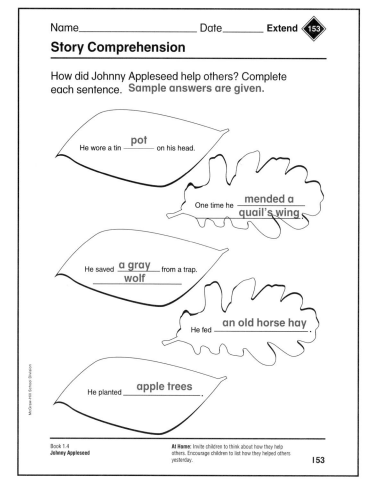

Name_____ Date_____ Extend 153

## Story Comprehension

How did Johnny Appleseed help others? Complete each sentence. **Sample answers are given.**

He wore a tin ___pot___ on his head.

One time he ___mended a quail's wing___

He saved ___a gray wolf___ from a trap.

He fed ___an old horse hay___

He planted ___apple trees___ .

Book 1.4
**Johnny Appleseed**

At Home: Invite children to think about how they help others. Encourage children to list how they helped others yesterday.

153

---

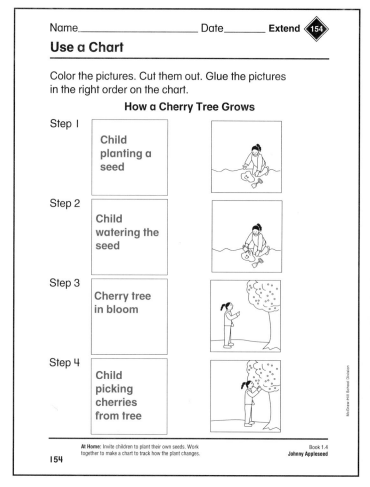

Name_____ Date_____ Extend 154

## Use a Chart

Color the pictures. Cut them out. Glue the pictures in the right order on the chart.

**How a Cherry Tree Grows**

Step 1 | Child planting a seed |

Step 2 | Child watering the seed |

Step 3 | Cherry tree in bloom |

Step 4 | Child picking cherries from tree |

At Home: Invite children to plant their own seeds. Work together to make a chart to track how the plant changes.

154

Book 1.4
**Johnny Appleseed**

---

# Johnny Appleseed • EXTEND

## Long *a: ay, ai*

| tray | hay | bay | pail | tail | rail |

Look at the words. Choose a word from the box that rhymes. Write it on the line. **Sample answers are given.**

1. clay _____tray_____

2. pay _____hay_____

3. snail _____pail_____

4. trail _____tail_____

5. say _____bay_____

6. mail _____rail_____

Book 1.4
**Johnny Appleseed**

**At Home:** Invite children to write a poem using some of the rhyming words.

155

---

## *ai, ay; u-e, o-e*

Color the picture that has the same middle sound as in the first picture.

snail

train

cube

rose

**At Home:** Have children write the word for each answer on one index card and a drawing of the word on another. Place the cards face down. Have the child play a memory game and match each word to its drawing.

156

Book 1.4
**Johnny Appleseed**

---

## Make Inferences

Look at the picture. Underline the sentence that is true.

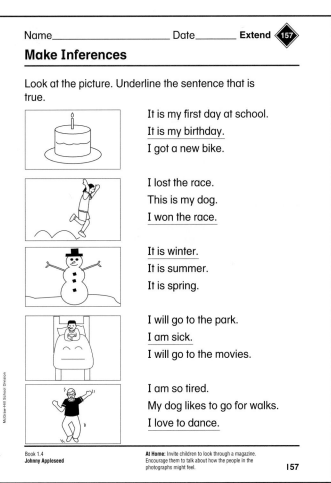

It is my first day at school.
It is my birthday.
I got a new bike.

I lost the race.
This is my dog.
I won the race.

It is winter.
It is summer.
It is spring.

I will go to the park.
I am sick.
I will go to the movies.

I am so tired.
My dog likes to go for walks.
I love to dance.

Book 1.4
**Johnny Appleseed**

**At Home:** Invite children to look through a magazine. Encourage them to talk about how the people in the photographs might feel.

157

---

## Inflectional Endings *-er, -est*

Look at the pictures. Write a sentence about each one. Use words from the box. **Sample sentences are given.**

| bigger | biggest | taller | tallest | faster | fastest |

1. _____Max is taller than Ben._____

2. _____The first duck is the biggest._____

3. _____She is the fastest rider._____

**At Home:** Invite children to compare two items or people. For example: My dog runs *faster* than me.

158

Book 1.4
**The Knee-High Man**

# Johnny Appleseed • GRAMMAR

---

### *See* and *Say*

- The verb *see* has a special form to tell about the past.
- Use *see* or *sees* to tell about the present.

    Johnny Appleseed **sees** pink buds.
- Use *saw* to tell about the past.

    He **saw** people going west.

Write the underlined verb so that it tells about the past.

1. Johnny sees the trees. _____ saw

2. He sees the people. _____ saw

3. They see his smile. _____ saw

4. Johnny sees the buds. _____ saw

5. Then he sees apples. _____ saw

Book 1.4
Johnny Appleseed
5
115

---

### *See* and *Say*

- The verb *say* has a special form to tell about the past.
- Use *say* and *says* to tell about the present.
- Use *said* to tell about something that happened in the past.

    I **say** something.    He **said** something.

Write the underlined verb so that it tells about the past.

1. Johnny says the ham was good. _____ said

2. He says he would rest. _____ said

3. He says the sun was up. _____ said

4. He says "I'm Johnny." _____ said

5. They say, "Hello, Johnny." _____ said

116
Book 1.4
Johnny Appleseed
5

---

### *See* and *Say*

- Use *see* or *sees* to tell about the present.

    We **see** pink flowers.
- Use *saw* to tell about something that happened in the past.

    We **saw** pink buds.

Circle the word that makes each sentence tell about the past.

1. Johnny (saw, see, sees) a wolf in a trap.

2. One day, he (saw, see, sees) an old horse.

3. People (saw, see, sees) his pets.

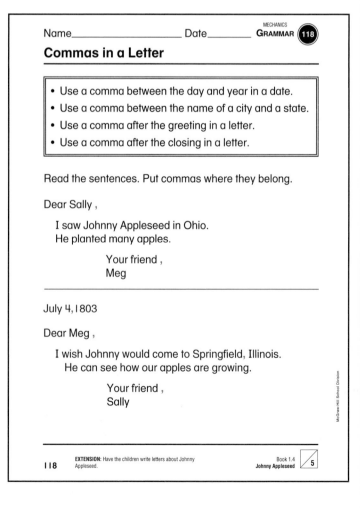

Circle the word that makes each sentence tell about the present.

4. Johnny (saw, see, sees) many plants.

5. He could (saw, see, sees) rain.

6. He (saw, see, sees) many people.

6
Book 1.4
Johnny Appleseed
EXTENSION: Have the children write present or past tense sentences about seeing apples.
117

---

### Commas in a Letter

- Use a comma between the day and year in a date.
- Use a comma between the name of a city and a state.
- Use a comma after the greeting in a letter.
- Use a comma after the closing in a letter.

Read the sentences. Put commas where they belong.

Dear Sally ,

I saw Johnny Appleseed in Ohio.
He planted many apples.

    Your friend ,
    Meg

July 4, 1803

Dear Meg ,

I wish Johnny would come to Springfield, Illinois.
He can see how our apples are growing.

    Your friend ,
    Sally

118
EXTENSION: Have the children write letters about Johnny Appleseed.
Book 1.4
Johnny Appleseed
5

---

# Johnny Appleseed • GRAMMAR

## Test

Draw a line under the verb that tells about the present. Circle the verb that tells about the past.

1. Johnny Appleseed (saw) apple trees.

2. Johnny Appleseed <u>sees</u> apple trees.

3. Johnny (said), "Plant apple seeds."

4. Johnny <u>says</u>, "Plant apple seeds."

5. Johnny <u>sees</u> people planting trees.

6. Johnny (saw) people planting trees.

7. Johnny (said) he liked animals.

8. He <u>says</u> he likes animals.

9. The people (said) they liked Johnny.

10. The people <u>say</u> they like Johnny.

## More Practice with *See* and *Say*

- Use *see* or *sees* to tell about the present.
- Use *saw* to tell about the past.
- Use *say* or *says* to tell about the present.
- Use *said* to tell about the past.

Read each sentence aloud. Circle the sentences that tell about the past. Underline the sentences that tell about the present.

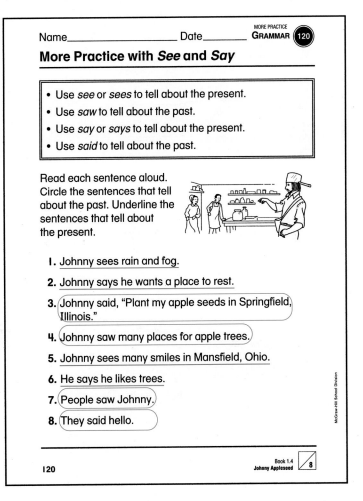

1. <u>Johnny sees rain and fog.</u>

2. <u>Johnny says he wants a place to rest.</u>

3. (Johnny said, "Plant my apple seeds in Springfield, Illinois.")

4. (Johnny saw many places for apple trees.)

5. <u>Johnny sees many smiles in Mansfield, Ohio.</u>

6. <u>He says he likes trees.</u>

7. (People saw Johnny.)

8. (They said hello.)

# Johnny Appleseed • SPELLING

## Words with Long a: ai, ay

**Pretest Directions**
Fold back the paper along the dotted line. Use the blanks to write each word as it is read aloud. When you finish the test, unfold the paper. Use the list at the right to correct any spelling mistakes. Practice the words you missed for the Posttest.

1. _____    1. rain
2. _____    2. wait
3. _____    3. way
4. _____    4. day
5. _____    5. say
6. _____    6. tail

**To Parents**
Here are the results of your child's weekly spelling Pretest. You can help your child study for the Posttest by following these simple steps for each word on the list:
1. Read the word to your child.
2. Have your child write the word, saying each letter as it is written.
3. Say each letter of the word as your child checks the spelling.
4. If a mistake has been made, have your child read each letter of the correctly spelled word aloud, and then repeat steps 1-3.

**Challenge Words**
_____
_____  how
_____
_____  light
_____
_____  live
_____
_____  pretty

5  Book 1.4
Johnny Appleseed                          115

---

## Words with Long a : ai, ay

**Using the Word Study Steps**
1. LOOK at the word.
2. SAY the word aloud.
3. STUDY the letters in the word.
4. WRITE the word.
5. CHECK the word.
   Did you spell the word right? If not, go back to step 1.

**Spelling Tip**
When there is a long vowel sound at the beginning or in the middle of a one-syllable word, it usually has two vowels.
   rain   say

**Word Scramble**
Unscramble each set of letters to make a spelling word.

1. nria ___rain___    2. yas ___say___

3. ady ___day___    4. ayw ___way___

5. iwat ___wait___    6. ilta ___tail___

**To Parents or Helpers:**
Using the Word Study Steps above as your child comes across any new words will help him or her spell well. Review the steps as you both go over this week's spelling words.
Go over the Spelling Tip with your child. Help your child write new one-syllable words that have a long vowel sound at the beginning or in the middle and have two vowels.
Help your child complete the spelling activity.

116                      Book 1. 4
                         Johnny Appleseed  6

---

## Words with Long a : ai-ay

Read the words. Circle the letters that are the same in each set of words.

1. rain      tail      wait
2. day       say       way

Write the letters that complete each spelling word.

3. r___ai___n    4. w___ai___t

5. w___ay___    6. d___ay___

7. s___ay___    8. t___ai___l

Read the rhyme. Circle the words that have the long a sound as in may.

I (wait) in the (rain) on a school (day),
Hoping the bus will come my (way).

Write the words you circled that have the long a spelled ay.

9. ___day___    10. ___way___

Write the words you circled that have the long a spelled ai.

11. ___wait___    12. ___rain___

16  Book 1.4
Johnny Appleseed                          117

---

## Words with Long a : ai, ay

Complete each spelling word by adding letters that spell the long a sound as in way.

1. The r___ai___n makes plants a grass grow.

2. D___ay___ is the opposite of night.

3. The dog wags her t___ai___l when she is happy.

4. We w___ai___t for the school bus together.

5. We s___ay___ "Hi!" to all our friends.

6. Then the bus goes on its w___ay___.

Circle the spelling word that means the same as the word tell.

7. ___say___

118                      Book 1.4
                         Johnny Appleseed  7

# Johnny Appleseed • SPELLING

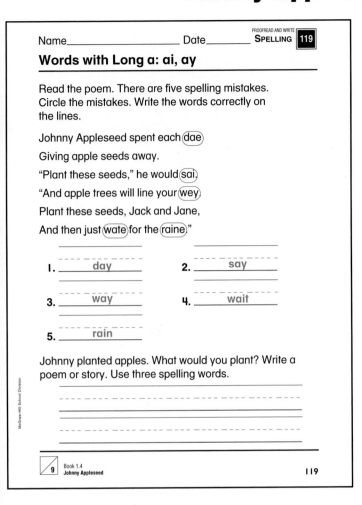

## Words with Long a: ai, ay

Read the poem. There are five spelling mistakes.
Circle the mistakes. Write the words correctly on
the lines.

Johnny Appleseed spent each (dae)

Giving apple seeds away.

"Plant these seeds," he would (sai.)

"And apple trees will line your (wey)

Plant these seeds, Jack and Jane,

And then just (wate) for the (raine)."

I. ___day___   2. ___say___

3. ___way___   4. ___wait___

5. ___rain___

Johnny planted apples. What would you plant? Write a
poem or story. Use three spelling words.

_____

_____

_____

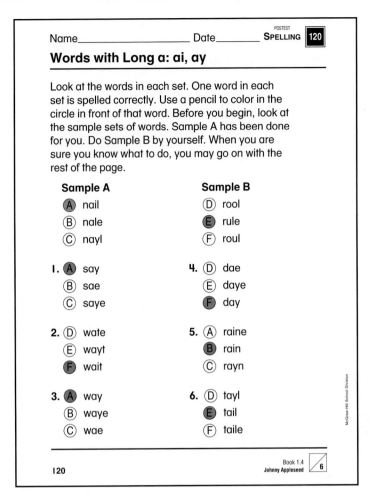

## Words with Long a: ai, ay

Look at the words in each set. One word in each
set is spelled correctly. Use a pencil to color in the
circle in front of that word. Before you begin, look at
the sample sets of words. Sample A has been done
for you. Do Sample B by yourself. When you are
sure you know what to do, you may go on with the
rest of the page.

**Sample A**          **Sample B**

Ⓐ nail            Ⓓ rool

Ⓑ nale            Ⓔ rule

Ⓒ nayl            Ⓕ roul

I. Ⓐ say          4. Ⓓ dae

   Ⓑ sae             Ⓔ daye

   Ⓒ saye            Ⓕ day

2. Ⓓ wate         5. Ⓐ raine

   Ⓔ wayt            Ⓑ rain

   Ⓕ wait            Ⓒ rayn

3. Ⓐ way          6. Ⓓ tayl

   Ⓑ waye            Ⓔ tail

   Ⓒ wae            Ⓕ taile

**Annotated Workbooks**

Name_____ Date_____ Practice **159**

## *ai, ay; u-e, o-e, i-e, a-e*

Write a word from the box to complete each sentence.

| fumes | smoke | spray | ride | rain |
|---|---|---|---|---|

1. The fire made black __smoke__.

2. They __spray__ water with a hose.

3. I want to __ride__ on a truck!

4. Do you smell the smoke __fumes__?

5. The __rain__ put out the fire.

5  Book 1.4
**Ring! Ring! Ring! Put Out the Fire!**

At Home: Have children draw a picture for the following words: slide, hose, rule, sail, and day.

159

McGraw-Hill School Division

Name_____ Date_____ Practice **160**

## High-Frequency Words

Write a word from the box to complete each sentence. The pictures show what each sentence means.

| how | clean | always | work | done |
|---|---|---|---|---|

1. I must __clean__ the rug.

2. This is __how__ I do it.

3. It is hard __work__.

4. I __always__ put things away.

5. When I am __done__, I have lunch.

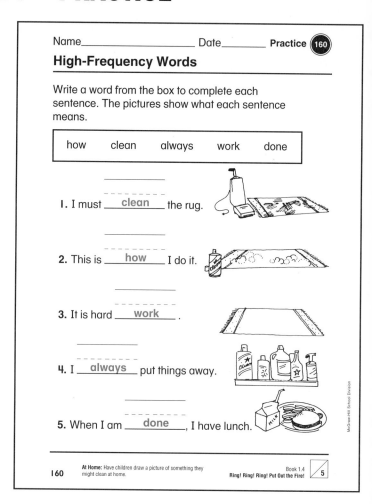

160  At Home: Have children draw a picture of something they might clean at home.

Book 1.4
**Ring! Ring! Ring! Put Out the Fire!**  5

McGraw-Hill School Division

# Hen and Snail

Snail went to Hen and asked for a bite to eat and a place to stay.

"From now on you must work." said Hen.
Snail said, "Yes." Hen and Snail became friends.

At Home: Have children talk about why work is important. What kinds of work are there? What kind of work do they like to do?

4   160a

2

The red hen always got her work done.
"How clean my pen is!" Hen said.
But the snail did not want to work. She sat in the sun.

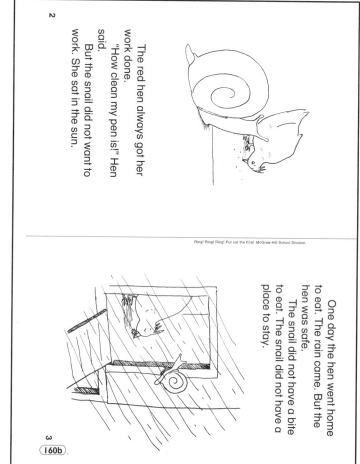

3   160b

One day the hen went home to eat. The rain came. But the hen was safe.
The snail did not have a bite to eat. The snail did not have a place to stay.

**T50**   *Annotated Workbooks*

# Put Out the Fire • PRACTICE

## Story Comprehension

Circle the sentences that tell what happened in
"Ring! Ring! Ring! Put Out the Fire!"

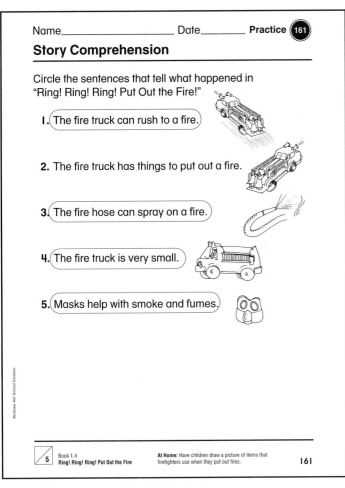

1. The fire truck can rush to a fire.

2. The fire truck has things to put out a fire.

3. The fire hose can spray on a fire.

4. The fire truck is very small.

5. Masks help with smoke and fumes.

Book 1.4
5  Ring! Ring! Ring! Put Out the Fire          **At Home:** Have children draw a picture of items that
firefighters use when they put out fires.                    161

---

## A Chart

Jon's class voted about where to go on a picnic.
They chose from four places. This **chart** tells you
how many votes each place got.

| Place | Number of Votes |
|---|---|
| Mill Pond Park | I I I I I I I I I I |
| Fish Creek | I I I I I I I |
| Sand Beach | I I I I I |
| Stone Hills | I I I I I I |

1. How many votes did Fish Creek get? _____ seven

2. How many votes did Stone Hills get? _____ six

3. Which place got the most votes? _____ Mill Pond Park

4. Which place got the least votes? _____ Sand Beach

162  **At Home:** Ask children to add the total number of votes to
determine how many students were in the class.         Book 1.4
Ring! Ring! Ring! Put Out the Fire!  4

---

## Cause and Effect

Read the question. Look at the picture. Underline
the answer.

**Effect**                    **Cause**

1. Why did the milk spill?   The cup was too full.
   The knight bumped the cup.
   The cup was too tall.

2. Why did the queen
   go away?                   No one was home.
   The king said to go away.
   The prince was late.

3. Why did the queen
   call the knight?           He tells good stories.
   She wants the dragon
   to go away.
   The king is missing.

4. Why did the cook
   run in?                    He saw a mouse.
   The food was not cooked.
   The pot was running over.

4  Book 1.4
Ring! Ring! Ring! Put Out the Fire!          **At Home:** Have children choose one of the effects and tell
what happens next.                         163

---

## Make Inferences

Read the sentences. Circle the word that tells how
the person might feel. Then write the word on the
line.

1. Jill wants a new toy.
   Her mom says no.
   Jill is _____.            _____ sad

   sad   happy   excited

2. Ann loves animals.
   Dad brings her a hamster.
   Ann is _____.             _____ happy

   sad   mad   happy

3. Ray wants a snack.
   He asks for an apple.
   Ray is _____.             _____ hungry

   silly   hungry   happy

4. Dad looks at the clock.
   He yawns.
   Dad is _____.             _____ sleepy

   sad   happy   sleepy

164  **At Home:** Have children cut out pictures of a person from a
magazine and then tell something about the person.         Book 1.4
Ring! Ring! Ring! Put Out the Fire!  4

# Put Out the Fire • PRACTICE

Name_____ Date_____ Practice (165)

## Inflectional Endings -ed, -s, -es

Add **-s** or **-es** to tell what one person or thing does **now**. Add **-ed** to tell what happened in the **past**.

Look at the underlined word in each sentence. Then look at the word after the sentence. Add **-s**, **-es**, or **-ed** to the underlined word and write the new word.

1. Dad <u>braid</u> Dale's hair.  past  braided

2. Lane <u>grill</u> the fish.  now  grills

3. Nash and I <u>plant</u> grapes.  past  planted

4. Gram <u>wish</u> for a soft quilt.  now  wishes

5. Jen <u>chain</u> up her bike.  past  chained

6. Pat <u>miss</u> the bus.  now  misses

6 | Book 1.4
**Ring! Ring! Ring! Put Out the Fire!**

**At Home:** Choose two sentences and act them out with children.

165

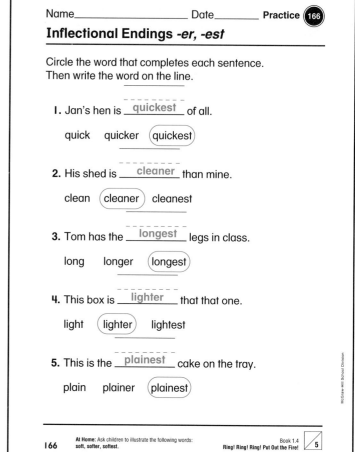

Name_____ Date_____ Practice (166)

## Inflectional Endings -er, -est

Circle the word that completes each sentence. Then write the word on the line.

1. Jan's hen is ____quickest____ of all.

   quick    quicker    (quickest)

2. His shed is ____cleaner____ than mine.

   clean    (cleaner)    cleanest

3. Tom has the ____longest____ legs in class.

   long    longer    (longest)

4. This box is ____lighter____ that that one.

   light    (lighter)    lightest

5. This is the ____plainest____ cake on the tray.

   plain    plainer    (plainest)

166 | **At Home:** Ask children to illustrate the following words: soft, softer, softest.

Book 1.4
**Ring! Ring! Ring! Put Out the Fire!** | 5

**T52** *Annotated Workbooks*

# Put Out the Fire • RETEACH

---

Name_____ Date_____ **Reteach** 159

## ai, ay; u-e, o-e, i-e, a-e

> Read these words.
>
> **s**ai**l**    **d**ay    **c**u**te**    **gl**o**be**    **t**i**me**    **g**a**me**

Draw lines to match the pictures to the words.

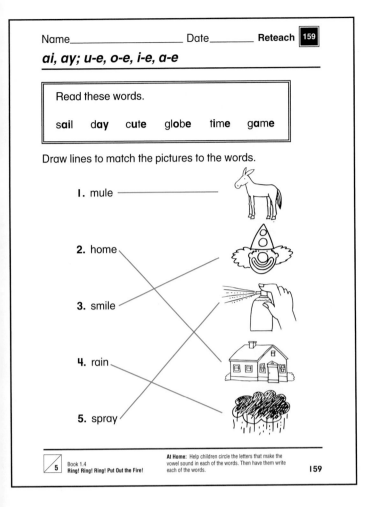

1. mule
2. home
3. smile
4. rain
5. spray

---

Name_____ Date_____ **Reteach** 160

## High-Frequency Words

Underline the word in the sentence that is also in the box. Then write the word.

> how    clean    always    work    done

1. I clean our house. _____clean_____
2. Mom always bakes on Sunday. _____always_____
3. The work is fun. _____work_____
4. Ken knows how to make cookies. _____how_____
5. We eat when we are done. _____done_____

---

Name_____ Date_____ **Reteach** 161

## Story Comprehension

Draw a line to match the words to the pictures.

1. fire truck
2. fire hose
3. fire
4. pole
5. mask

---

Name_____ Date_____ **Reteach** 162

## A Chart

> A vote and tally **chart** helps you figure out the results of an election.

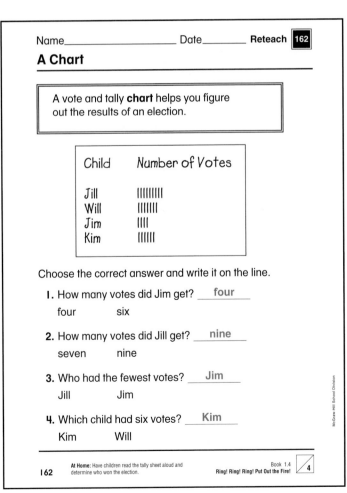

| Child | Number of Votes |
|-------|-----------------|
| Jill  | \|\|\|\|\|\|\|\|\| |
| Will  | \|\|\|\|\|\|\| |
| Jim   | \|\|\|\| |
| Kim   | \|\|\|\|\|\| |

Choose the correct answer and write it on the line.

1. How many votes did Jim get? _____four_____
   four        six
2. How many votes did Jill get? _____nine_____
   seven        nine
3. Who had the fewest votes? _____Jim_____
   Jill        Jim
4. Which child had six votes? _____Kim_____
   Kim        Will

Name_____ Date_____ Reteach **163**

## Cause and Effect

A **cause** is the reason why something happens. An **effect** is what happens.

| Cause | Effect |
|-------|--------|
| The king called the dog. | The dog came to the king. |

Look at the picture. Draw a line to another picture to show what happened.

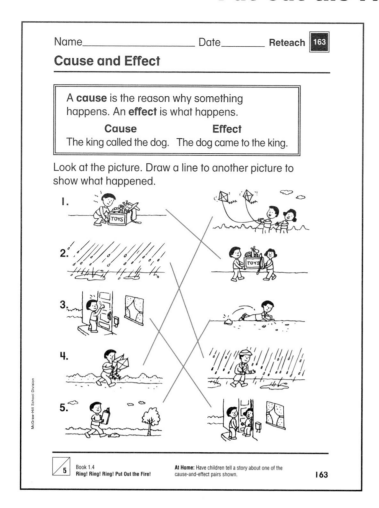

1.
2.
3.
4.
5.

---

Name_____ Date_____ Reteach **164**

## Make Inferences

You can use what you read and what you already know to answer questions about stories.

Read each story and look at the pictures. Circle the word or the picture clue that answers each question about the story.

Mom and Dad gave Tara a present.
Tara sees a toy animal.
The animal has a great big body.
The nose is very long.
The ears are big.
The tail is not very long.
Tara said, "This is great!"

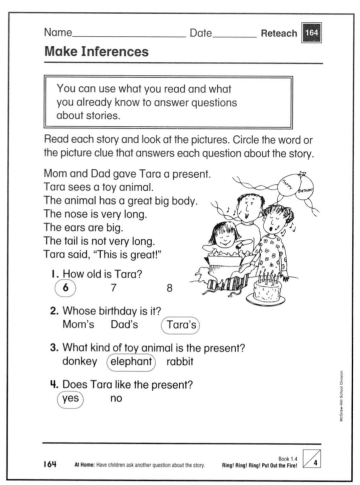

1. How old is Tara?
   (6)     7     8

2. Whose birthday is it?
   Mom's     Dad's     (Tara's)

3. What kind of toy animal is the present?
   donkey     (elephant)     rabbit

4. Does Tara like the present?
   (yes)     no

---

Name_____ Date_____ Reteach **165**

## Inflectional Endings *-ed, -s, -es*

Add **-ed** to tell what happened in the past.
Last week, Jay wash**ed** his cars.

Add **-s** or **-es** to tell what one person or thing is doing now.
Today Jay wax**es** his cars.

Circle **-ed** words that tell what happened in the past. Underline **-s** or **-es** words that tell what happens now.

1. Tom (fixed) the van.

2. The ship (sailed) away.

3. Beth mends her pants.

4. Jane (wiped) the glass.

5. Dad tosses the salad.

6. Mom plays with the cat.

7. The firefighter sprays the flames.

8. Max (fetched) the stick.

---

Name_____ Date_____ Reteach **166**

## Inflectional Endings *-er, -est*

Add **-er** to compare two things.
round + **er** = round**er**
This grape is round**er** than that one.

Add **-est** to compare three or more things.
round + **est** = round**est**
This plum is the round**est** of all.

Draw one line under the word that compares two things. Draw two lines under the word that compares three or more things.

1. This tree is older than that one.

2. White is the lightest color of all.

3. Your rug is softer than mine.

4. A truck is faster than a bike.

5. Is this dog smaller than that one?

6. This is the plainest skirt.

# Put Out the Fire • EXTEND

## ai, ay; u-e, o-e, i-e, a-e

Red words: Rome, note, home, phone, pole

Color words that have the long **o** sound as in
**Rome** red.          Yellow words: say, clay, pay

Color words that have **ay** as in **say** yellow.

Color words that have the long **i** sound as in
**mime** green.     Green words: mime, time, slime

Color words that have the long **u** sound as in
**tune** blue.

Blue words: tune, rude, prune, flute, tube, dune.

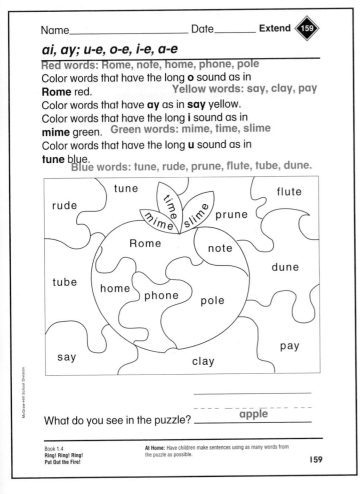

What do you see in the puzzle? _____ apple

Book 1.4
Ring! Ring! Ring!
Put Out the Fire!

At Home: Have children make sentences using as many words from
the puzzle as possible.

159

---

## High-Frequency Words

Use the words in the box to finish the poem.

| how | clean | always | work | done |
|-----|-------|--------|------|------|

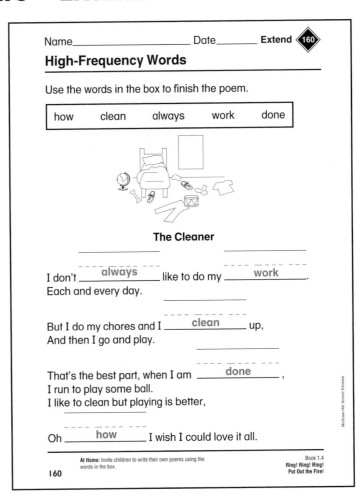

**The Cleaner**

_____

I don't ___always___ like to do my ___work___.
Each and every day.          _____

But I do my chores and I ___clean___ up,
And then I go and play.     _____

That's the best part, when I am ___done___,
I run to play some ball.
I like to clean but playing is better,

Oh ___how___ I wish I could love it all.

160

At Home: Invite children to write their own poems using the
words in the box.

Book 1.4
Ring! Ring! Ring!
Put Out the Fire!

---

## Story Comprehension

Look at the pictures. Put a 1 in the box to show
what happens first. Put a 2 in the box to show what
happens next. Put a 3 in the box to show what
happens last.

What are some other things firefighters do? Draw a
picture.

Book 1.4
Ring! Ring! Ring!
Put Out the Fire!

At Home: Have children talk about what they want to be
when they grow up. Ask them to draw a picture and write
a story about it.

161

---

## Use a Chart

What does a firefighter need? Read the list.
Use ✓ check marks to fill in the chart.

Answers may vary.

| What Does a Firefighter Need? | A Firefighter Needs . . . | A Firefighter Does Not Need . . . |
|---|---|---|
| hose | ✔ | |
| cat | | ✔ |
| fire truck | ✔ | |
| iron | | ✔ |
| fire hat | ✔ | |
| horse | | ✔ |
| sneakers | | ✔ |
| boots | ✔ | |
| lamp | | ✔ |
| ladder | ✔ | |

Use / tally marks to answer.
How many things does a firefighter need? ЖΙ
How many things does a firefighter not need? ЖΙ

162

At Home: Invite children to add to the list any other items
that a firefighter might need.

Book 1.4
Ring! Ring! Ring!
Put Out the Fire!

# Put Out the Fire • EXTEND

## Cause and Effect

Look at each picture. ✔ the sentence that happens next.

[ ] The water turns to ice.
[ ] The water gets cold.
[✔] The water gets hot.

[ ] The bank will fly.
[✔] The bank will break.
[ ] The bank will stop in the air.

Look at each picture. ✔ the sentence that happened before.

[ ] Sam fell off his bike.
[ ] Sam played with a friend.
[✔] Sam cleaned his bike.

[✔] Jane heard a joke.
[ ] Jane did her homework.
[ ] Jane ate an apple.

Book 1.4
Ring! Ring! Ring!
Put Out the Fire!

**At Home:** Take turns playing a **Why/Because** game with children. One person makes a simple statement. The other person asks **Why?** and the first person responds.

163

---

## Make Inferences

Look at the chart. Read the words. Make the ☐ red if it is a word that tells about a firefighter.

| brave | June | trained |
| strong | good | while |
| busy | lake | hard-working |
| when | fast | helpful |

Shade in these spaces: brave, strong, trained, good, helpful, busy, hard-working, fast

**At Home:** Invite children to think about other brave or helpful people. Who are they? Ask children to make drawings of them.

164

Book 1.4
Ring! Ring! Ring!
Put Out the Fire!

---

## Inflectional Endings -ed -s, -es

Choose the right word. Write it in the blank.

A firefighter can put out a **(fire fires)** _____fire_____.

My mom **(smile smiled)** _____smiled_____ at me.

How many **(grape grapes)** _____grapes_____ can you hold?

The **(fume fumes)** _____fumes_____ made me sick.

There were **(flame flames)** _____flames_____ in the fireplace.

The firefighter **(chop chopped)** _____chopped_____ down the door.

Book 1.4
Ring! Ring! Ring!
Put Out the Fire!

**At Home:** On individual index cards, write **-es, -s,** and these base words: **flame, muffin, fire, can, fume,** and **grape.** Turn the word cards face down on a table. Have the child pick a card and point to the correct ending.

165

---

## Inflectional Endings -er, -est

Name each picture. Use the words in the box to help you.

| long longer longest | small smaller smallest |
| tall taller tallest | big bigger biggest |

1.
___long___  ___longer___  ___longest___

2.
___small___  ___smaller___  ___smallest___

3.
___tall___  ___taller___  ___tallest___

4.
___biggest___  ___bigger___  ___big___

**At Home:** Invite children to make sentences with the words in the box.

166

Book 1.4
Ring! Ring! Ring!
Put Out the Fire!

---

**T56** *Annotated Workbooks*

# Put Out the Fire • GRAMMAR

## More Contractions with *Not*

- A **contraction** is a short form of two words.
- A **contraction** is a short way of saying two words.
- An **apostrophe** (') takes the place of the letters that are left out.

| | |
|---|---|
| was not | wasn't |
| were not | weren't |

Read the sentences. Circle the short form of two words.

1. The house (wasn't) on fire.
2. They (weren't) going to a fire.
3. They (weren't) in the truck.
4. There (wasn't) any work to do.
5. He (wasn't) putting out a fire.
6. They (weren't) going down the pole.
7. The pole (wasn't) tall.
8. The trucks (weren't) blue.

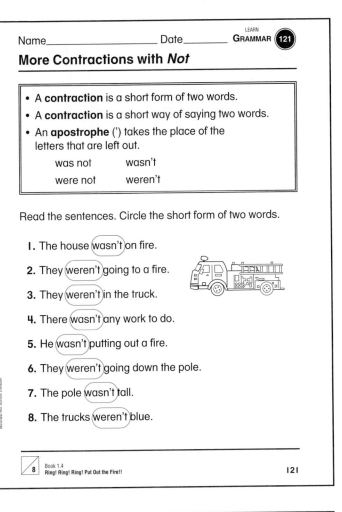

## More Contractions with *Not*

- A **contraction** is a short form of two words.
- An **apostrophe** (') takes the place of the letters that are left out.

| | |
|---|---|
| do not | don't |

Read the sentences. Find the short form of two words. Draw a circle around the contraction.

1. (Didn't) you see the fire truck?
2. The fire truck (didn't) stop.
3. I (don't) see the fire.
4. They (didn't) need to work.
5. We (don't) have a fire here.

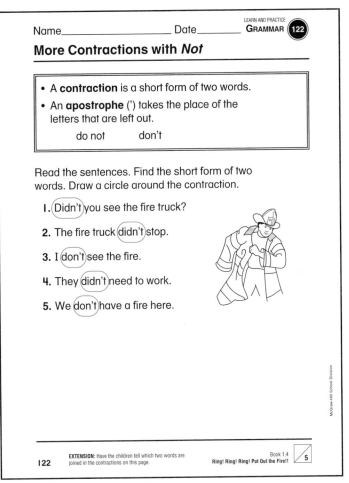

## More Contractions with *Not*

- A **contraction** is a short form of two words.
- An **apostrophe** (') takes the place of the letters that are left out.

| | |
|---|---|
| was not | wasn't |
| were not | weren't |
| do not | don't |
| did not | didn't |

Read the sentences. Circle the two words that make the contraction in each sentence.

1. The firefighters don't always need masks.
   (do not)   was not   did not
2. The firefighters weren't on their way.
   (were not)   was not   do not
3. They didn't rush away.
   (did not)   was not   do not
4. They didn't go down the pole.
   (did not)   was not   do not
5. That wasn't the ladder.
   (was not)   did not   do not

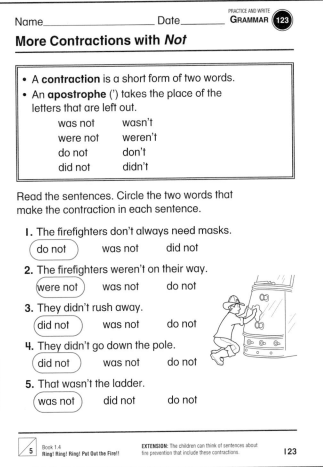

## More Contractions with *Not*

- A **contraction** is a short form of two words.
- Use an **apostrophe** (') in place of <u>o</u> in a contraction with <u>not</u>.

| | |
|---|---|
| was not | wasn't |

On the lines, write the contractions for the words in ( ).

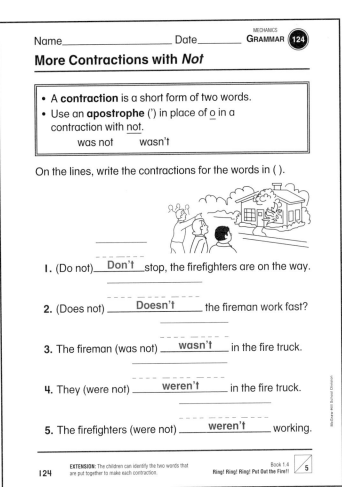

1. (Do not)____Don't____stop, the firefighters are on the way.
2. (Does not) ____Doesn't____ the fireman work fast?
3. The fireman (was not) ____wasn't____ in the fire truck.
4. They (were not) ____weren't____ in the fire truck.
5. The firefighters (were not) ____weren't____ working.

# Put Out the Fire • GRAMMAR

Name_____ Date_____

## Test

Write the contraction for the underlined words.

1. The house <u>was not</u> on fire.

   ------ wasn't ------

2. The men <u>did not</u> rush.

   ------ didn't ------

3. <u>Do not</u> go near the fire.

   ------ Don't ------

4. They <u>were not</u> at home.

   ------ weren't ------

5. She <u>did not</u> see the truck.

   ------ didn't ------

---

Name_____ Date_____

## More Practice With Contractions

- A **contraction** is a short form of two words.
- An **apostrophe** (') takes the place of the letters that are left out.

Look at the picture. Read the sentences about it. Circle the contraction for the underlined words.

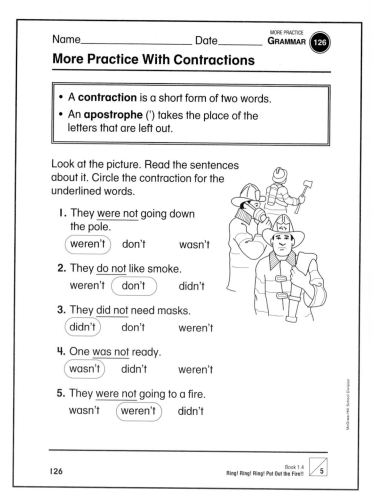

1. They <u>were not</u> going down the pole.

   (weren't)   don't   wasn't

2. They <u>do not</u> like smoke.

   weren't   (don't)   didn't

3. They <u>did not</u> need masks.

   (didn't)   don't   weren't

4. One <u>was not</u> ready.

   (wasn't)   didn't   weren't

5. They <u>were not</u> going to a fire.

   wasn't   (weren't)   didn't

---

**T58**   *Annotated Workbooks*

# Put Out the Fire • SPELLING

## Words from Science

**Pretest Directions**

Fold back the paper along the dotted line. Use the blanks to write each word as it is read aloud. When you finish the test, unfold the paper. Use the list at the right to correct any spelling mistakes. Practice the words you missed for the Posttest.

1. _____  1. truck
2. _____  2. smoke
3. _____  3. bell
4. _____  4. pole
5. _____  5. ring
6. _____  6. brave

**Challenge Words**

_____ clean
_____ always
_____ work
_____ done

**To Parents**

Here are the results of your child's weekly spelling Pretest. You can help your child study for the Posttest by following these simple steps for each word on the list:

1. Read the word to your child.
2. Have your child write the word, saying each letter as it is written.
3. Say each letter of the word as your child checks the spelling.
4. If a mistake has been made, have your child read each letter of the correctly spelled word aloud, and then repeat steps 1-3.

---

## Words from Social Studies

**Using the Word Study Steps**

1. LOOK at the word.
2. SAY the word aloud.
3. STUDY the letters in the word.
4. WRITE the word.
5. CHECK the word. Did you spell the word right? If not, go back to step 1.

**Spelling Tip**

Keep a notebook with a list of words you have trouble spelling.

**Find and Circle**

Where are the spelling words?

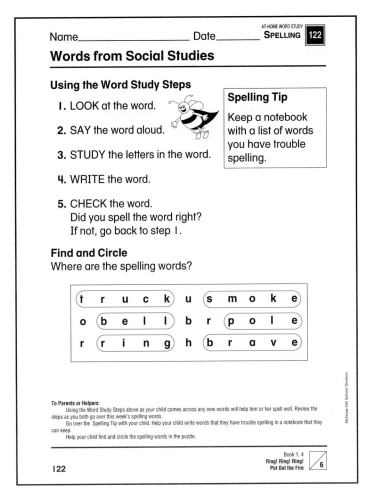

---

## Words from Social Studies

Look at the spelling words in the box. Write each word in the correct helmet.

| truck | smoke | bell | pole | ring | brave |

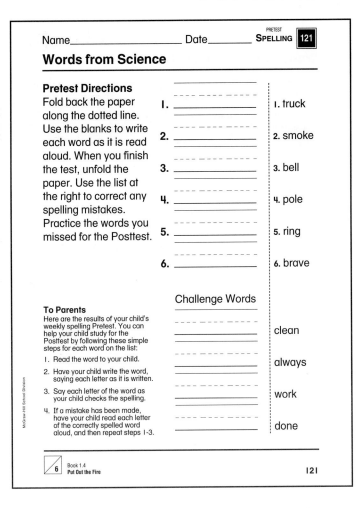

words with short vowel sounds
1. truck
2. bell
3. ring

words with long vowel sounds
1. smoke
2. pole
3. brave

---

## Words from Social Studies

Write the spelling word that goes with each picture.

1. _____ truck
2. _____ smoke
3. _____ bell
4. _____ pole

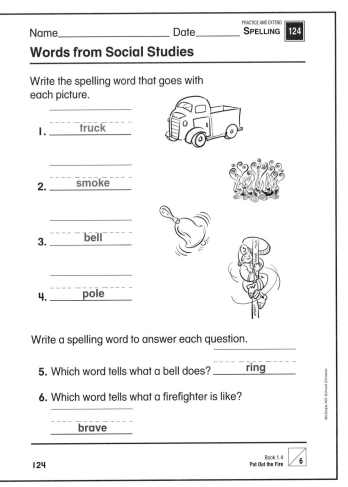

Write a spelling word to answer each question.

5. Which word tells what a bell does? _____ ring

6. Which word tells what a firefighter is like?

_____ brave

**T59**

# Put Out the Fire • SPELLING

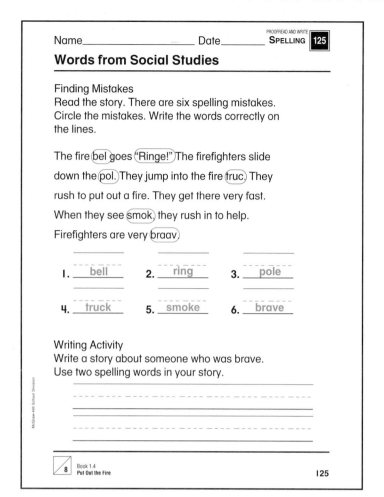

## Words from Social Studies

Finding Mistakes
Read the story. There are six spelling mistakes.
Circle the mistakes. Write the words correctly on
the lines.

The fire bel goes "Ringe!" The firefighters slide

down the pol. They jump into the fire truc. They

rush to put out a fire. They get there very fast.

When they see smok, they rush in to help.

Firefighters are very braav.

1. ___bell___    2. ___ring___    3. ___pole___

4. ___truck___    5. ___smoke___    6. ___brave___

Writing Activity
Write a story about someone who was brave.
Use two spelling words in your story.

_____

_____

_____

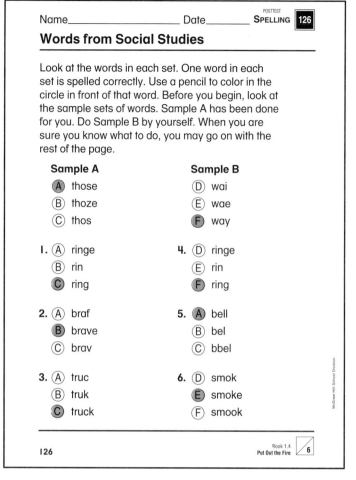

## Words from Social Studies

Look at the words in each set. One word in each
set is spelled correctly. Use a pencil to color in the
circle in front of that word. Before you begin, look at
the sample sets of words. Sample A has been done
for you. Do Sample B by yourself. When you are
sure you know what to do, you may go on with the
rest of the page.

**Sample A**
- (A) those ●
- (B) thoze
- (C) thos

**Sample B**
- (D) wai
- (E) wae
- (F) way ●

1.
- (A) ringe
- (B) rin
- (C) ring ●

2.
- (A) braf
- (B) brave ●
- (C) brav

3.
- (A) truc
- (B) truk
- (C) truck ●

4.
- (D) ringe
- (E) rin
- (F) ring ●

5.
- (A) bell ●
- (B) bel
- (C) bbel

6.
- (D) smok
- (E) smoke ●
- (F) smook

# Unit 4 Review • PRACTICE and RETEACH

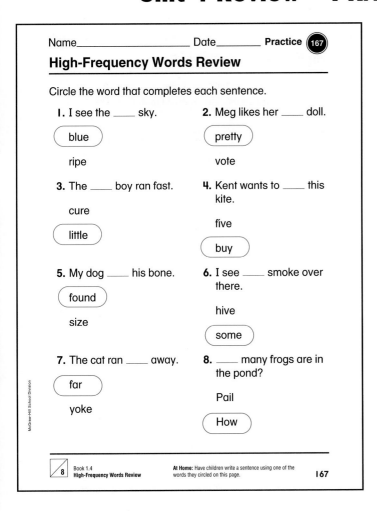

Name_____ Date_____

## High-Frequency Words Review

Circle the word that completes each sentence.

1. I see the ____ sky.
   (blue)
   ripe

2. Meg likes her ____ doll.
   (pretty)
   vote

3. The ____ boy ran fast.
   cure
   (little)

4. Kent wants to ____ this kite.
   five
   (buy)

5. My dog ____ his bone.
   (found)
   size

6. I see ____ smoke over there.
   hive
   (some)

7. The cat ran ____ away.
   (far)
   yoke

8. ____ many frogs are in the pond?
   Pail
   (How)

McGraw-Hill School Division

8 Book 1.4
High-Frequency Words Review
At Home: Have children write a sentence using one of the words they circled on this page.
167

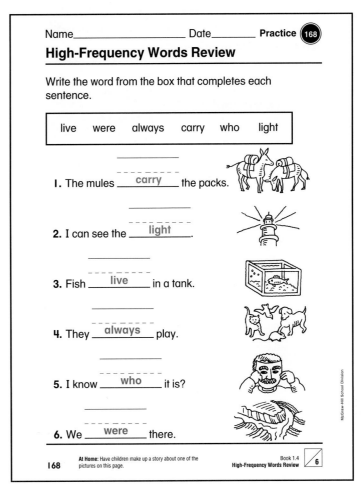

Name_____ Date_____

## High-Frequency Words Review

Write the word from the box that completes each sentence.

| live | were | always | carry | who | light |

1. The mules __carry__ the packs.

2. I can see the __light__.

3. Fish __live__ in a tank.

4. They __always__ play.

5. I know __who__ it is?

6. We __were__ there.

168 At Home: Have children make up a story about one of the pictures on this page.
Book 1.4
High-Frequency Words Review 6

McGraw-Hill School Division

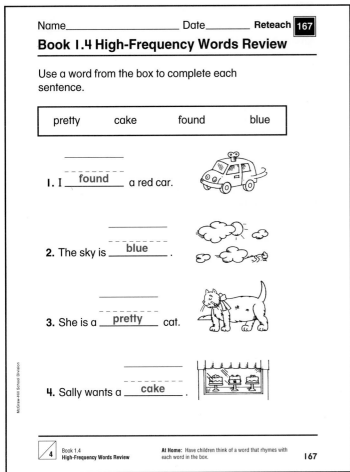

Name_____ Date_____

## Book 1.4 High-Frequency Words Review

Use a word from the box to complete each sentence.

| pretty | cake | found | blue |

1. I __found__ a red car.

2. The sky is __blue__.

3. She is a __pretty__ cat.

4. Sally wants a __cake__.

McGraw-Hill School Division

4 Book 1.4
High-Frequency Words Review
At Home: Have children think of a word that rhymes with each word in the box.
167

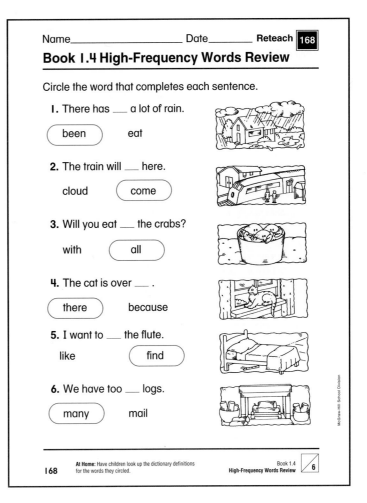

Name_____ Date_____

## Book 1.4 High-Frequency Words Review

Circle the word that completes each sentence.

1. There has ____ a lot of rain.
   (been)    eat

2. The train will ____ here.
   cloud    (come)

3. Will you eat ____ the crabs?
   with    (all)

4. The cat is over ____ .
   (there)    because

5. I want to ____ the flute.
   like    (find)

6. We have too ____ logs.
   (many)    mail

McGraw-Hill School Division

168 At Home: Have children look up the dictionary definitions for the words they circled.
Book 1.4
High-Frequency Words Review 6

**T61**

# Unit 4 Review • EXTEND and GRAMMAR

Name_____ Date_____ **Extend** 167

## High-Frequency Words Review

Draw a line from the sentence to its picture.

The duck is **after** the dog.

The lake is **blue**.

I use the lamp for **light**.

I **found** a frog.

We **live** in a home.

She is **clean** after a bath.

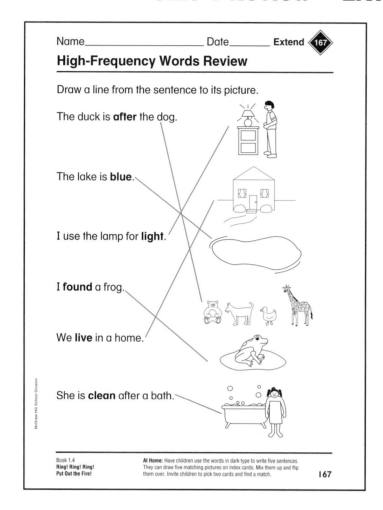

At Home: Have children use the words in dark type to write five sentences. They can draw five matching pictures on index cards. Mix them up and flip them over. Invite children to pick two cards and find a match.  **167**

---

Name_____ Date_____ **Extend** 168

## High-Frequency Words Review

Read the sentences. Use the words in the box. Write the word on the line. Then write the word in the puzzle.

| some | because | who | always |
|------|---------|-----|--------|

**Across**

1. Mike is home

   ____because____ he is sick.

3. ____Who____ will go with you?

4. ____Some____ cars are new but this car is old.

**Down**

2. I ____always____ like to play.

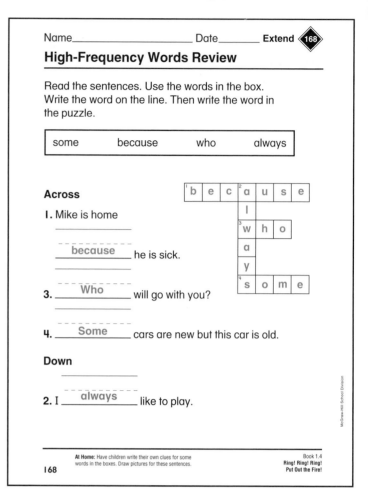

At Home: Have children write their own clues for some words in the boxes. Draw pictures for these sentences.   Book 1.4
**Ring! Ring! Ring!**
**Put Out the Fire!**

---

Name_____ Date_____ REVIEW **GRAMMAR** 127

## More About Verbs

Read the sentences in the box. Look at the part with the line under it. Is there a mistake? How do you make it right? Mark your answer.

> Five plums were in a bag. <u>A jar of jam were on the shelf.</u>
> (1)

1. Ⓐ Take away *were*.
   Ⓑ Change *were* to *was*.
   Ⓒ Do not change.

> The child has ducks. <u>The children has many ducks.</u>
> (2)

2. Ⓐ Change *has* to *have*.
   Ⓑ Take away *has*.
   Ⓒ Do not change.

> <u>Yasmin have many ducks.</u> The ducks have a home.
> (3)

3. Ⓐ Take away *have*.
   Ⓑ Change *have* to *has*.
   Ⓒ Do not change.

> Sam went to get help. <u>Sam go up the tree.</u>
> (4)

4. Ⓐ Change *go* to *went*.
   Ⓑ Take away *go*.
   Ⓒ Do not change.

Go on

---

Name_____ Date_____ REVIEW **GRAMMAR** 128

## More About Verbs

> Sam went to see Bob the Bull. <u>Where do Sam go?</u>
> (5)

5. Ⓐ Change *do* to *did*.
   Ⓑ Change *go* to *went*.
   Ⓒ Do not change.

> Long ago, <u>Johnny says he liked apples.</u> He planted apple trees.
> (6)

6. Ⓐ Take away *says*.
   Ⓑ Change *says* to *said*.
   Ⓒ Do not change.

> People saw apple trees. <u>Johnny see people smile.</u>
> (7)

7. Ⓐ Change *see* to *saw*.
   Ⓑ Take away *see*.
   Ⓒ Do not change.

> <u>We do'nt like smoke.</u> We aren't going to the fire.
> (8)

8. Ⓐ Change *do'nt* to *don't*.
   Ⓑ Change *do'nt* to *doesn't*.
   Ⓒ Do not change.

# Unit 4 Review • SPELLING

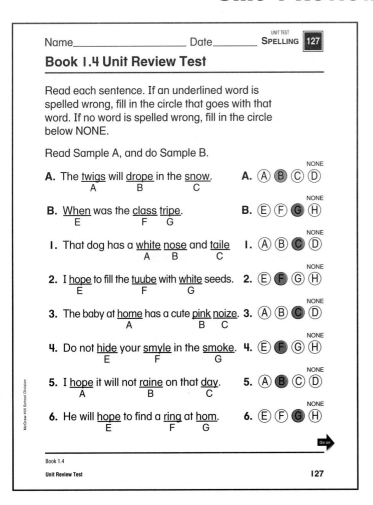

## Book 1.4 Unit Review Test

Read each sentence. If an underlined word is spelled wrong, fill in the circle that goes with that word. If no word is spelled wrong, fill in the circle below NONE.

Read Sample A, and do Sample B.

A. The <u>twigs</u> will <u>drope</u> in the <u>snow</u>.
   A        B              C

A. Ⓐ Ⓑ Ⓒ Ⓓ  NONE

B. <u>When</u> was the <u>class</u> <u>tripe</u>.
   E              F      G

B. Ⓔ Ⓕ Ⓖ Ⓗ  NONE

1. That dog has a <u>white</u> <u>nose</u> and <u>taile</u>.
   A       B        C

1. Ⓐ Ⓑ Ⓒ Ⓓ  NONE

2. I <u>hope</u> to fill the <u>tuube</u> with <u>white</u> seeds.
   E              F          G

2. Ⓔ Ⓕ Ⓖ Ⓗ  NONE

3. The baby at <u>home</u> has a cute <u>pink</u> <u>noize</u>.
   A                  B     C

3. Ⓐ Ⓑ Ⓒ Ⓓ  NONE

4. Do not <u>hide</u> your <u>smyle</u> in the <u>smoke</u>.
   E        F              G

4. Ⓔ Ⓕ Ⓖ Ⓗ  NONE

5. I <u>hope</u> it will not <u>raine</u> on that <u>day</u>.
   A              B          C

5. Ⓐ Ⓑ Ⓒ Ⓓ  NONE

6. He will <u>hope</u> to find a <u>ring</u> at <u>hom</u>.
   E               F         G

6. Ⓔ Ⓕ Ⓖ Ⓗ  NONE

Go on →

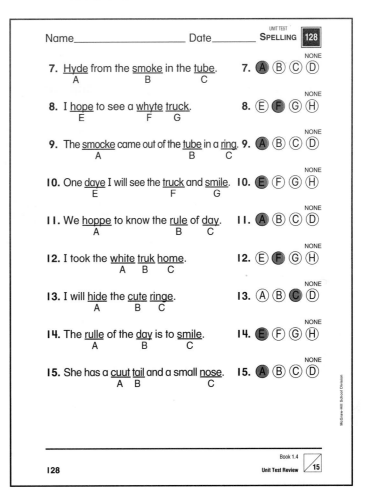

7. <u>Hyde</u> from the <u>smoke</u> in the <u>tube</u>.
   A              B            C

7. Ⓐ Ⓑ Ⓒ Ⓓ  NONE

8. I <u>hope</u> to see a <u>whyte</u> <u>truck</u>.
   E            F      G

8. Ⓔ Ⓕ Ⓖ Ⓗ  NONE

9. The <u>smocke</u> came out of the <u>tube</u> in a <u>ring</u>.
   A                        B          C

9. Ⓐ Ⓑ Ⓒ Ⓓ  NONE

10. One <u>daye</u> I will see the <u>truck</u> and <u>smile</u>.
    E                    F          G

10. Ⓔ Ⓕ Ⓖ Ⓗ  NONE

11. We <u>hoppe</u> to know the <u>rule</u> of <u>day</u>.
    A                 B       C

11. Ⓐ Ⓑ Ⓒ Ⓓ  NONE

12. I took the <u>white</u> <u>truk</u> <u>home</u>.
    A        B      C

12. Ⓔ Ⓕ Ⓖ Ⓗ  NONE

13. I will <u>hide</u> the <u>cute</u> <u>ringe</u>.
    A         B      C

13. Ⓐ Ⓑ Ⓒ Ⓓ  NONE

14. The <u>rulle</u> of the <u>day</u> is to <u>smile</u>.
    A           B          C

14. Ⓔ Ⓕ Ⓖ Ⓗ  NONE

15. She has a <u>cuut</u> <u>tail</u> and a small <u>nose</u>.
    A     B              C

15. Ⓐ Ⓑ Ⓒ Ⓓ  NONE

# Long *i*: *i–e*

**OBJECTIVES** Children will be introduced to words containing the combination of the long *i* sound and a silent *e*.

## Alternate Activities

### *Visual*

#### SECRET AGENTS

**Materials:** outline drawing of a secret agent, crayons, markers, pencils

Use the following activity to introduce children to words containing the combination of long *i* with a silent *e*.

- Draw a large outline of a secret agent in a trench coat, sunglasses, and a slouch hat with "silent *e*" written on it.

- Have children color in the drawing.

- Below the drawing, list the following words: *win, hip, din, bin, fin, pin, dip, dim, Tim, gin, lip*.

- Ask children to be "long *i* silent *e* sleuths" and find the words which, when an *e* is added to them, become words with the long *i* sound. ▶**Linguistic**

### *Kinesthetic*

#### ALL TOGETHER NOW

**Materials:** cardboard, markers

Have children work with letter cards, combining them to form words with long *i* and silent *e*.

- Make up cardboard cards that have the letters *v, w, m, d, f, l, n*, and *p* printed on them.

- Hand out the cards to eight children, and ask them to hold them up in front of the class.

- Choose eight other children to hold up cards with the word *in* printed on them. Ask these children to pick a letter to stand next to.

- Choose one child to be the "silent *e*." Ask the child to stand at the end of each of the three-letter groups.

- Ask the remainder of the class to read the word that is formed. ▶**Bodily/Kinesthetic**

### *Auditory*

#### LISTEN FOR THE I

**Materials:** recordings of popular songs with long *i* words in the lyrics, for example, The Beatles' "I, Me, Mine"

Encourage children to listen to the music and see if they recognize words with the long *i* sound, distinguishing those that have a silent *e*.

- Play a recording of a popular song which contains some long *i* words (*mine, fine, line, etc.*).

- Ask children to listen for the long *i* sound.

- Have children say the words and list them on the chalkboard. Ask for volunteers to underline the silent *e* on the end of the words. ▶**Musical**

 **CD-ROM**

**See Reteach 127, 131, 132, 140, 148, 159**

# Charts

 **OBJECTIVES** Children will learn to interpret information on charts.

## Alternate Activities

## *Visual*

### HEIGHT CHARTS

 **Materials:** examples of charts, large sheet of paper, markers, tape

Draw a chart on the chalkboard to show the heights of all the children. Have them fill it in and then use it and other charts as models to make their own height charts.

- Have on display in the classroom various charts for children to view.

- Using large sheets of paper taped to the wall, measure the heights of all children in the class. Ask each child to label his or her name and height on the chart you have drawn on the chalkboard.

- Ask children to return to their seats and create a chart of their own showing statistics for four of their classmates. ▶Spatial

## *Kinesthetic*

### PHYSICAL CHART

 **Materials:** masking tape, cardboard, markers, index cards

Help children learn to interpret chart information by creating a "physical chart."

- Make a grid with masking tape on the floor. Explain to children that you are making a physical chart of different types of shoes worn in the classroom.

- Ask a child wearing laced shoes to stand in one square, a child wearing sneakers to stand in one square, a child wearing black shoes to stand in one square, and so on.

- Ask each of the children standing in a square to count the number of children in the class who fit the criterion of his or her square.

- Give each child standing in a square a card with the number of children who fit the category written on it.

- Talk the class through ways of interpreting the data on the chart. ▶Logical/Mathematical

## *Auditory*

### CHART THIS

**Materials:** examples of charts, paper, markers

Give children additional practice with interpreting information on charts by having groups make up their own charts.

- Divide the class into small groups, and hand out examples of charts for them to study and discuss.

- Ask groups to decide on something within the classroom to chart and a format to copy from the examples in the handouts.

- Have groups share their charts with the class, so that children have an opportunity to practice interpreting charts. ▶Spatial

**See Reteach 130, 138, 146, 154, 162**

# Cause and Effect

**OBJECTIVES** Children will learn to recognize cause and effect.

## Alternate Activities

### Visual

**CAN YOU PREDICT?**

**Materials:** magazines, scissors, pencils

Use magazine illustrations to help children understand cause and effect.

* Provide children with magazines that have a lot of illustrations.

* Explain the meaning of cause and effect by discussing everyday examples, such as: *If you knock over the glass of milk, the milk will spill.*

* Ask children to look through magazines for photographs which demonstrate cause and effect. Explain that although both the cause and the effect may not be apparent in the photos, the child may be able to make up either the cause or the effect. For example, if one photo shows a glass of milk, the student can invent the scenario of knocking it over.

**WRITING** Have children cut out the photographs and write a cause-and-effect statement under them. ▶**Logical/Mathematical**

### Kinesthetic

**ACT IT OUT**

**PARTNERS** Have children work in pairs to demonstrate cause and effect.

* Ask one child in each pair to be the CAUSE and the other child to be the EFFECT.

* Ask each pair to come up with a pantomime of a cause-and-effect situation, such as: *John tickles Joe, and Joe giggles.*

* Have the pairs act out their scenarios, and ask the audience to state the cause and effect.
  ▶**Bodily/Kinesthetic**

### Auditory

**WORD FANS**

**GROUP** **Materials:** large sheets of paper, pencils

Use this activity to show children that one cause may have several different effects.

* Ask children to think of several cause-and-effect situations. They may be drawn from the book they have just read or from real-life observations.

**WRITING** Ask children to write the cause at the top of a sheet of paper and pass it to the classmate on their left. Have those children fill in a plausible effect underneath the cause.

* Have children fold the paper so that the effect is not visible and pass the paper once more to the left.

* Have that child fill in another plausible effect to match the initial cause.

* Do this several times, then return the papers to their originators, and share the results with the group. ▶**Interpersonal**

**See Reteach 133, 141, 163**

# Inflectional endings -s, -es

## Alternate Activities

### Visual

**TRADING LISTS**

**PARTNERS** Have children work with partners to make plural words.

- Ask children to make lists of ten words in their singular form.

- Assign each child a partner, and have partners exchange lists.

- Ask each child to write the plural of the words on the partner's list. Remind children that some plurals require just an -s, and others need an -es.

- To ensure that some of the words will require the less common -es ending, you can suggest several words (ax, box, fox, etc.) which should be included on everyone's list. ▶Linguistic

### Kinesthetic

**LABELS**

**Materials:** blue and white index cards

**ONE** Review -s and -es endings by having children write the plurals of the names of objects in the classroom.

- Ask children to use white index cards to label items in the classroom.

- Have children write on the card the name of the object and tape it to the surface of the object if possible.

- Once the labels are in place, ask children to use blue index cards to label each object with the word in its plural form. For example, if the white index card says *window*, the blue index card would say *windows*.

- Suggest several items in the classroom whose names require -es to form the plural, such as *box*.
  ▶**Bodily/Kinesthetic**

### Auditory

**WORD CARDS**

**Materials:** index cards or white paper

**PARTNERS** Have children make word cards, and then have partners take turns quizzing each other about the words' plurals.

- Write the words *fox, box, mix, cat, dog, ball,* and *hat* on the chalkboard.

- Ask children to copy each word onto an index card or slip of white paper.

- Ask children to write on the back of each card whether the word requires -s or -es to make it plural.

- Have children work in pairs, taking turns holding up the cards and asking each other the following: *What is the word, and how do you make it plural?*
  ▶**Linguistic**

**See Reteach 134, 165**

# Long o: o–e

**OBJECTIVES** Children will be introduced to words containing the long o sound.

## Alternate Activities

### Visual

**LOOKING FOR LONG O'S**

 **Materials:** books, magazines, newspapers, paper, pencils or crayons

Use this activity to introduce words with long o and silent e, helping children recognize these words in books, magazines, and newspapers.

- Have each child draw several letter o's on a sheet of paper, leaving plenty of space between them to add letters.

- Have children decorate the o's to look like eyes by adding pupils and eyelashes.

- Ask children to use their eyes to look through books, magazines, and newspapers in search of long o words with silent e endings.

- Have children write the words on their sheet of paper, using the eyes to represent the o's in the words. ▶Spatial

### Kinesthetic

**ADD THE SILENT E**

 **Materials:** index cards, bulletin board, thumbtacks

Have children tack on silent e's to review words with the long o sound.

- Ask children to help make a list of long o words with silent e endings. If children suggest words which have the long o sound but not the silent e,

such as *soap*, make a separate list of those words, and discuss them afterward.

- Write the long o words on cards, leaving off the final *e*, and use thumbtacks to attach the cards to a bulletin board.

- Make cards with only the letter *e* on them, and hand these out to children.

- Ask children to tack on the final *e* to the words on the bulletin board. Pronounce the words correctly aloud. ▶Linguistic

### Auditory

**IS IT OR ISN'T IT?**

**Materials:** cardboard, markers

Have children use letter cards to help them listen for words containing long o and silent e.

- Read a passage from *Yasmin's Ducks*, making sure to choose a section which has words containing the long o sound and silent e on the end.

- Ask children to make up two cards, one which has long o on it and one which has an e on it.

- Ask children to listen to the passage and to raise their long o cards when they hear a long o word.

- When they raise their cards, ask: *If you think this word has a silent e on the end, raise your e card.*

- Write the word on the chalkboard so they can see the spelling. ▶Interpersonal

 CD-ROM

**See Reteach 135, 139, 140, 148, 156, 159**

# Long *u: u-e*

**TESTED OBJECTIVES** Children will be introduced to words with the long *u* sound.

## Alternate Activities

### *Visual*

#### WORD GRID

**ONE**

**Materials:** paper with grid drawn on it, pencils

To introduce children to words containing long *u* and silent *e*, have them create word grids.

- Provide each child with a nine-box grid. On the chalkboard, write the following words: *rule, use, June, cute, tune, tube, mule, flute.*

- Ask children to write one of the words in each square, in any order they choose.

- Read a word from the list, and ask children to find the word on their grid.

- Once they have located the word, ask children to say the word out loud and then to underline the silent *e* in the word.

- Continue until all of the words have been called.
  ▶**Logical/Mathematical**

### *Kinesthetic*

#### GONE FISHING

**PARTNERS**

**Materials:** construction-paper fish, pencils or markers

Play *Go Fish* with words containing long *u* and silent *e*.

- Cut out fish shapes from colored construction paper.

- Have each child write on the fish: *rule, mule, rude, dude, tube, huge, use, fuse, fume, plume, dune, June, tune, prune, cute, lute, flute.*

- Children pick a partner and combine their fish.

- Have each pair play *Go Fish* with the words.

- Explain the rules. Each player starts with three fish. A player asks for a particular word. If the other player doesn't have it in his or her hand, then the first player must draw a fish from the pile. The player with the most word pairs is the winner. ▶**Interpersonal**

### *Auditory*

#### LISTENING FOR THE LONG *U*

**GROUP**

**Materials:** oak tag, markers

Have children use smiling and frowning faces when they hear words with long *u* sound.

- Ask children to draw two pictures, one on either side of a piece of oak tag. One side has a smiling face, the other a frowning face.

- Read the following list of words: *rule, rub, use, mule, mud , tube, tub, huge, hug, fuss, fume, plum, June, prune, run, fun, flute, sun.*

- Ask children to hold up the happy face when they hear a long *u* word with a silent *e* ending and to hold up the sad face when they hear a word that does *not* have the long *u* sound.
  ▶**Bodily/Kinesthetic**

 **CD-ROM**

**See Reteach 143, 147, 148, 156, 159**

**T69**

# Make Inferences

## Alternate Activities

### Visual

#### WHAT DO YOU REALLY KNOW?

**GROUP** Use this activity to show children how to make inferences based on the information the author gives.

- Explain that authors do not always tell readers everything.

- Write the following statement on the chalkboard: *John picked up his pen and thought very, very hard.*

- Ask children the following: *What information has the author given you?* (The person's name is John; He has a pen; He is thinking.)

- Explain that an inference is something which is implied, rather than stated directly.

- Ask children: *What inferences can you make based on that sentence?*

- Encourage children to ask "why" questions. For example, *Why did John pick up the pen?* (He is about to write something.) *Why is John thinking very, very hard?* (He is trying to decide what to write about.) ►**Logical/Mathematical**

### Kinesthetic

#### INFERENCE CHARADES

Have children play a game of *Charades* and **GROUP** make inferences.

- Write out a series of simple actions for children to act out (*pick up the book, close your eyes*).

- Have a child act out the action. Have the class tell what the action is: *He is picking up the book.*

- On the bottom of each action statement, add another statement, such as *you want to read a story, you are angry,* or *you are in a hurry.*

- Ask the child to repeat the action, including the second statement in the pantomime.

- Based on the action, have the class guess how the child feels.

- Encourage children to ask "why" questions: *Why is he picking up the book?* (He wants to read a story.) ►**Bodily/Kinesthetic**

### Auditory

#### DID THE AUTHOR TELL US?

Show children how to make inferences **GROUP** using the "Five W's."

- Ask children to listen to a passage as you read aloud from the featured text.

- After you have read the passage, write the following question words on the chalkboard: *Who? What? Where? When? Why?*

- Ask children to ask and answer questions about the text using the words on the chalkboard.

- List the answers on the chalkboard and ask: *Did the author tell us this, or did we figure it out on our own?* ►**Interpersonal**

**See Reteach 149, 157, 164**

# Inflectional endings -er, -est

 **OBJECTIVES** Children will be introduced to the concept of adding *-er* and *-est* to compare objects.

## Alternate Activities

## Visual

**FILL IN THE BLANKS**

 **Materials:** duplicate sheets, as described below

Use this activity to introduce the inflectional endings *-er* and *-est*.

- Hand out duplicate sheets with charts consisting of three boxes in a row. In the top row of boxes write the words *big, bigger,* and *biggest.*

- In each subsequent row, one of the boxes will contain a word, and the other two boxes will be blank. For example, box 1 would be blank, box 2 would contain the word *faster,* and box 3 would be blank.

- Ask children to fill in the blank boxes.

- When they have completed their charts, ask children to underline *-er* and *-est* in the comparative forms. ▶**Linguistic**

## Kinesthetic

**THREE OF A KIND**

 **Materials:** paper, markers

Have children show the differences between *big, bigger,* and *biggest* by drawing comparative pictures.

- Have each child draw three pictures illustrating the concepts of *big, bigger,* and *biggest.*

- Encourage children to share their illustrations with the class, using comparative words when describing the three drawings. For example, *The first bear is big. The second bear is bigger. The third bear is the biggest.* ▶**Spatial**

## Auditory

**BIG, BIGGER, BIGGEST**

**Materials:** boxes or baskets, items to be compared

Have children review the inflected endings *-er* and *-est* by comparing various objects.

- Place three baskets or boxes on a table.

- Box 1 has no label, box 2 is labeled *-er,* and box 3 is labeled *-est.*

- Gather several three-object sets that can be easily compared; for example, use three pencils of varying lengths.

- Ask children to place the objects in the boxes according to the criterion by which they are categorizing them, for example, l*ong, longer, longest.* ▶**Logical/Mathematical**

See Reteach 150, 158, 166

# Long *a*: *ai, ay*

**OBJECTIVES** Children will be introduced to words with the long *a* sound spelled *ai* or *ay*.

## Alternate Activities

### Visual

#### AY OR AI?

**Materials:** index cards, two shoe boxes

Use index cards with long *a* words to help children distinguish words spelled *ai* from those spelled *ay*.

- On the chalkboard, tack up index cards with the following words written on them: *bay, day, hay, lay, may, pay, play, ray, say, way, aid, paid, laid, maid, raid, paint, saint, pain, gain, main, rain.*

- Ask children to read a word, remove it from the board and place it in one of two boxes—one marked "*ay* words" and one marked "*ai* words."

- After all cards have been removed, draw them out of the boxes and read them aloud one at a time.

- Ask children whether it is an *ay* word or an *ai* word. If they answer correctly, put the card back on the chalkboard. If they answer incorrectly, put it back in the box.

- Continue until all of the cards are back on the chalkboard. ▶**Logical/Mathematical**

### Kinesthetic

#### THE LONG *A* TEAM

Have children work in teams to decide whether *ai* or *ay* is used in spelling words with the long *a* sound.

- Divide the class into two teams—the *ai* team and the *ay* team.

- Read sentences containing one of the following words: *bay, day, hay, lay, may, pay, play, ray, say, way, aid, paid, laid, maid, paint, pain, gain, main, rain.* After you've read the sentences, repeat the word with the long *a* sound.

- Alternating teams, choose one player to decide whether the long *a* sound in the word you read is represented by the letters *ai* or *ay*.

- If the player guesses correctly, he or she writes the word on the chalkboard, and his or her team gets one point. If the player guesses incorrectly, the other team writes the word on the chalkboard and gets the point. ▶**Interpersonal**

### Auditory

#### WHICH IS IT?

 Review *ai* and *ay* by having children list words with the long *a* sound.

- Read a passage from the featured text or a newspaper article, or write and read a passage of your own which contains both *ai* and *ay* words.

- Ask children to raise their hands when they hear a word with the long *a* sound.

- If the word they hear has *ai* or *ay* in it, ask children to write it on a piece of paper.

- Review the list with the whole group.
  ▶**Intrapersonal**

 **CD-ROM**

**See Reteach 151, 155, 156, 159**

# Notes

## Writing Readiness

Before children begin to write, fine motor skills need to be developed. Here are examples of activities that can be used:

- **Simon Says** Play Simon Says using just finger positions.
- **Finger Plays and Songs** Sing songs such as "Where Is Thumbkin" or "The Eensie, Weensie, Spider" or songs that use Signed English or American Sign Language.
- **Mazes** Use or create mazes, especially ones that require moving the writing instruments from left to right.

## The Mechanics of Writing

### POSTURE

- Chair height should allow for the feet to rest flat on the floor.
- Desk height should be two inches above the elbows.
- There should be an inch between the child and the desk.
- Children sit erect with the elbows resting on the desk.
- Letter models should be on the desk or at eye level.

### PAPER POSITION

- **Right-handed children** should turn the paper so that the  lower left-hand corner of the paper points to the abdomen.

- **Left-handed children** should turn the paper so that the lower right-hand corner of the paper points to the abdomen.

- The nondominant hand should anchor the paper near the top so that the paper doesn't slide.
- The paper should be moved up as the child nears the bottom of the paper. Many children won't think of this.

## The Writing Instrument Grasp

For handwriting to be functional, the writing instrument must be held in a way that allows for fluid dynamic movement.

### FUNCTIONAL GRASP PATTERNS

- **Tripod Grasp** The writing instrument is held with the tip of  the thumb and the index finger and rests against the side of the third finger. The thumb and index finger form a circle.

- **Quadrupod Grasp** The writing instrument is held with the tip of the thumb and index finger and rests against the fourth finger. The thumb and index finger form a circle.

### INCORRECT GRASP PATTERNS

- **Fisted Grasp** The writing instrument is held in a fisted hand.

- **Pronated Grasp** The instrument is held diagonally within the hand with the tips of the thumb and index finger but with no support from other fingers.

- **Five-Finger Grasp** The writing instrument is held with the tips of all five fingers.

- **Flexed or Hooked Wrist** Flexed or bent wrist is typically seen with left-handed writers but is also present in some right-handed writers.

- To correct wrist position, have children check their writing posture and paper placement.

### TO CORRECT GRASPS

- Have children play counting games with an eye dropper and water.
- Have children pick up small objects with a tweezer.
- Do counting games with children picking up small coins using just the thumb and index finger.

# Evaluation Checklist

### Formation and Strokes

- ☑ Does the child begin letters at the top?
- ☑ Do circles close?
- ☑ Are the horizontal lines straight?
- ☑ Do circular shapes and extender and descender lines touch?
- ☑ Are the heights of all upper-case letters equal?
- ☑ Are the heights of all lower-case letters equal?
- ☑ Are the lengths of the extenders and descenders the same for all letters?

### Directionality

- ☑ Do the children form letters starting at the top and moving to the bottom?
- ☑ Are letters formed from left to right?

### Spacing

- ☑ Are the spaces between letters equidistant?
- ☑ Are the spaces between words equidistant?
- ☑ Do the letters rest on the line?
- ☑ Are the top, bottom and side margins on the paper even?

# Write the Alphabet

Trace and write the letters.

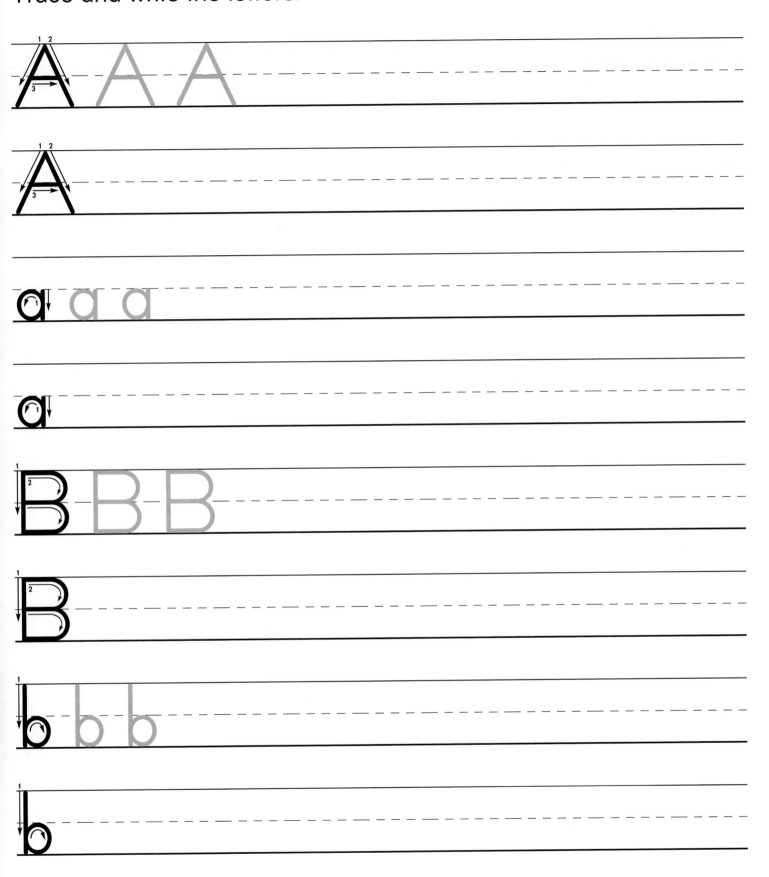

Trace and write the letters.

C C C C

C

c c c

c

D D D D

D

d d d

d

# Trace and write the letters.

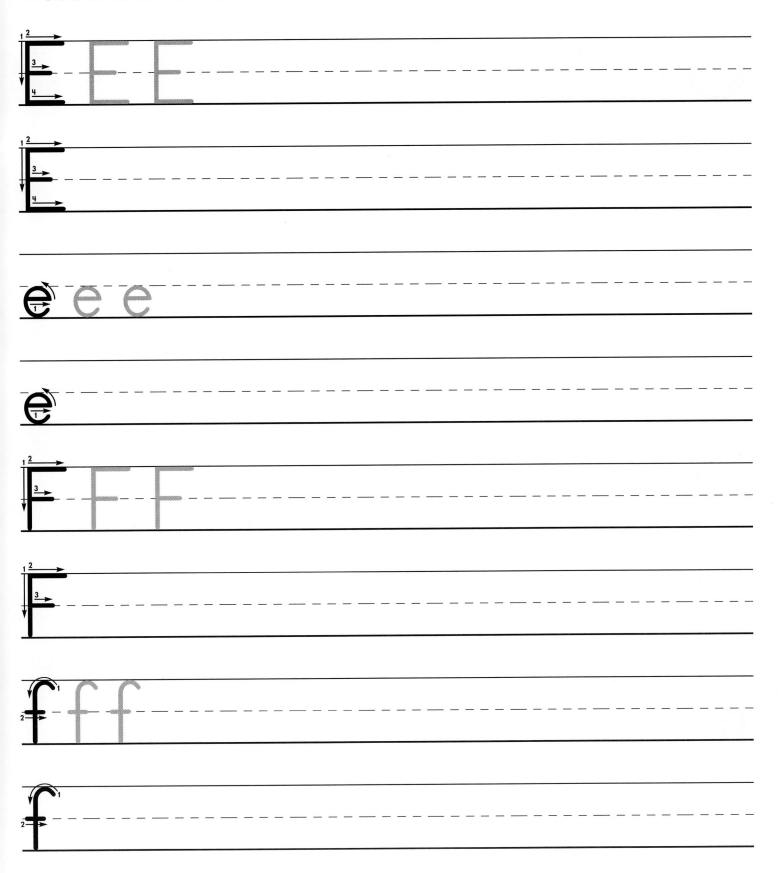

# Trace and write the letters.

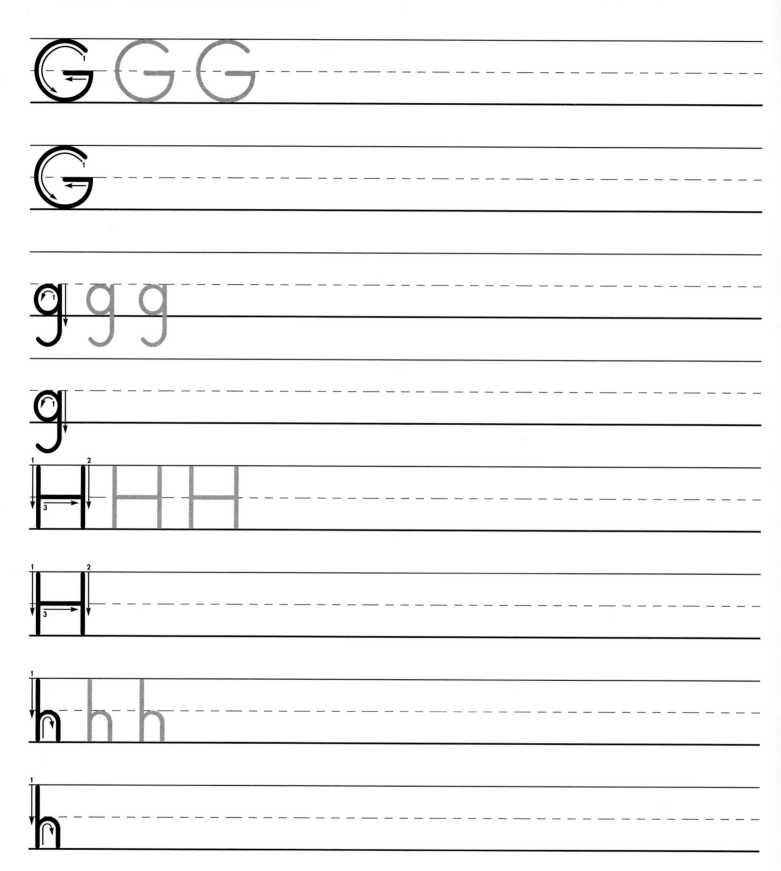

Trace and write the letters.

I I I

I

i i i

i

J J J J

J J

j j j j

j

# Trace and write the letters.

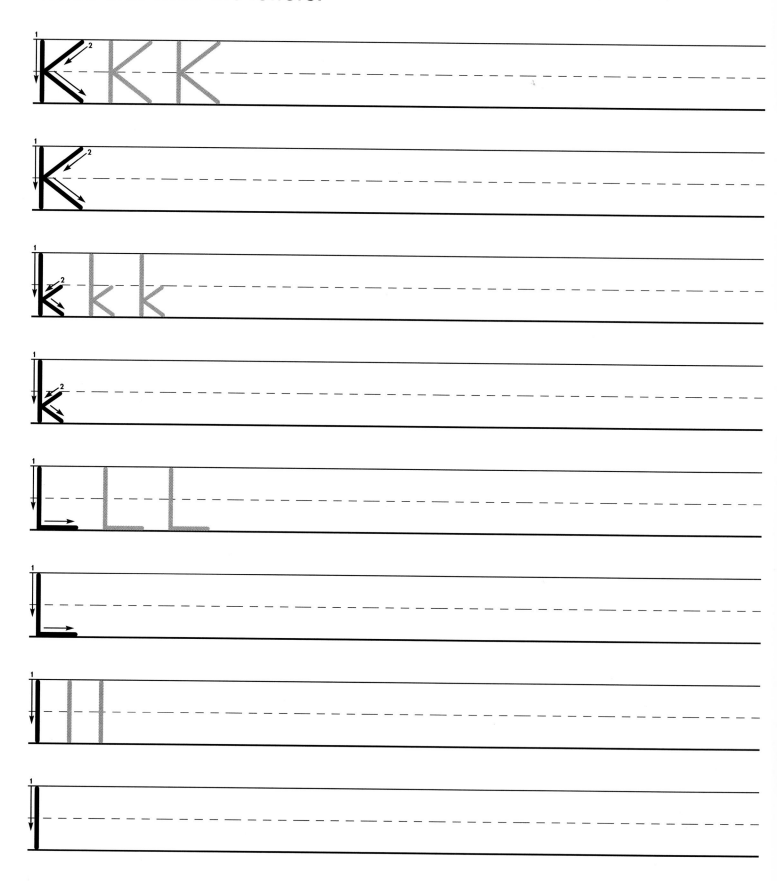

Trace and write the letters.

M M M M

M M

m m m

m

N N N N

N N

n n n

n

# Trace and write the letters.

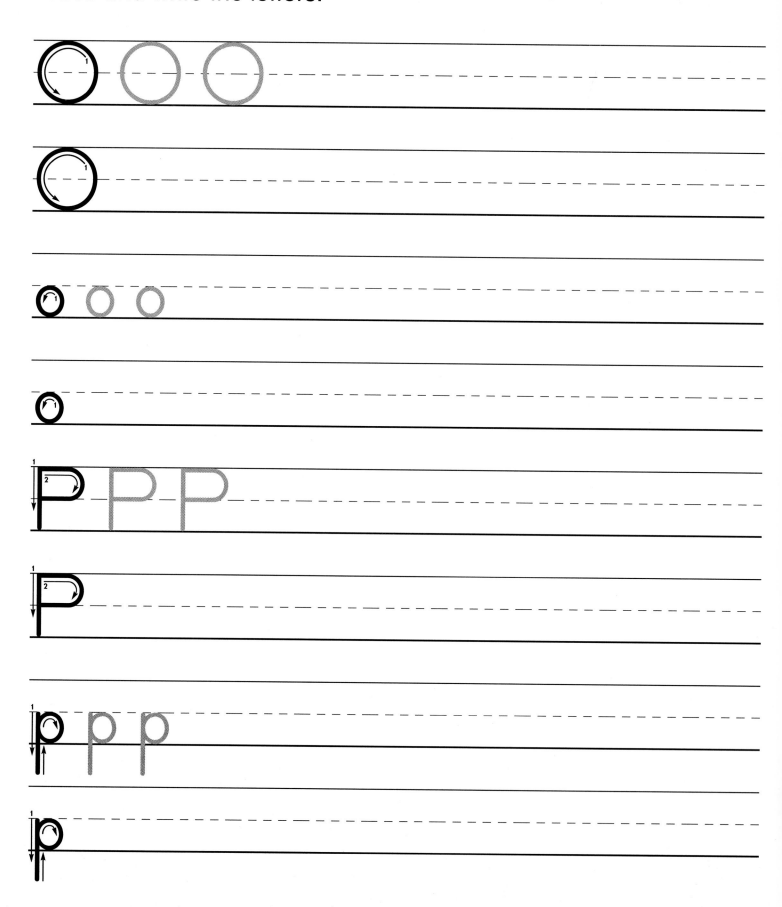

Trace and write the letters.

Q Q Q

Q

q q q

q

R R R

R

r r r

r

Trace and write the letters.

S S S

S

s s s

s

T T T

T

t t t

t

Trace and write the letters.

U U U U

U

u u u

u

V V V

V

V V V

V

# Trace and write the letters.

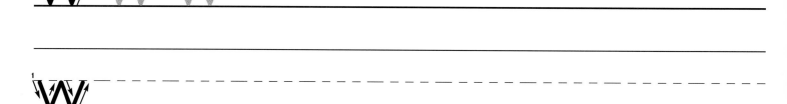

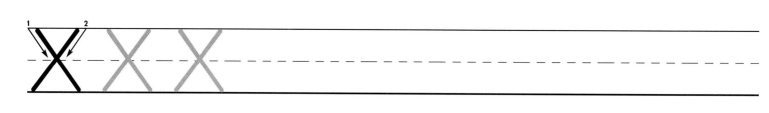

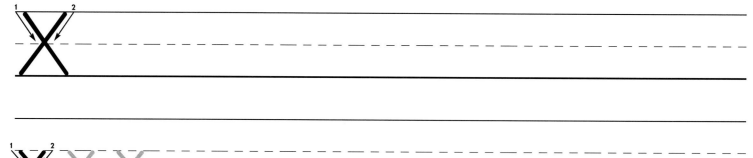

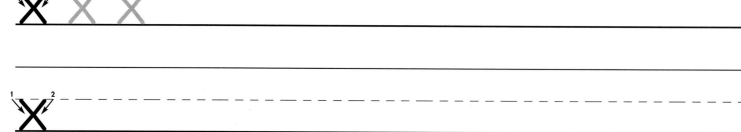

Trace and write the letters.

Y Y Y

Y

y y y

y

Z Z Z

Z

z z z

z

## Selection Titles

## Honors, Prizes, and Awards

**QUACK**
Book 1, p.34
by *Judy Barrett*

**Author/Illustrator:** *Judy Barrett*, winner of IRA-CBC Children's Choice Award (1978) for *Cloudy With a Chance of Meatballs*

**WHAT DOES PIG DO?**
Book 1, p.58
by *Angela Shelf Medearis*
Illustrated by *Barbara Reid*

**Author:** *Angela Shelf Medearis*, winner of IRA-Teachers' Choice Award (1995) for *Our People*
**Illustrator:** *Barbara Reid*, winner of Canada Council Award (1985) for Children's Illustrations for *Have You Seen Birds?*; Ezra Jack Keats Award (1988); Mr. Christie Book Award (1991) for the *Zoe* series; ALA Notable (1994) for *Two By Two*; IBBY Honor List (1996) for *Gifts*; Governor General's Award for Illustration (1997) for *The Party*

**A YEAR LATER**
Book 1, p.122
by *Mary Ann Hoberman*

**Poet:** *Mary Ann Hoberman*, winner of American Book Award Paper Picture Book Award (1983) for *A House Is a House for Me*

**ONE GOOD PUP**
Book 2, p.10
by *Frank Asch*

**Author/Illustrator:** *Frank Asch*, winner of American Book Award Pick of the List Award (1997) for *Barnyard Animals*

**WHAT BUG IS IT?**
Book 2, p.98
by *Pat Cummings*

**Author/Illustrator:** *Pat Cummings*, winner of Coretta Scott King Award (illustration; 1984) for *My Mama Needs Me*; National Council of Teachers of English Orbis Pictus Award, Boston Globe-Horn Book Award (1992), ALA Notable (1993) for *Talking with Artists*; ALA Notable (1996) for *Talking with Artists, Vol. 2*

| Selection Titles | Honors, Prizes, and Awards |
|---|---|
| **STAN'S STUNT**<br>Book 3, p.10<br>By *Lynn Plourde*<br>Illustrated by *Pam Levy* | **Illustrator: *Pam Levy,*** winner of 1996 Society of Children's Book Writers and Illustrators Magazine Merit Award for *Cricket* magazine |
| **GREG'S MASK**<br>Book 3, p.40<br>by *Ann McGovern* | **Author: *Ann McGovern***, winner of Boston Globe-Horn Book Honor (1975) for *Scram Kids* |
| **THE SHOPPING LIST**<br>Book 4, p.10<br>by *Gary Apple*<br>Illustrated by *Shirley Beckes* | **Illustrator: *Shirley Beckes,*** winner of The 39th Annual Book Exhibit, The Chicago Book Clinic Honor Book Certificate Award for *Irwin the Sock* |
| **THE KNEE-HIGH MAN**<br>Book 4, p.68<br>by *Ellen Dreyer*<br>Illustrated by *Tim Raglin* | **Illustrator: *Tim Raglin,*** winner of Silver Medal by the Society Illustrators, 39th Exhibition |

| Selection Titles | Honors, Prizes, and Awards |
|---|---|
|  **BABY CHICK**<br>Book 5, p.8<br>by *Aileen Fisher* | **Poet:** *Aileen Fisher*, winner of National Council of Teachers of English Award for Excellence in Poetry for Children (1978) |
|  **SHRINKING MOUSE**<br>Book 5, p.48<br>by *Pat Hutchins* | **Author/Illustrator:** *Pat Hutchins*, winner of Boston Globe-Horn Book Honor (1968) for *Rosie's Walk;* New York Times Best Illustrated (1972) for *You'll Soon Grow Into Them, Titch;* IBBY Honor Award (1974); ALA Notable (1997) for *The Doorbell Rang* |
|  **YOU CAN'T SMELL A FLOWER WITH YOUR EAR**<br>Book 5, p.84<br>by *Joanna Cole* | **Author:** *Joanna Cole*, winner of ALA Notable (1983) for *Bony-Legs* and *Cars and How They Go;* ALA Notable, Golden Kite Honor Book (1984) for *How You Were Born;* Boston Globe-Horn Book Honor (1987) for *The Magic School at the Waterworks;* Texas Blue Bonnet Master List (1995) for *On the Bus with Joanna Cole;* IRA-CBC Children's Choice (1997) for *The Magic School Bus Blows Its Top: A Book About Volcanos* |
|  **OWL AND THE MOON**<br>Book 5, p.120<br>by *Arnold Lobel* | **Author/Illustrator:** *Arnold Lobel*, Caldecott Honor (1970) for *Frog and Toad Are Friends,* (1972) for *Hildilid's Night;* Christopher Award (1972) for *On the Day Peter Stuyvesant Sailed Into Town;* Newbery Honor (1973) for *Frog and Toad Together;* Christopher Award (1977) for *Frog and Toad All Year;* Caldecott Medal (1981) for *Fables;* ALA Notable, Caldecott Honor (1982), Boston Globe-Horn Book Honor, New York Times Best Illustrated (1981) for *On Market Street;* Boston Globe-Horn Book Honor (1984) for *Rose in My Garden;* ALA Notable (1984) for *Book of Pigericks/Pig Limericks;* ALA Notable (1986) for *Three Day Hat;* Golden Kite Award Book (1987) for *The Devil and Mother Crump* |

| Selection Titles | Honors, Prizes, and Awards |
|---|---|

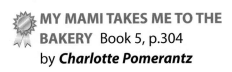

**NEW SHOES FOR SILVIA**
Book 5, p.194
by *Johanna Hurwitz*
Illustrated by *Jerry Pinkney*

**Author:** *Johanna Hurwitz*, winner of Texas Blue Bonnet Award (1987) for *The Hot and Cold Summer;* ALA Notable (1984) for *Rip-Roaring Russell;* Texas Blue Bonnet Master List (1996–97) for *Birthday Surprises: Ten Great Stories to Unwrap*

**Illustrator:** *Jerry Pinkney,* winner of Coretta Scott King Award, ALA Notable, Christopher Award (1986) for *Patchwork Quilt;* Newbery Medal, Boston Globe-Horn Book Honor (1977) for *Roll of Thunder, Hear My Cry;* Boston Globe-Horn Book Honor (1980) *Childtimes: A Three Generation Memoir;* Coretta Scott King Award (1987) for *Half a Moon and One Whole Star;* ALA Notable (1988) for *Tales of Uncle Remus: The Adventures of Brer Rabbit;* ALA Notable, Caldecott Honor, Coretta Scott King Award (1989) for *Mirandy and Brother Wind;* ALA Notable, Caldecott Honor, Coretta Scott King Honor (1990) for *Talking Eggs: A Folktale for the American South;* Golden Kite Award Book (1990) for *Home Place;* ALA Notable (1991) for *Further Tales of Uncle Remus: The Misadventures of Brer Rabbit, Brer Fox ...;* ALA Notable (1993) for *Back Home;* ALA Notable, Boston Globe-Horn Book Award, Caldecott Honor (1995) for *John Henry;* ALA Notable, Blue Ribbon (1997) for *Sam and the Tigers;* ALA Notable, Christopher Award, Coretta Scott King Award, Golden Kite Honor Book (1997) for *Minty: A Story of Young Harriet Tubman;* Aesop Prize (1997) for *The Hired Hand;* National Council for Social Studies Notable Children's Book Award (1998) for *The Hired Hand* and *Rikki-Tikki-Tavi;* Rip Van Winkle Award (1998); 1998 Hans Christian Andersen nominee

**MY MAMI TAKES ME TO THE BAKERY** Book 5, p.304
by *Charlotte Pomerantz*

**Poet:** *Charlotte Pomerantz,* winner of Jane Addams Book Award (1975) for *Princess and the Admiral;* ALA Notable (1994) for *Outside Dog*

## Trade Books

**A**dditional fiction and nonfiction trade books related to each selection can be shared with children throughout the unit.

### Don't Forget the Bacon
*Pat Hutchins (William Morrow, 1994)*

A young boy goes shopping for his mother and tries very hard to remember her instructions.

### To Market, To Market
*Anne Miranda, illustrated by Janet Stevens (Harcourt Brace, 1997)*

Starting with the familiar Mother Goose nursery rhyme, this tale then takes off to describe a series of unruly animals that run amok.

### Bunny Money
*Rosemary Wells (Dial Books for Young Readers, 1997)*

When Max and his sister Ruby go shopping for Grandma's birthday gift, they almost run out of money before they find the right present.

### Building a House
*Byron Barton (Greenwillow Books, 1981)*

The steps in building a house are briefly described and colorfully illustrated.

### Cleversticks
*Bernard Ashley, illustrated by Derek Brazell (Crown, 1991)*

Ling Sung is very unhappy in his new school until he has the chance to teach the other children something that they didn't know how to do.

### The Art Lesson
*Tomie dePaola (G. P. Putnam's Sons, 1989)*

Tommy learns that the art lesson in school is much different than drawing at home.

## Technology

**M**ultimedia resources can be used to enhance children's understanding of the selections.

 ***Alexander Who Used To Be Rich*** (Weston Woods) Video, 14 min. When Alexander's grandparents give him five dollars, Alexander discovers more ways to spend his money than to save it.

 ***Money Town*** (Simon and Schuster/Davidson) CD-ROM, Macintosh and Windows. Players earn money to keep the Greenstreet Town Park open. Teaches money identification, adding, and making change.

***Adventure Enough*** (Phoenix/BFA) A young boy's trip to the grocery store is anything but usual.

 ***Living or Nonliving?*** (National Geographic Educational Services) Video, 16 min. Teaches the differences between living and nonliving things. Explores how living things are nourished, grow, and respond to the world around them.

 ***Art for Beginners: Fun With Lines*** (Coronet/MTI) Video, 11 min. An introduction to using lines in drawing, and recognizing lines in nature.

## THE KNEE-HIGH MAN

### I Want to Be
*Thylias Moss, illustrated by Jerry Pinkney (Dial Press, 1993)*

After much exploration, a girl discovers the kind of person she wants to be.

### The Most Wonderful Egg in the World
*Helme Heine (Atheneum, 1983)*

Three hens learn that it is not what you look like that's the most important thing.

### So What!
*Miriam Cohen, illustrated by Lillian Hoban (Bantam Doubleday Dell Books for Young Readers, 1988)*

After much insecurity, a first grader learns to accept himself as he is.

## JOHNNY APPLESEED

### One Bean
*Anne Rockwell, illustrated by Megan Halsey (Walker, 1998)*

Watch what happens to a bean when it is soaked, planted, and watered, and eventually produces pods.

### The Giving Tree
*Shel Silverstein (Harper & Row, 1964)*

The story of a boy who loved a tree throughout his entire life and how the tree responded to his love.

### The Apple Pie Tree
*Zoe Hall, illustrated by Shari Halpern (Scholastic, 1996)*

Two sisters describe the changes that occur as they watch an apple tree grow in their backyard. A recipe for apple pie is included at the end of the story.

## RING! RING! RING! PUT OUT THE FIRE!

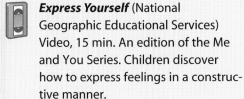

### Fire Engines
*Anne Rockwell, (E. P. Dutton, 1986)*

The parts of a fire engine and how firefighters use them are described.

### Fire Truck
*Peter Sis (Greenwillow Books, 1998)*

Matt loves fire trucks so much that one day he turns into one and saves the community with his heroic deeds.

### Fire Fighters
*Norma Simon, illustrated by Pam Paparone (Simon & Schuster Books for Young Readers, 1995)*

The vehicles, equipment, and procedures used by firefighters are described and illustrated.

---

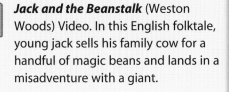 ***Express Yourself*** (National Geographic Educational Services) Video, 15 min. An edition of the Me and You Series. Children discover how to express feelings in a constructive manner.

 ***Jack and the Beanstalk*** (Weston Woods) Video. In this English folktale, young jack sells his family cow for a handful of magic beans and lands in a misadventure with a giant.

 ***Johnny Appleseed*** (Weston Woods) Video or cassette. Narrated by Garrison Keillor, this video tells the story of naturalist Johnny Appleseed's life of goodwill.

 ***The Giving Tree*** (Weston Woods) Video, 10 min. Shel Silverstein narrates his classic story of the many lessons of giving and receiving.

 ***Trees for Life*** (National Geographic Educational Services) Video, 22 min. Children discover the profusion of life that lives in a tree and how trees are important to life on Earth.

 ***The Fire Station*** (National Geographic Educational Services) Video, 13 min. Children learn about the important work of firefighters and paramedics.

 ***The Police Station*** (National Geographic Educational Services) Video, 15 min. Find out the multitude of ways in which police officers serve their communities.

***Tonka Search and Rescue*** (Hasbro Interactive) CD-ROM, Macintosh and Windows. Teaches following directions and listening.

# Publishers Directory

**Abdo & Daughters**
4940 Viking Drive, Suite 622
Edina, MN 55435
(800) 458-8399 • www.abdopub.com

**Aladdin Paperbacks**
(Imprint of Simon & Schuster Children's Publishing)

**Atheneum**
(Imprint of Simon & Schuster Children's Publishing)

**Bantam Doubleday Dell Books for Young Readers**
(Imprint of Random House)

**Blackbirch Press**
1 Bradley Road, Suite 205
Woodbridge, CT 06525
(203) 387-7525 • (800) 831-9183

**Blue Sky Press**
(Imprint of Scholastic)

**Boyds Mills Press**
815 Church Street
Honesdale, PA 18431
(570) 253-1164 • Fax (570) 251-0179 •
(800) 949-7777

**Bradbury Press**
(Imprint of Simon & Schuster Children's Publishing)

**BridgeWater Books**
(Distributed by Penguin Putnam)

**Candlewick Press**
2067 Massachusetts Avenue
Cambridge, MA 02140
(617) 661-3330 • Fax (617) 661-0565

**Carolrhoda Books**
(Division of Lerner Publications Co.)

**Charles Scribners's Sons**
(Imprint of Simon & Schuster Children's Publishing)

**Children's Press** (Division of Grolier, Inc.)
P.O. Box 1796
Danbury, CT 06813-1333
(800) 621-1115 • www.grolier.com

**Child's World**
P.O. Box 326
Chanhassen, MN 55317-0326
(612) 906-3939 • (800) 599-READ •
www.childsworld.com

**Chronicle Books**
85 Second Street, Sixth Floor
San Francisco, CA 94105
(415) 537-3730 • (415) 537-4460 • (800) 722-6657 • www.chroniclebooks.com

**Clarion Books**
(Imprint of Houghton Mifflin, Inc.)
215 Park Avenue South
New York, NY 10003
(212) 420-5800 • (800) 726-0600 •
www.hmco.com/trade/childrens/shelves.html

**Crowell** (Imprint of HarperCollins)

**Crown Publishing Group**
(Imprint of Random House)

**Dial Books**
(Imprint of Penguin Putnam Inc.)

**Dorling Kindersley** (DK Publishing)
95 Madison Avenue
New York, NY 10016
(212) 213-4800 • Fax (800) 774-6733 •
(888) 342-5357 • www.dk.com

**Doubleday** (Imprint of Random House)

**E. P. Dutton Children's Books**
(Imprint of Penguin Putnam Inc.)

**Farrar Straus & Giroux**
19 Union Square West
New York, NY 10003
(212) 741-6900 • Fax (212) 633-2427 •
(888) 330-8477

**Four Winds Press**
(Imprint of Macmillan, see Simon & Schuster Children's Publishing)

**Greenwillow Books**
(Imprint of William Morrow & Co, Inc.)

**Grosset & Dunlap**
(Imprint of Penguin Putnam, Inc.)

**Harcourt Brace & Co.**
525 "B" Street
San Diego, CA 92101
(619) 231-6616 • (800) 543-1918 •
www.harcourtbooks.com

**Harper & Row** (Imprint of HarperCollins)

**HarperCollins Children's Books**
10 East 53rd Street
New York, NY 10022
(212) 207-7000 • Fax (212) 202-7044 •
(800) 242-7737 •
www.harperchildrens.com

**Henry Holt and Company**
115 West 18th Street
New York, NY 10011
(212) 886-9200 • (212) 633-0748 • (888) 330-8477 • www.henryholt.com/byr/

**Holiday House**
425 Madison Avenue
New York, NY 10017
(212) 688-0085 • Fax (212) 421-6134

**Houghton Mifflin**
222 Berkeley Street
Boston, MA 02116
(617) 351-5000 • Fax (617) 351-1125 •
(800) 225-3362 • www.hmco.com/trade

**Hyperion Books**
(Imprint of Buena Vista Publishing Co.)
114 Fifth Avenue
New York, NY 10011
(212) 633-4400 • (800) 759-0190 •
www.disney.com

**Ideals Children's Books**
(Imprint of Hambleton-Hill Publishing, Inc.)
1501 County Hospital Road
Nashville, TN 37218
(615) 254-2480 • (800) 336-6438

**Joy Street Books**
(Imprint of Little, Brown & Co.)

**Just Us Books**
356 Glenwood Avenue
E. Orange, NJ 07017
(973) 672-0304 • Fax (973) 677-7570

**Alfred A. Knopf**
(Imprint of Random House)

**Lee & Low Books**
95 Madison Avenue
New York, NY 10016
(212) 779-4400 • Fax (212) 683-1894

**Lerner Publications Co.**
241 First Avenue North
Minneapolis, MN 55401
(612) 332-3344 • Fax (612) 332-7615 •
(800) 328-4929 • www.lernerbooks.com

**Little, Brown & Co.**
3 Center Plaza
Boston, MA 02108
(617) 227-0730 • Fax (617) 263-2864 •
(800) 343-9204 • www.littlebrown.com

**Lothrop Lee & Shepard**
(Imprint of William Morrow & Co.)

**Macmillan**
(Imprint of Simon & Schuster Children's Publishing)

**Marshall Cavendish**
99 White Plains Road
Tarrytown, NY 10591
(914) 332-8888 • Fax (914) 332-1082 •
(800) 821-9881 •
www.marshallcavendish.com

**William Morrow & Co.**
1350 Avenue of the Americas
New York, NY 10019
(212) 261-6500 • Fax (212) 261-6619 •
(800) 843-9389 •
www.williammorrow.com

**Morrow Junior Books**
(Imprint of William Morrow & Co.)

**Mulberry Books**
(Imprint of William Morrow & Co.)

**National Geographic Society**
1145 17th Street, NW
Washington, DC 20036
(202) 828-5667 • (800) 368-2728 •
www.nationalgeographic.com

**Northland Publishing**
(Division of Justin Industries)
P.O. Box 62
Flagstaff, AZ 86002
(520) 774-5251 • Fax (800) 257-9082 •
(800) 346-3257 • www.northlandpub.com

**North-South Books**
1123 Broadway, Suite 800
New York, NY 10010
(212) 463-9736 • Fax (212) 633-1004 •
(800) 722-6657 • www.northsouth.com

**Orchard Books** (A Grolier Company)
95 Madison Avenue
New York, NY 10016
(212) 951-2600 • Fax (212) 213-6435 •
(800) 621-1115 • www.grolier.com

**Owlet** (Imprint of Henry Holt & Co.)

**Willa Perlman Books**
(Imprint of Simon & Schuster Children's Publishing)

**Philomel Books**
(Imprint of Putnam Penguin, Inc.)

**Puffin Books**
(Imprint of Penguin Putnam, Inc.)

**G.P. Putnam's Sons Publishing**
(Imprint of Penguin Putnam, Inc.)

**Penguin Putnam, Inc.**
345 Hudson Street
New York, NY 10014
(212) 366-2000 • Fax (212) 366-2666 •
(800) 631-8571 •
www.penguinputnam.com

**Random House**
201 East 50th Street
New York, NY 10022
(212) 751-2000 • Fax (212) 572-2593 •
(800) 726-0600 • www.randomhouse/kids

**Rourke Corporation**
P.O. Box 3328
Vero Beach, FL 32964
(561) 234-6001 • (800) 394-7055 •
www.rourkepublishing.com

**Scholastic**
555 Broadway
New York, NY 10012
(212) 343-6100 • Fax (212) 343-6930 •
(800) SCHOLASTIC • www.scholastic.com

**Sierra Junior Club**
85 Second Street, Second Floor
San Francisco, CA 94105-3441
(415) 977-5500 • Fax (415) 977-5799 •
(800) 935-1056 • www.sierraclub.org

**Simon & Schuster Children's Books**
1230 Avenue of the Americas
New York, NY 10020
(212) 698-7200 • (800) 223-2336 •
www.simonsays.com/kidzone

**Smith & Kraus**
4 Lower Mill Road
N. Stratford, NH 03590
(603) 643-6431 • Fax (603) 643-1831 •
(800) 895-4331 • www.smithkraus.com

**Teacher Ideas Press**
(Division of Libraries Unlimited)
P.O. Box 6633
Englewood, CO 80155-6633
(303) 770-1220 • Fax (303) 220-8843 •
(800) 237-6124 • www.lu.com

**Ticknor & Fields**
(Imprint of Houghton Mifflin, Inc.)

**Usborne** (Imprint of EDC Publishing)
10302 E. 55th Place, Suite B
Tulsa, OK 74146-6515
(918) 622-4522 • (800) 475-4522 •
www.edcpub.com

**Viking Children's Books**
(Imprint of Penguin Putnam Inc.)

**Watts Publishing**
(Imprint of Grolier Publishing;
see Children's Press)

**Walker & Co.**
435 Hudson Street
New York, NY 10014
(212) 727-8300 • (212) 727-0984 • (800)
AT-WALKER

**Whispering Coyote Press**
300 Crescent Court, Suite 860
Dallas, TX 75201
(800) 929-6104 • Fax (214) 319-7298

**Albert Whitman**
6340 Oakton Street
Morton Grove, IL 60053-2723
(847) 581-0033 • Fax (847) 581-0039 •
(800) 255-7675 • www.awhitmanco.com

**Workman Publishing Co., Inc.**
708 Broadway
New York, NY 10003
(212) 254-5900 • Fax (800) 521-1832 •
(800) 722-7202 • www.workman.com

# Multimedia Resources

**AGC/United Learning**
6633 West Howard Street
Niles, IL 60714-3389
(800) 424-0362 • www.unitedlearning.com

**AIMS Multimedia**
9710 DeSoto Avenue
Chatsworth, CA 91311-4409
(800) 367-2467 •
www.AIMS-multimedia.com

**BFA Educational Media**
(see Phoenix Learning Group)

**Broderbund**
(Parsons Technology;
also see The Learning Company)
500 Redwood Blvd
Novato, CA 94997
(800) 521-6263 • Fax (800) 474-8840 •
www.broderbund.com

**Carousel Film and Video**
260 Fifth Avenue, Suite 705
New York, NY 10001
(212) 683-1660 • e-mail:
carousel@pipeline.com

**Cloud 9 Interactive**
(888) 662-5683 • www.cloud9int.com

**Computer Plus** (see ESI)

**Coronet/MTI**
(see Phoenix Learning Group)

**Davidson** (see Knowledge Adventure)

**Direct Cinema, Ltd.**
P.O. Box 10003
Santa Monica, CA 90410-1003
(800) 525-0000

**Disney Interactive**
(800) 900-9234 •
www.disneyinteractive.com

**DK Multimedia** (Dorling Kindersley)
95 Madison Avenue
New York, NY 10016
(212) 213-4800 • Fax: (800) 774-6733 •
(888) 342-5357 • www.dk.com

**Edmark Corp.**
P.O. Box 97021
Redmond, CA 98073-9721
(800) 362-2890 • www.edmark.com

**Encyclopaedia Britannica Educational Corp.**
310 South Michigan Avenue
Chicago, IL 60604
(800) 554-9862 • www.eb.com

**ESI/Educational Software**
4213 S. 94th Street
Omaha, NE 68127
(800) 955-5570 • www.edsoft.com

**GPN/Reading Rainbow**
University of Nebraska-Lincoln
P.O. Box 80669
Lincoln, NE 68501-0669
(800) 228-4630 • www.gpn.unl.edu

**Hasbro Interactive**
(800) 683-5847 • www.hasbro.com

**Humongous**
13110 NE 177th Pl., Suite B101, Box 180
Woodenville, WA 98072
(800) 499-8386 • www.humongous.com

**IBM Corp.**
1133 Westchester Ave.
White Plains, NY 10604
(770) 863-1234 • Fax (770) 863-3030 •
(888) 411-1932 •
www.pc.ibm.com/multimedia/crayola

**ICE, Inc.**
(Distributed by Arch Publishing)
12B W. Main St.
Elmsford, NY 10523
(914) 347-2464 • (800) 843-9497 •
www.educorp.com

**Knowledge Adventure**
19840 Pioneer Avenue
Torrence, CA 90503
(800) 542-4240 • (800) 545-7677 •
www.knowledgeadventure.com

**The Learning Company**
6160 Summit Drive North
Minneapolis, MN 55430
(800) 685-6322 • www.learningco.com

**Listening Library**
One Park Avenue
Greenwich, CT 06870-1727
(800) 243-4504 • www.listeninglib.com

**Macmillan/McGraw-Hill**
(see SRA/McGraw-Hill)

**Maxis**
2121 N. California Blvd
Walnut Creek, CA 94596-3572
(925) 933-5630 • Fax (925) 927-3736 •
(800) 245-4525 • www.maxis.com

**MECC**
(see the Learning Company)

**Microsoft**
One Microsoft Way
Redmond, WA 98052-6399
(800) 426-9400 • www.microsoft.com/kids

**National Geographic Society Educational Services**
P.O. Box 10597
Des Moines, IA 50340-0597
(800) 368-2728 •
www.nationalgeographic.com

**National School Products**
101 East Broadway
Maryville, TN 37804
(800) 251-9124 • www.ierc.com

**PBS Video**
1320 Braddock Place
Alexandria, VA 22314
(800) 344-3337 • www.pbs.org

**Phoenix Films**
(see Phoenix Learning Group)

**The Phoenix Learning Group**
2348 Chaffee Drive
St. Louis, MO 63146
(800) 221-1274 • e-mail:
phoenixfilms@worldnet.att.net

**Pied Piper** (see AIMS Multimedia)

**Scholastic New Media**
555 Broadway
New York, NY 10003
(800) 724-6527 • www.scholastic.com

**Simon & Schuster Interactive**
(see Knowledge Adventure)

**SRA/McGraw-Hill**
220 Daniel Dale Road
De Soto, TX 75115
(800) 843-8855 • www.sra4kids.com

**SVE/Churchill Media**
6677 North Northwest Highway
Chicago, IL 60631
(800) 829-1900 •www.svemedia.com

**Tom Snyder Productions** (also see ESI)
80 Coolidge Hill Rd.
Watertown, MA 02472
(800) 342-0236 • www.teachtsp.com

**Troll Associates**
100 Corporate Drive
Mahwah, NJ 07430
(800) 929-8765 • Fax (800) 979-8765 •
www.troll.com

**Voyager** (see ESI)

**Weston Woods**
12 Oakwood Avenue
Norwalk, CT 06850
(800) 243-5020 • Fax (203) 845-0498

**Zenger Media**
10200 Jefferson Blvd., Room 94,
P.O. Box 802
Culver City, CA 90232-0802
(800) 421-4246 • (800) 944-5432 •
www.Zengermedia.com

# BOOK 1

| | Decodable Words | | | Spelling | Vocabulary |
|---|---|---|---|---|---|

## MAX, THE CAT

### Short *a*

| | | | Short *a* | High-Frequency Words |
|---|---|---|---|---|
| **and** | **has** | pan | **bad** | **give** |
| bad | hat | pat | **can** | **likes** |
| bag | jam | rag | had | **one** |
| bat | lap | ran | **hat** | **this** |
| cab | **mad** | **sad** | **mat** | |
| **can** | man | Sam | pan | |
| **cap** | map | sat | | |
| **cat** | **mat** | tag | | |
| dad | **Max** | tan | | |
| Dan | nag | tap | | |
| fan | **nap** | van | | |
| fat | **naps** | wag | | |
| had | pad | wax | | |
| ham | **Pam** | yam | | |

## QUACK

### Digraph *ck*

| | | | Digraph *ck* | High-Frequency Words |
|---|---|---|---|---|
| **back** | **pack** | rack | **back** | **on** |
| **Jack** | **packs** | sack | **pack** | **they** |
| **Mack** | **quack** | tack | **quack** | **what** |
| | | | rack | **your** |
| | | | sack | |
| | | | tack | |

## WHAT DOES PIG DO?

### Short *i*

| | | | Short *i* | High-Frequency Words |
|---|---|---|---|---|
| bib | hip | lip | **dig** | **does** |
| big | his | mix | **kick** | **her** |
| bit | hit | Nick | **pick** | **look** |
| Dick | **is** | nip | **pig** | **there** |
| did | jig | **pick** | pin | |
| **dig** | Jim | **picks** | win | |
| **digs** | **kick** | **pig** | | |
| dip | **kicks** | pin | | |
| fin | kid | pit | | |
| fit | Kim | quick | | |
| fix | kit | quit | | |
| hid | lick | rib | | |
| him | lid | **wig** | | |

**Boldfaced** words appear in the selection.

# BOOK 1

| | Decodable Words | | | Spelling | Vocabulary |
|---|---|---|---|---|---|
| **A Path on the Map** | **Digraphs *sh, th*** | | | **Digraphs *sh, th*** | **High-Frequency Words** |
| | bath | **path** | that | dish | **be** |
| | cash | rash | thick | **path** | **could** |
| | dash | **shack** | thin | **shack** | **down** |
| | dish | shin | **this** | that | **see** |
| | **fish** | ship | wish | thin | |
| | mash | than | with | wish | |
| | math | | | | |
| **Time for Kids: Ships** | **Phonics Review** | | | **Words from Social Studies** | **Review High-Frequency Words** |
| | | | | bus    map | **look** |
| | | | | fast    **ship** | **this** |
| | | | | go    stop | **one** |
| | | | | | **what** |

# BOOK 2

| | Decodable Words | | | Spelling | Vocabulary |
|---|---|---|---|---|---|
| **One Good Pup** | **Short *u*** | | | **Short *u*** | **High-Frequency Words** |
| | bud | hum | rut | buck | **no** |
| | bug | hush | shut | **but** | **out** |
| | bun | hut | sub | cut | **ride** |
| | bus | jug | suck | duck | **small** |
| | **but** | luck | sum | rug | |
| | cub | mud | sun | **tug** | |
| | cup | mug | sup | | |
| | cut | nut | thud | | |
| | duck | **pup** | **tub** | | |
| | dug | rub | tuck | | |
| | **fun** | rug | **tug** | | |
| | gum | run | yum | | |
| | hug | rush | | | |
| **The Bug Bath** | **Short *o*** | | | **Short *o*** | **High-Frequency Words** |
| | **Bob** | **hot** | pop | hop | saw |
| | box | job | pot | **hot** | two |
| | cob | jog | rock | lock | very |
| | cot | jot | **rocked** | **not** | want |
| | dock | lock | rod | rock | |
| | dog | log | shock | **top** | |
| | dot | lot | sob | | |
| | fog | mop | sock | | |
| | fox | nod | tock | | |
| | **got** | **not** | **top** | | |
| | hog | **on** | tot | | |
| | hop | pod | | | |

# BOOK 2

| Decodable Words | Spelling | Vocabulary |
|---|---|---|

## SPLASH!

| Short *e* | | | Short *e* | High-Frequency Words |
|---|---|---|---|---|
| bed | led | pen | **hen** | **away** |
| beg | leg | pet | pet | **good** |
| Ben | **legs** | **pets** | **red** | **into** |
| bet | let | **red** | **shed** | **put** |
| deck | **Meg** | set | **then** | |
| den | men | **shed** | **wet** | |
| fed | met | Ted | | |
| get | **neck** | ten | | |
| hem | Ned | **them** | | |
| **hen** | net | **then** | | |
| jet | peck | vet | | |
| Ken | peg | **wet** | | |
| | | yet | | |

## WHAT BUG IS IT?

| Blends | | | Blends | High-Frequency Words |
|---|---|---|---|---|
| bass | hiss | **slim** | doll | **about** |
| bill | huff | slip | **flat** | **again** |
| bluff | hull | slit | miss | **around** |
| **buzz** | ill | slob | **pass** | **use** |
| cuff | **Jill** | slop | puff | |
| doll | kiss | slot | **snap** | |
| dull | lull | slug | | |
| fill | mass | slush | | |
| **flap** | mill | **smack** | | |
| flash | **Miss** | smash | | |
| **flat** | muff | smock | | |
| flick | **Nell** | smug | | |
| flip | **pass** | snack | | |
| flock | pill | **snag** | | |
| flop | puff | **snap** | | |
| fluff | quill | sniff | | |
| frill | ruff | snip | | |
| frock | sill | snob | | |
| frog | slam | snub | | |
| fuss | slap | snug | | |
| gill | slash | thrill | | |
| gull | slick | till | | |
| **hill** | slid | **will** | | |

## TIME FOR KIDS: A VET

| Phonics Review | Words from Social Studies | Review High-Frequency Words |
|---|---|---|
| | **cat**   **vet** | **small**   **good** |
| | **help** | **out**   **want** |
| | **hog** | |
| | job | |
| | pat | |

# BOOK 3

## Decodable Words  ## Spelling  ## Vocabulary

STAN'S STUNT

### Blends

| | | |
|---|---|---|
| **asked** | mask | spend |
| bang | melt | spent |
| belt | mend | spill |
| bend | milk | spin |
| bent | mint | spot |
| best | mist | stack |
| **bump** | must | staff |
| camp | nest | stag |
| damp | pant | stamp |
| dent | past | **Stan** |
| dump | pest | **Stan's** |
| dust | pump | stand |
| end | quilt | stem |
| fang | raft | step |
| fast | ramp | stick |
| felt | rang | stiff |
| fist | rent | still |
| fling | rest | sting |
| flung | ring | stomp |
| gang | risk | **stop** |
| gasp | rung | stub |
| gift | rust | stuck |
| gust | sang | stuff |
| hang | scab | stump |
| **held** | scat | stung |
| help | scuff | **stunt** |
| hint | send | **stunts** |
| hump | sent | sung |
| hung | shelf | swim |
| hunt | shift | swing |
| jest | sift | swung |
| **jump** | silk | task |
| just | sing | tend |
| Kent | skid | tent |
| king | skill | test |
| lamp | skimp | theft |
| last | skin | **thing** |
| left | skip | thump |
| lend | skit | tilt |
| lent | skull | trust |
| lift | slant | vent |
| limp | soft | vest |
| lint | span | **went** |
| list | spat | west |
| loft | speck | wilt |
| lump | sped | wing |
| lung | spell | |

### Blends

**bump**
**jump**
spell
spill
tent

**went**

### High-Frequency Words

**fall**
**their**
**try**
**would**

T99

# BOOK 3

| | Decodable Words | | | Spelling | Vocabulary |
|---|---|---|---|---|---|

## GREG'S MASK

**Blends**

| | | |
|---|---|---|
| black | clock | Greg's |
| blast | clog | grill |
| blend | club | grip |
| blimp | clump | gruff |
| blob | crab | grump |
| block | crack | grunt |
| blond | craft | plan |
| blot | cramp | plant |
| blush | crib | plop |
| Brad | crisp | plot |
| brag | crop | plug |
| brand | crush | plum |
| brass | crust | plump |
| bring | draft | plus |
| brisk | drag | press |
| brush | dress | print |
| clack | drift | prop |
| clam | drill | track |
| clamp | **drip** | tramp |
| clang | **drop** | trap |
| clap | drum | **trash** |
| clasp | glad | trick |
| **class** | glass | trim |
| click | Glen | trip |
| cliff | **glob** | trot |
| cling | grab | truck |
| **clip** | grant | trust |
| | **Greg** | **twist** |

**Spelling — Blends**

clap
**class**
dress
**drop**
track
trip

**Vocabulary — High-Frequency Words**

**any**
**grow**
**new**
**old**

## SAM'S SONG

*ch, wh, nk*

| | | |
|---|---|---|
| bank | **Chuck** | ranch |
| bench | chunk | rank |
| blank | clank | **sank** |
| **branch** | crank | **sink** |
| brunch | **crunch** | spank |
| Chad | drank | such |
| champ | Frank | tank |
| check | French | thank |
| chess | Hank | **think** |
| **chest** | inch | **when** |
| Chet | lunch | whip |
| **chick** | **much** | **whish** |
| chill | munch | whisk |
| **chin** | pinch | **wink** |
| chip | **plink** | yank |
| chomp | **plunk** | |
| chop | punch | |

**Spelling — *ch, wh, nk***

**chick**
**chin**
sink
**think**
**when**
**wink**

**Vocabulary — High-Frequency Words**

**eat**
**now**
**together**
**too**

# BOOK 3

| | Decodable Words | Spelling | Vocabulary |
|---|---|---|---|
| **SNAKES** | Long *a: a-e* | Long *a: a-e* | **High-Frequency Words** |

**SNAKES**

### Decodable Words
**Long *a: a-e***

| | | |
|---|---|---|
| bake | game | sale |
| base | gate | same |
| blame | gave | save |
| brake | gaze | scale |
| brave | grade | **scales** |
| cake | grape | shade |
| came | hate | shake |
| cane | Jake | shame |
| cape | Jane | shape |
| case | Kate | shave |
| cave | **lake** | skate |
| chase | lane | **snake** |
| date | late | **snake's** |
| Dave | **made** | state |
| daze | **make** | take |
| drape | mane | tale |
| fade | name | tame |
| fake | pane | tape |
| fame | plane | trade |
| flake | plate | vase |
| flame | rake | wade |
| frame | **safe** | wake |
| | | wave |

### Spelling
**Long *a: a-e***

came
**lake**
**made**
name
shade
**snake**

### Vocabulary
**High-Frequency Words**

**know**
**under**
**where**
**why**

---

**TIME FOR KIDS: LET'S CAMP OUT**

### Phonics Review

### Words from Science

| | |
|---|---|
| **fire** | **sticks** |
| mud | **sun** |
| snow | **twigs** |

### Review High-Frequency Words

**old**
**eat**
**together**
**under**

# BOOK 4

| | Decodable Words | | Spelling | Vocabulary |
|---|---|---|---|---|

## THE SHOPPING LIST

### Decodable Words

**Long i: i–e**

| | | |
|---|---|---|
| bike | lime | **smile** |
| bite | line | **smiled** |
| bribe | live | snipe |
| bride | **Mike** | spike |
| chime | **Mike's** | spine |
| chive | mile | stride |
| crime | mime | strike |
| dime | mine | stripe |
| dine | mite | swine |
| dive | Nile | swipe |
| drive | nine | tide |
| file | pike | tile |
| fine | pile | **time** |
| fire | pine | tire |
| **five** | pipe | tribe |
| glide | pride | vile |
| grime | prime | vine |
| gripe | prize | while |
| hide | quite | whine |
| hike | ride | **white** |
| hire | **ripe** | **wide** |
| hive | shine | wife |
| jive | side | wine |
| kite | size | wipe |
| life | slide | wire |
| like | slime | |

### Spelling

**Long i: i–e**

bite
hide
**smile**
while
**white**
**wide**

### Vocabulary

**High-Frequency Words**

**after**
**always**
**blue**
**were**
**who**

## YASMIN'S DUCKS

### Decodable Words

**Long o: o–e**

| | | |
|---|---|---|
| bone | home | **Rome's** |
| broke | **hope** | rope |
| choke | hose | rose |
| chose | **hoses** | scope |
| clone | **joke** | shone |
| close | mope | slope |
| clove | **nope** | smoke |
| code | nose | spoke |
| coke | note | stone |
| cone | poke | stove |
| cope | pope | strode |
| cove | pose | stroke |
| dome | probe | those |
| drone | prone | tone |
| drove | prose | vote |
| **globe** | quote | woke |
| grove | rode | yoke |
| | | zone |

### Spelling

**Long o: o–e**

hole
**home**
**hope**
nose
rope
those

### Vocabulary

**High-Frequency Words**

**because**
**buy**
**found**
**some**
**work**

# BOOK 4

| | Decodable Words | Spelling | Vocabulary |
|---|---|---|---|

## THE KNEE-HIGH MAN

**Decodable Words — Long *u: u–e***

| | | |
|---|---|---|
| **brute** | dune | prune |
| cube | flute | pure |
| cure | fume | rude |
| cute | fuse | **rule** |
| dude | **June** | tube |
| duke | **mule** | tune |

**Spelling — Long *u: u–e***

cute
flute
mule
**rule**
tube
tune

**Vocabulary — High-Frequency Words**

**been**
**carry**
**clean**
**done**
**far**

## JOHNNY APPLESEED

**Decodable Words — Long *a: ai, ay***

| | | |
|---|---|---|
| bail | **jays** | sail |
| bait | laid | **sailed** |
| bay | lay | **say** |
| braid | maid | snail |
| brain | mail | Spain |
| chain | main | sprain |
| clay | **May** | spray |
| **day** | nail | stain |
| **days** | paid | stay |
| **explained** | pail | strain |
| drain | pain | stray |
| fail | pay | sway |
| faint | plain | tail |
| frail | play | trail |
| Gail | praise | train |
| gay | quail | tray |
| grain | **quail's** | vain |
| **gray** | raid | wail |
| **hail** | rail | wait |
| hay | **rain** | **way** |
| jail | raise | |
| jay | ray | |

**Spelling — Long *a: ai, ay***

**day**
**rain**
say
tail
**wait**
**way**

**Vocabulary — High-Frequency Words**

**how**
**light**
**little**
**live**
**pretty**

## TIME FOR KIDS: RING! RING! RING! PUT OUT THE FIRE!

**Decodable Words — Phonics Review**

**Spelling — Words from Social Studies**

| | |
|---|---|
| **bell** | **ring** |
| **brave** | **smoke** |
| **pole** | **truck** |

**Vocabulary — Review High-Frequency Words**

**work**
**always**
**done**

# BOOK 5, UNIT 1

| Decodable Words | Spelling | Vocabulary |
|---|---|---|

## SEVEN SILLIES

**Long e: e, ee** (Decodable Words)

| | | |
|---|---|---|
| be | green | she |
| bee | greet | sheet |
| beef | he | **sheep** |
| beep | heel | sleep |
| beet | jeep | sleet |
| bleed | keep | speech |
| cheek | Lee | steel |
| cheep | me | steep |
| creek | meet | steer |
| creep | need | street |
| deed | peek | sweep |
| deep | peel | sweet |
| deer | peep | tee |
| fee | queen | teen |
| feed | reef | **three** |
| **feel** | screech | tree |
| feet | screen | tweet |
| flee | **see** | we |
| fleet | seed | weed |
| free | seek | week |
| freed | seem | weep |
| greed | seen | wheel |

**Spelling — Long e: e, ee**

bee
she
**sheep**
**three**
tree
we

**Vocabulary — High-Frequency Words**

**all**
**four**
**many**
**over**
**so**

## SHRINKING MOUSE

**Long e: ie, ea** (Decodable Words)

| | | |
|---|---|---|
| **be** | **he** | **really** |
| beach | **he'll** | scream |
| bead | **he's** | sea |
| beak | heal | seal |
| bean | hear | seat |
| beast | heat | shield |
| beat | Jean | sneak |
| bleach | lead | speak |
| cheat | leak | squeàk |
| chief | leap | steal |
| clean | least | steam |
| clear | **me** | streak |
| cream | meal | stream |
| deal | mean | tea |
| Dean | meat | teach |
| dear | near | team |
| dream | neat | tear |
| fear | pea | thief |
| feast | peach | **we** |
| field | peak | weak |
| flea | reach | year |
| grief | **reached** | yield |
| **fields** | read | |

**Spelling — Long e: ie, ea**

**fields**
leaf
piece
**reached**
read
sea

**Vocabulary — High-Frequency Words**

**before**
**come**
**off**
**our**
**right**

# BOOK 5, UNIT 1

| | Decodable Words | Spelling | Vocabulary |
|---|---|---|---|

## YOU CAN'T SMELL A FLOWER WITH YOUR EAR!

### Long *o: o, oa, oe, ow*

| | | |
|---|---|---|
| blow | go | **opening** |
| blown | goal | **pillow** |
| boat | goat | road |
| bold | **goes** | roast |
| **both** | groan | roll |
| bow | grow | row |
| coach | grown | scold |
| coal | **hold** | show |
| coast | **holding** | shown |
| coat | Joan | slow |
| **cold** | Joe | snow |
| croak | load | so |
| crow | loan | soak |
| don't | low | sold |
| float | moan | throat |
| flow | **moment** | toad |
| flown | most | toast |
| foal | mow | toe |
| foam | no | told |
| fold | oat | toll |
| glow | old | won't |

### Spelling — Long *o: o, oa, oe, ow*

boat
**cold**
**goes**
**hold**
road
show

### High-Frequency Words

**by**
**find**
**kind**
**high**
**more**

## OWL AND THE MOON

### Long *i: i, y, igh*

| | | |
|---|---|---|
| blind | fright | **night** |
| bright | fry | **right** |
| by | grind | shy |
| child | high | sigh |
| cry | **kind** | sight |
| dry | **light** | **sky** |
| fight | might | slight |
| find | mild | sly |
| flight | mind | tight |
| fly | **my** | wild |
| | | wind |

### Long *i: i, y, igh*

child
**my**
**night**
**shy**
**sky**
tight

### High-Frequency Words

**everything**
**eyes**
**gone**
**head**
**room**

## TIME FOR KIDS: THE NIGHT ANIMALS

### Phonics Review

### Words from Science

| | |
|---|---|
| **bugs** | **owl** |
| frog | pond |
| logs | **rat** |

### Review High-Frequency Words

**many**
**off**
**all**

# BOOK 5, UNIT 2

| | Decodable Words | Spelling | Vocabulary |
|---|---|---|---|

## A FRIEND FOR LITTLE BEAR

**Decodable Words — /ü/ oo**

bloom, boo, boom, boot, booth, broom, cool, doom, droop, food, fool, groom, hoop, hoot, loom, loop, moo, mood, moon, noon, pool, proof, **roof**, **room**, root, scoop, shoot, snoop, soon, spool, spoon, stool, stoop, too, tool, tooth, troop, zoo, zoom

**Spelling — /ü/ oo**

cool, fool, moon, **roof**, soon, zoo

**Vocabulary — High-Frequency Words**

**called**, **friend**, **only**, **pulled**, **these**

## NEW SHOES FOR SILVIA

**Decodable Words — /ä/ ar**

ark, arm, art, bar, bark, barn, Bart, **car**, Carl, cart, charm, chart, Clark, dark, dart, **far**, farm, hard, harm, harp, Lark, march, mark, park, part, shark, sharp, spark, star, start, tart, yard

**Spelling — /ä/ ar**

bark, **car**, dark, park, part, star

**Vocabulary — High-Frequency Words**

**every**, **morning**, **once**, **or**, **took**

## THE STORY OF BLUE BIRD

**Decodable Words — /ûr/ ir, ur, er**

**bird**, **birds**, birth, burn, churn, clerk, curb, curl, dirt, fern, fir, first, fur, girl, hurt, jerk, shirt, sir, skirt, stern, squirt, stir, **surprised**, term, third, thirst, turn, twirl, verb, whirl

**Spelling — /ûr/ ir, ur, er**

**bird**, burn, first, girl, hurt, serve

**Vocabulary — High-Frequency Words**

**brother**, **from**, **mother**, **sister**, **walked**

# BOOK 5, UNIT 2

| Decodable Words | Spelling | Vocabulary |
|---|---|---|

## YOUNG AMELIA EARHART

### Decodable Words

*/ou/ou, ow; /oi/oi, oy*

| | | |
|---|---|---|
| boil | frown | our |
| bound | gown | out |
| bow | grouch | plow |
| boy | ground | point |
| **boys** | growl | pound |
| broil | **her** | pout |
| brow | **herself** | proud |
| brown | hound | prowl |
| cloud | **how** | round |
| clown | howl | Roy |
| coin | **Howland** | scout |
| couch | join | soil |
| count | joint | sound |
| cow | joy | sour |
| crown | loud | south |
| **down** | moist | spoil |
| drown | mound | sprout |
| flour | mount | town |
| foil | mouth | toy |
| found | now | wound |
| fowl | oil | |

### Spelling

*/ou/ou, ow;*
*/oi/oi, oy*

| | |
|---|---|
| **boys** | sound |
| mouse | town |
| noise | toy |

### Vocabulary

**High Frequency Words**

**father**
**horse**
**people**
**should**
**woman**

## TIME FOR KIDS: ON THE GO!

### Phonics Review

### Words from Math

| | |
|---|---|
| feet | miles |
| **five** | sum |
| **less** | **ten** |

### Review High Frequency Words

| | |
|---|---|
| **from** | **or** |
| **these** | horse |
| **called** | people |

# Listening, Speaking, Viewing, Representing

☑ Tested Skill

Tinted panels show skills, strategies, and other teaching opportunities

| LISTENING | K | 1 | 2 | 3 | 4 | 5 | 6 |
|---|---|---|---|---|---|---|---|
| Learn the vocabulary of school (numbers, shapes, colors, directions, and categories) | | | | | | | |
| Identify the musical elements of literary language, such as rhymes, repeated sounds, onomatopoeia | | | | | | | |
| Determine purposes for listening (get information, solve problems, enjoy and appreciate) | | | | | | | |
| Listen critically and responsively | | | | | | | |
| Ask and answer relevant questions | | | | | | | |
| Listen critically to interpret and evaluate | | | | | | | |
| Listen responsively to stories and other texts read aloud, including selections from classic and contemporary works | | | | | | | |
| Connect own experiences, ideas, and traditions with those of others | | | | | | | |
| Apply comprehension strategies in listening activities | | | | | | | |
| Understand the major ideas and supporting evidence in spoken messages | | | | | | | |
| Participate in listening activities related to reading and writing (such as discussions, group activities, conferences) | | | | | | | |
| Listen to learn by taking notes, organizing, and summarizing spoken ideas | | | | | | | |
| **SPEAKING** | | | | | | | |
| Learn the vocabulary of school (numbers, shapes, colors, directions, and categories) | | | | | | | |
| Use appropriate language and vocabulary learned to describe ideas, feelings, and experiences | | | | | | | |
| Ask and answer relevant questions | | | | | | | |
| Communicate effectively in everyday situations (such as discussions, group activities, conferences) | | | | | | | |
| Demonstrate speaking skills (audience, purpose, occasion, volume, pitch, tone, rate, fluency) | | | | | | | |
| Clarify and support spoken messages and ideas with objects, charts, evidence, elaboration, examples | | | | | | | |
| Use verbal and nonverbal communication in effective ways when, for example, making announcements, giving directions, or making introductions | | | | | | | |
| Retell a spoken message by summarizing or clarifying | | | | | | | |
| Connect own experiences, ideas, and traditions with those of others | | | | | | | |
| Determine purposes for speaking (inform, entertain, give directions, persuade, express personal feelings and opinions) | | | | | | | |
| Demonstrate skills of reporting and providing information | | | | | | | |
| Demonstrate skills of interviewing, requesting and providing information | | | | | | | |
| Apply composition strategies in speaking activities | | | | | | | |
| Monitor own understanding of spoken message and seek clarification as needed | | | | | | | |
| **VIEWING** | | | | | | | |
| Demonstrate viewing skills (focus attention, organize information) | | | | | | | |
| Respond to audiovisual media in a variety of ways | | | | | | | |
| Participate in viewing activities related to reading and writing | | | | | | | |
| Apply comprehension strategies in viewing activities | | | | | | | |
| Recognize artists' craft and techniques for conveying meaning | | | | | | | |
| Interpret information from various formats such as maps, charts, graphics, video segments, technology | | | | | | | |
| Evaluate purposes of various media (information, appreciation, entertainment, directions, persuasion) | | | | | | | |
| Use media to compare ideas and points of view | | | | | | | |
| **REPRESENTING** | | | | | | | |
| Select, organize, or produce visuals to complement or extend meanings | | | | | | | |
| Produce communication using appropriate media to develop a class paper, multimedia or video reports | | | | | | | |
| Show how language, medium, and presentation contribute to the message | | | | | | | |

# Reading: Alphabetic Principle, Sounds/Symbols

☑ Tested Skill

☐ Tinted panels show skills, strategies, and other teaching opportunities

| | K | 1 | 2 | 3 | 4 | 5 | 6 |
|---|---|---|---|---|---|---|---|
| **PRINT AWARENESS** | | | | | | | |
| Know the order of the alphabet | | | | | | | |
| Recognize that print represents spoken language and conveys meaning | | | | | | | |
| Understand directionality (tracking print from left to right; return sweep) | | | | | | | |
| Understand that written words are separated by spaces | | | | | | | |
| Know the difference between individual letters and printed words | | | | | | | |
| Understand that spoken words are represented in written language by specific sequence of letters | | | | | | | |
| Recognize that there are correct spellings for words | | | | | | | |
| Know the difference between capital and lowercase letters | | | | | | | |
| Recognize how readers use capitalization and punctuation to comprehend | | | | | | | |
| Recognize the distinguishing features of a paragraph | | | | | | | |
| Recognize that parts of a book (such as cover/title page and table of contents) offer information | | | | | | | |
| **PHONOLOGICAL AWARENESS** | | | | | | | |
| Identify letters, words, sentences | | | | | | | |
| Divide spoken sentence into individual words | | | | | | | |
| Produce rhyming words and distinguish rhyming words from nonrhyming words | | | | | | | |
| Identify, segment, and combine syllables within spoken words | | | | | | | |
| Identify and isolate the initial and final sound of a spoken word | | | | | | | |
| Add, delete, or change sounds to change words (such as *cow* to *how*, *pan* to *fan*) | | | | | | | |
| Blend sounds to make spoken words | | | | | | | |
| Segment one-syllable spoken words into individual phonemes | | | | | | | |
| **PHONICS AND DECODING** | | | | | | | |
| Alphabetic principle: Letter/sound correspondence | ☑ | ☑ | ☑ | | | | |
| Blending CVC words | ☑ | | | | | | |
| Segmenting CVC words | ☑ | | | | | | |
| Blending CVC, CVCe, CCVC, CVCC, CVVC words | ☑ | ☑ | ☑ | | | | |
| Segmenting CVC, CVCe, CCVC, CVCC, CVVC words | ☑ | ☑ | ☑ | | | | |
| Initial and final consonants: /n/n, /d/d, /s/s, /m/m, /t/t, /k/c, /f/f, /r/r, /p/p, /l/l, /k/k, /g/g, /b/b, /h/h, /w/w, /v/v, /ks/x, /kw/qu, /j/j, /y/y, /z/z | ☑ | ☑ | | | | | |
| Initial and medial short vowels: *a, i, u, o, e* | ☑ | ☑ | ☑ | | | | |
| Long vowels: *a-e, i-e, o-e, u-e* (vowel-consonant-e) | | ☑ | ☑ | | | | |
| Long vowels, including *ay, ai; e, ee, ie, ea, o, oa, oe, ow; i, y, igh* | | ☑ | ☑ | | | | |
| Consonant Digraphs: *sh, th, ch, wh* | | ☑ | | | | | |
| Consonant Blends: continuant/continuant, including *sl, sm, sn, fl, fr, ll, ss, ff* | | ☑ | | | | | |
| Consonant Blends: continuant/stop, including *st, sk, sp, ng, nt, nd, mp, ft* | | ☑ | | | | | |
| Consonant Blends: stop/continuant, including *tr, pr, pl, cr, tw* | | ☑ | | | | | |
| Variant vowels: including /u/oo; /ô/a, aw, au; /ü/ue, ew* | | ☑ | ☑ | | | | |
| Diphthongs, including /ou/ou, ow; /oi/oi, oy* | | ☑ | ☑ | | | | |
| r-controlled vowels, including /âr/are; /ôr/or, ore; /îr/ear* | | | ☑ | | | | |
| Soft *c* and soft *g* | | | ☑ | | | | |
| *nk* | | ☑ | ☑ | | | | |
| Consonant Digraphs: *ck* | ☑ | ☑ | | | | | |
| Consonant Digraphs: *ph, tch, ch* | | | ☑ | | | | |
| Short *e: ea* | | | ☑ | | | | |
| Long *e: y, ey* | | | ☑ | | | | |
| /ü/oo | | ☑ | ☑ | | | | |
| /är/ar; /ûr/ir, ur, er | | ☑ | ☑ | | | | |
| Silent letters: including *l, b, k, w, g, h, gh* | | | ☑ | | | | |
| Schwa: /ər/er; /ən/en; /əl/le; | | | ☑ | | | | |
| Reading/identifying multisyllabic words | | ☑ | ☑ | | | | |

# Reading: Vocabulary/Word Identification

☑ Tested Skill

☐ Tinted panels show skills, strategies, and other teaching opportunities

| WORD STRUCTURE | K | 1 | 2 | 3 | 4 | 5 | 6 |
|---|---|---|---|---|---|---|---|
| Common spelling patterns | | | | | | | |
| Syllable patterns | | | | | | | |
| Plurals | | | | | | | |
| Possessives | | | | | | | |
| Contractions | | | | | | | |
| Root, or base, words and inflectional endings (-s, -es, -ed, -ing) | | | | | | | |
| Compound Words | | | | | | | |
| Prefixes and suffixes (such as un-, re-, dis-, non-; -ly, -y, -ful, -able, -tion) | | | | | | | |
| Root words and derivational endings | | | | | | | |
| **WORD MEANING** | | | | | | | |
| Develop vocabulary through concrete experiences | | | | | | | |
| Develop vocabulary through selections read aloud | | | | | | | |
| Develop vocabulary through reading | | | | | | | |
| Cueing systems: syntactic, semantic, phonetic | | | | | | | |
| Context clues, including semantic clues (word meaning), syntactical clues (word order), and phonetic clues | ☑ | ☑ | ☑ | ☑ | ☑ | ☑ | ☑ |
| High-frequency words (such as the, a, an, and, said, was, where, is) | | | | | | | |
| Identify words that name persons, places, things, and actions | | | | | | | |
| Automatic reading of regular and irregular words | | | | | | | |
| Use resources and references dictionary, glossary, thesaurus, synonym finder, technology and software, and context) | | | | | | | |
| Synonyms and antonyms | | | | | | | |
| Multiple-meaning words | | | | | | | |
| Figurative language | | | | | | | |
| Decode derivatives (root words, such as like, pay, happy with affixes, such as dis-, pre-, -un) | | | | | | | |
| Systematic study of words across content areas and in current events | | | | | | | |
| Locate meanings, pronunciations, and derivations (including dictionaries, glossaries, and other sources) | | | | | | | |
| Denotation and connotation | | | | | | | |
| Word origins as aid to understanding historical influences on English word meanings | | | | | | | |
| Homophones, homographs | | | | | | | |
| Analogies | | | | | | | |
| Idioms | | | | | | | |

# Reading: Comprehension

| PREREADING STRATEGIES | K | 1 | 2 | 3 | 4 | 5 | 6 |
|---|---|---|---|---|---|---|---|
| Preview and Predict | | | | | | | |
| Use prior knowledge | | | | | | | |
| Establish and adjust purposes for reading | | | | | | | |
| Build background | | | | | | | |
| **MONITORING STRATEGIES** | | | | | | | |
| Adjust reading rate | | | | | | | |
| Reread, search for clues, ask questions, ask for help | | | | | | | |
| Visualize | | | | | | | |
| Read a portion aloud, use reference aids | | | | | | | |
| Use decoding and vocabulary strategies | | | | | | | |
| Paraphrase | | | | | | | |
| Create story maps, diagrams, charts, story props to help comprehend, analyze, synthesize and evaluate texts | | | | | | | |

*(continued on next page)*

*(Reading: Comprehension continued)*

| SKILLS AND STRATEGIES | K | 1 | 2 | 3 | 4 | 5 | 6 |
|---|---|---|---|---|---|---|---|
| Story details | ☑ | | | | | | |
| Use illustrations | ☑ | ☑ | | | | | |
| Reality and fantasy | ☑ | ☑ | ☑ | ☑ | | | |
| Classify and categorize | ☑ | | | | | | |
| Make predictions | ☑ | ☑ | ☑ | ☑ | ☑ | ☑ | ☑ |
| Sequence of events (tell or act out) | ☑ | ☑ | ☑ | ☑ | ☑ | ☑ | ☑ |
| Cause and effect | | ☑ | ☑ | ☑ | ☑ | ☑ | ☑ |
| Compare and contrast | ☑ | ☑ | ☑ | ☑ | ☑ | ☑ | ☑ |
| Summarize | ☑ | ☑ | ☑ | ☑ | ☑ | ☑ | ☑ |
| Make and explain inferences | | ☑ | ☑ | ☑ | ☑ | ☑ | ☑ |
| Draw conclusions | | ☑ | ☑ | ☑ | ☑ | ☑ | ☑ |
| Important and unimportant information | | | | ☑ | ☑ | ☑ | ☑ |
| Main idea and supporting details | ☑ | ☑ | ☑ | ☑ | ☑ | ☑ | ☑ |
| Form conclusions or generalizations and support with evidence from text | | | | ☑ | ☑ | ☑ | ☑ |
| Fact and opinion (including news stories and advertisements) | | | | ☑ | ☑ | ☑ | ☑ |
| Problem and solution | | | | ☑ | ☑ | ☑ | ☑ |
| Steps in a process | | ☑ | ☑ | ☑ | ☑ | ☑ | ☑ |
| Make judgments and decisions | | | | | ☑ | ☑ | ☑ |
| Fact and nonfact | | | | | ☑ | ☑ | ☑ |
| Recognize techniques of persuasion and propaganda | | | | | ☑ | ☑ | ☑ |
| Evaluate evidence and sources of information | | | | | ☑ | ☑ | ☑ |
| Identify similarities and differences across texts (including topics, characters, problems, themes, treatment, scope, or organization) | | | | | | | |
| Practice various questions and tasks (test-like comprehension questions) | | | | | | | |
| Paraphrase and summarize to recall, inform, and organize | | | | | | | |
| Answer various types of questions (open-ended, literal, interpretative, test-like such as true-false, multiple choice, short-answer) | | | | | | | |
| Use study strategies to learn and recall (preview, question, reread, and record) | | | | | | | |
| **LITERARY RESPONSE** | | | | | | | |
| Listen to stories being read aloud | | | | | | | |
| React, speculate, join in, read along when predictable and patterned selections are read aloud | | | | | | | |
| Respond through talk, movement, music, art, drama, and writing to a variety of stories and poems | | | | | | | |
| Show understanding through writing, illustrating, developing demonstrations, and using technology | | | | | | | |
| Connect ideas and themes across texts | | | | | | | |
| Support responses by referring to relevant aspects of text and own experiences | | | | | | | |
| Offer observations, make connections, speculate, interpret, and raise questions in response to texts | | | | | | | |
| Interpret text ideas through journal writing, discussion, enactment, and media | | | | | | | |
| **TEXT STRUCTURE/LITERARY CONCEPTS** | | | | | | | |
| Distinguish forms of texts and the functions they serve (lists, newsletters, signs) | | | | | | | |
| Understand story structure | | | | | | | |
| Identify narrative (for entertainment) and expository (for information) | | | | | | | |
| Distinguish fiction from nonfiction, including fact and fantasy | | | | | | | |
| Understand literary forms (stories, poems, plays, and informational books) | | | | | | | |
| Understand literary terms by distinguishing between roles of author and illustrator | | | | | | | |
| Understand title, author, and illustrator across a variety of texts | | | | | | | |
| Analyze character, character's point of view, plot, setting, style, tone, mood | | ☑ | ☑ | ☑ | ☑ | ☑ | ☑ |
| Compare communication in different forms | | | | | | | |
| Understand terms such as *title, author, illustrator, playwright, theater, stage, act, dialogue,* and *scene* | | | | | | | |
| Recognize stories, poems, myths, folktales, fables, tall tales, limericks, plays, biographies, and autobiographies | | | | | | | |
| Judge internal logic of story text | | | | | | | |
| Recognize that authors organize information in specific ways | | | | | | | |
| Identify texts to inform, influence, express, or entertain | | | | | | | |
| Describe how author's point of view affects text | | | | | | | |
| Recognize biography, historical fiction, realistic fiction, modern fantasy, informational texts, and poetry | | | | | | | |
| Analyze ways authors present ideas (cause/effect, compare/contrast, inductively, deductively, chronologically) | | | | | | | |
| Recognize flashback, foreshadowing, symbolism | | | | | | | |

*(continued on next page)*

*(Reading: Comprehension continued)*

| VARIETY OF TEXT | K | 1 | 2 | 3 | 4 | 5 | 6 |
|---|---|---|---|---|---|---|---|
| Read a variety of genres | | | | | | | |
| Use informational texts to acquire information | | | | | | | |
| Read for a variety of purposes | | | | | | | |
| Select varied sources when reading for information or pleasure | | | | | | | |

| FLUENCY | K | 1 | 2 | 3 | 4 | 5 | 6 |
|---|---|---|---|---|---|---|---|
| Read regularly in independent-level and instructional-level materials | | | | | | | |
| Read orally with fluency from familiar texts | | | | | | | |
| Self-select independent-level reading | | | | | | | |
| Read silently for increasing periods of time | | | | | | | |
| Demonstrate characteristics of fluent and effective reading | | | | | | | |
| Adjust reading rate to purpose | | | | | | | |
| Read aloud in selected texts, showing understanding of text and engaging the listener | | | | | | | |

| CULTURES | K | 1 | 2 | 3 | 4 | 5 | 6 |
|---|---|---|---|---|---|---|---|
| Connect own experience with culture of others | | | | | | | |
| Compare experiences of characters across cultures | | | | | | | |
| Articulate and discuss themes and connections that cross cultures | | | | | | | |

| CRITICAL THINKING | K | 1 | 2 | 3 | 4 | 5 | 6 |
|---|---|---|---|---|---|---|---|
| Experiences (comprehend, apply, analyze, synthesize, evaluate) | | | | | | | |
| Make connections (comprehend, apply, analyze, synthesize, evaluate) | | | | | | | |
| Expression (comprehend, apply, analyze, synthesize, evaluate) | | | | | | | |
| Inquiry (comprehend, apply, analyze, synthesize, evaluate) | | | | | | | |
| Problem solving (comprehend, apply, analyze, synthesize, evaluate) | | | | | | | |
| Making decisions (comprehend, apply, analyze, synthesize, evaluate) | | | | | | | |

## Study Skills

| INQUIRY/RESEARCH | K | 1 | 2 | 3 | 4 | 5 | 6 |
|---|---|---|---|---|---|---|---|
| Follow directions | | | | | | | |
| Use alphabetical order | | | | | | | |
| Identify/frame questions for research | | | | | | | |
| Obtain, organize, and summarize information: classify, take notes, outline | | | | | | | |
| Evaluate research and raise new questions | | | | | | | |
| Use technology to present information in various formats | | | | | | | |
| Follow accepted formats for writing research, including documenting sources | | | | | | | |
| Use test-taking strategies | | | | | | | |
| Use text organizers (book cover; title page—title, author, illustrator; contents; headings; glossary; index) | | ☑ | ☑ | ☑ | ☑ | ☑ | ☑ |
| Use graphic aids, including maps, diagrams, charts, graphs | | ☑ | ☑ | ☑ | ☑ | ☑ | ☑ |
| Read and interpret varied texts including environmental print, signs, lists, encyclopedia, dictionary, glossary, newspaper, advertisement, magazine, calendar, directions, floor plans | | ☑ | ☑ | ☑ | ☑ | ☑ | ☑ |
| Use reference sources, such as glossary, dictionary, encyclopedia, telephone directory, technology resources | | ☑ | ☑ | ☑ | ☑ | ☑ | ☑ |
| Recognize Library/Media center resources, such as computerized references; catalog search—subject, author, title; encyclopedia index | | ☑ | ☑ | ☑ | ☑ | ☑ | ☑ |

# Writing

| MODES AND FORMS | K | 1 | 2 | 3 | 4 | 5 | 6 |
|---|---|---|---|---|---|---|---|
| Interactive writing | | | | | | | |
| Personal narrative (Expressive narrative) | | | ☑ | ☑ | ☑ | ☑ | ☑ |
| Writing that compares (Informative classificatory) | | | ☑ | ☑ | ☑ | ☑ | ☑ |
| Explanatory writing (Informative narrative) | | ☑ | ☑ | ☑ | ☑ | ☑ | ☑ |
| Persuasive writing (Persuasive descriptive) | | | ☑ | ☑ | ☑ | ☑ | ☑ |
| Writing a story | | ☑ | ☑ | ☑ | ☑ | ☑ | ☑ |
| Expository writing | | ☑ | ☑ | ☑ | ☑ | ☑ | ☑ |
| Write using a variety of formats, such as advertisement, autobiography, biography, book report/report, comparison-contrast, critique/review/editorial, description, essay, how-to, interview, invitation, journal/log/notes, message/list, paragraph/multi-paragraph composition, picture book, play (scene), poem/rhyme, story, summary, note, letter | | | | | | | |
| **PURPOSES/AUDIENCES** | | | | | | | |
| Dictate messages such as news and stories for others to write | | | | | | | |
| Write labels, notes, and captions for illustrations, possessions, charts, and centers | | | | | | | |
| Write to record, to discover and develop ideas, to inform, to influence, to entertain | | | | | | | |
| Exhibit an identifiable voice in personal narratives and stories | | | | | | | |
| Use literary devices (suspense, dialogue, and figurative language) | | | | | | | |
| Produce written texts by organizing ideas, using effective transitions, and choosing precise wording | | | | | | | |
| **PROCESSES** | | | | | | | |
| Generate ideas for self-selected and assigned topics using prewriting strategies | | | | | | | |
| Develop drafts | | | | | | | |
| Revise drafts for varied purposes | | | | | | | |
| Edit for appropriate grammar, spelling, punctuation, and features of polished writings | | | | | | | |
| Proofread own writing and that of others | | | | | | | |
| Bring pieces to final form and "publish" them for audiences | | | | | | | |
| Use technology to compose text | | | | | | | |
| Select and use reference materials and resources for writing, revising, and editing final drafts | | | | | | | |
| **SPELLING** | | | | | | | |
| Spell own name and write high-frequency words | | | | | | | |
| Words with short vowels (including CVC and one-syllable words with blends CCVC, CVCC, CCVCC) | | | | | | | |
| Words with long vowels (including CVCe) | | | | | | | |
| Words with digraphs, blends, consonant clusters, double consonants | | | | | | | |
| Words with diphthongs | | | | | | | |
| Words with variant vowels | | | | | | | |
| Words with r-controlled vowels | | | | | | | |
| Words with /ər/, /əl/, and /ən/ | | | | | | | |
| Words with silent letters | | | | | | | |
| Words with soft *c* and soft *g* | | | | | | | |
| Inflectional endings (including plurals and past tense and words that drop the final *e* when adding -*ing*, -*ed*) | | | | | | | |
| Compound words | | | | | | | |
| Contractions | | | | | | | |
| Homonyms | | | | | | | |
| Suffixes including -*able*, -*ly*, or -*less*, and prefixes including *dis-*, *re-*, *pre-*, or *un-* | | | | | | | |
| Spell words ending in -*tion* and -*sion*, such as *station* and *procession* | | | | | | | |
| Accurate spelling of root or base words | | | | | | | |
| Orthographic patterns and rules such as *keep/can; sack/book; out/now; oil/toy; match/speech; ledge/cage;* consonant doubling, dropping *e,* changing *y* to *i* | | | | | | | |
| Multisyllabic words using regularly spelled phonogram patterns | | | | | | | |
| Syllable patterns (including closed, open, syllable boundary patterns) | | | | | | | |
| Synonyms and antonyms | | | | | | | |
| Words from Social Studies, Science, Math, and Physical Education | | | | | | | |
| Words derived from other languages and cultures | | | | | | | |
| Use resources to find correct spellings, synonyms, and replacement words | | | | | | | |
| Use conventional spelling of familiar words in writing assignments | | | | | | | |
| Spell accurately in final drafts | | | | | | | |

*(continued on next page)*

☑ Tested Skill

Tinted panels show skills, strategies, and other teaching opportunities

| GRAMMAR AND USAGE | K | 1 | 2 | 3 | 4 | 5 | 6 |
|---|---|---|---|---|---|---|---|
| Understand sentence concepts (word order, statements, questions, exclamations, commands) | | | | | | | |
| Recognize complete and incomplete sentences | | | | | | | |
| Nouns (common; proper; singular; plural; irregular plural; possessives) | | | | | | | |
| Verbs (action; helping; linking; irregular) | | | | | | | |
| Verb tense (present, past, future, perfect, and progressive) | | | | | | | |
| Pronouns (possessive, subject and object, pronoun-verb agreement) | | | | | | | |
| Use objective case pronouns accurately | | | | | | | |
| Adjectives | | | | | | | |
| Adverbs that tell how, when, where | | | | | | | |
| Subjects, predicates | | | | | | | |
| Subject-verb agreement | | | | | | | |
| Sentence combining | | | | | | | |
| Recognize sentence structure (simple, compound, complex) | | | | | | | |
| Synonyms and antonyms | | | | | | | |
| Contractions | | | | | | | |
| Conjunctions | | | | | | | |
| Prepositions and prepositional phrases | | | | | | | |

| PENMANSHIP | K | 1 | 2 | 3 | 4 | 5 | 6 |
|---|---|---|---|---|---|---|---|
| Write each letter of alphabet (capital and lowercase) using correct formation, appropriate size and spacing | | | | | | | |
| Write own name and other important words | | | | | | | |
| Use phonological knowledge to map sounds to letters to write messages | | | | | | | |
| Write messages that move left to right, top to bottom | | | | | | | |
| Gain increasing control of penmanship, pencil grip, paper position, beginning stroke | | | | | | | |
| Use word and letter spacing and margins to make messages readable | | | | | | | |
| Write legibly by selecting cursive or manuscript as appropriate | | | | | | | |

| MECHANICS | K | 1 | 2 | 3 | 4 | 5 | 6 |
|---|---|---|---|---|---|---|---|
| Use capitalization in sentences, proper nouns, titles, abbreviations and the pronoun *I* | | | | | | | |
| Use end marks correctly (period, question mark, exclamation point) | | | | | | | |
| Use commas (in dates, in addresses, in a series, in letters, in direct address) | | | | | | | |
| Use apostrophes in contractions and possessives | | | | | | | |
| Use quotation marks | | | | | | | |
| Use hyphens, semicolons, colons | | | | | | | |

| EVALUATION | K | 1 | 2 | 3 | 4 | 5 | 6 |
|---|---|---|---|---|---|---|---|
| Identify the most effective features of a piece of writing using class/teacher generated criteria | | | | | | | |
| Respond constructively to others' writing | | | | | | | |
| Determine how his/her own writing achieves its purpose | | | | | | | |
| Use published pieces as models for writing | | | | | | | |
| Review own written work to monitor growth as writer | | | | | | | |

For more detailed scope and sequence including page numbers and additional phonics information, see McGraw-Hill Reading Program scope and sequence (K-6)

*been,* 68D, 95A-C
*blue,* 10D, 37A-C
*buy,* 38D, 65A-C
*carry,* 68D, 95A-C
*clean,* 68D, 95A-C
*done,* 68D, 95A-C
*far,* 68D, 95A-C
*found,* 38D, 65A-C
*how,* 98D, 123A-C
*light,* 98D, 123A-C
*little,* 98D, 123A-C
*live,* 98D, 123A-C
*pretty,* 98D, 123A-C
*some,* 38D, 65A-C
*were,* 10D, 37A-C
*who,* 10D, 37A-C
*work,* 38D, 65A-C

**High utility vocabulary,** 10D, 37A-C, 40D, 65A-C, 68D, 95A-C, 98D, 123A-C, 126D, 133A-C

**Illustrations, using,** 69, 70, 79, 81, 82, 83, 84, 88, 99, 116. *See also* Comprehension strategies.

**Imagery,** 7

**Independent reading,** 8B, 37B, 38B, 65B, 66B, 95B, 96B, 123B, 124B, 133B

**Inferences, making,** 71, 74, 79, 86, 95I-J, 96E, 98-123, 123I-J, 126-133, 133G-H, T70

**Inflectional endings,** 37K, 37L, 65K, 133I, 133K, 133L, T67, T71

**Informal assessment,** 6G, 33, 61, 91, 119, 129

**Initial consonants,** 8/9, 38/39, 66/67, 96/97, 124/12. *See also* Phonics and decoding.

**Inquiry and research,** 7, 37D, 65D, 95D, 123D, 133D, 135

**Integrated Language Arts.** *See* Cross-curricular.

**Internet connection,** 7, 37D, 65D, 72, 80, 93, 95D, 106, 121, 123D, 133D, 135

**Intervention/prevention.** *See* Prevention/intervention.

*Johnny Appleseed,* 98-123

**Journal writing,** 33, 37D, 37N, 37R, 61, 65D, 65N, 65R, 91, 95N, 95D, 95R, 119, 123D, 123N, 123R, 129, 133D, 133N, 133R

**Knee-High Man,** 68-95

**Language Arts link,** 8E, 38E, 66E, 96E, 124E

**Language control,** 135C

**Language support,** 10C, 11, 37A-C, 37F, 37H, 37J, 37L, 37N, 37O, 37Q, 40C, 41, 65A-C, 65F, 65H, 65J, 65L, 65N, 65O, 65Q, 68C, 69, 95A-C, 95F, 95H, 95J, 95L, 95N, 95O, 95Q, 98C, 99, 123A-C, 123F, 123H, 123J, 123L, 123N, 123O, 123Q, 126C, 127, 133A-C, 133F, 133H, 133J, 133L, 133N, 133O, 133Q, 135C

**Learning styles,**
   auditory, 10D, 37F, 37H, 98D, 124E
   kinesthetic, 10C, 37J, 40B, 40C, 76, 84, 86, 98C, 102, 104, 124E, 133J
   linguistic, 10C, 10D, 37F, 37H, 40C, 65F, 65H, 80, 86, 98C, 106, 123H, 123J, 123L
   logical, 76, 110
   spatial, 40B, 65F
   visual, 8E, 10C, 10D, 37J, 38E, 40C, 80, 84, 96E, 98D, 104, 106, 116, 123H, 123J, 123L

**Leveled books,** 8B, 37A-D, 38B, 65A-D, 66B, 95A-D, 96B, 123A-D, 124B, 133A-D

**Limited English proficiency.** *See* Language support.

**Liatsos, Sandra,** 6

**Listening and speaking activities,** 8E, 10C, 10D, 32, 33, 37D, 37N, 37O, 38E, 40C, 40D, 60, 61, 65D, 65N, 65O, 66E, 68C, 68D, 90, 91, 95D, 95N, 95O, 96E, 98C, 98D, 118, 119, 123D, 123N, 123O, 124E, 126C, 126D, 128, 129, 133D, 133N, 133O. *See also* Speaking and listening. Presentation ideas.

**Listening library,** 6, 8A, 38A, 66A, 96A, 124A

**Lists, making,** 6, 7, 10C, 37C, 37F, 37R, 65M, 65R, 75, 86, 95M, 95R, 123M, 123R, 133R

**Literacy support.** *See* Language support.

**Literary devices,** 7, 135
   imagery, 7
   rhyme, 135

**Literary genre,** 10, 40, 68, 98, 126 134
   informational story, 134
   play, 134

**Literary response,** 7, 33, 37A-C, 61, 65A-C, 91, 95A-C, 119, 123A-C, 129, 133A-C, 135

**Long vowels and phonograms**
   long a: *ai, ay,* 98A-B, 98-123, 123A-C, 123E-F,
   123G-H, 126A-B
   long i: i-e, 10A-B, 10-37, 37A-C, 37E-F, 37G-H, 65G-H, 95G-H
   long o: o-e, 40A-B, 40-65, 65A-C, 65E-F, 65G-H, 95G-H, 123G-H, 126A-B
   long u: u-3, 68A-B, 68-95, 95A-C, 95E-F, 95G-H, 123G-H, 126A-B. *See also* Phonics and decoding.

**Main idea/supporting details, identifying,** 100, 111, 135C

**Math link,** 76, 110

**Mechanics and usage,** 37P, 65P, 95P, 123P, 133P
   apostrophes in contractions, 117P
   capitalizing proper nouns, 37P, 95P
   commas in letters, 123P
   sentence punctuation, 65P. *See also* Grammar, mechanics and usage.

**Meeting individual needs**
   for comprehension, 37J, 65J, 95J, 123J, 133J
   for phonics, 10B, 37F, 37H, 40B, 65F, 65H, 68B, 95F, 95H, 98B, 123F, 123H, 126B, 133F, 133H
   for vocabulary, 37L, 65L, 95L, 123L, 133L
   grouping suggestions for strategic reading, 10, 34, 37A-C, 40, 64, 67A-C. 70, 94, 97A-C, 100, 122, 125A-C, 128, 136, 139A-C
   leveled books, 8B, 37D, 38B, 65D, 66B, 95D, 96B, 123D, 124B, 133D
   resources for, 6F, 8B, 38B, 66B, 96B, 124B

**Metacognition,** 10A, 37E, 37G, 37I, 37K, 40A, 65E, 65G, 65I, 65K, 68A, 95E, 95G, 95I, 95K, 98A, 123E, 123G, 123I, 123K, 126A, 133E, 133G, 133I, 133K

**Minilessons,** 13, 17, 19, 23, 25, 27, 29, 75, 79, 87, 89, 101, 105, 107, 109, 113, 115, 117
   cause/effect, 73, 115
   character, 109
   context clues, 75, 101
   high frequency words, 77
   main idea, 89
   make inferences, 79
   make predictions, 113
   setting, 107
   spatial relationships, 87
   vowels, 105
   summarize, 117

**Modalities, learning.** *See* Learning styles

**Modeling skills,** 10A, 37E, 37G, 37I, 37K,

# Scoring Chart

The Scoring Chart is provided for your convenience in grading your students' work.

- Find the column that shows the total number of items.
- Find the row that matches the number of items answered correctly.
- The intersection of the two rows provides the percentage score.

**TOTAL NUMBER OF ITEMS**

| NUMBER CORRECT | 1 | 2 | 3 | 4 | 5 | 6 | 7 | 8 | 9 | 10 | 11 | 12 | 13 | 14 | 15 | 16 | 17 | 18 | 19 | 20 | 21 | 22 | 23 | 24 | 25 | 26 | 27 | 28 | 29 | 30 |
|---|---|---|---|---|---|---|---|---|---|---|---|---|---|---|---|---|---|---|---|---|---|---|---|---|---|---|---|---|---|---|
| 1 | 100 | 50 | 33 | 25 | 20 | 17 | 14 | 13 | 11 | 10 | 9 | 8 | 8 | 7 | 7 | 6 | 6 | 6 | 5 | 5 | 5 | 5 | 4 | 4 | 4 | 4 | 4 | 4 | 3 | 3 |
| 2 | | 100 | 66 | 50 | 40 | 33 | 29 | 25 | 22 | 20 | 18 | 17 | 15 | 14 | 13 | 13 | 12 | 11 | 11 | 10 | 10 | 9 | 9 | 8 | 8 | 8 | 7 | 7 | 7 | 7 |
| 3 | | | 100 | 75 | 60 | 50 | 43 | 38 | 33 | 30 | 27 | 25 | 23 | 21 | 20 | 19 | 18 | 17 | 16 | 15 | 14 | 14 | 13 | 13 | 12 | 12 | 11 | 11 | 10 | 10 |
| 4 | | | | 100 | 80 | 67 | 57 | 50 | 44 | 40 | 36 | 33 | 31 | 29 | 27 | 25 | 24 | 22 | 21 | 20 | 19 | 18 | 17 | 17 | 16 | 15 | 15 | 14 | 14 | 13 |
| 5 | | | | | 100 | 83 | 71 | 63 | 56 | 50 | 45 | 42 | 38 | 36 | 33 | 31 | 29 | 28 | 26 | 25 | 24 | 23 | 22 | 21 | 20 | 19 | 19 | 18 | 17 | 17 |
| 6 | | | | | | 100 | 86 | 75 | 67 | 60 | 55 | 50 | 46 | 43 | 40 | 38 | 35 | 33 | 32 | 30 | 29 | 27 | 26 | 25 | 24 | 23 | 22 | 21 | 21 | 20 |
| 7 | | | | | | | 100 | 88 | 78 | 70 | 64 | 58 | 54 | 50 | 47 | 44 | 41 | 39 | 37 | 35 | 33 | 32 | 30 | 29 | 28 | 27 | 26 | 25 | 24 | 23 |
| 8 | | | | | | | | 100 | 89 | 80 | 73 | 67 | 62 | 57 | 53 | 50 | 47 | 44 | 42 | 40 | 38 | 36 | 35 | 33 | 32 | 31 | 30 | 29 | 28 | 27 |
| 9 | | | | | | | | | 100 | 90 | 82 | 75 | 69 | 64 | 60 | 56 | 53 | 50 | 47 | 45 | 43 | 41 | 39 | 38 | 36 | 35 | 33 | 32 | 31 | 30 |
| 10 | | | | | | | | | | 100 | 91 | 83 | 77 | 71 | 67 | 63 | 59 | 56 | 53 | 50 | 48 | 45 | 43 | 42 | 40 | 38 | 37 | 36 | 34 | 33 |
| 11 | | | | | | | | | | | 100 | 92 | 85 | 79 | 73 | 69 | 65 | 61 | 58 | 55 | 52 | 50 | 48 | 46 | 44 | 42 | 41 | 39 | 38 | 37 |
| 12 | | | | | | | | | | | | 100 | 92 | 86 | 80 | 75 | 71 | 67 | 63 | 60 | 57 | 55 | 52 | 50 | 48 | 46 | 44 | 43 | 41 | 40 |
| 13 | | | | | | | | | | | | | 100 | 93 | 87 | 81 | 76 | 72 | 68 | 65 | 62 | 59 | 57 | 54 | 52 | 50 | 48 | 46 | 45 | 43 |
| 14 | | | | | | | | | | | | | | 100 | 93 | 88 | 82 | 78 | 74 | 70 | 67 | 64 | 61 | 58 | 56 | 54 | 52 | 50 | 48 | 47 |
| 15 | | | | | | | | | | | | | | | 100 | 94 | 88 | 83 | 79 | 75 | 71 | 68 | 65 | 63 | 60 | 58 | 56 | 54 | 52 | 50 |
| 16 | | | | | | | | | | | | | | | | 100 | 94 | 89 | 84 | 80 | 76 | 73 | 70 | 67 | 64 | 62 | 59 | 57 | 55 | 53 |
| 17 | | | | | | | | | | | | | | | | | 100 | 94 | 89 | 85 | 81 | 77 | 74 | 71 | 68 | 65 | 63 | 61 | 59 | 57 |
| 18 | | | | | | | | | | | | | | | | | | 100 | 95 | 90 | 86 | 82 | 78 | 75 | 72 | 69 | 67 | 64 | 62 | 60 |
| 19 | | | | | | | | | | | | | | | | | | | 100 | 95 | 90 | 86 | 83 | 79 | 76 | 73 | 70 | 68 | 66 | 63 |
| 20 | | | | | | | | | | | | | | | | | | | | 100 | 95 | 91 | 87 | 83 | 80 | 77 | 74 | 71 | 69 | 67 |
| 21 | | | | | | | | | | | | | | | | | | | | | 100 | 95 | 91 | 88 | 84 | 81 | 78 | 75 | 72 | 70 |
| 22 | | | | | | | | | | | | | | | | | | | | | | 100 | 96 | 92 | 88 | 85 | 81 | 79 | 76 | 73 |
| 23 | | | | | | | | | | | | | | | | | | | | | | | 100 | 96 | 92 | 88 | 85 | 82 | 79 | 77 |
| 24 | | | | | | | | | | | | | | | | | | | | | | | | 100 | 96 | 92 | 89 | 86 | 83 | 80 |
| 25 | | | | | | | | | | | | | | | | | | | | | | | | | 100 | 96 | 93 | 89 | 86 | 83 |
| 26 | | | | | | | | | | | | | | | | | | | | | | | | | | 100 | 96 | 93 | 90 | 87 |
| 27 | | | | | | | | | | | | | | | | | | | | | | | | | | | 100 | 96 | 93 | 90 |
| 28 | | | | | | | | | | | | | | | | | | | | | | | | | | | | 100 | 97 | 93 |
| 29 | | | | | | | | | | | | | | | | | | | | | | | | | | | | | 100 | 97 |
| 30 | | | | | | | | | | | | | | | | | | | | | | | | | | | | | | 100 |

# Persuasive Writing: Writing a Letter

## Scoring Rubric: 6-Trait Writing

### 6. Exceptional

- **Ideas & Content** crafts a strong argument that could affect a reader's opinion; thoughtful details support the writer's position.
- **Organization** well-planned structure allows a reader to follow each point of the argument; has an inviting beginning and a solid ending.
- **Voice** shows originality and deep involvement with the argument; matches a genuine personal message to the purpose and audience.
- **Word Choice** makes creative use of new and everyday words; advanced vocabulary conveys a strong opinion.
- **Sentence Fluency** varied sentences flow naturally and add interest to the argument; writing is easy to follow and read aloud.
- **Conventions** is skilled in most writing conventions; proper use of the rules of English enhances clarity and meaning; editing is largely unnecessary.

### 5. Excellent

- **Ideas & Content** creates a carefully-detailed argument that could influence a reader.
- **Organization** creates a careful strategy, in an order that helps the reader follow the argument's logic; has a solid beginning and ending.
- **Voice** shows originality and strong involvement with the topic; brings a personal message to the topic and audience.
- **Word Choice** makes thoughtful use of both new and everyday words; message is clear and interesting.
- **Sentence Fluency** crafts well-paced sentences with a variety of lengths, beginnings, and patterns that fit together well.
- **Conventions** is skilled in most writing conventions; proper use of the rules of English enhances clarity and meaning; editing is largely unnecessary.

### 4. Good

- **Ideas & Content** presents a solid, clear argument, with details that help the reader understand the main idea.
- **Organization** presents facts and ideas in a logical order; has a clear beginning and ending; reader can follow the writer's logic.
- **Voice** attempts to convey a real personal message; shows involvement with the topic; message matches the argument, and attempts to reach an audience.
- **Word Choice** uses a variety of words that fit the argument; explores some new words, or makes fresh use of familiar words.
- **Sentence Fluency** careful, easy-to-follow sentences vary in length, beginnings, and patterns; writing is easy to read aloud.
- **Conventions** may make some errors in spelling, capitalization, punctuation, or usage, but these do not interfere with understanding the text; some editing is needed.

### 3. Fair

- **Ideas & Content** attempts to argue a position; may include ideas or details which are not clear, or do not fit the topic.
- **Organization** attempts to argue a position, but the logic is sometimes hard to follow; some ideas don't belong where they are placed; beginning and ending may be too short or may ramble.
- **Voice** may not show involvement with the topic; opinion comes across, but may not convey who is behind the writing.
- **Word Choice** states the argument, but in an ordinary way; may try to use a variety of words, but some do not fit; may overuse some words/expressions.
- **Sentence Fluency** most sentences are readable, but are limited in lengths and patterns; some rereading is necessary to follow the meaning; some sentences are choppy or overlong.
- **Conventions** has basic control of conventions, but makes enough errors to interfere with a smooth reading of the text; significant editing is needed.

### 2. Poor

- **Ideas & Content** has little control of task to persuade, or seems unsure of the topic; ideas are vague; details are few, repeated, or inaccurate.
- **Organization** has no clear structure; order of ideas is hard to follow; details don't fit where they are placed; beginning and ending are missing or undeveloped.
- **Voice** is not involved in sharing ideas with a reader; writing may be lifeless, with no sense of who is behind the words.
- **Word Choice** does not choose words that convey a clear opinion; some words may detract from the meaning or impact of the argument.
- **Sentence Fluency** sentences may be incomplete or awkward; patterns are similar or monotonous; text may be hard to follow or read aloud.
- **Conventions** makes frequent errors in spelling, word choice, punctuation and usage; paper is difficult to read; needs extensive revision and editing.

### 1. Unsatisfactory

- **Ideas & Content** does not state an opinion; writer is unsure of what s/he wants to say.
- **Organization** has an extreme lack of structure; ideas and details are disconnected; details, if given, are inaccurate or vague.
- **Voice** does not address an audience at all; does not show a sense of sharing a personal message or style.
- **Word Choice** uses words that do not fit, or are vague and confusing; no new words are attempted.
- **Sentence Fluency** uses incomplete, rambling, or confusing sentences that make the text hard to follow and read aloud.
- **Conventions** makes severe errors in most conventions; spelling errors may make it hard to guess what words are meant; some parts of the text may be impossible to follow or understand.

**0:** This piece is either blank, or fails to respond to the writing task. The topic is not addressed, or the student simply paraphrases the prompt. The response may be illegible or incoherent.

TAAS WRITING

# Persuasive Writing: Writing a Letter

## 8-Point Writing Rubric

| 8 | 7 | 6 | 5 | 4 | 3 | 2 | 1 |
|---|---|---|---|---|---|---|---|
| The writer<br>• presents an exceptionally well-constructed article, containing vivid descriptions of a place.<br>• uses interesting facts and finely observed or researched description to elaborate each aspect of the place.<br>• uses sophisticated language and compelling images to enhance the facts.<br>• uses a logical structure with an intriguing beginning, detailed middle, and apt end.<br>• reaches a well-thought out conclusion based on facts and reasons in the report. | The writer<br>• crafts a well-organized article vivid with fine descriptions of a place.<br>• elaborates with facts and observations about the place.<br>• uses sophisticated vocabulary and interesting images to highlight the facts.<br>• clearly presents a logical structure with a beginning, middle, and ending.<br>• reaches a thoughtful conclusion based on the facts. | The writer<br>• presents an organized article with descriptions of a place.<br>• uses facts that present a clear picture of the place.<br>• chooses vocabulary and images that highlight the facts.<br>• presents a logical structure.<br>• reaches a conclusion in the report. | The writer<br>• attempts an organized, detailed article on a place.<br>• elaborates with some facts and description.<br>• may vary word choice but doesn't include personal observation.<br>• may exhibit organization difficulty with lapses in conventions.<br>• may not offer an entirely logical conclusion. | The writer<br>• has made an adequate attempt at an article on a place.<br>• may not consistently elaborate on the facts or observations.<br>• may show lapses in logical ordering of ideas.<br>• exhibits recurring problems with conventions.<br>• may not offer a relevant conclusion. | The writer<br>• attempts a minimally-successful report on a place.<br>• exhibits organizational problems, such as an illogically-structured list of facts without a beginning, middle, or end.<br>• may not elaborate on factual information.<br>• may exhibit limited control of grammar, mechanics, and usage.<br>• may not draw a pertinent conclusion. | The writer<br>• makes a largely unsuccessful attempt at reporting on a place.<br>• exhibits organizational problems great enough to interfere with comprehension of the text.<br>• has not used pertinent facts or descriptions about a place.<br>• may show repeated errors in basic grammar, mechanics, and usage.<br>• does not draw a conclusion or concludes with a comment unrelated to facts, reasons, or the topic itself. | The writer<br>• makes little attempt at expository writing and exhibits a lack of awareness of the topic.<br>• lacks any sense of organization.<br>• has used only generalities, with no attempt to include specific facts, descriptions, or observations.<br>• shows serious and repeated errors in basic grammar, mechanics, and usage.<br>• leaves writing unfinished without even an attempt at a conclusion. |

**0:** This piece is either blank, or fails to respond to the writing task. The topic is not addressed, or the student simply paraphrases the prompt. The response may be illegible or incoherent.

# Notes

# Notes

# Notes

# Notes

# Notes

# Notes